D1389880

ECONOMETRIC MODELING OF CHINA

**ECONOMETRICS IN THE INFORMATION AGE:
THEORY AND PRACTICE OF MEASUREMENT**

Series Editors: Lawrence R Klein *(Univ. of Pennsylvania)*
Kanta Marwah *(Carleton Univ.)*

Published

Vol. 1 Selected Papers of Lawrence R Klein: Theoretical Reflections and
Econometric Applications
edited by Kanta Marwah

Forthcoming

Vol. 2 The Chinese Economy in the Twenty-First Century
— An Econometric Approach
Lawrence J Lau

Econometrics in the Information Age: Theory and Practice of Measurement — Vol. 3

Series Editors: Lawrence Klein & Kanta Marwah

ECONOMETRIC MODELING OF CHINA

Editors

Lawrence R. Klein
University of Pennsylvania, USA

Shinichi Ichimura
ICSEAD, Japan

World Scientific
Singapore • New Jersey • London • Hong Kong

Published by

World Scientific Publishing Co. Pte. Ltd.

P O Box 128, Farrer Road, Singapore 912805

USA office: Suite 1B, 1060 Main Street, River Edge, NJ 07661

UK office: 57 Shelton Street, Covent Garden, London WC2H 9HE

British Library Cataloguing-in-Publication Data
A catalogue record for this book is available from the British Library.

ECONOMETRIC MODELING OF CHINA

Copyright © 2000 by World Scientific Publishing Co. Pte. Ltd.

All rights reserved. This book, or parts thereof, may not be reproduced in any form or by any means, electronic or mechanical, including photocopying, recording or any information storage and retrieval system now known or to be invented, without written permission from the Publisher.

For photocopying of material in this volume, please pay a copying fee through the Copyright Clearance Center, Inc., 222 Rosewood Drive, Danvers, MA 01923, USA. In this case permission to photocopy is not required from the publisher.

ISBN 981-02-4383-9

Printed in Singapore by World Scientific Printers

To Sonia and Yukiko

Foreword

These are the up-to-date fruits of our efforts in econometric modeling of China at the International Center for the Study of East Asian Development, Kitakyushu, Japan. ICSEAD was established as a joint undertaking with the University of Pennsylvania in 1989, and ever since its inception, it has followed the suggestion of Professor Lawrence R. Klein to maintain econometric models and their data banks of East Asian economies. It has held the work-shops for this purpose and published a number of proceedings. Moreover, on the basis of our own econometric models we have made the predictions of the East Asian Economies available in our quarterly journals every year.

In particular, we have emphasized the quantitative studies of the Chinese economy among others. Inviting a number of economists from China, we have been working with them on the econometric models of China. We will continue to do so in the future. This book tries to make available all the econometric models of China presented at our workshop held at ICSEAD in 1998, together with the statistical data used for their model building. The editors asked all the authors not only to revise their original papers considering the comments given at the workshop but also to provide the reader with almost all the basic statistical data that they used to estimate their own models. We believe that the most important and difficult part of econometric work on the Chinese economy is indeed the preparation of reliable statistical data. The reader will have the benefit of learning about reliable data and their sources.

The benefit of this statistical information can hardly be over-emphasized, not only for the studies of Chinese economy but more generally for the advancement of econometric work. The progress of empirical work in econometrics will be improved substantially if the data used in the estimation and tests of the models are offered at the same time. As theoretical physics and experimental physics naturally develop side by side, so econometrics should develop in theory and its empirical applications side by side. But unlike physics, the empirical work in econometrics requires enormous efforts in searching for and compiling the statistical data needed for model building. For this reason we believe that despite the difficulties we must try to make the data as well as the models available to the reader. Only then can the re-examination and testing of published econometric works be meaningful and easily used by other econometricians. The benefit will be for both initial research workers and their followers. The cumulative process of empirical research will be much faster and productive, so that further improvement in applied econometrics may be expected. This is particularly important for econometric work on the Chinese economy, where statistical data are still unsatisfactory and require careful treatment.

Almost half a century has passed since I first met Sonia and Lawrence R. Klein in Ann Arbor in 1953. Moreover, our family association has lasted more than forty years. We have learned a great deal from the association with their family. This may not be too common nowadays. As a token of our many years of friendship and professional and family association, we would like to dedicate this joint effort to our two wives whose dedication made it possible to produce this unique volume at this time.

March 3, 2000

Shinichi Ichimura

CONTENTS

Foreword .... *vii*

Contents .... *ix*

List of Tables and Figures .... *xiv*

Introduction to: Econometric Modeling of China 1

**Chapter 1   A Model Study of Balance of Payments and
                       Money Supply of China** 9

Introduction 9

1. Characteristics of the Chinese Balance of Payments 12

2. Current Balance 15

    2.1. Trade Balance 15

    2.2 Non-Trade Balance 20

3. Capital Account 23

    3.1 Characteristics of Capital Account 23

    3.2 Analysis of Long-Term Capital Account 25

    3.3 Short-Term Capital Items 29

4. Balance of Payments and Money Supply 31

    4.1 Balance of Payments and Foreign Exchange Reserves 31

    4.2 Formation of Reserve Money 33

    4.3 Money Supply 34

    4.4 Influence of Monetary Supply on the Economy 37

    4.5 Relationship between Money Supply M_1 and Nominal GDP 38

    4.6 Relationship between Money Supply and Price Level 39

5. Structure and Test of the Model 40

    5.1 Structure of the Model 40

    5.2 Test of the Model 41

References 47

Appendix 1—List of Equations 47

Appendix 2—List of Variables 56

Appendix 3—List of Data Used in the Model 59

Chapter 2   ICSEAD'S Econometric Model of the Chinese Economy 67

1. Introduction 67

2. Econometric Models of the Chinese Economy: Brief Historic Review 68

3. Outline of the Model 69

    3.1 Basic Principles of Model Building 69

    3.2 Outline of the Model 70

4. Some Simulation Analyses 93

4.1. Effects of FDI Increase 93
4.2. Effects of Money Supply Expansion 93
4.3. Effects of Increase in Government Consumption 94
4.4. Effects of Increase in Public Investment...94
4.5. Effects of World GDP Increase 95
5. Reference 95
Appendix A—China Macro Econometric Model 1997 Version Equation List........96
Appendix B—Simulation...118
Appendix C—Statistical Data 138

Chapter 3   Outline of the PAIR China-Hong Kong Link Model 151
1. PAIR Project 151
2. Data Problems...152
   2.1 China...152
   2.2 Hong Kong...157
   2.3 Merchandise Trade Statistics 159
3. Model Specification 161
   3.1 Background..161
   3.2 Trade Link 162
   3.3 Domestic Block..163
4. Estimation Results and Simulation Analysis.......................................165
   4.1 Estimation Results 165
   4.2 Simulation Analyses of Exchange Rate Policy 166
Appendix 1. Estimation Results of RRXM 171
Appendix 2. Structure of Trade Block in PCHLM....................................172
Appendix 3. Price Determination Structure of China Block 173
Appendix 4. List of Equation (PLM ver.98.1) 173
Appendix 5-1-1. List of Variables for China 175
Appendix 5-1-2. Data Set for China...177
Appendix 5-2-1. List of Variable for Hong Kong......................................179
Appendix 5-2-2. Data Set for Hong Kong 181
Appendix 6. Estimation Results of Equations..185
Appendix 7. Final Test (1985–1996) 199

Chapter 4   China's Econometric Model for Project PAIR 201
1. Introduction...201
2. Data...202
3. Structure of the Model 205
   3.1 Private Consumption Expenditures...205
   3.2 Investment Function...206
   3.3 Production Functions 207

3.4 Export and Import Functions 208
3.5 The Price Index Equations 209
3.6 Fiscal and Private Income Equations 212
4. List of the Equations 213
   4.1 Domestic Demand Block 213
   4.2 Production and Gross Domestic Product Block 214
   4.3 Finance and Private Income Block 216
   4.4 Price Block... 217
   4.5 Foreign Trade Block 218
5. Explanation of Variables... 220
   5.1 Endogenous Variables 220
   5.2 Exogenous Variables 222
6. Dynamic Simulation Test.. 223
7. Policy Simulations 223
   7.1 Impacts of an Increase of 10% in Nominal Public Consumption. 223
   7.2 Impacts of a 10% Increase in Fixed Investment Loans........................... 224
   7.3 Impacts of an Increase of 10% in Tax Revenues on Agriculture,
       Industry and Commerce.. 224
   7.4 Impacts of an Increase of 10% in Exports 225
8. Concluding Remarks... 225
APPENDIX: China's Economic Model for Project LINK............................... 239
1. List of Equations 239
2. Explanation of Variables... 246
   (1) Endogenous Variables... 246
   (2) Exogenous Variables... 247
References... 248

**Chapter 5   A Computable General Equilibrium Model for
                 the Chinese Economy**.. 249
1. Introduction... 249
2. Methodology—Why a CGE Model ?... 251
3. The Structure of DRCCGE2 252
   3.1 Production and Factor Market.. 253
   3.2 Trade.. 255
   3.3 Demand... 256
   3.4 Income Distribution 258
   3.5 Government and the Extra-Budget Public Sector 259
   3.6 Equilibrium and Macro Closure... 259
   3.7 Recursive Dynamics 260
4. Model Calibration and the Benchmark Equilibrium Data Set........................ 261
   4.1 Trade Data 262

4.2 Sectoral Taxes Data 264
4.3 Splits of Sectors 264
4.4 Estimating the Input-Output Matrix of Production for Processing Exports
....264
5. Some Major Applications of DRCCGE Model...265
References:...269
Appendix A—Sector Classification in DRCCGE2 and Their SSB-IO Sector
Concordance..270
Appendix B—Algebraic Specification of CGE Model for China 273
1. Sector Definition..273
2. Definition of Variables 274
3. Definition of Parameters 278
4. Equation List..280

**Chapter 6   Natural Decomposition of Total Factor Productivity
Growth**...291
1. Abstract..291
2. Growth in Total Factor Productivity 291
3. Output Elasticities in Terms of Costs [2] 292
4. Decomposition of Total Factor Productivity Growth...................................294
5. Decomposition of Product Output Growth 296
References...301
Appendix I 301
Results of OLS Estimation..302
Appendix II 304
Results of OLS Estimation..304
Appendix III..305
Results of OLS Estimation..306

Chapter 7   China's Macro Econometric Annual Model 307
1. Summary of the Model...307
2. Model Structure..308
2.1. Production Block 309
2.2. Population and Labor Force Block 310
2.3. Residents' Income Block 312
2.4. Consumption Block 313
2.5. Investment and Capital Stock Block..313
2.6. Finance and Banking Block 314
2.7. Price Block..316
2.8. Foreign Capital and Foreign Trade Block..317
3. Model Application and Problems..318

Chapter 8   A Retrospective View of the Asian Financial Crisis:
             Special Reference to Exchange Rate Policy 321
1. Introduction 321
2. Dollar Pegs 322
3. How Large is the Effect of Exchange Rate Policy? 326
4. Conclusions 327
Appendix A: Estimated Equations and the Coefficients 328
Appendix B: Summary of Simulation Results 339
Appendix C: Swap Rate 341
Appendix D: New Data 342

Chapter 9   Output and Price Determination in Chinese
             Macroeconometric Models 363
1. Introduction 363
2. The Case of Liang's Model 363
3. The Case of Shen's Model 364
4. Concluding Remarks 365
References 366

Chapter 10   A Note on the Statistical Data of China: Population
              and Labor 367
1. Introduction 367
2. Data of Population and Labor 367
3. Economically Active Population and Employed Persons 368
4. The Number of Staff and Workers 368

Index 371

LIST of TABLES and FIGURES

Chapter 1 A Model Study of Balance of Payments and Money Supply of China

Table 1-1   Chinese Balance of Payments (1982–1996) 13
Table 2-1   Structural Changes of the Imports and Exports of China 16
Table 2-2   Influential Factors of Different Categories of Exports 18
Table 2-3   Influential Factors of Different Categories of Imports 19
Table 2-4   Contribution of Foreign-Funded Enterprises to Total Exports 19
Table 2-5   Non-Trade Balance and Its Components 21
Table 3-1   Structure of Utilization of Foreign Capital 24
Table 3-2   Balances of Types of Long-Term Capital 26
Table 3-3   The Flow of Short-Term Capital and Its Structure 30
Table 4-1   China's Reserves and Its Components 32
Table 4-2   Balance Sheet of Monetary Authorities (End of 1996) 33
Table 4-3   Main Asset Items of Monetary Authorities And Reserve Money 34
Table 4-4   Balance Sheet of Deposit Money Banks (1996-End) 35
Table 4-5 M_2, Reserve Money MB And Monetary Multiplier m 36
Table 4-6   Ratio of Domestic Credit To M_2 38
Table 5-1   Final Test (1991–1996) 44
Figure 5-1   Flow Chart of The Model 41
Figure 5-2   Final Test of The Model For Some Variables 43

Chapter 2 ICSEAD'S Econometric Model of the Chinese Economy

Table 1   Estimation Results of the Production Function 75
Table 2   Gross Domestic Product and Expenditure 76
Table 3-1   Flow of Funds (National Bank Basis) 89
Table 3-2   Monetary Survey Table: 1995 90
Figure 1-(a) Composition of Real GDP 71
Figure 1-(b) Composition of Real GDP 71
Figure 2-(a) Real Industrial Output by Sector 72
Figure 2-(b) Real Industrial Output by Sector 72
Figure 3   Growth of Output, Employment and FDI in Non State-Owned
                   Industry 74
Figure 4-(a) Fixed Investment and Source of Funds 80
Figure 4-(b) Composition of Source of Funds for Fixed Investment 80
Figure 5   Income Difference and Urban Population Ratio 84
Figure 6-(a) Inflation Development 1 85
Figure 6-(b) Inflation Development 2 85
Figure 6-(c) Factor Decomposition of Retail Price Inflation 86
Figure 7   Growth of Total Loan and Bank Credits 91

Chapter 3 Outline of the PAIR China-Hong Kong Link Model
Table 1   Estimates of Export/Import Deflators 155
Table 2   Assumptions for Simulation..167
Table 3   Summary of Simulation Results..167
Table 4   Impacts on Merchandise Trade(US Dollar Term: 1990 Prices)..........168
Table 5   Impacts on Trade Prices(Local Currency Term)................................168
Table 6   Impacts on Trade Prices(US Dollar Term) 169
Figure1   China's Trade Statistics 153
Figure2   Estimates of RRXM 158
Figure3   Trade between China and Hong Kong..159
Figure4-1   Share of Main Destination in China's Export......................................160
Figure4-2   Share of Main Origin in China's Imports 161

Chapter 4 China's Econometric Model for Project PAIR
Table 1   Simulation Results 226
Table 2   Impacts of 10% Increase in Public Consumption
            on Major Endogenous Variables..227
Table 3   Impacts of 10% Increase in Fixed Investment Loan on
            Major Endogenous Variables..229
Table 4   Impacts of a Sustained Increase of 10% in Tax Revenues
            on Agriculture, Industry and Commerce over The Period
            1987–1992 on Major Endogenous Variables. 233
Table 5   Impacts of 10% Increase in Exports of Goods and Services
            on Endogenous Variables..235

**Chapter 5   A Computable General Equilibrium Model for the Chinese
             Economy**
Table 1   Standard Accounting Matrix and Related
            Sectoral Classification..263
Table 2   Some Major Applications of DRCCGE 265
Table 3   A Marco SAM Chinese Economy, 1995 (100Mn Yuan)....................266
Figure 1.   Structure of Production 254
Figure 2.   Structure of Demand 257

Chapter 6 Natural Decomposition of Total Factor Productivity Growth
Table 1   Comparison of China's and the US Economies 299

Chapter 7 China's Macroeconometric Annual Model
Table 1   Total Population and Forecast (Mid-year) 311
Figure 1   Diagram of China's Macro Econometric Annual Model 309

Chapter 8 Estimation of Effects of Exchange Rate Policies: China and Other East Asian Economies

Table 1 Current Account of East Asian Economies..323
Table 2 Long Run Elasticity of Relative Prices and Real Income 339
Table 3 Long Run Elasticity of Relative Prices and Real Income 340
Table 4 Summary of Simulation Results..340

Chapter 9 Output and Price Determination in Chinese Macroeconometric Models

Figure 1: Price Determination in Liang Model 364
Figure 2: Price Determination in Shen Model..365

Introduction to:
Econometric Modeling of China

L.R. Klein and S. Ichimura

The University of Pennsylvania and ICSEAD

Prior to the starting of the economic reform initiated by Deng Xiaoping in the Peoples' Republic of China in 1978, the concepts of modern economic analysis played little formal role inside the country. As for econometrics, neither was it part of the academic curriculum nor were the statistical materials for empirical model building to be found.

Outside the PRC, some economists with deep special interest in the economy of China attempted to try to follow economic events externally, using crude estimates of macroeconomic data and rough estimates of parametric specifications that were not necessarily in the minds of Chinese decision makers but more familiar to those schooled in "Western" economics. As early as 1968, such efforts produced a very comprehensive volume on trends and prospects of the Chinese economy around that time: *Economic Trends in Communist China*, edited by Alexander Eckstein, Walter Galenson and Ta-chung Liu, Aldine Publishing Co., Chicago, 1968. This was followed by a series of publications on the Chinese Economy by the Joint Economic Committee of the US Congress in 1967, 72, 75 and 78.[1] They were incisively summed up by Alexander Eckstein as *China's Economic Revolution*, Cambridge University Press, 1977.[2] These studies have tried hard to collect all the scanty statistical data available then and knit them together to peep into the working of the Chinese economy and find out the trends or prospects for the Chinese economy after the Cultural Revolution or economic reform. In

---

[1] They are: *An Economic Profile of Mainland China*, 1967; *People's Republic of China: An Economic Assessment*, 1972; *China: An Economic Reassessment*, 1975; *Chinese Economy Post-Mao*, 1978. As for the summary of these studies, see S. Ichimura's introduction to the translation of the Eckstein-Galenson-Liu monograph: *Chugoku Keizai no Hatten (Development of Chinese Economy)*, Sobunsha, Tokyo, 1979.

[2] The book was translated into Japanese under the supervision of Shigeru Ishikawa: Chugoku no Keizai Kakumei (China's Economic Revolution), University of Tokyo Press, 1980. He added an interesting note as a postscript.

the 80's a significant amount of statistical data gradually began to flow out, even to foreign researchers. Modeling the Chinese economy in the macro-econometric way appeared to be possible.

A pioneer in this respect was Lawrence J. Lau of Stanford University, who undertook the task of interpreting the economy of the PRC through the medium of a macroeconometric model that would function in a compatible way with the other models of Project LINK, a system of models that aimed to analyze the total world economy by building up all the separate pieces that represented individual countries or regional groupings of a few countries. In some respects, Professor Lau's approach resembled those used in LINK for the USSR and other countries in the Warsaw Pact agreements. Where data or other information were lacking, neo-classical economic theory with judgmental coefficient estimates were used for some of the equation specifications. Well-known production function specifications were used for estimating the technological equations and their factor demands or requirements. Trade relations with other countries were guided by movements in world markets and by pieces of information about such things as harvest conditions or other major primary activities.

In Japan the first pioneering work was undertaken by Professor Haruki Niwa then of Kyoto Sangyo University, and it was published as "Chapter 12: China Model" in S. Ichimura & M. Ezaki (ed), *Econometric Models of Asian LINK*, Springer-Verlag, 1985. It suffered, however, from the shortage of reliable statistics, so that Niwa had to convert some heterogeneous time-series to indices. Regrettably this made it difficult to integrate it into the Asian LINK system of econometric models.

In 1979, the Committee on Scholarly Communication with the Peoples' Republic of China (CSCPRC–US National Academy of Sciences, Social Science Research Council, and American Council of Learned Societies) visited China in order to establish academic contacts, and two members of that delegation were Lawrence J. Lau and Irving B. Kravis. Professor Lau lectured to Chinese economists, other social scientists, and governmental officials about statistical model building for China, while Professor Kravis lectured on methods of comparing macroeconomic magnitudes (especially GDP) among countries. The attendees at these and other economic lectures, who had been through the Cultural Revolution and its aftermath, responded enthusiastically to the delegation's expositions of modern economics, including econometrics. In the next year, a six-week seminar on econometrics drew an intensely interested group of participants. Measurement for model-building and measurement for insightful international comparisons took root and helped to generate interest in quantitative economics through-out China.[3]

In the meantime, some Chinese economists also visited Japanese universities and learned the methods of econometric modeling. In particular, Professor Tang Guoxing visited the Institute of Economic Research, Kyoto University and produced his first macroeconometric model of the Chinese economy in cooperation with Professor Chikashi Moriguchi in 1984.[4] His later improved model was published as "Economy of China: 1969-89, A Macroeconometric Model," in: S. Ichimura & Y. Matsumoto (ed.), *Econometric Models of Asian-Pacific Countries*, Springer-Verlag, 1994.

It is truly remarkable that within 10 years, a corps of Chinese scholars were taught to go their own way and develop statistical data files, in the modern sense, and estimate econometric relationships of world class for use in forecasting, scenario analysis, policy formation, and other aspects of Chinese economic relationships—at home and abroad. After two decades, a considerable literature has grown on the subject of econometric analysis of the PRC.[5]

The International Centre for the Study of East Asian Development (ICSEAD) at Kitakyushu has also devoted considerable resources to hosting Chinese visiting research scholars and has also drawn upon local Japanese talent in building econometric models of China ever since its foundation in 1989. It is the objective of the present collection in this volume to demonstrate the considerable achievement of econometricians in putting the economy of China into dynamic equation systems that model the country for the purposes of econometric study. It is an enormous achievement, considering the situation that prevailed in China when the delegation from CSCPRC visited in 1979.

---

[3] The detailed report of this delegation is availabe as *Report of the CSCPRC Economics Delegation to the People's Republic of China, October 1979 with an Appendix by Irving B. Kravis on "An Approximation of the RelativeReal Per Capita GDP of the People's Republic of China,"* National Academy of Sciences, Washington, D.C., 1980 pp. 86.

[4] It was presented at the LINK Project meeting, Staford University in August, 1984. His later works are made available as working papers at Osaka Sangyo University (with the help of Professor Ippei Sugiura) and Osaka International University earlier than in the Ichimura-Matsumoto volume.

[5] The surveys of model-building in East and Southeast Asian countries including China are provided by S. Ichimura: Chapter 1: A Survey of Econometric Model-Building in East and Southeast Asia, in Ichimura-Ezaki, *op. cit.* and Chapter 1: Development of Econometric Models in Asian-Pacific Countries, Ichimura-Matsumoto, *op. cit.*

Some of the contributors to the chapters in this book are Chinese scholars. Now, they have independent knowledge and resources to carry on the econometric work that was started by outsiders. The internal scholars are much better situated to obtain data efficiently in large volume and with the least reporting delay. They are also well trained to know what to look for by way of Chinese behavioral or technological or institutional characteristics that are essential for meaningful econometric analysis.[6]

At ICSEAD and other research Centres, Chinese economic scholars have interacted for nearly 20 years with foreigners who would like to examine the econometrics of China, too. In this volume we find contributions by Japanese as well as Chinese econometricians, and there has been much fruitful sharing of information on data interpretation or assessment, on model specification, and on computational treatment of the data.

A feature of the book is to have data appendixes in which the authors indicate where the data originated, the conceptual issues of social accounting, and some of the data revisions that have occurred or are to be expected in the future. This puts Chinese econometric modeling into "international play", a situation that is conducive to constructive appraisal, criticism, and testing. China has done so well in becoming a leading world economic power in the past two decades, that there can now be a two-way (feedback) relationship in this field of scholarly investigation as well.

All the contributions are not total-economy macroeconometric models, although that is the central theme. There are chapters on the econometrics of China's balance of payments, substitution elasticities in foreign trade, technical progress, and other specific aspects of Chinese economics.

The paper by Tang Guoxing focuses attention on a model of China's balance of payments, but covers other aspects of the macroeconomy as well. Given the turmoil and surprise caused by the Asian financial crisis (not involving China directly) it is entirely appropriate for model builders to pay increasing attention to payments flows between China and the rest-of-the-

---

[6] More recent publications in China are numerous. Here we quote only four books which seem to have collected most important econometric models and input-output models: The State Council Development Research Center (ed.), *China's Economic Development and Models (Zhongguo Jing Ji De Fazhan Yu Moxing)*, Zhongguo Calizheng Jingji Chuban She, Beijing, 1990; Chen Xikang (ed.), *Chinese Urban Economy and Input Output Analysis (Zhongguo Chengxiang Jingji Touru Ahanyong Chanchu Fenxi)*, Kexue Chubanshe, Beijing, 1992, and Wang Huijiong, Li Boxi and Li Shantong (eds.) *Chinese Practical Macroeconometric Models (Ahong Shiyong Hongguan Jingji Moxing, 1993 and also 1999)*, Zhon Guo Kaizheng Jingji Cheban She, Beijing, 1993 and also 1999.

world. This paper is definitely a step forward in treating balance of payments items from an econometric point of view.

Dr. Shen Lisheng, who has often attended meetings of Project LINK and worked on Asia-Pacific models at Pennsylvania and Stanford University, has built a macroeconometric model along the lines of Professor Lau's work. That forms the subject of his chapter.

Mr. Zhou-Fang's contribution is more specialized in dealing with the estimates of total factor productivity growth. That is a subject of immense importance in Asian development and has received much attention in the past five years. The lines of analysis that were developed by Professor Lau in estimating production functions have been very illuminating. Other less careful analyses have not been constructive. Zhou-Fang follows an aggregate production function approach and makes the very interesting separation between disembodied technical change (independent of the *scale* of production) and embodied technical change, where economies of scale are important. In this paper, the author shows how to separate the estimates of the two sources of technical change and develops that concept from econometric treatment of production functions.

Macroeconometric models based on methods of statistical inference are predominantly produced in this volume, but other approaches to quantitative analysis of macroeconomic performance are also explored. The chapter by Ms. Shantong Li and Mr. Fan Zhai is based on a computable general equilibrium (CGE) model of China. The CGE models are usually partially based on statistical samples but some parameters are estimated subjectively or from separate analyses (univariate time averages, *e.g.*) and are not constrained by available degrees of freedom, in the statistical sense. They are mainly concerned with long-run development and may be based on a variety of information sources. In an economy such as China's, where the statistical base is still in a development phase, the CGE approach is very attractive.

Mr. Youcai Liang, like Mr. Shen Lisheng, has frequently participated in LINK meetings and also spent much time at the University of Pennsylvania. His model for China is prepared in the present instance, for Project PAIR, centered at the Institute for Developing Economies, Japan. It covers the economy as a whole and is not confined to limited aspects of the Chinese economy. Mr. Liang pays much attention to data issues in his works.

Professor Soshichi Kinoshita does not, in his chapter[7], estimate a total macro model for China; he reviews the equations for output and price determination in two Chinese econometric models, the model of Youcai Liang and the model of Shen Lisheng. Both models have related lineage but Dr. Liang is associated in China with the State Information Center, while Dr. Shen represents the Chinese Academy of Social Sciences.

Professor Yoshihisa Inada is associated with the staff at ICSEAD; so his model of China, covering the economy as a whole is built for the World LINK Model of ICSEAD. He too received much training at Pennsylvania and Stanford. He is able to provide an excellent Japanese assessment of the structure of the Chinese economy.

In all the models, authors fully recognized the need for data improvement and enlargement in China, in order to provide better estimation bases for the economy. Professor Shoichi Ito is very well qualified to examine Chinese statistical data. He shows how contradictions arise in estimating long run statistical series on Chinese demography. Special attention is paid to estimates of the total population, which is already a key factor in assessing China's growth prospects–econometrically based and otherwise. It is very good to know that the data for this entire project are being examined by a person of Dr. Ito's importance.

Finally Mr. So Umezaki's chapter outlines another component of the PAIR project, namely a prototype model for both China and Hong Kong. It is evident that Hong Kong's prosperity is closely tied to that of China. This is another extremely valuable PAIR project involving the Institute for Developing Economies.

A chapter is included that deals with the estimated elasticity of substitution between the exports of China, on the one hand, and the exports of each of several Asian countries that experienced financial crises in 1997 and 1998. The purpose of this econometric exercise was to see if the exchange rate policies of several East Asian countries like South Korea, Thailand, Malaysia, Indonesia, and the Philippines, by which they informally pegged their currencies to the US dollar, were responsible for the loss of world export trade to China. China unified currency rates in 1994 and then held the exchange rate of the reminbi steady during the crisis period.

---

[7] Kinoshita presented his own regional model of Asia-Pacific economies in his "A Linked International Model for the Pacific-Basin Economies," in Ichimura-Matsumoto, *op. cit.* It did not include China, however.

Two significant data problems confronted Professor Y. Inada, Junichi Makino, and me at the onset of the crisis. In order to deal with the fast-moving currency values after July 1997, we resorted to monthly data to see if there was world substitution in favor of China's exports. Lags are quite long in international adjustments and our sample period was brief, January, 1994, through December, 1998. To determine the rate change when China unified rates, January, 1994, we used the swap rates (Shanghai, Shenzen, and Hong Kong–averaged). We found evidence of significant elasticity of substitution with respect to relative prices vis-à-vis China and also vis-à-vis Japan, whose currency fluctuated in the relevant period.

Econometric modeling involves statistical approximations of live economies. The approximations can always be improved by the availability of more data, better data, more insight into national (and world) economic behavior. It is useful to take stock of the present situation in the econometric modeling of China, reflect on the results, and return to the drawing boards for improved products.

1.   A MODEL STUDY OF BALANCE OF PAYMENTS AND MONEY SUPPLY OF CHINA[*]

Tang Guoxing

Fudan University

Introduction

A Balance of Payments is a total record of specific but comprehensive economic transactions between an economic entity[1] (a country or an area) and others that happened in a certain period. The balance of payments statement is a financial statement that represents international payments and receipts according to specialized accounting classifications with double-entry bookkeeping. It includes the following:

- The transactions of expenditures and receipts for merchandise, services and investment income between an economic entity and others in the world.
- Ownership of monetary gold, special drawing rights and the changes in credits and debits between the economic entity and others.
- A total balance that allows for statistical errors and missing information.

According to the International Monetary Fund (IMF), the balance of international payment accounts mainly covers four items: current items, capital items, errors and omissions, and reserves and related items.

(1) Current items
Current items constitute the *current account*; this includes three component accounts, that is, the foreign trade account, the invisible trade account (also called non-trade or services and income account) and unrequited transfers.

[*] This research is supported by Chinese Natural Science Fund (79790130).

[1] Economic entity: according to the definition in the fifth edition of the balance of Payments Manual, an economic entity is compared with some economic entities who are closely related in the special domain. It is mostly an independent country or area.

(2) Capital items

These items constitute the capital account. It reflects capital transfers with other countries, that is, international capital flows, which include both capital inflows and outflows. Capital outflows point to the increase of foreign assets, that is, the increase in the foreign rights of domestic citizens[2] with respect to non-citizens, or the decrease of corresponding debts. Capital inflows point to an increase in foreign liabilities or the decrease in foreign assets. The capital account includes two second-level-accounts: long-term capital account and short-term capital account.

(3) Errors and omissions

Because the statistics of international payments adopt the rule of double-entry bookkeeping, the credit account and debit account as totals must be equal; their difference is zero. But in practice it seldom balances because of differences among data sources and statistical measurements in the entry of practical international payments statistics. There is often a net credit or net debit; so account keepers force the two sides to balance by adding a separate item—errors and omissions.

(4) Reserves and related items

Reserves and related items are the foreign assets held by the monetary authorities aimed at balancing international payments directly and intervening in markets to influence exchange rates or for other purposes. It includes monetary gold, foreign exchange, SDRs, reserve position in the IMF and other credit items.

The above items should add to zero in the balance of payments accounts:

$$\begin{pmatrix} Current \\ balance \end{pmatrix} + \begin{pmatrix} Capital \\ balance \end{pmatrix} + \begin{pmatrix} Errors\,and \\ Omissions \end{pmatrix} + \begin{pmatrix} Change\,of \\ reserves \end{pmatrix} = 0$$

So a negative change of reserves represents an increase of the sum of the other items in the balance identity.

Since its foundation, the IMF set about establishing a global unified international payment system, and published the first edition of *Balance of Payment Manual*. The IMF then adapted it continually in 1950, 1961 1977 and 1993, and added new items. Now most of the member countries of the IMF adopt the concept and classifications of Balance of Payments,

---

[2] citizen: citizens in an economic entity include its governments and agencies, the individuals and all kinds of enterprises and institutions who exist or live one year or more in this domain.

from the fourth edition in 1977. Editing and publishing balance of payments accounts have been obligations of the member countries and enable them to take part in activities of other international economic organizations.

Before the reforms and open-door policy, Chinese foreign economic statistics were limited to the statistics of foreign trade and foreign exchange payments. Due to the relatively smaller quantity of import and export trade and services and income items, and not being a member of IMF. There were no international payments statistics. After the open door policy and reform, great changes have taken place in Chinese foreign trade and capital flows. In 1980, the Chinese Import and Export Management Commission suggested the lay out of a corresponding system for Chinese balance of payments statistics. In the same year, China obtained membership status in the IMF and World Bank. According to the rules of the IMF, a member country must periodically provide relevant data, including the balance of payments, as a necessary condition of getting loans on favorable terms from the two international finance organizations. The State Statistics Bureau and the Bank of China took the responsibility for drawing up a Chinese balance of payment tabulation. In 1981, based on Chinese economic practices and general international statistical methods, the State General Bureau of Foreign exchange Management laid out the first statistical system of the Chinese balance of payments. Since then, the statistical work began formally for the Chinese balance of payments.

In October 1984, adapting to the economic development and the need for further opening and reform, based on the suggestion of relevant institutions, the State Statistics Bureau and the General Bureau of Foreign Exchange Management supplemented and revised original statistics to conform with international practice and tried to be more perfect, and set out the current *Balance of Payments Statistics System*. On September 1, 1985, the State General Bureau of Foreign Exchange Management formally published a summary balance of payments of China from 1982 to 1984, which is the PRC's first publication of a balance of payments. In 1987, China published the balance of payments for 1985 and 1986. Since 1988, China has annually been publishing the balance of payments of the previous year, in detail.

Domestic publication of the balance of payments, laid out according to the fourth edition of the "Balance of Payments Manual", and the counterpart published in *International Financial Statistics* of the IMF, laid out according to the fifth edition differ in the following ways:

(1) The latter put transportation, travel, financial services of the non-trade account into the service account, and investment income from interest, profits, dividends and compensation of employees into the income account;

(2) The latter does not distinguish between long-term and short-term capital, because with the development of international financial freedom and financial instruments, the distinguishing of capital terms becomes less significant; long or short term is only a difference in the type of financial commodities.

This research is based on the data for domestic publication, and the sample period of most data is from 1982 to 1996. With the expansion of the Chinese opening, especially after the East Asian financial crisis, the Chinese balance of payments has been widely highlighted.

The Balance of Payments Model is an important part of the overall Chinese econometric model. We can see in what follows that the items of international payments are closely related with the domestic economy and with the outside environment. They affect economic growth and inflation through their influence on money supply, domestic supply capacity, and aggregate demand.

1. Characteristics of the Chinese Balance of Payments

Table 1-1 is a summary of the Chinese balance of payments from 1982 to 1996, from which we can see the following characteristics:

(1) Imports and exports of China have developed rapidly since the opening and reform. The average annual rate of increase of total trade is high at 16.3%, surpassing 8% for world trade, and the amount of foreign trade in 1996 equaled the level of Japan in 1985 and of the United States in 1977.

(2) The current account has not been in balance, which is obviously different from the situation before 1978. There is a surplus in some years, such as 1982, 1990, 1991. The surplus surpassed 10% of total imports and exports, and there was a huge deficit in other years, such as 1985, 1986, 1993.

Table 1-1 Chinese balance of payments (1982-1996)   Unit: 100 million USD

Item	1982	1983	1984	1985	1986	1987	1988	1989
1. Current balance	56.74	42.40	20.30	-114.17	-70.34	3.00	-38.02	-43.17
a. Trade balance	42.49	19.90	0.14	-131.23	-91.40	-16.61	-53.15	-56.20
Exports(fob)	211.25	207.07	239.05	251.08	257.56	347.34	410.54	432.20
Imports(fob)	168.76	187.17	238.91	382.31	348.96	363.95	463.69	488.40
b. Non-trade	9.39	17.39	15.74	14.63	17.27	17.37	10.94	9.22
Revenue	36.04	40.28	48.19	45.33	49.27	54.13	63.27	64.97
Expenditure	26.65	22.89	32.45	30.70	32.00	36.76	52.33	55.75
c.Unrequited transfer	4.86	5.11	4.42	2.43	3.79	2.24	4.19	3.81
Private net	5.30	4.36	3.05	1.71	2.55	2.48	4.17	2.37
Official net	-0.44	0.75	1.37	0.72	1.24	-0.24	0.03	1.43
2. Capital balance	3.38	-2.26	-10.03	89.72	59.43	60.02	71.32	37.21
a. Long-term capital	3.89	0.49	-1.13	67.01	82.38	57.90	70.56	52.40
Inflow	33.12	7.02	41.28	95.31	113.94	97.40	111.14	121.33
Outflow	29.23	26.53	42.41	28.30	31.56	39.50	40.58	68.93
b. Short-term capital	-0.51	-2.75	-8.90	22.71	-22.93	2.12	0.77	-15.19
Inflow	2.44	0.59	2.23	113.46	93.43	94.26	91.49	63.46
Outflow	2.95	3.34	11.13	90.75	116.36	92.14	90.72	78.65
3. Errors & omissions	2.79	-3.66	-9.32	0.92	-1.84	-14.50	-10.94	-0.17
4. Change in reserves	-62.91	-36.48	-0.95	23.53	12.75	-48.52	-22.36	6.13

Item	1990	1991	1992	1993	1994	1995	1996
1. Current balance	119.97	132.72	64.02	-119.02	76.57	16.18	72.43
a. Trade balance	91.65	87.43	51.83	-106.55	72.90	180.50	195.35
Exports(fob)	515.19	589.19	695.68	756.60	1025.60	1281.10	1510.70
Imports(fob)	423.54	501.76	643.85	863.10	952.70	1100.60	1315.40
b. Non-trade	25.58	36.98	0.63	-24.20	-9.69	-178.67	-144.22
Revenue	88.72	106.98	148.44	155.83	223.57	243.21	279.19
Expenditure	63.14	70.00	147.81	177.06	230.73	421.88	423.40
c.Unrequited transfer	2.74	8.31	11.57	11.73	13.37	14.35	21.29
Private net	2.22	4.44	8.05	8.84	8.36	8.10	18.28
Official net	0.52	3.87	3.52	2.89	5.01	6.25	3.01
2. Capital balance	32.57	2.20	-2.50	234.72	326.44	386.74	399.67
a. Long-term capital	64.54	76.70	6.56	274.11	357.56	382.49	415.54
Inflow	116.11	128.58	276.42	503.54	607.89	660.67	697.21

Outflow	51.57	51.88	269.86	229.43	250.33	278.18	281.67
b. Short-term capital	-31.98	3.62	-9.06	-39.39	-31.12	4.25	-15.87
Inflow	87.67	74.65	25.80	4.75	10.04	16.44	12.56
Outflow	119.65	71.03	34.86	44.14	41.16	12.19	28.43
3. Errors & omissions	-31.26	5.97	-84.19	-98.03	-97.75	-178.10	-155.59
4. Change in reserves	-121.27	-140.89	22.67	-17.67	-305.27	-224.81	-316.51

Sources : Chinese Financial Statistics1952--1987, China Statistical Yearbook, Almanac of China's Finance and Banking

(3) In general, the balance on goods and services tends to improve. In the period from 1978 to 1996, there are eight years in deficit, but from 1991 to 1996, only in 1993 is there a deficit, and its size relative to total imports and exports is only 7%, lower than that of 1978, 1979, 1985 and 1986.

(4) Usually the goods and services surplus occurs in periods of low economic growth, such as 1981-1983, 1990-1991; otherwise, a deficit occurs in periods of high economic growth, such as 1978-1980, 1985-1989. But since 1992, the Chinese economy has maintained high growth rates (over 10%), and only in 1993 is there a deficit. The surplus has become a basic trend. This fact makes clear that the industrial structure of China has been reasonable, and especially, that Chinese export ability and import substitution have been greatly increased due to large foreign direct investment.

(5) The balance on non-trade has changed to deficit since 1993; the main reason is the rapid increase of the investment income expenditure. The net investment income expenditure is 11.8 billion US dollars in 1995, and 12.4 billion US dollars in 1996. However, the balance on goods and services in these years is 12.0 billion US dollars and 17.5 billion US dollars, respectively. The net outflow of investment income has become a major factor in restraining the growth of the current balance of China.

(6) The proportion of short-term capital in the balance of payments is small, and that of long-term capital is relatively high; so the Chinese balance of payments pattern is not sensitive to the effects of international financial speculation and has stability.

(7) Since 1979, long-term capital supports a positive net inflow, and there are obvious differences among the period before 1984, from 1985 to

1991 and the years after 1992. These relate to the different phases of the opening and reform.

(8) The errors and omissions are quite high.

Due to the opening and reform, the trade balance of China has improved since 1990. Although the net outflow of investment income has risen rapidly, the current balance still remains in surplus in most years; so net foreign assets have an upward trend. Until 1996, Chinese net foreign assets were estimated at 16.0 billion US dollars; so the Chinese balance of payments pattern has been in the stage from debtor country to creditor country.

2. Current Balance

2.1. Trade Balance

2.1.1 Statistics and Goods Structure of Imports and Exports

There are three kinds of import and export statistics in China.

(1) Statistics of the Ministry of Foreign Trade, which are based on foreign trade contracts.
(2) Customs statistics based on customs documents of imports and exports. Imports are calculated CIF, while exports are calculated FOB.
(3) Statistics of international payments based on the rules of IMF. The value of imports and exports are all calculated FOB, but imported and exported goods for processing and assembling, only the processing charges, in the services balance.

Due to the statistical differences, we take two steps to estimate the trade balance. (1) Estimate customs imports and exports by commodity category and then combine them to get total imports (CIF) and total exports (FOB); (2) Use statistical equations, to change import and export statistics from a customs basis to those for international payments.

Customs statistics of China are made on the basis of SITC (Standard International Trade Classification) specified by the United Nations; its one-digit classifications are the following:

Primary Goods:

SITC0 – food and live animals for food (such as corn, meat, aquatic products, getables and fruits)

SITC1 – beverages and tobacco (such as tea, coffee, cacao, sugar, cigarettes)

SITC2 – non-edible raw materials (such as wood, cotton, raw silk, wool, chemical fibers, medicinal materials, ore)

SITC3 – mineral fuels, lubricants and related materials (such as coal, crude oil, petroleum products)

SITC4 – animal and vegetable oil, fats and wax

Manufactured Goods:

SITC5 – chemicals and related products (such as medicine, fertilizers, industrial chemicals, fireworks)

SITC6 – light and textile products, rubber products, mineral and metallurgical products (such as tires, paper, steel, cement)

SITC7 – machinery and transportation equipment (such as TV sets, computers, machine tools, bicycles, automobiles, ships, planes)

SITC8 – miscellaneous products (such as clothes, shoes, toys, medical appliances, cameras)

SITC9 – other products not classified.

The contents in the above categories are major import and export goods of China. In the model we separately list SITC0 and SITC1, SITC2/SITC4, SITC3, and SITC5~SITC9 goods (as one classification to estimate).

Table 2-1 Structural Changes of the Imports and Exports of China (%)

Year	SITC 0~1 Ex-ports	SITC 2, 4 Ex-ports	SIT 3 Ex-ports	SITC 5~9 Ex-ports	SITC 0~1 Im-ports	SITC 2, 4 Im-ports	SITC 3 Im-ports	SITC 5~9 Im-ports
1980	17.0	9.8	23.6	49.8	14.8	18.9	1.0	65.2
1981	13.5	9.4	23.7	53.3	17.4	18.7	0.4	63.5
1982	13.5	7.8	23.8	55.0	22.5	16.2	0.9	60.4
1983	13.3	9.0	21.0	56.7	14.8	11.8	0.5	72.8
1984	12.8	9.8	23.1	54.3	8.9	9.6	0.5	81.0
1985	14.3	10.2	26.1	49.4	4.2	7.9	0.4	87.5

1986	14.8	9.8	11.9	63.6	4.2	7.8	1.2	86.8
1987	12.6	9.5	11.5	66.5	6.3	8.5	1.2	84.0
1988	12.9	9.1	8.3	69.7	6.9	9.9	1.4	81.8
1989	12.3	8.2	8.2	71.3	7.4	9.7	2.8	80.1
1990	11.2	6.0	8.4	74.4	6.5	9.5	2.4	81.5
1991	10.8	5.1	6.6	77.5	4.7	9.0	3.3	83.0
1992	10.6	3.9	5.5	80.0	4.2	7.8	4.4	83.6
1993	10.1	3.6	4.5	81.8	2.4	5.7	5.6	86.3
1994	9.1	3.8	3.4	83.7	2.8	8.0	3.5	85.7
1995	7.6	3.2	3.6	85.6	4.9	9.7	3.9	81.5
1996	7.7	2.9	3.9	85.5	4.4	8.9	5.0	81.7

Source: China Statistical Yearbook 1997

The structure of Chinese imports and exports has undergone great changes since 1980 (see Table 2-1). In exports, the proportion of primary goods SITC0~4, especially that of mineral fuel SITC3, has steadily fallen, while the proportion of manufactured goods has risen. It was over 85% in 1996. In imports, it is remarkable that the proportion of SITC3 rises. Since 1993, China has become a net importer of energy (mainly crude oil).

2.1.2 Specification of the Import and export Equations

(1) Export Function

Export (*EX*) is the foreign demand for domestic products, so it depends on foreign income (*Y*) and export price. On the assumption that China is a "little country", the price of Chinese export merchandise (*PEX*) does not affect the world export price of the same merchandise (*PEW*), so a reduction of the export price of China results in the reduction of relative price *PEX/PEW*, thus enhancing the price-competitive capacity of Chinese goods and promotes exports. The export price *PEX* is assumed to be the domestic price *P* divided by the yuan-dollar exchange rate, *REX*; so the relative price can be expressed as *P/REX/PEW*.

For some merchandise, there are supply capacity constraints for export from China, especially in primary products, such as agricultural and mineral products. Due to the influence of climate and the land constraint, supply of these products is less than their demand. With the rise of domestic demand, the supply for export will decline. Based on the above analysis, we specify the export function as:

$$EX = f(+Y, -P/REX/PEW, +S, -D)$$

where Y expresses world economic level, S is the supply capacity for export, and D is the domestic demand. For the different categories of export goods, the economic indicators that represent the above influential factors may vary, as listed in Table 2-2, based on the results of data analysis.

Table 2-2 Influential Factors of Different Categories of Exports

Influential Factors	SITC0, 1	SITC2, 4	SITC3	SITC5~9
World economy	World exports			World exports
World export price			Average crude oil price	
Domestic price	Purchasing Price of farm products	Purchasing price of farm products		
Exchange rate	Exchange rate Yuan/$		Exchange rate Yuan/$, Yen/$	Exchange rate Yuan/$
Supply capacity	Gross agricultural output	Gross agricultural output	Output of crude oil	Accumulated FDI
Domestic demand		Gross industrial output		

(2) Import Function

Import (*IM*) is China's demand for the products of the rest of the world; so we consider following influential factors as explanatory variables:
(1) Domestic economic level X;
(2) Import substitution capacity represented by K;
(3) Relative price of imports to domestic products;
(4) Payment capacity for imports Z.

The specification of an import function can be expressed as:

$$IM = f(+X, -K, -PIM*REX/P, +Z)$$

Because the foreign-funded enterprises can produce many products, that must be imported at the beginning of openness, Chinese import substitution capacity will be enhanced after introducing foreign direct invest-ment. For this reason, we make the accumulated foreign direct investment (*KXDI*) an explanatory variable representing import substitution capacity for estimating the import function of manufactured goods.

Import prices in US dollars *PIM* can be valued in *RMB* Yuan (*PIM* * *REX*). If the ratio to domestic price $P - (PIM*REX/P)$ rises, it means that imported goods are more expensive and imports will be restrained. They are negatively related to price. We choose foreign exchange reserves *KFXG* as an explanatory variable representing the payment capacity *Z*. As in the export case, for different categories of imports the representative indicators may be different. Table 2-3 lists the results of the real data analysis.

Table 2-3 Influential Factors of Different Categories of Imports

Influential Factors	SITC0, 1	SITC2, 4	SITC3	SITC5~9
Domestic economic level	Population	Gross indust-rial product	Gross indust-rial product	Output value of agriculture and industry
Domestic price	Purchase price of farm products	Purchase price of farm products		
Import price			World price of crude oil	
Exchange rate	Exchange rate Yuan/$		Exchange rate Yuan/$	
Import substi-ution capacity	Grain output	Gross agricul-tural Output		Accumulated FDI
Payment capacity	For'n exchange reserve			

(3) Influence of Foreign Direct Investment on Chinese Foreign Trade

Table 2-4 Contribution of Foreign-Funded Enterprises to Total Exports

Year	Exports of For-eign-Funded Enterprises (100m $) (a)	Growth Rate of (a) (%)	Ratio of (a) to Total Exports (%)	Contribution Rate of Foreign-Funded Enterprises to Total Exports*(%)
1985	3.2		1.1	
1986	4.8	50.0	1.6	4.4
1987	12.0	150.0	3.0	7.5
1988	24.6	105.0	5.2	15.6
1989	49.2	100.0	8.3	49.0

1990	78.0	58.8	12.5	30.2
1991	121.0	54.2	16.8	49.2
1992	174.0	44.2	20.4	40.5
1993	252.4	45.4	27.5	114.9
1994	347.1	37.5	28.7	32.4
1995	468.7	35.0	36.6	47.5
1996	615.1	31.2	40.8	642.1

*Contribution rate of foreign funded enterprises to total exports = increment of exports of foreign-funded enterprises ÷ increment of total exports

Source: China Statistical Yearbook

Since the opening and reform, the most remarkable aspect of Chinese foreign trade is the rapid increase of imports and exports of foreign-funded enterprises, as is shown by Table 2-4. During 'the eighth five-year plan' (1991-1995) period, the average annual rate of increase of Chinese export value was 19.1%, while that of the foreign-funded enterprises was as high as 50.8%. In the total imports and exports of China, the proportion of the foreign-funded enterprises has risen from lower than 15% in 1990 to 46% in 1996. The export ratio is 41%, and the import ratio is 51%. Foreign-funded enterprises play a very important role in Chinese foreign trade. In many equations of the model there is a variable *KXDI*, the accumulated foreign direct investment (FDI), which is used to reflect the productive capacity of foreign-funded enterprises, as well as their import demand for raw materials.

2.2 Non-Trade Balance

Non-merchandise trade in the current items includes such services as freight transportation and insurance, port services, tourism, investment income (profits, interest, transaction fees of banks) and other services, such as communications, processing charges, contracted projects abroad, patent fees, financial services, etc. (See Table 2-5.)

2.2.1 Balance on transportation and Insurance

The balance on transportation and insurance relates to the amount of imports and exports, freight fares and transport capacity. The marine transport capacity of China cannot keep up with the rapid increase of foreign trade; so the balance on transportation stays in deficit continuously.

After 1992, due to the fast development of foreign trade, the deficit expanded rapidly. It is estimated that this situation will continue.

Freight transportation income is mainly explained by imports and exports, and the exchange rate, because of its influence on the price of transportation service. The depreciation of the RMB yuan would reduce the service price calculated in US dollars and would expand demand.

Besides the export quantity, the expenditure on transportation will depend on the increase of exports. The increase of domestic transport capacity cannot keep up with the increase of exports. This results in more expenditure paid to foreign shipping companies. Moreover, the increase of the imports of machinery, equipment and raw materials due to the foreign direct investment is also one reason to expand the expenditure on transportation.

Table 2-5 Non-Trade Balance and Its Components (100 million USD)

Year	Transportation and Insurance	Tourism	Investment Income	Other	Balance
1982	0.4	7.8	3.8	−2.5	9.4
1983	0.9	8.9	11.6	−2.1	17.4
1984	1.7	9.8	15.3	−7.7	15.7
1985	−3.7	9.4	8.4	0.5	14.6
1986	−3.6	12.2	−0.2	8.9	17.3
1987	−3.4	14.6	−2.2	8.3	17.4
1988	−5.3	16.1	−1.6	1.7	10.9
1989	−12.5	14.3	2.3	5.1	9.2
1990	−8.9	17.5	10.6	6.4	25.6
1991	−8.6	23.3	8.4	13.9	37.0
1992	−24.5	14.4	2.5	8.3	0.6
1993	−37.5	18.9	−12.8	7.3	-24.2
1994	−49.8	42.9	−10.4	7.6	−9.7
1995	−86.0	50.4	−117.7	−25.4	−78.7
1996	−73.5	57.3	−124.4	−3.6	−144.2

Source: China Statistical Yearbook Almanac of China's Finance and Banking

2.2.2 Balance on Tourism and Travel

Tourism is the main advantageous item in the Chinese non-trade balance, it remains in surplus in the long-term, and it was a main source for maintaining the non-trade balance surplus before 1992. Since 1992, because of the development of international business and the relaxation of restrictions on tourism abroad, expenditure on tourism and travel has increased rapidly, and the balance was reduced on one occasion.

Tourism income has a stable increasing trend, so we choose its lag as an explanatory factor. Besides, the changes of the exchange rate and the level of foreign economic activities represented by total exports have influence on tourism income.

For tourism expenditure we mainly consider the following explanatory factors: (a) the level of foreign economic activities, represented by total imports and exports and foreign direct investment; (b) the exchange rate of RMB to the US dollar; (c) payment capacity, represented by foreign exchange reserves.

2.2.3 Balance on Investment Income

There was a reverse of the positive balance on investment income in 1993, changing it to a deficit, amounting to 11.7 billion and 12.4 billion US dollars deficit in 1995 and 1996. It has become a main source of non-trade deficit. The deficit on investment income is related to the profit outflow of foreign-funded enterprises and the interest payments on foreign loans. The outflow of investment income may increase due to the large inflows of foreign capital.

While direct investment abroad is a small quantity, the main funding source is from the income of the Bank of China, by operations of its foreign assets, which cannot be increased rapidly. In a word, the balance on investment income of China may be in a deficit for a long period of time.

The expenditure of investment income can mainly be explained by the accumulated foreign direct investment (*KXDI*), but also by the change of exchange rate. It seems that the depreciation of RMB has an effect of reducing the outflow of investment income.

A main source of the revenue from the investment income of China is the interest from operating with the short-term foreign assets of banks and the foreign exchange reserves. The former are related to trade credit; so we choose total imports and exports as explanatory variables. The latter can be explained by the current balance and foreign exchange reserves. With the increase of foreign-funded enterprises, the financing of foreign exchange for these enterprises has been increasing. But because these enterprises are owned by Chinese citizens, according to the definitions of international payments, this part of income is not listed in international investment income. This means that the increase of foreign-funded enterprises will reduce the revenue of investment income from abroad; so the amount of foreign-funded enterprises, represented by accumulated foreign direct investment (*KXDI*), is considered as an explanatory variable to reflect this negative factor.

2.2.4 Balance on Other Service Items

Other service items include communication, finance service, non-cargo insurance, patent use, entrusted processing, project contract, information service and consulting, etc.; the commissions and fares charged to these items belong in the balance on other services.

The revenue for other services comes mainly from projects contracted abroad, labor service cooperation with foreign countries and negotiated processing. The revenue from labor service cooperation is explained by the total value of imports and exports, which is representative of the level of foreign economic activities. Inflation will influence production cost including wage, and be disadvantageous to the negotiated processing, so the price, a negative factor, is also used as an explanatory variable.

Expenditure has been increasing rapidly after 1992, mainly in the form of foreign employees' wages. It is related to the increased presence of foreign-funded enterprises; so we chose the accumulated foreign direct investment (*KXDI*) as a major explanatory variable. Also we considered the total inflow and outflow of other long-term capital and the foreign exchange rate.

3. Capital Account

3.1 Characteristics of Capital Account

From 1979 to 1996, China has utilized 284.0 billion US dollars of foreign capital in total, of which the foreign direct investment is 175.0 billion US dollars, 62% of the total; foreign loans amount to 104.1 billion US dollars,

37% of the total. During the period, the utilization of foreign capital has gone through three different stages:

(1) 1979-1982, during this period, foreign loans predominated. In the composition of foreign capital, the share of foreign loans was 85.82%, while the foreign direct investment was only 9.36%.

(2) 1983-1991, China increased the utilization of foreign direct investment year by year. Although foreign loans were still a major form of utilization of foreign capital, the share of foreign direct investment increased sharply from less than 10% to one-third. This structure held until 1991.

(3) After Deng Xiaoping's inspection in 1992, foreign direct investment in-creased rapidly and came to be the major form of foreign capital. In 1992, its share was 57.32%; in recent years it has been above 70%.

Seen from the whole capital account in Table 3-1, there was a small deficit in 1983, 1984 and 1992; otherwise there was surplus. The capital account has become the important source of covering the current balance deficit and increasing foreign exchange reserves. The changes in the net capital flow from 1982 to 1992, were steady; later they increased significantly. From 1982 to 1992, the total net inflow of foreign capital was 42.0 billion US dollars, while in only four years, from 1993 to 1996, it reached 134.0 billion US dollars. It means that the utilization of foreign capital in China essentially started in 1992.

Table 3-1 Structure of Utilization of Foreign Capital

Year	Foreign Capital Actually Used (100m $)	Foreign Loans		Foreign Direct Investment	
		Value (100m $)	Ratio (%)	Value (100m $)	Ratio (%)
1979-82	124.57	106.90	85.82	11.66	9.36
1983	19.81	10.65	53.76	6.36	32.10
1984	27.05	12.86	47.54	12.58	46.51
1985	46.47	26.88	57.84	16.61	35.74
1986	72.58	50.14	69.08	18.74	25.82
1987	84.52	58.05	68.68	23.14	27.38
1988	102.26	64.87	63.44	31.94	31.23
1989	100.59	62.86	62.49	33.92	33.72
1990	102.89	65.34	63.50	34.87	33.89
1991	115.54	68.88	59.62	43.66	37.79

1992	192.02	79.11	41.20	110.07	57.32
1993	389.60	111.89	28.72	275.15	70.62
1994	432.13	92.67	21.44	337.67	78.14
1995	481.33	103.37	21.48	375.21	77.95
1996	548.04	126.69	23.12	417.26	76.14

Source: China Statistical Yearbook

We can see from the structure of the capital account, that long-term capital is the major form. The surpluses for long-term capital over the years have governed the basic pattern of the capital balance. In the short-term capital balance, there appears to be a deficit pattern, more or less, but it does not have much influence on the trend of the capital balance of China. It has accessory status.

3.2 Analysis of Long-Term Capital Account

Long-term capital is the capital whose term is longer than one year, and it includes the following items:
a) Direct investment,
b) Long-term securities investment,
c) Long-term foreign loans(including government loans, loans from international financial organizations, bank loans and local government and central department loans from abroad),
d) Other long-term capital (including deferred payment, deferred receipt, equipment fund of compensation trade, international lease).

Table 3-2 lists the inflow, outflow and balance of the items of long-term capital. The table shows that the main net inflow of long-term capital is from foreign direct investment. Long-term loans and repayments tend to balance, and the utilization of capital in the form of securities developed after 1993.

3.2.1 Inflow of Long-Term Capital

(1) Foreign direct investment
There are many factors that influence foreign direct investment. First, the steady rapid development of the Chinese economy over ten years has created lucrative chances for foreign-funded enterprises, thus increasing

the Chinese appeal to foreign investors; second, the 1.2 billion population in this deve-loping country means a huge potential market. Many favor-able policies lure foreign capital.

Table 3-2 Balances of types of long-term capital (100 million USD)

Year	Direct investment			Securities investment		
	inflow	outflow	balance	inflow	outflow	balance
1982	4.3	0.4	3.9	0.4	0.2	0.2
1983	6.4	0.9	5.4	1.5	7.7	-6.2
1984	12.6	1.3	11.2	9.4	25.8	-16.4
1985	16.6	6.3	10.3	30.5	0.2	30.3
1986	18.8	4.5	14.3	16.1	0.4	15.7
1987	23.1	6.5	16.7	11.9	1.4	10.5
1988	31.9	8.5	23.4	12.2	3.4	8.8
1989	33.9	7.8	26.1	1.4	3.2	-1.8
1990	34.9	8.3	26.6	0.0	2.4	-2.4
1991	43.7	9.1	34.5	5.7	3.3	2.4
1992	111.6	40.0	71.6	3.9	9.2	-5.3
1993	275.2	44.0	231.2	36.5	19.9	16.5
1994	337.9	20.0	317.9	44.9	9.5	35.4
1995	377.4	38.9	338.5	17.2	10.9	6.3
1996	401.8	21.1	380.7	23.3	6.3	17.0
Year	Foreign loan			Other long-term capital		
	inflow	outflow	balance	inflow	outflow	balance
1982	11.9	12.3	-0.3	16.5	16.3	0.2
1983	10.9	7.6	3.4	8.2	10.3	-2.1
1984	11.7	1.9	9.8	7.6	13.4	-5.8
1985	39.5	5.6	33.9	8.7	16.2	-7.5
1986	63.9	8.4	55.5	15.3	18.3	-3.1
1987	50.3	22.1	28.2	12.0	9.5	2.5
1988	59.2	13.5	45.7	7.8	15.1	-7.3
1989	72.3	46.1	26.2	13.7	11.9	1.9
1990	62.3	26.6	35.8	18.9	14.3	4.6
1991	60.8	27.0	33.8	18.5	12.5	6.0
1992	65.1	97.6	-32.5	95.8	123.1	-27.3
1993	64.9	47.9	17.0	127.0	117.6	9.5
1994	100.0	96.3	3.7	125.1	124.6	0.6
1995	125.9	94.0	32.0	140.1	134.4	5.7
1996	94.6	85.0	9.7	177.5	169.3	8.2

Source: *China Statistical Yearbook, Almanac of China's Finance and Banking*

The specification of foreign direct investment *XDI* follows the accelerator theory of investment as follows:

$$XDI = f(+Y, -KXDI(-1), -Z)$$

where *Y* is GDP of China in US dollars, *KXDI* is the accumulated foreign direct investment, and *Z* is a factor reflecting cost change, represented by the change of consumer prices. The rise of consumer prices results in an increase of raw material prices and wages, which would affect foreign direct investment.

(2) Securities investment

In 1985 Chinese enterprises began to raise funds by issuing stocks and bonds abroad. Usually during a period of rapid economic development, enterprises are short of funds and issue stocks or bonds abroad; so for the inflow of securities investment, the growth rate of GDP can be considered as the first explanatory variable. Besides, the change of the exchange rate minus the inflation rate is the change of real domestic purchasing power of foreign exchange. The higher the indicator, the bigger the effect of raising funds. Thus we specify the following equation to explain foreign securities investment in China:

$$XPI = f(DGDP, +\Delta REX, -DP)$$

where *DGDP* is the growth rate of GDP, *ΔREX* is the change of exchange rate, and *DP* is the rate of inflation.

(3) Foreign loans

Chinese foreign loans are mainly loans from a foreign government, such as Japan, and an international financial organization, such as the World Bank. Others are foreign commercial bank loans to Chinese banks and local governments. The quantity of loans is relatively stable, and its change is related to domestic demand for funds, so the change of GDP would be an explanatory variable. The increase of foreign direct investment *XDI* and foreign exchange reserves *KFXG* may alleviate the shortage in fund supply and reduce the demand for foreign loans, so they are negatively related to foreign loans. Adding the influence of the exchange rate, the specification for foreign loans is:

$$XL = f(+\Delta GDP, -XDI, -KFXG(-1), +REX, -U)$$

where U is the long-term interest rate in US dollars as representative of borrowing cost.

(4) Other long-term capital

The inflows of other long-term capital are mainly related to the receivable and payable accounts of imports and exports; so we choose the increment of exports as an explanatory variable.

3.2.2 Outflow of Long-Term Capital

In the Chinese balance of payments, Table 1-1, the outflow of long-term capital is not very large before 1991. It is about 4.0 billion US dollars, and its major form is the payment of foreign debt. But in 1992, the outflow of long-term capital increased abruptly to 27.0 billion US dollars. There are some reasons that explain this fact. First, according to the international definition of reserves and Chinese conditions, from the third quarter of 1992, the declared foreign exchange reserve includes only the foreign exchange holdings of the People's Bank of China, not that of the Bank of China. The latter is listed in the capital items. This increases the loans of banks and changes the balance sheet of 1992; second, in this year direct investment abroad increased sharply, from less than 1.0 billion US dollars to over 4.0 billion US dollars; third, the outflow on deferred payment increased rapidly in 1992.

(1) Direct investment abroad

Direct investment abroad has risen by a large step since 1992. It is caused by the rapid increase of exports, the further opening and the strengthening of the country's power. For this we use the lagged increase of exports, increase of foreign direct investment and change of lagged real GDP as the explanatory variables. Due to special conditions in 1992, we add a dummy variable.

(2) Payment of foreign debt

Foreign government loans and World Bank loans usually have long maturity; so the repaid debt now is basically commercial debt. We suppose that the payment of foreign debt is related to the status of the current balance and capital balance, and also to the increase of exports, thus we specify the following equation:

$$ML = f(+CB, +LC, +\Delta EX)$$

where the explanatory variables are current balance, long-term capital balance and the increase of exports, in that given order.

(3) Outflow of other long-term capital

Outflows of other long-term capital are mainly related to the deferred receivable and payable account in foreign trade. The major explanatory variables are the foreign exchange reserve *KFXG* to indicate payment ability and the accumulated foreign direct investment *KXDI*, for the scale of foreign-funded enterprises, which play an important role in foreign trade as mentioned above.

(4) Securities investment abroad

Due to its small amount and irregularity, securities investment abroad is treated as a residual. For this, we estimate an equation of the total outflow of long-term capital first, with the foreign direct investment and its change as the explanatory variables, then substitute other outflows from it to have the outflow of securities investment.

3.3 Short-Term Capital Items

In Table 3-3, we see that the flows of short-term capital are very changeable. Although the balance on short-term capital fluctuates sharply in these years, it can still be divided into three phases. The first phase was from 1982 to 1984. During this period, the absolute amount of flows of short-term capital were very small, and its main part was deferred payment and receipt. The second phase was from 1985 to 1991. During the period, deferred receipts and payments increased rapidly, especially deferred receipts, its inflow or outflow in each year is about 5.0 to 8.0 billion US dollars, but the inflow and the outflow basically stayed in balance. The third phase is from 1992 to now, where the deferred payments and receipts change to zero, which reduce the quantity of flows of short-term capital abruptly. In the "other items", there are outflows of about 4.0 billion US dollars from 1992, but the corresponding inflows are close to zero.

In recent years, the net outflow of short-term capital of China has tended to increase and the balance on errors and omissions has been more than (minus) 10.0 billion US dollars; leading some analysts to think that international speculative funds have entered China to arbitrage.

Table 3-3 the flow of short-term capital and its structure   (100 million $)

Year	Inflow					
	Bank-borrowing	Local & dept. borrowing	Deferred payments	Deferred receipts	Others	Total
1982	0.4	0.2	1.8	0.0	0.0	2.4
1983	0.0	0.6	0.0	0.0	0.0	0.6
1984	0.0	0.8	1.4	0.0	0.0	2.2
1985	25.2	1.5	5.2	81.6	0.0	113.5
1986	0.0	7.0	3.3	78.9	4.3	93.4
1987	2.8	4.6	5.3	80.4	1.8	94.3
1988	4.6	3.1	11.1	72.7	0.0	91.5
1989	0.0	0.9	10.1	52.5	0.0	63.5
1990	26.8	0.0	7.0	53.9	0.0	87.7
1991	5.6	0.0	11.4	58.6	0.1	74.7
1992	24.4	1.4	0.0	0.0	0.0	25.8
1993	0.0	4.8	0.0	0.0	0.0	4.8
1994	0.0	10.0	0.0	0.0	0	10.0
1995	0.0	11.5	0.0	0.0	4.9	16.4
1996	0.0	12.6	0.0	0.0	0.0	12.6

Year	Outflow						Balance
	Bank-borrowing	Local & dept. borrowing	Deferred payments	Deferred receipts	Others	Total	
1982	0.0	0.4	0.0	2.6	0.0	3.0	-0.5
1983	0.2	0.3	0.0	2.8	0.0	3.3	-2.8
1984	0.1	0.8	0.0	0.9	9.4	11.1	-8.9
1985	0.0	8.1	4.9	84.6	0.5	90.8	22.7
1986	32.9	1.9	3.5	78.2	0.0	116.4	-22.9
1987	0.0	5.7	6.4	80.1	0.0	92.1	2.1
1988	0.2	1.1	9.4	72.7	7.3	90.7	0.8
1989	5.8	0.4	12.4	53.4	6.6	78.7	-15.2
1990	54.4	1.2	6.3	54.5	3.3	119.7	-32.0
1991	0.0	0.0	11.1	59.9	0.0	71.0	3.6
1992	0.0	0.0	0.0	0.0	34.9	34.9	-9.1
1993	5.5	3.0	0.0	0.0	35.7	44.1	-39.4
1994	4.1	0.0	0.0	0.0	37.0	41.7	-31.1
1995	12.2	0.0	0.0	0.0	0.0	12.2	4.3
1996	19.3	0.0	0.0	0.0	9.1	28.4	-15.9

Source: Almanac of China's Finance and Banking

In the model we put short-term capital balance and errors and omissions together, and believe that they are related to such foreign transactions as imports, exports and foreign direct investment. The estimation results show that this item is negatively related to exports, that is, the more exports, the more the unreasonable net outflows, which may be a result of the fact; that many enterprises do not bring back export income. It is positively related to foreign direct investment. Maybe, due to that, there are many fake foreign-funded enterprises.

4. Balance of Payments and Money Supply

Since 1993, with the increase of foreign exchange reserves, the ratio of net foreign assets to total assets of the People's Bank of China increased gradually, from 11.3% in 1993 to 35.3% in 1996, and the purchasing of foreign exchange has become the major factor in expansion of the fundamental money supply. In order to counteract this kind of expansion of fundamental money, the monetary authorities adjusted its asset structure by greatly reducing loans to deposit money banks. But due to the rigidity of the credit loan quantity, the huge increase of foreign exchange will probably bring about excessive money supply and increase the difficulty of implementation of monetary policy.

4.1 Balance of Payments and Foreign Exchange Reserves

The surplus or deficit of the balance of payments results in the increase or decrease of international reserves. International reserves include (1) foreign exchange, (2) special drawing rights (SDRs), (3) reserve position in the IMF and (4) monetary gold. Different countries have different structures of international reserves. For example, the United States held total reserves of 75.0 billion US dollars in 1996, of which monetary gold was $11.05 billion and accounted for 14.7% of the total, SDRs were $10.31 billion and 13.7%, the reserve position in IMF was $15.43 billion and 20% and foreign exchange was $38.3 billion and 51%. The United States holds a small amount of foreign exchange for two reasons. One is that the US dollar is a freely exchangeable currency, which can be directly used in international payment; the other is that the United States holds other international reserves valued at 26.0 billion US dollars.

In contrast with the developed countries, international reserves of the developing countries use free foreign exchange as their major form of reserves; so does China. From Table 4-1 we see that, in the total reserves (minus gold), foreign exchange accounts for over 90% and nearly 100% in recent years.

Total reserves K is the accumulation of the overall balance OB, that is:

$$K = K(-1) + OB$$

and the overall balance OB is defined as

$$OB = CB + LC + SCEO,$$

where CB is the current balance, LC is the long-term capital balance, and $SCEO$ is the total short-term capital balance plus net errors and omissions.

Because Chinese international reserves are mainly foreign exchange reserves, the change of foreign exchange reserves should be approximately equal to the overall balance OB; thus we use the following equation to estimate foreign exchange reserves.

$$KFXG = f(+KFXG(-1), +OB, +\Delta R_1)$$

where KFXG is a country's foreign exchange reserve, ΔR_1 is the change of interest rate. When the interest rate rises, people are willing to sell foreign exchange and get RMB, which will increase the foreign exchange reserve of the monetary authorities; so ΔR_1 correlates positively with foreign exchange reserves.

Table 4-1   China's Reserves and Its Components

Year	Total Reserves Minus Gold (100m USD)	SDRs (100m USD)	Reserve Position in IMF (100mUSD)	Foreign Exchange (100m USD)	Ratio of Foreign Exchange to Total Reserves (%)
1980	25.45	0.92	1.91	22.62	88.9
1985	127.28	4.83	3.32	119.13	93.6
1990	295.86	5.62	4.30	285.94	96.6
1991	436.74	5.77	4.33	426.64	97.7
1992	206.20	4.19	7.58	194.43	94.3
1993	223.87	4.84	7.04	211.99	94.7
1994	529.14	5.39	7.55	516.20	97.6
1995	753.77	5.82	12.16	735.79	97.6
1996	1070.10	6.14	13.96	1050.00	98.1

Source: International Financial Statistics, Yearbook 1997, IFM

4.2 Formation of Reserve Money

Table 4-2 is a balance sheet of the monetary authorities, in which the major parts of the liabilities are the reserve money *MB* and the deposits of the central government *DG*. Reserve money includes the currency issued by the People's Bank of China M_0, the required deposit reserves and the deposits of financial and non-financial institutions.

Table 4-2 Balance Sheet of Monetary Authorities (End of 1996)

Assets		Liabilities	
Foreign assets (FS)	9562	Reserve money (MB)	26889
Claims on central government		Currency issue (M0)	9435
(LG)	1583	Liabilities to financial	
Claims on deposit money		institutions (RM)	14354
banks (LB)	14518	Depos. financial instit.	3099
Claims on NMFI*	118	Depos.of central gov.(DG)	1225
Claims on non-financial sectors	686	Own capital	367
		Other items (net)	–2041

*NMFI – non-financial institutions; Unit: 100 million-yuan
Source: Almanac of China's Finance and Banking (1997)

Major items of the assets are the foreign assets (net) FS, the claims on the deposit money banks LB and the central government LG. The change of each asset item, *ceteris paribus*, will cause changes in reserve money eventually.

The main part of net foreign assets is foreign exchange. Its change is formed by the trade of foreign exchange for RMB yuan, and the trade will result in the increasing or decreasing of reserve money, eventually.

The net claims on central government are the monetary complements for the financial deficit. The expenditure of government is used to purchase goods and services; so the financial deficit will increase the deposits and currencies held by enterprises and residents. It will then cause an increase of required deposit reserve and currency issue. Both result in the increase of reserve money.

Because the assets are equal to the liabilities, according to Table 4-2, our neglect of small items, means that we have the following approximate equality:

$$MB + DG \approx FS + LG + LB \qquad (4.1)$$

and for the reserve money *MB*, there is

$$MB \approx FS + LB + (LG - DG) \qquad (4.2)$$

which means that the reserve money is approximately the total of net foreign assets FS, claims on deposit money banks LB, and net claims on central government $(LG - DG)$. As seen in Table 4-3. We estimated the following relationship statistically:

$$MB = -561.23 + 1.122*(FS + LB + LG - DG)$$
$$(-2.6) \quad (112.7)$$
$$adj. \ R^2 = 0.999 \ SE = 234.8 \qquad DW = 0.621 \qquad (1985\text{-}1996)$$

Table 4-3 Main Asset Items of Monetary Authorities and Reserve Money

(100m Y)

Year	Loans to Deposit Banks *LB*	Net Foreign Assets *FS*	Net Claims on C'tral Gov'nt *(LG-DG)*	*LB+FS+ (LG–DG)*	Reserve Money *MB*
1986	2681.6	37.0	58.6	2777.2	2827.7
1987	2756.5	181.0	208.0	3145.5	3223.6
1988	3364.4	208.9	305.6	3878.9	4056.6
1989	4209.5	329.5	246.6	4785.6	4919.3
1990	5090.7	684.8	420.7	6196.2	6398.1
1991	5918.1	1317.4	582.0	7817.5	8255.9
1992	6780.2	1195.1	1010.5	8985.8	9717.4
1993	9625.7	1563.4	1094.8	12283.9	13147.0
1994	10451.0	4451.3	854.4	15756.0	17217.8
1995	11510.0	6669.5	609.4	18788.0	20759.8
1996	14518.0	9562.2	357.4	24437.0	26888.5

Source: Almanac of China's Finance and Banking

4.3 *Money Supply*

From the balance sheet of deposit money banks (Table 4-4), we can see that the assets are mainly claims on other sectors L and reserve assets RM, which include required reserves, deposits in the People's Bank of China, cash in vault and central bank bonds. The liabilities are mainly the liabilities to non-financial sectors D (all kinds of deposits) and the liabilities to the central bank LB.

Because the net foreign assets and other items are all relatively small, we have the following approximate relationship:

$$D + LB \approx L + RM \qquad (4.3)$$

Combining to the balance sheets of monetary authorities and deposit money banks give the monetary survey. Now add equation (4.1) and (4.3) and arrange them, then we get:

$$D + (MB - RM) = L + FS + (LG - DG)$$

where $MB - RM$ is nearly equal to the currency in circulation M_0.

Table 4-4 Balance Sheet of Deposit Money Banks (1996-end)   (100.m.yuan)

Assets		Liabilities	
Foreign assets	4200	Foreign liabilities	4240
Reserve assets (RM)	13695	Liabilities on non-financial sectors	
Claims on central government		(D)	61716
	1804	Liabilities on central bank (LB)	14210
Claims on other sectors (L)	58232	Liabilities on NMFI	579
Claims on NMFI	776	Bonds	288
		Owner's equity	3298
		Other items (net)	−5624

Source: Almanac of China's Finance and Banking 1997

According to definitions of money:

M_0 = currency in the circulation

M_1 (money) = M_0 + demand deposits

M_2 (money plus quasi-money) = M_0 + demand deposits + time deposits
+ savings deposits + other deposits,

we get

$$M_2 = M_0 + D = D + (MB - RM) = L + FS + (LG - DG) \qquad (4.4);$$

that is, M_2 is the total of the loans of deposit money banks to other sectors L, the net foreign assets of monetary authorities FS and the net claims on central government $(LG - DG)$.

Suppose that in M_2 and the reserve money MB there is the following multiple relation:

$$M_2 = mMB$$

then from (4.2)

$$M_2 = m(LB + FS + (LG - DG))$$

this points out that, besides LB, net foreign assets FS and the net claims on central government $(LG - DG)$ can influence M_2 through a multiplier relation. This means that the balance of payments and the financial balance can greatly influence the money supply M_2.

The monetary multiplier m is determined by the following equation:

$$m = M_2/MB = (M_0 + D)/(M_0 + RM)$$

$$m = M_2/MB = (M_0 + D)/(M_0 + RM)$$
$$= (M_0 + D)/(M_0 + RD + RE)$$
$$= (cu + 1)/(cu + rd + re)$$

where $cu = M_0/D$ is the ratio of currency M_0 to deposits D; $re = RE/D$ and $rd = RD/D$ are separately the ratio of required reserves RE to deposits D and excess reserve RD to deposits D. These ratios, particularly the currency-deposit ratio cu and the excess reserve ratio rd, are not constant; so the monetary multiplier m varies.

Table 4-5 M_2, Reserve Money MB and Monetary Multiplier m

Year	M_0 (100m yuan)	D (100myuan)	M_2 (100m yuan)	RD (100m yuan)	RE (100m yuan)
1986	1218	5503	6721	565	966
1987	1454	6896	8350	670	1021
1988	2134	7966	10100	841	978
1989	2344	9606	11950	1042	1406
1990	2644	12650	15294	1391	2219
1991	3178	16172	19350	1810	3110
1992	4336	21066	25402	2335	2808
1993	5865	25636	31501	2885	3999
1994	7289	37538	44827	3961	5373
1995	7885	50367	58252	5247	6939
1996	8802	64811	73613	7612	9841

Year	MB (100m yuan)	Rd (%)	re (%)	cu (%)	m
1986	2828	10.3	17.5	22.1	2.377
1987	3223	9.7	14.8	21.1	2.590
1988	4057	10.6	12.3	26.8	1.490
1989	4920	10.8	14.6	24.4	2.429
1990	6398	11.0	17.5	20.9	2.390
1991	8256	11.2	19.2	19.7	2.344
1992	9718	11.1	13.3	20.6	2.614
1993	13172	11.3	15.6	22.9	2.391
1994	17218	10.6	14.3	19.4	2.604
1995	20760	10.4	13.8	15.7	2.806
1996	26888	11.7	15.2	13.6	2.738

Source: Almanac of China's Finance and Banking

As seen in Table 4-5, the monetary multiplier of China is about 2.5 on average, fluctuates between 2.3 and 2.8 and has an increasing trend. Because the actual required reserve ratio re changes little, the change of the monetary multiplier is mainly caused by the change of cu and re. Usually, the rise of interest rates would increase re and reduce cu; inflation reduces rd and increases cu.

Considering the influence of interest rate on the monetary multiplier, we adopt the following specification for the money supply M_2:

$$M_2 = m \ (LB + FS + (LG - DG))$$
$$= (cu + 1)/(cu + rd + re) * (LB + FS + (LG - DG))$$
$$= f(LB + FS + (LG - DG), R_1, U)$$

where R_1 is the interest rate on one-year deposits, U is other influential factors, and the net foreign assets FS are specified as:

$$FS = f(FS(-1), OB*REX, \Delta R_1)$$

it relies mainly on the overall balance OB and the exchange rate REX.

4.4 Influence of Monetary Supply on the Economy

The objectives of monetary policy are (1) to keep the stability of the price level, that is, maintain the value of national currency; (2) maintain a stable growth of the economy and the stability of employment; (3) keep the stability of foreign exchange markets. There may be contradictions in meeting the objectives, but to keep a stable value of the national currency is the most important task.

Under the original system of economic management or guidance of China, the major tools of monetary policy have been reserve requirements, fundamental loans, rediscounts and interest rates. Because the first tool has very strong effects it is seldom used; so the latter three are relied upon. But interest rates are not determined by market conditions, and the effect of controlling interest rate levels is not obvious. The major tools are actually rediscounts and fundamental loans.

In the 1990s, there has been an obvious change in banking for China. The increasing growth rate of money supply has made M_2 exceed domestic credit (see Table 4-6), due especially to the expansion of foreign exchange assets generated by the huge surplus of international payments.

Table 4-6 Ratio of Domestic Credit to M_2

Year	Domestic Credit (a) (100m yuan)	Money and Quasi-Money M_2 (b) (100m yuan)	Ratio of (a) to (b)
1990	15729	15293	1.03
1991	19614	19350	1.01
1992	26147	25402	1.03
1993	34811	34880	1.00
1994	43103	46923	0.92
1995	53338	60750	0.88
1996	66410	76095	0.87

Source: *Almanac of China's Finance and Banking*

At the end of 1993, based on the deficiencies of the policy of controlling domestic credit, the People's Bank of China laid out a new financial reform plan, determined to make the money supply the primary object of monetary policy.

M_1, the total of currency in circulation M_0 and demand deposits, is the medium of transactions for trade in commodities, services and securities. It is also the means for paying wages, rent and interest; so it is a financial asset with high liquidity. Undoubtedly, the amount of M_1, is closely related to the level of economic activity and prices.

4.5 Relationship Between Money Supply M_1 and Nominal GDP

As above mentioned, M_1 has direct influence on the economy, but the Chinese agricultural sector has a weaker demand for money than any other sector. Considering this fact, we estimate nominal *GDP* with the gross output value of agriculture, money supply M_1 and government expenditure *GE* as explanatory variables and get the following equation:

$$GDP = 527.664 + 0.0888*(IGA*PIA) + 0.7973*M_1 + 0.8887*M_1(-1)$$
$$\quad\quad (2.3) \quad\quad (4.4) \quad\quad\quad\quad\quad (5.9) \quad\quad (3.4)$$
$$\quad + 0.6873 * GE$$
$$\quad\quad (4.5)$$

$$adj.\ R^2 = 0.9999 \quad SE = 196.96 \quad DW = 1.913 \quad (1980\text{-}1996)$$

where IGA * PIA is the product of the agriculture output index IGA and the purchasing price index of farm and sideline products PIA, as estimates of agricultural output in current prices. This equation shows that money supply M_1 has important effect on the nominal GDP, the long-term multiplier of M_1 with respect to GDP is about 1.7 (0.7973 + 0.8887).

4.6 Relationship Between Money Supply and Price Level

Money supply has an obvious relationship with price level, but the different definitions of money have different effects on the price index. M_0 has a close relationship with the retail price index or the consumer price index, while M_1 has a close relationship with the *GDP* deflator *PGDP*, as seen in the following estimated equation:

$$PGDP = -21.775 + 1.262 * PGDP (-1) + 0.0106 * M_1 (-1)$$
$$(-1.5) \quad (9.0) \qquad\qquad (6.40)$$
$$- 0.0146 * M_1 (-2)$$
$$(-6.70)$$

$$adj. \ R^2 = 0.997 \quad\quad SE = 4.543 \quad\quad DW = 1.910 \quad\quad (1979\text{-}1996)$$

and we can see from the above equation that the money supply M_1 has lagged effects on the GDP deflator, but slightly stronger and negative. M_2 is the total of M_1 and quasi-money, and quasi-money is the total of deposits of lower liquidity such as time deposits, savings deposits, etc. Quasi-money cannot be used directly as a medium for commercial and service transactions, but it may be transformed to currency or demand deposits after drawing. Currency and demand deposits can be deposited in banks and changed into quasi-money; thus quasi-money and M_1 are substitutable for each other. Because of this relationship between quasi-money and M_1, M_1 can be seen as only the amount of circulating money, not the amount of all money. M_2 is the total money stock. There is a close relationship between M_1 and M_2, which can be seen from the following estimated equation:

$$Log (M_1) = 0.9161 + 0.9247 * Log (M_2)$$
$$(10.1) \quad (58.7)$$
$$-0.1232 * Log (R_1) - 0.1477 * Log (R_1(-1)) - 0.1368 * Log (R_1(-2))$$
$$(-2.0) \qquad\qquad (-2.3) \qquad\qquad\qquad (-2.2)$$

$$adj. \ R^2 = 0.999 \quad\quad SE = 0.023 \quad\quad DW = 2.257 \quad\quad (1985\text{-}1996)$$

where R_1 is the interest rate for one-year time deposits.   Since the coefficient of $log\ M_2$ is almost 1.0, this equation shows that the *ratio* of M_1 to M_2 depends inversely on R_1

5. Structure and Test of the Model

5.1 Structure of the Model

The balance of payments and money supply model of China consists of 50 equations (see Appendix 1) and is divided into five sectors as follows:

(1) Imports and exports and trade balance	(equations 1-3)
(2) Non-trade (services and income) balance	(equations 4-6)
(3) Capital balance	(equations 8-11)
(4) Money supply	(equations 13-15)
(5) Nominal GDP	(equations 16-17)

This model is build as a sub-model of the macro econometric model of China, and the flow chart of the relationship among the sectors is represented in Figure 5-1. Because it is a sub-model, the indicators relative to production, demand, price and income are seen as exogenous variables, which are determined in other blocks. The main exogenous variables in the model are:

(1) Real indicators – grain output GRAIN, output of crude oil OIL, index of gross agricultural output IGA, index of gross industrial output IGI.
(2) Price indicators – purchase price of farm and sideline products PIA, retail price PIS, world oil price POIL, exchange rate REX, interest rate R_1, and average wage W.
(3) Other indicators – population POP, financial expenditure GE, claims of monetary authorities on deposit money banks (fundamental loans) LB, net claims of monetary authorities on central government LG-DG, world exports EXW, etc.

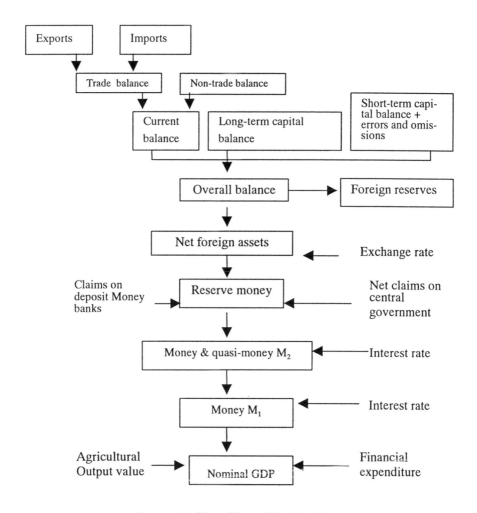

Figure 5-1 Flow Chart of the Model

5.2 Test of the Model

In estimating the equations of the model, the sample period of most variables is from 1982 to 1996 because the international payments statistics of China originate from 1982. Data for exports and imports from customs are from 1980 to 1996. Because the People's Bank of China began to function as a central bank after 1984, so the statistics of money supply are provided from 1985.

The test period of the model is from 1991 to 1996, because Chinese international payments have changed greatly in the reform period. The selected test is the final test, that is, a dynamic test. There are two kinds of criteria for evaluating the test errors.

For variables such as exports, and imports that have basic trends, we choose mean absolute percentage error *MAPE*, whose definition is:

$$MAPE = \frac{1}{n}\sum_{t=1}^{n} APE_t = \frac{1}{n}\sum_{t=1}^{n}\left|\frac{Y_t - \hat{Y}_t}{Y_t}\right| * 100(\%)$$

where, $\hat{Y}_t$, Y_t are actual and fitted values respectively.

For the balance variables such as current balance, capital balance, the value of which may probably be close to zero, which could cause *MAPE* to tend to infinity, we choose the mean error *ME* defined by

$$ME = \frac{1}{n}\sum_{t=1}^{n} ER_t = \frac{1}{n}\sum_{t=1}^{n}(Y_t - \hat{Y}_t)$$

The test results for main variables are presented in Figure 5-2 and listed in Table 5-1. We can see from the tables that most of MAPE are lower than 3%, especially the indicators in which we are interested. For example, MAPE of foreign exchange reserves is 3.7%, of long-term capital inflow 2.5%, of M_2 0.77%, of nominal GDP 0.88%. For the balance variables which use ME as test error criterion, ME of trade balance is –$1.73 billion, of current balance – $0.98 billion, long-term capital balance –$0.32 billion, short-term capital balance and errors and omissions $0.46 billion. All these MEs are relatively small compared with their average level, besides it is more important that the fitted value and the actual value of these variables have almost the same trend.

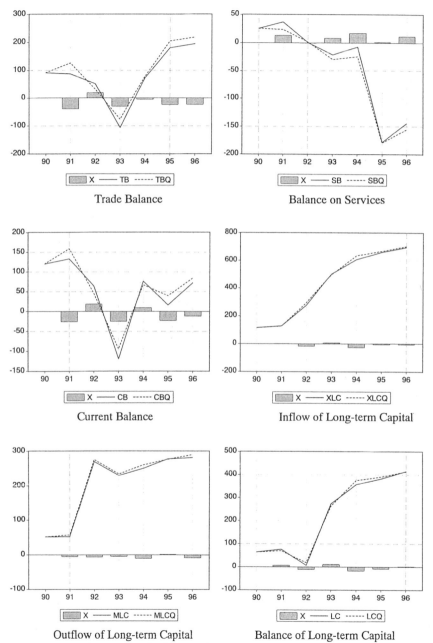

Figure 5-2 Final Test of the Model for Some Variables

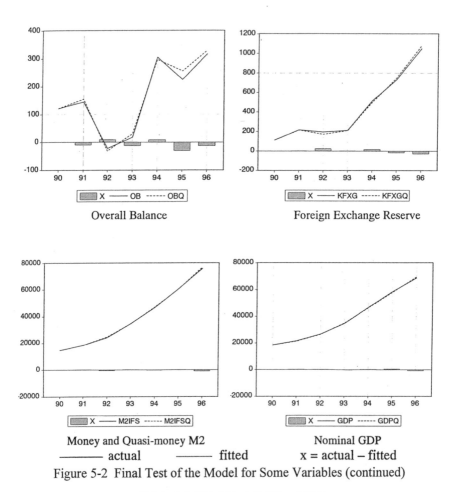

Overall Balance

Foreign Exchange Reserve

Money and Quasi-money M2

Nominal GDP

——— actual   -------- fitted   x = actual − fitted

Figure 5-2 Final Test of the Model for Some Variables (continued)

Table 5-1 Final Test (1991 – 1996)

Year	Exports EXFOB			Imports IMCIF		
	Actual	Fitted	APE	Actual	Fitted	APE
1991	718.43	737.05	2.59	637.91	608.08	4.68
1992	849.40	829.71	2.32	805.31	807.15	0.23
1993	917.44	945.00	3.00	1039.59	1032.21	0.71
1994	1210.66	1215.63	0.46	1156.14	1156.90	0.07
1995	1487.70	1490.14	0.16	1320.78	1304.29	1.25
1996	1510.70	1516.23	0.37	1388.40	1368.97	1.40
		MAPE	1.48		MAPE	1.39

Trade Balance TB				Non-Trade Revenue EXS		
Year	Actual	Fitted	ER	Actual	Fitted	APE
1991	87.43	126.66	−39.23	106.98	110.02	2.84
1992	51.83	32.69	19.14	148.44	146.59	1.24
1993	−106.50	−76.05	−30.45	155.83	149.59	4.01
1994	72.90	78.38	−5.48	223.57	216.97	2.95
1995	180.50	204.76	−24.26	243.21	244.40	0.49
1996	195.35	218.73	−23.38	279.19	282.70	1.26
		ME	−17.28		MAPE	2.13
Non-Trade Expenditure IMS				Non-Trade Balance SB		
Year	Actual	Fitted	APE	Actual	Fitted	ER
1991	70.00	86.33	23.33	36.98	23.69	13.29
1992	147.81	145.17	1.79	0.63	1.43	−0.80
1993	177.06	179.22	1.22	−21.23	−29.64	8.41
1994	230.73	241.37	4.61	−7.16	−24.41	17.25
1995	421.89	424.25	0.56	−178.68	−179.85	1.17
1996	423.39	438.31	3.52	−144.20	−155.60	11.40
		MAPE	5.84		ME	8.45
	Current Balance CB			Long-Term Capital Inflow XLC		
Year	Actual	Fitted	ER	Actual	Fitted	APE
1991	132.72	158.66	−25.94	128.58	127.31	0.98
1992	64.02	45.69	18.33	276.42	294.36	6.49
1993	−119.02	−93.96	−25.06	503.54	497.53	1.19
1994	76.57	67.34	9.23	607.89	635.85	4.60
1995	16.18	39.26	−23.08	660.61	667.64	1.06
1996	72.43	84.42	−11.99	697.21	703.76	0.94
		ME	−9.75		MAPE	2.55

	Long-Term Capital Outflow MLC			Long-Term Captial BalanceLC		
Year	Actual	Fitted	APE	Actual	Fitted	ER
1991	51.88	56.94	9.74	76.70	70.38	6.32
1992	269 .86	275.98	2.27	6.56	18.38	−11.82
1993	229.43	234.13	2.05	274.11	263.40	10.71
1994	250.33	260.43	4.04	357.56	375.42	−17.86
1995	278.18	276.69	0.53	382.43	390.95	−8.52
1996	281.67	290.16	3.01	415.54	413.60	1.94
		MAPE	3.61		ME	−3.20

	Balance on Short-Term Capital and Errors and Omissions SCEO			Overall Balance OB		
Year	Actual	Fitted	ER	Actual	Fitted	ER
1991	−64.30	−73.71	9.41	145.12	155.33	−10.21
1992	−93.25	−95.74	2.47	−22.67	−31.66	8.99
1993	−137.42	1.18	1.18	17.67	30.84	−13.17
1994	−128.87	−145.78	16.91	305.26	296.99	8.27
1995	−173.85	−174.68	0.83	224.81	255.53	−30.72
1996	−171.46	−168.44	−3.02	316.51	329.59	−13.08
		ME	4.63		ME	−8.32
	Foreign Exchange Reserves KFXG			Net Foreign Assets FS		
Year	Actual	Fitted	APE	Actual	Fitted	APE
1991	217.12	215.89	0.56	1399.6	1504.2	7.47
1992	194.43	170.44	12.34	1330.4	1302.8	2.08
1993	211.99	210.00	0.74	1549.5	1636.4	5.61
1994	516.20	499.55	3.22	4451.3	4439.8	0.26
1995	735.80	753.52	2.41	6669.5	6850.2	2.71
1996	1050.00	1073.40	2.80	9562.2	9929.9	3.84
		MAPE	3.71		MAPE	3.66
	Money and Quasi-Money M2			Money M1		
Year	Actual	Fitted	APE	Actual	Fitted	APE
1991	18598.9	18522.7	0.41	8987.8	8754.0	2.60
1992	24327.3	24818.3	2.02	11714.3	12110.5	3.38
1993	34739.9	34652.8	0.25	16761.1	16662.1	0.59
1994	46920.3	47162.9	0.52	21539.9	21243.0	1.38
1995	60744.0	60649.5	0.16	25597.3	25428.7	0.66
1996	76095.3	77057.4	1.26	30662.6	31778.8	3.64
		MAPE	0.77		MAPE	2.04

	Nominal GDP GDP			Index of GDP IGDP		
Year	Actual	Fitted	APE	Actual	Fitted	APE
1991	21617.8	21365.4	1.17	307.6	305.2	0.78
1992	26638.1	26488.2	0.56	351.4	349.1	0.67
1993	34634.4	34943.6	0.89	398.8	407.1	2.08
1994	46759.4	46486.1	0.58	449.3	447.8	0.34
1995	58478.1	57976.3	0.86	496.5	491.1	1.08
1996	68593.8	69429.4	1.22	544.2	557.2	2.39
		MAPE	0.88		MAPE	1.22

References

Ichimura, S. and Y. Matsumoto (eds.), (1994), "Econometric Models of Asian-Pacific Countries," pp. 27-75, Springer-Verlag.

Tang, Guoxing (1988), "Opening and Economic Growth of China," (in Japanese), Discussion Paper KIER8801, Kyoto Institute of Economic Research.

Tang, Guoxing (1997), "The Effects of Monetary Policy of China on Its Current Balance," (in Chinese) *Guang Dong Finance*, No. 11, 12.

Xu, Bin and Liu Xuesheng (1994), "An Outline of Chinese Balance of Payments," (in Chinese) Finance Publishing.

Appendix 1—List of Equations

Exports

1.1 SITC0+1

$$EX01 = -34.337 + 0.002645 * EXW - 0.1440 * PIA (-1)$$
$$(-12.7) \quad (12.4) \quad (-7.0)$$
$$+ 0.2980 * IGA (-1) + 1.6721 * (REX-REX(-1))$$
$$(7.6) \quad (2.0)$$

adj $R^2 = 0.995$ \quad SE = 2.029 \quad DW = 2.060 \quad (1980-1996)

1.2 SITC2+4

$$EX24 = 3.738 + 0.2499 * IGA - 0.1886 * (IGI(-1)) - 0.0652 * REXJPA$$
$$(0.5) \quad (7.5) \quad (-7.1) \quad (-3.4)$$
$$+ 0.4680 * ((PIA/PIA(-1)-1) * 100$$
$$(7.0)$$

adj $R^2 = 0.962$ \quad SE = 1.996 \quad DW = 2.401 \quad (1980-1996)

1.3 SITC3

$$EX3 = -161.555 + 0.0105 * OIL + 1.4797 * POIL + 0.2419 * REXJP$$
$$(-7.7) \quad (9.2) \quad (6.9) \quad (6.5)$$
$$+ 2.9917 * (REX(-1) - REX(-2))$$
$$(2.8)$$

adj $R^2 = 0.903$ \quad SE = 2.803 \quad DW = 1.803 \quad (1980-1996)

1.4 SITC5~9

$$EXMG = -185.63 + 0.01317 * EXW + 0.5517 * XDI$$
$$(-5.0) \quad (5.0) \quad (3.5)$$

$$+ 0.4523 * EXMG(-1) + 31.1028 * (REX-REX(-1))$$
$$(3.5) \qquad\qquad\qquad (3.0)$$
$$+ 45.5918 * (REX(-1) - REX(-2))$$
$$(4.7)$$

adj $R^2 = 0.998$ SE $= 19.89$ DW $= 2.680$ (1980-1996)

1.5 Exports, Total (F.O.B.)

EXFOB = EX01 + EX24 + EX3 + EXMG

2. Imports

2.1 SITC0 + 1

$$IM01 = 88.170 + 0.1855 * PIA - 6.467 * REX - 0.2004 * GRN(-1)$$
$$(4.0) \qquad (5.1) \qquad\qquad (-3.7) \qquad\qquad (-3.3)$$
$$+ 0.0572 * KFXG(-1) - 0.0815 * KFXG(-2)$$
$$(3.6) \qquad\qquad\qquad (-4.2)$$

adj $R^2 = 0.933$ SE $= 3.393$ DW $= 1.886$ (1980-1996)

2.2 SITC2 + 4

$$IM24 = 34.1836 - 0.364 * IGA + 0.2838 * PIA + 0.0407 * IGI$$
$$(2.9) \qquad (-3.8) \qquad\qquad (5.2) \qquad\qquad (1.7)$$

adj $R^2 = 0.974$ SE $= 5.068$ DW $= 2.098$ (1980-1996)

2.3 SITC3

$$IM3 = -19.445 + 0.2822 * POIL - 1.9546 * (REX - REX(-1))$$
$$(-4.8) \qquad (2.7) \qquad\qquad (-2.3)$$
$$+ 0.0909 * IGI(-1) + 0.1741 * XDI - 0.2289 * XDI(-1)$$
$$(9.7) \qquad\qquad (10.9) \qquad\qquad (-11.1)$$

adj $R^2 = 0.990$ SE $= 2.193$ DW $= 2.979$ (1980-1996)

2.4 SITC5~9

$$IMMG = -235.52 + 1.2209 * IGI - 0.4458 * KXDI(-1)$$
$$(-5.7) \qquad (11.6) \qquad\qquad (-8.0)$$
$$+ 1.2035 * IGA(-1) + 10.1382 * DGDP(-1)$$
$$(3.1) \qquad\qquad\qquad (7.2)$$

adj $R^2 = 0.997$ SE $= 18.065$ DW $= 1.669$ (1980-1996)

2.5 Imports, Total (C.I.F.)
IMCIF = IM01 + IM24 + IM3 + IMMG

3. Trade Balance (IMF)

TB= 20.764 +0.9088 *EXFOB – 0.9547*IMCIF + 0.0614 * KXDI(-1)
(6.4)   (49.3)   (-58.6)   (5.5)
+ 5.145 * (REX-REX(-1)) + 3.035 * (REX(-1) – REX(-2))
(2.3)   (1.1)
+ 15.887 * (REX(-2) – REX(-3))
(4.3)
adj R^2 = 0.998   SE = 4.300   DW = 2.414   (1980-1996)

4. Credit, Services and Income

4.1 Freight, Transportation and Port Services
RTRA = -2.213 + 7.312 * (REX – REX(-1)) + 6.256 * (REX(-1)
(-1.2)   (8.1)   (7.5)
– REX(-2))+ 0.0129 * EXFOB + 0.285 * IM01 – 7.335 * DD91
(6.7)   (4.5)   (-3.4)
adj R^2 = 0.974   SE = 1.957   DW = 2.287   (1982-1996)

4.2 Tourism
RTOU = -2.879 + 0.939 * RTOU(-1) + 4.459 * (REX-REX(-1))
(-3.4)   (11.2)   (6.1)
+ 0.01505 * EXFOB – 7.729 * DD89 – 6.299 * DD90
(3.3)   (-4.5)   (-3.5)
adj R^2 = 0.997   SE 1.658   DW = 2.484   (1982-1996)

4.3 Other Services
ROTH=7.832+ 0.01232*(EXFOB + IMCIF) + 0.04677 * (EXFOB(-1)
(2.3)   (3.0)   (10.9)
+ IMCIF(-1)) – 0.257 * PIS – 0.418 * DPIS – 5.234 * DD88
(-5.1)   (-5.0)   (-3.9)
adj R^2 = 0.996   SE = 1.250   DW = 2.904   (1982-1996)

4.4 Investment Income

RINV = -10.716 + 0.0336 * (EXFOB + IMCIF) + 0.1443 * KFXG(-1)
     (-7.0)   (18.1)   (11.8)
     + 0.0552 * CB – 0.0935 * KXDI(-1) + 4.810 * (REX-REX(-1))
        (8.3)   (-12.2)   (5.1)
     –5.536 * (REX(-1) – REX(-2))
      (-7.3)
adj R^2 = 0.993   SE = 1.766   DW = 2.733   (1982-1996)

4.5 Credit, Services and Income

EXS = RTRA + RTOU + ROTH + RINV

5. Debit, Services and Income

5.1 Freight, Transportation and Port Services

ETRA = 19.512 + 0.2132 * EXFOB – 0.1298 * EXFOB(-1)
      (3.6)   (6.3)   (-5.4)
     + 0.166 * XDI(-1) -12.273 * REX
      (5.8)   (-3.9)
adj R^2 = 0.985   SE = 4.796   DW = 2.528   (1982-1996)

5.2 Tourism

ETOU = - 0.1777 + 0.007129 * (EXFOB + IMCIF) + 0.06664 * XDI
     (-0.2)   (3.1)   (8.9)
     –1.3636 * REX + 0.0164 * KFXG(-2) + 11.7643 * DD92
      (-2.3)   (3.9)   (10.5)
adj R^2 = 0.996   SE = 0.982   DW = 1.914   (1982-1996)

5.3 Other Services

EOTH = 8.531 + 0.0427 * KXDI + 0.0674 * (XLCO + MLCO)
     (5.1)   (17.4)   (6.8)
     –3.408 * REX + 7.283 * (REX(-1) – REX(-2)) + 8.701 * DD84
      (-6.7)   (11.0)   (4.8)
adj R^2 = 0.996   SE = 1.662   DW = 2.047   (1982-1996)

5.4 Investment Income

$$EINV = 2.500 + 0.148 * KXDI(-1) - 9.262 * (REX - REX(-1))$$
$$\quad (2.1) \quad (70.5) \qquad\qquad (-8.4)$$
$$+ 7.545 * (REX(-1) - REX(-2)) + 14.313 * DD92$$
$$\quad (6.0) \qquad\qquad\qquad (4.6)$$
adj R^2 = 0.997 　　 SE = 2.955 　　 DW = 2.604 　　 (1982-1996)

5.5 Debit, Services and Income

$$IMS = ETRA + ETOU + EOTH + EINV$$

6. Balance on Services and Income

$$SB = EXS - IMS$$

7. Current Account Balance

$$CB = TB + SB + TRS$$

8. Credit, Long-term Capital Investment

8.1 Foreign Direct Investment in China

$$XDI = -42.784 + 1.632 * IGDP - 1.524 * IGDP(-1) - 0.063 * KXDI(-1)$$
$$\quad (-3.0) \quad (4.26) \qquad (-3.65) \qquad\qquad (-1.65)$$
$$+ 1.055 * XDI(-1) + 106.48 * DD93$$
$$\quad (9.64) \qquad\qquad (7.95)$$
adj R^2 = 0.999 　　 SE = 2.384 　　 DW = 2.219 　　 (1980-1996)

8.2 Securities Investment in China

$$XPI = -11.206 + 2.073 * DGDP(-1) - 0.5408 * DPIS(-1)$$
$$\quad (-2.3) \quad (4.6) \qquad\qquad (-2.1)$$
$$+ 7.7256 * (REX-REX(-1)) + 0.0477 * XDI$$
$$\quad (3.7) \qquad\qquad\qquad (3.8)$$
adj R^2 = 0.845 　　 SE = 5.499 　　 DW = 2.673 　　 (1982-1996)

8.3 Loans from Abroad

XL   = 61.439 − 0.2111 * XDI + 0.01346 * (GDP(-1) − GDP(-2))
      (5.4)   (-8.0)   (11.3)
      -0.0824 * KFXG(-1) − 5.048 * RBUS + 6.6264 * REX
      (-6.6)   (-6.3)   (4.4)
adj R^2 = 0.987   SE = 3.700   DW = 2.392   (1982-1996)

8.4 Other Capital Inflow

XLCO = 8.321 + 0.433* XDI − 0.1037 * (EXFOB − EXFOB(−1))
       (4.8)   (41.1)   (-5.8)
      + 52.777 * DD92
      (10.7)
adj R^2 = 0.994   SE = 4.680   DW = 1.829   (1982-1996)

8.5 Inflow of Long-term Capital

XLC = XDI + XPI + XL + XLCO

8.6 Foreign Direct Investment, Contracts and Agreements

FCDC = -29.6272 + 4.0228 * KXDI(-1) − 5.2194 * KXDI(-2)
        (-2.3)   (29.0)   (-25.6)
      + 0.5622 * EXFOB(-1) − 0.3278 * IMCIF(-1)
      (5.6)   (-4.2)
      + 467.56 * DD92 + 761.02 * DD93
      (20.9)   (34.0)
adj R^2 = 0.998   SE = 16.69   DW = 1.857   (1978-1996)

9. Debit, Long-term Capital Investment

9.1 Direct Investment Abroad

MDI = -14.7038 + 0.0956 * (EXFOB(-1) − EXFOB(-2))
       (-5.3)   (8.8)
      + 0.2249 * (XDI-XDI(-1))+ 0.5066 * IGDP(-1) − 0.6772 * IGDP(-2)
      (15.8)   (5.8)   (-6.1)
      + 5.2799 * R1(-1) + 22.3409 * DD92
      (6.4)   (11.8)
adj R^2 = 0.989   SE = 1.580   DW = 2.762   (1982-1996)

9.2 Securities Investment Abroad

MPI = MLC – MDI – ML – MLCO

9.3 Payment on Foreign Loans

ML = 0.4971 + 0.0776 $*$ CB + 0.1878 $*$ LC
         (0.3)   (5.1)   (19.2)
      + 0.0707$*$(EXFOB-EXFOB(-1))+35.54 $*$ DD89 + 81.62 $*$ DD92
         (4.3)   (8.1)   (17.6)
adj R^2 = 0.987   SE = 4.084   DW = 1.881   (1992-1996)

9.4 Other Capital Outflow

MLCO = 9.2182 + 0.0901 $*$ KFXG(-2) – 0.1542 $*$ MLCO(-1)
            (11.0)   (7.6)   (-5.4)
      + 0.0257 $*$ KXDI(-1) + 99.84 $*$ D92
         (6.0)   (43.1)
adj R^2 = 0.999   SE = 2.209   DW = 2.331   (1982-1996)

9.5 Outflow of Long-term Capital

MLC = 23.531 + 0.8222$*$ XDI – 0.1811 $*$ XDI(-1) + 23.292 $*$ DD89
         (12.7)   (23.2)   (-4.4)   (4.2)
      + 162.50 $*$ DD92
         (28.5)
adj R^2 = 0.997   SE = 5.210   DW = 2.586   (1982-1996)

10. Long-term Capital Investment Balance

LC = XLC – MLC

11. Short-term Capital Balance, Errors and Omissions

SCEO = 14.674 – 0.2236 $*$ EXFOB + 0.1400 $*$ IMCIF
           (1.1)   (-4.4)   (2.3)
      – 0.4859 $*$ XDI + 0.4234 $*$ XDI(-1)
         (-3.8)   (3.6)
adj R^2 = 0.959   SE = 13.295   DW = 2.696   (1982-1996)

12. Overall Balance

OB = CB + LC + SCEO

13. Foreign Exchange Reserve

KFXG = -10.2844 + 1.0885 * KFXG(-1) + 11.7264 * R1
      (-0.4)   (35.0)   (3.4)
    − 13.9273 * R1(-1) + 0.9557 * OB
      (-3.3)   (14.8)
adj R^2 = 0.997   SE = 16.060   DW = 3.331   (1982-1996)

14. Foreign Assets of Monetary Authorities

FS = 48.445 + 1.0673 * FS(-1) + 1.0496 * (OB * REX) + 70.974 * R1
    (0.2)   (62.8)   (27.8)   (4.1)
    -87.071 * R1(-1)
    (-4.4)
adj R^2 = 0.999   SE = 69.81   DW = 2.369   (1985-1996)

15. Money Supply

15.1 Money and Quasi-money M2

M2 = 1006.73 + 2.1479 * (LB + FS + LG) − 397.95 * R1
    (0.9)   (15.7)   (-2.8)
    − 833.01 * R1(-1)+ 0.789 * (IGA* PIA) + 459.026 * DGA
    (-5.7)   (8.7)   (3.7)
adj R^2 = 0.999   SE = 560.5   DW = 2.530   (1985-1996)

15.2 Money M_1

Log(M1) = 0.9161 + 0.9247 * Log(M2) − 0.1232* Log(R1)
      (10.1)   (58.7)   (-2.0)
    −0.1477 * Log(R1(-1)) − 0.1368 * Log(R1(-2))
    (-2.3)   (-2.2)
adj R^2 = 0.999   SE = 0.023   DW = 2.257   (1985-1996)

15.3 Currency in Circulation M_0

M0 = -1281.75 + 0.4715 * M1 − 0.3705 * M1(-1) + 22.9052 * PIS
$\quad$ (-21.3)$\quad$ (41.4)$\qquad$ (-25.3)$\qquad\qquad$ (29.2)
$\quad$ −9.9112 * PIS(-1) + 383.07 * DD92
$\quad\quad$ (-12.0)
adj R^2 = 0.999$\qquad$ SE = 33.24$\qquad$ DW = 2.381$\qquad$ (1980-1996)

16. Nominal GDP

GDP = 527.664 + 0.0888 * (IGA * PIA) + 0.7973 * M1
$\qquad$ (2.3)$\qquad$ (4.4)$\qquad\qquad\qquad$ (5.9)
$\quad$ + 0.8887 * M1(-1)+ 0.6873 * GE
$\qquad$ (3.40)$\qquad\qquad$ (4.5)
adj R^2 = 0.9999$\qquad$ SE = 196.96$\qquad$ DW = 1.913$\qquad$ (1980-1996)

17. GDP Deflator

PGDP = 13.061 + 0.255 * PIS + 0.0352 * (W-W(-1)) + 2.5210 * REX
$\qquad$ (7.5)$\qquad$ (6.0)$\qquad$ (13.4)$\qquad\qquad$ (3.0)
$\quad$ −0.0476 * (GRN-GRN(-1)) + 0.5823 * PGDP(-1)
$\quad$ (-2.2)$\qquad\qquad\qquad$ (11.2)
adj R^2 = 0.999$\qquad$ SE = 1.456$\qquad$ SE = 2.928$\qquad$ (1978-1996)

18. Definitions

18.1 GDP Index
IGDP = GDP/PGDP/36.24 * 100

18.2 Grain Output Per Capita
GRN = GRAIN/((POP + POP(-1))/2) * 1000

18.3 Accumulated Foreign Direct Investment
KXDI = KXDI(-1) + XDI

18.4 Accumulated Current Balance
KCB = KCB(-1) + CB

18.5 Rate of Change of Retail Price Index
DPIS = (PIS/PIS(-1)-1) * 100

18.6 Growth Rate of Agricultural Output
DGA = (IGA/IGA(-1)-1) * 100

18.7 Rate of Change of GDP Deflator
DPGDP = (PGDP/PGDP(-1)-1) * 100

18.8 Growth Rate of Nominal GDP
DGDPN = (GDP/GDP(-1)-1) * 100

Appendix 2—List of Variables

Variable	Description	Unit	Period	Source	Note
CB	Current Balance	100m US$	82-96	SYC	E
DGA	= (IGA/IGA(-1)-1)*100, Growth Rate of Agriculture	%	78-96		E
DGDP	= (IGDP/IGDP(-1)-1)*100, Growth Rate of GDP	%	78-96		E
DPIS	= (PIS/PIS(-1)-1)*100	%	78-96		E
EINV	Expenditure on Investment	100m US$	82-96	SYC	E
EOTH	Expenditure on Other Services	100m US$	82-96	SYC	E
ETOU	Expenditure on Tourism	100m US$	82-96	SYC	E
ETRA	Expenditure on Freight Trans-portation and Port services	100m US$	82-96	SYC	E
EX01	Exports of SITC0+1 (Customs Statistics: CS)	100m US$	80-96	SYC	E
EX24	Exports of SITC2+4 (CS)	100m US$	80-96	SYC	E
EX3	Exports of SITC3 (CS)	100m US$	80-96	SYC	E
EXFOB	Total Exports (F.O.B.) (CS)	100m US$	80-96	SYC	E
EXMG	Exports of SITC5 ~ 9 (CS)	100m US$	80-96	SYC	E
EXS	Revenue on Services and Income	100m US$	82-96	SYC	E

FCDC	Foreign Direct Investment, Signed Contract Agreements	100m US$	82-96	SYC	E
FS	Foreign Assets of Monetary Authorities	100m Yuan	85-96	SYC	E
GDP	Nominal GDP	100m Yuan	78-96	SYC	E
GRN	=GRAIN/((POP+POP(-1))/2) *1000	Kg/Psn	78-96		E
IM01	Imports of SITC0+1 (CS)	100m US$	80-96	SYC	E
IM24	Imports of SITC2+4 (CS)	100m US$	80-96	SYC	E
IM3	Imports of SITC3 (CS)	100m US$	80-96	SYC	E
IMCIF	Imports (C.I.F.) (CS)	100m US$	80-96	SYC	E
IMMG	Imports of SITC5 ~ 9 (CS)	100m US$	80-96	SYC	E
IMS	Expenditure on Services and Income	100m US$	82-96	SYC	E
KFXG	Foreign Exchange Reserve	100m US$	78-96	SYC	E
KXDI	= KXDI(-1) + XDI	100m US$	78-96		E
LC	Balance of Long-term Capital Investment	100m US$	82-96	SYC	E
M0	Currency in Circulation M0	100m Yuan	78-96	SYC	E
M1	Money M1	100m Yuan	78-96	IFS	E
M2	Money and Quasi-money M2	100m Yuan	78-96	IFS	E
MDI	Direct Investment Abroad	100m US$	82-96	SYC	E
ML	Payments on Foreign Loans	100m US$	82-96	SYC	E
MLC	Outflow of Long-term Capital	100m US$	82-96	SYC	E
MLCO	Other Outflow of Long-term Capital	100m US$	82-96	SYC	E
MPI	Securities Investment Abroad	100m US$	82-96	SYC	E
OB	Overall Balance	100m US$	82-96	SYC	E
PGDP	GDP Deflator, = GDP/IGDP/36.24*100	1978 = 100	78-96		E
RINV	Revenue from Investment	100m US$	82-96	SYC	E
ROTH	Revenue from Other Services	100m US$	82-96	SYC	E
RTOU	Revenue from Tourism	100m US$	82-96	SYC	E
RTRA	Revenue from Freight Transportation and Port Services	100m US$	82-96	SYC	E
SB	Balance on Services and Income	100m US$	82-96	SYC	E
SCEO	Short-term Capital Balance and Errors and Omissions	100m US$	82-96	SYC	E
TB	Trade Balance (IMF Stat.)	100m US$	82-96	SYC	E
XDI	Foreign Direct Investment	100m US$	82-96	SYC	E
XL	Loans from Abroad	100m US$	82-96	SYC	E
XLC	Inflow of Long-term Capital	100m US$	82-96	SYC	E
XLCO	Other Long-term Capital Inflow	100m US$	82-96	SYC	E

XPI	Foreign Securities Investment	100m US$	82-96	SYC	E
DD84	Dummy = 1for 84; = 0 for other				X
DD89	Dummy = 1fpr 89; = 0 for other				X
DD91	Dummy = 1for 91; = 0 for other				X
DD92	Dummy =1 for 92; = 0 for other				X
DD93	Dummy = 1for93; = 0 for other				X
EXW	World Exports	100m US$	78-96	IFS	X
GE	Financial Expenditure	100m Yuan	78-96	SYC	X
GRAIN	Output of Grain	10,000 tn	78-96	SYC	X
IGA	Index of Gross Output Value, Agricultural	1978 = 100	78-96	SYC	X
IGDP	Index of Real GDP	1978 = 100	78-96	SYC	X
IGI	Index of Gross Output Value, Industrial	1978 = 100	78-96	SYC	X
LB	Claims on Deposit Money Banks	100m Yuan	86-96	ACFB	X
LG	Net Claims on Central Gov'nt	100m Yuan	86-96	ACFB	X
OIL	Output of Crude Oil	10,000 tn	78-96	SYC	X
PIA	Purchasing Price Index of Farm Products	1978 = 100	78-96	SYC	X
PIS	Price Index of Retail sales	1978 = 100	78-96	SYC	X
POIL	Average Crude Oil Price	US$/barrel	78-96	IFS	X
POP	Population	10,000 Psn	78-96	SYC	X
R1	Interest Rate, One-year time deposit	%	78-96	SYC	X
RBUS	Govt. Securities Yield of U.S.: Long-term	%	78-96	IFS	X
REX	Exchange Rate, Yuan to US$	Yuan/US$	78-96	IFS	X
REXJP	Exchange Rate, JYen to US$	Yen/US$	78-96	IFS	X
RTUS	US Treasury Bill Rate annual	%	78-96	IFS	X
TRS	Unrequited Transfer	100m US$	82-96	SYC	X
W	Average Annual Wage of Staff and Workers	Yuan/Psn	78-96	SYC	X
YEAR	Time Trend	1978 = 0	78-96		X

Source: SYC – Statistic Yearbook of China,   IFS – International Financial Statistics
   ACFB – Almanac of China's Finance and Banking

Note: E – Endogenous Variable,   X – Exogenous Variable

Appendix 3—List of Data Used in the Model

Year	CB	EINV	EOTH	ETOU	ETRA
1978	-13.37	0.00	n.a.	n.a.	n.a.
1979	-24.89	6.24	n.a.	n.a.	n.a.
1980	-32.81	6.12	n.a.	n.a.	n.a.
1981	13.20	8.12	n.a.	n.a.	n.a.
1982	56.74	6.41	6.22	0.66	13.36
1983	42.40	2.95	4.78	0.53	14.63
1984	20.30	3.88	12.65	1.50	14.42
1985	-114.17	5.46	6.17	3.14	15.92
1986	-70.34	9.24	3.65	3.08	16.02
1987	3.00	11.91	3.15	3.87	17.84
1988	-38.02	16.30	4.80	6.33	24.90
1989	-43.17	16.65	5.42	4.28	29.39
1990	119.27	19.62	5.43	4.70	33.39
1991	132.72	28.79	8.88	5.11	27.16
1992	64.02	53.67	23.23	25.12	46.00
1993	-119.02	56.96	33.99	27.97	58.40
1994	76.57	68.73	37.62	30.36	95.01
1995	16.18	169.75	77.36	36.88	137.99
1996	72.43	197.55	75.65	44.74	105.45

Year	EX01	EX24	EX3	EXFOB	EXMG
1978	n.a.	n.a.	n.a.	99.55	n.a.
1979	n.a.	n.a.	n.a.	136.14	n.a.
1980	30.72	17.71	42.80	180.99	90.05
1981	29.84	20.72	52.28	220.43	117.59
1982	30.05	17.31	53.14	223.21	122.71
1983	29.57	19.97	46.66	222.26	126.06
1984	33.42	25.65	60.27	261.39	142.05
1985	39.08	27.88	71.32	273.50	135.22
1986	45.67	30.22	36.83	309.42	196.70
1987	49.56	37.31	45.44	394.37	262.06
1988	61.25	43.31	39.50	475.16	331.10
1989	64.59	42.98	43.21	525.38	374.60
1990	69.51	36.98	52.37	620.91	462.05
1991	77.57	36.34	47.54	718.43	556.98
1992	90.04	33.13	46.72	849.40	679.51
1993	93.00	32.57	41.09	917.44	750.78
1994	110.19	46.27	40.69	1210.06	1012.98
1995	113.24	48.29	53.32	1487.70	1272.95
1996	115.74	44.22	59.29	1510.70	1291.41

Year	EXS	FCDC	FS	GDP	IM01
1978	9.99	n.a.	n.a.	3624.1	n.a.
1979	16.93	2.00	n.a.	4038.2	n.a.
1980	24.09	4.00	n.a.	4517.8	29.63
1981	31.00	15.00	n.a.	4862.4	38.35
1982	36.04	20.00	n.a.	5294.7	43.31
1983	40.28	36.00	n.a.	5934.5	31.68
1984	48.19	26.51	n.a.	7171.0	24.47
1985	45.33	59.32	145.7	8964.6	17.59
1986	49.27	28.34	144.0	10202.1	17.97
1987	54.13	37.09	254.7	11962.5	27.06
1988	63.27	52.97	282.2	14958.3	38.22
1989	64.97	56.00	405.0	16909.2	43.94
1990	88.72	65.96	820.5	18547.9	34.92
1991	106.98	119.77	1399.6	21617.8	29.99
1992	148.44	581.24	1330.4	26638.1	33.85
1993	155.83	1114.36	1549.5	34634.4	24.51
1994	223.57	826.80	4451.3	46759.4	31.87
1995	243.21	912.82	6669.5	58478.1	65.26
1996	279.19	732.76	9562.2	68593.8	61.69

Year	IM24	IM3	IMCIF	IMMG	IMS
1978	n.a.	n.a.	111.31	n.a.	11.69
1979	n.a.	n.a.	156.21	n.a.	22.54
1980	37.93	2.03	200.17	130.58	27.03
1981	41.26	0.83	220.15	139.71	33.33
1982	31.20	1.83	192.85	116.51	26.65
1983	25.29	1.11	213.90	155.82	22.89
1984	26.22	1.39	274.10	222.02	32.45
1985	33.58	1.72	422.52	369.63	30.70
1986	33.48	5.04	429.04	372.55	32.00
1987	36.70	5.39	432.16	363.01	36.76
1988	54.59	7.87	552.75	452.07	52.33
1989	57.10	16.50	591.40	473.86	55.75
1990	50.89	12.72	533.45	434.92	63.14
1991	57.22	21.14	637.91	529.56	70.00
1992	62.85	35.46	805.31	673.15	147.81
1993	59.40	58.19	1039.59	879.49	177.06
1994	92.47	40.34	1156.14	991.28	230.73
1995	127.64	51.27	1320.78	1076.67	421.89
1996	123.94	68.77	1388.40	1133.98	423.39

Year	KFXG	KXDI	LC	M0	M1
1978	1.67	0.00	n.a.	212.0	580.4
1979	8.40	0.50	n.a.	267.7	921.5
1980	-12.96	1.80	n.a.	346.2	1148.8
1981	27.08	5.70	n.a.	396.4	1345.2
1982	69.86	11.66	3.89	439.1	1488.4
1983	89.01	18.02	0.49	529.8	1748.9
1984	82.20	30.60	-1.13	792.1	2449.4
1985	26.40	47.19	67.01	987.8	3017.3
1986	20.72	65.94	82.38	1218.4	3859.0
1987	29.23	89.08	57.90	1454.5	4574.0
1988	33.72	121.02	70.56	2134.0	5487.4
1989	55.50	154.94	52.40	2344.2	5834.2
1990	110.93	189.81	64.54	2644.4	7009.5
1991	217.12	233.47	76.70	3177.8	8987.8
1992	194.43	345.03	6.56	4336.0	11714.3
1993	211.99	620.18	274.11	5864.7	16761.1
1994	516.20	958.05	357.56	7288.6	21539.9
1995	735.80	1335.41	382.43	7885.3	25597.3
1996	1050.00	1748.84	415.54	8802.0	30662.6

Year	M2	MDI	ML	MLC	MLCO
1978	889.7	n.a.	n.a.	n.a.	n.a.
1979	1327.8	n.a.	n.a.	n.a.	n.a.
1980	1627.1	n.a.	n.a.	n.a.	n.a.
1981	1977.7	n.a.	n.a.	n.a.	n.a.
1982	2265.7	0.44	12.27	29.23	16.32
1983	2712.8	0.93	7.55	26.53	10.31
1984	3598.5	1.34	1.89	42.41	13.38
1985	4874.9	6.29	5.60	28.30	16.19
1986	6348.6	4.50	8.35	31.56	18.31
1987	7957.4	6.45	22.11	39.50	9.54
1988	9602.1	8.50	13.54	40.58	15.14
1989	11393.1	7.80	46.08	68.93	11.85
1990	14681.9	8.30	26.58	51.57	14.28
1991	18598.9	9.13	26.99	51.88	12.46
1992	24327.3	40.00	97.57	269.86	123.07
1993	34739.9	44.00	47.93	229.43	117.57
1994	46920.3	20.00	96.25	250.33	124.58
1995	60744.0	38.87	93.98	278.18	134.41
1996	76095.3	21.14	84.99	281.67	169.26

Year	MPI	OB	RINV	ROTH	RTOU
1978	n.a.	n.a.	2.36	n.a.	2.63
1979	n.a.	n.a.	3.05	n.a.	4.50
1980	n.a.	n.a.	5.12	n.a.	6.17
1981	n.a.	n.a.	6.97	n.a.	7.85
1982	0.20	62.91	10.92	3.69	8.43
1983	7.74	36.48	15.49	2.64	9.41
1984	25.80	0.95	20.08	4.98	11.31
1985	0.22	-23.53	14.78	6.68	12.50
1986	0.40	-12.73	11.00	12.55	15.31
1987	1.40	48.52	10.27	11.48	18.62
1988	3.40	22.37	15.04	6.55	22.47
1989	3.20	-6.13	19.47	10.49	18.60
1990	2.41	121.27	30.69	11.84	22.18
1991	3.30	145.12	37.93	22.80	28.40
1992	9.22	-22.67	56.55	31.54	39.47
1993	19.93	17.67	44.37	41.27	46.83
1994	9.50	305.26	58.54	45.18	73.23
1995	10.92	224.81	51.91	51.96	87.30
1996	6.28	316.51	73.18	72.08	102.00

Year	RTRA	SB	SCEO	TB	XDI
1978	n.a.	-1.70	n.a.	-17.64	n.a.
1979	n.a.	-5.61	n.a.	-25.54	0.50
1980	n.a.	-2.94	n.a.	-35.57	1.10
1981	n.a.	-2.33	n.a.	9.80	3.80
1982	13.75	9.39	2.28	42.49	4.30
1983	13.70	17.39	-6.41	19.90	6.36
1984	12.68	15.74	-18.22	0.14	12.58
1985	12.27	14.63	23.63	-131.23	16.59
1986	12.40	17.27	-24.77	-91.40	18.75
1987	14.44	17.37	-12.38	-16.61	23.14
1988	19.57	10.94	-10.17	-53.15	31.94
1989	16.49	9.22	-15.36	-56.20	33.92
1990	24.19	25.58	-63.24	91.65	34.87
1991	18.58	36.98	-64.30	87.43	43.66
1992	21.48	0.63	-93.25	51.83	111.56
1993	20.88	-21.23	-137.42	-106.50	275.15
1994	45.25	-7.16	-128.87	72.90	337.87
1995	52.04	-178.68	-173.85	180.50	377.36
1996	31.93	-144.20	-171.46	195.35	401.80

Year	XL	XLC	XLCO	XPI	EXW
1978	n.a.	n.a.	n.a.	n.a.	12465
1979	n.a.	n.a.	n.a.	n.a.	16051
1980	n.a.	n.a.	n.a.	n.a.	19218
1981	n.a.	n.a.	n.a.	n.a.	19008
1982	11.94	33.12	16.47	0.41	17538
1983	10.91	27.02	8.22	1.53	17129
1984	11.72	41.28	7.56	9.42	18187
1985	39.50	95.31	8.73	30.49	18494
1986	63.85	113.94	15.26	16.08	20353
1987	50.34	97.40	12.01	11.91	23927
1988	59.20	111.14	7.84	12.16	27305
1989	72.27	121.33	13.74	1.40	19667
1990	62.34	116.11	18.90	0.00	33776
1991	60.80	128.58	18.47	5.65	34775
1992	65.11	276.42	95.82	3.93	37314
1993	64.88	503.54	127.04	36.47	37249
1994	99.95	607.89	125.14	44.93	42383
1995	125.93	660.61	140.08	17.24	50791
1996	94.64	697.21	177.50	23.27	52496

Year	GE	GRAIN	IGA	IGDP	IGI
1978	1111	30477	100.00	100.0	100.00
1979	1274	33512	107.51	107.6	108.82
1980	1213	32056	109.06	166.0	188.88
1981	1115	32502	115.37	122.0	124.00
1982	1153	35450	128.38	133.3	133.68
1983	1293	38728	138.39	148.2	148.63
1984	1546	40731	155.36	170.5	172.83
1985	1845	37911	160.66	192.9	209.81
1986	2331	39151	166.37	209.9	234.29
1987	2449	40298	175.68	234.1	275.74
1988	2707	39408	182.63	260.7	333.07
1989	3040	40755	188.29	271.3	361.50
1990	3452	44624	202.60	281.7	389.70
1991	3814	43529	210.11	307.6	447.26
1992	4390	44266	223.52	351.4	557.73
1993	5287	45649	240.99	398.8	709.99
1994	5793	44510	261.71	449.3	881.81
1995	6824	46662	290.24	496.5	1060.81
1996	7938	50454	317.52	544.2	1236.81

Year	LB	LG	OIL	PIA	PIS
1978	n.a.	n.a.	10405	100.0	100.00
1979	n.a.	n.a.	10615	122.1	101.99
1980	n.a.	n.a.	10595	130.8	108.09
1981	n.a.	n.a.	10122	138.5	110.67
1982	n.a.	n.a.	10212	141.5	112.80
1983	n.a.	n.a.	10607	147.7	114.50
1984	n.a.	n.a.	11461	153.6	117.73
1985	2248.6	-93.3	12490	166.8	128.11
1986	2681.6	58.6	13069	177.5	135.76
1987	2756.5	208.0	13414	198.8	145.70
1988	3364.4	305.6	13705	244.5	172.63
1989	4209.5	246.6	13764	281.2	203.38
1990	5090.7	420.7	13831	273.9	207.65
1991	5918.1	582.0	14099	268.4	213.67
1992	6780.2	1010.5	14210	277.5	225.21
1993	9625.7	1094.8	14524	314.7	254.94
1994	10451.0	854.4	14608	440.3	310.26
1995	11510.0	609.4	15004	527.9	356.19
1996	14518.0	357.4	15852	550.1	377.56

Year	POIL	POP	R1	RBUS	REX
1978	12.95	96269	3.24	8.41	1.68
1979	29.22	97542	3.96	9.44	1.55
1980	36.68	98705	5.40	11.46	1.50
1981	35.27	100072	5.40	13.91	1.71
1982	32.45	101590	5.76	13.00	1.89
1983	29.66	103008	5.76	11.11	1.98
1984	28.56	104357	5.76	12.52	2.32
1985	27.31	105851	6.72	10.62	2.94
1986	14.23	107507	7.20	7.68	3.45
1987	18.15	108073	7.20	8.38	3.72
1988	14.72	111026	7.68	8.85	3.72
1989	17.84	112704	11.12	8.50	3.77
1990	22.97	114333	9.90	8.55	4.78
1991	19.33	115823	8.09	7.86	5.32
1992	19.03	117171	7.56	7.01	5.51
1993	16.82	118517	9.43	5.82	5.76
1994	15.90	119850	10.98	7.11	8.62
1995	17.16	121121	10.98	6.58	8.35
1996	20.42	122389	9.16	6.44	8.31

Year	REXJP	RTUS	TRS	W	YEAR
1978	210.44	7.22	5.97	615	0
1979	219.14	10.04	6.26	668	1
1980	226.74	11.62	5.70	762	2
1981	220.54	14.08	5.72	772	3
1982	249.05	10.72	4.86	798	4
1983	237.51	8.62	5.11	826	5
1984	237.52	9.57	4.42	974	6
1985	238.54	7.49	2.43	1148	7
1986	168.52	5.97	3.79	1329	8
1987	144.64	5.83	2.24	1459	9
1988	128.15	6.67	4.19	1747	10
1989	137.96	8.11	3.81	1935	11
1990	144.79	7.51	2.74	2140	12
1991	134.71	5.41	8.31	2340	13
1992	126.65	3.46	11.57	2711	14
1993	111.20	3.02	11.73	3371	15
1994	102.21	4.27	13.37	4538	16
1995	94.06	5.51	14.35	5500	17
1996	108.75	5.04	21.29	6210	18

2 ICSEAD'S ECONOMETRIC MODEL OF THE CHINESE ECONOMY
—1997 Version—

Yoshihisa Inada

Konan University

1. Introduction

One of the purposes of this Chapter is to explain the features of the revised econometric model of China as a part of the ICSEAD World LINK model. Also the evaluation and examination of our model's properties through simulation serves another purpose. The ICSEAD World LINK model was developed and has been maintained by many co-researchers at ICSEAD. With respect to the development of the ICSEAD World LINK model, various papers such as Inada and Wescott (1993), Inada and Fujikawa (1993), Inada and Ichino (1995 and 1996) are helpful for understanding it at its various stages. The latest ICSEAD model as of 1997 covers the following country/regional models: Japan, US, South Korea, Taiwan, China, ASEAN, EU and the Rest of the World (ROW). The system of the ICSEAD World LINK model is completed through a trade matrix, in which country/regional models are linked together via bilateral trade flows[1].

As a step in further development of the ICSEAD World model, we are engaged in revision of the China model. As China has been playing an important role in the world economy, we can not ignore its economic development for prognosticating the outlook of the Pacific-Rim Economies. The revised China model to be introduced here is based on the earlier works of Inada and Ichino (1995) and Nogami and Zhu (1994). We also incorporate recent developments of Chinese statistics.

---

1 Among county models, Japan, the US and China models are relatively large in size and composed of production, expenditure, income distribution, price and monetary blocs. However, other country/regional models are compact and contain limited blocs such as expenditure, employment and price, *etc.*

In the next section, we first give a brief review of econometric models of China's economy and point out some underlying problems. In section 3, the outline of the revised China model is examined bloc by bloc. Then, in section 4, we show simulation results and examine properties of the model. For furhnter understanding of our model, we present a full list of equations and variables in **Appendix A**.

2. Econometric Models of the Chinese Economy: Brief Historic Review

Econometric model-building for China has been actively tried both in and outside China since the start of "Reform and Open Door Policy" in 1978[2]. According to Ichimura (1993), outside China we can cite pioneering works such as Tang Guoxing's model (visiting Kyoto University), Haruki Niwa model (Kyoto Industrial University), Lawrence J. Lau's model (Stanford University). Inside China, as far as we know, the State Information Center model, which is adopted as an official China model in the Project LINK, the Chinese Academy of Social Science and the Stanford model, and the Fudan University model[3] are representative.[4] These models have been modified as national income statistics have been developed and maintained. We can point out the following features common to these models:

(1) They are supply-oriented and production functions play important roles;
(2) In the model, there is no closure between GDP and GDE, which are theoretically equal in the SNA;
(3) The labor market does not play an important role in the model;
(4) The financial market is not taken seriously.

As to (1), it is quite natural because China had a long tradition of production-oriented planed economy. As to (2), closure problems arise because Chinese statistics had been based on Material Production System (MPS). The national accounting system is now gradually moving from MPS

---

2 According to Ichimura   (1993), full-scale macroeconometric model building had started in 1985. There were isolated efforts by Chinese scholars outside the PRC to model the economy by using meager statistics.

3 Other than these models, the Japan-US-China LINK model was developed by the joint work of Klein, Lau, Inada and CASS. See also Zhang (1993).

[4] See also Introduction to this book for some other references.

to SNA. Thus, this problem will soon be solved. [5] As to (3), so far, there is no comprehensive labor market in China to clear the demand-supply gap. In principle, demand and supply for labor are supposed to be balanced. However, problems concerned with wage differentials and unemployment will emerge as the market mechanism prevails. Thus, we should pay much attention to the proper modeling of the labor market. As to (4), so far, indirect fiscal and monetary policies as a tool of macro control do not work and function well. However, macro control will become more important in the future. For that reason, it is strategically important for the financial bloc in the model to be improved.

3. Outline of the Model

3.1 Basic Principles of Model Building

In the previous section, we reviewed briefly representative econometric models of China's economy. We also pointed out some problems in these models. In this revised China model to be reported here, we try to overcome specific problems. Our basic principles and model's features for development and maintenance are summarized as follows:

(1) First of all, the sample period for estimating behavior equations starts after 1978, when China moved to market economy and the government hammered out "Reform and Open Door" policies.

(2) So far, many model builders have stressed the supply-side. In their models, the following transmission mechanism played a central part. The determination of value added by industry leads to the determination of GDP and then income and employment. In this type of model, for example, an exogenous increase in investment contributes to an expansion of production and income through the supply-side channel. However, the multiplier-expansion channel aiming at demand-side effects is not incorporated in this model. Thus, a supply-oriented model can't trace the recent typical growth pattern of China's economy, in which an

---

5 For example, Liang (1994) tried to settle this problem by defining the discrepancy between production and expenditure as an increase in inventory.

increase in exports leads to an expansion of production and employment[6]. It is a feature of our model to incorporate this direct route.

(3) What stands out in China's recent economy is the different behavior between state-owned and non state-owned companies. Thus we divide industrial output into those of state-owned enterprises (SOE) and non state-owned enterprises (NSOE). We explicitly discriminate between their ways for determining output and employment.

(4) China has a long history of planned economy. Since 1949, many data have been created, but they are not familiar to us. Concretely, the "value" concept in the socialist economy is fundamentally based on material production, and many statistics are designed according to the method of Material Production System (MPS). This is different from the System of National Account (SNA) in which we use a broader definition of "value", including services or imputed value. However, the accounting system has been moving from MPS to SNA. For some series, data based on SNA have been reported recently. Thus we adopt the latest statistical system (SNA) as much as possible for model building.

3.2 Outline of the Model

Our China model is composed of seven blocs: (A) production, (B) expenditure, (C) income distribution and other, (D) labor, (E) wage and price, (F) money and finance and (G) international trade. Here we explain the features of our model bloc by bloc.

3.2.1. Production Bloc

In this bloc, GDP and its components at current and constant prices are determined. First, real GDP components are explained from behavior equations and their nominal values are determined by multiplying corresponding deflators. In China's recent national income statistics, series of GDP by industry such as primary, secondary and tertiary are available. In addition, secondary industry GDP is divided into manufacturing and construction industry GDP. For the sub-categories of tertiary industry, series for transportation, telecommunication, and commerce are available, but other series are not reported.

---

6 For this point, we owe to Dr. Toida's suggestion at IDE. See, also Toida-Liang (1990).

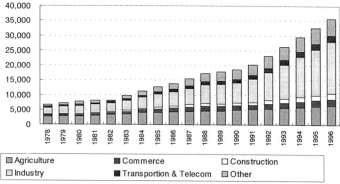

Figure 1-(a) Composition of Real GDP
(100M Yuan: at 1990 Prices)

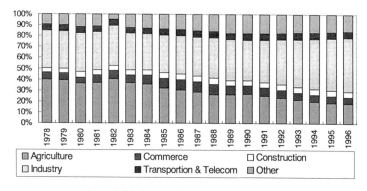

Figure 1-(b) Composition of Real GDP (%)

Before explaining a production function, let us sketch China's industrial structure. Figure 1(a) and 1(b) depict the industrial structure of real GDP since the start of "Open Door Policy" in 1978. Under this policy, the share of agriculture has declined from 40% to nearly 20%. In contrast, the share of industry has increased by 14 percentage points to 49% (see figure 1(b)). From this figure, we can easily understand that industry has been a main contributor to high growth in these twenty years.

Next, figure 2(a) and 2(b) show industrial output and share by sectors (sate-owned and non state-owned units). Industrial output, here, is a gross value because industrial GDP by sector is not available in the GDP statistics. It should be noted that gross value of output is not value added, and it includes some intermediate input. The share of non state-owned units in industrial

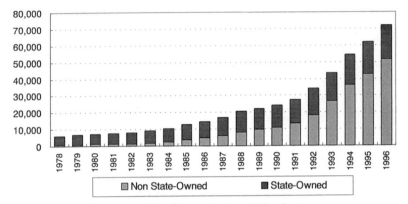

Figure 2-(a) Real Industrial Output by Sector
(100M Yuan: at 1990 Prices)

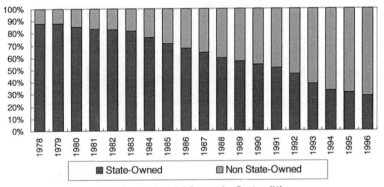

Figure 2-(b) Real Industrial Output by Sector (%)

output has widened from 12% to 72% in this period. Thus, high growth in industry or the rapid expansion of China's economy is attributable to the growth in non state-owned units.

In our model, we estimated industrial production functions following a conventional classification, such as primary, secondary and tertiary industries. Secondary industry is composed of manufacturing and construction industries. For secondary industry, we endogenize only the manufacturing sector. Thus, secondary industry GDP is explained by manufacturing GDP in a bridge equation. In addition, manufacturing GDP is divided into state-owned and non state-owned GDP. We estimate corresponding production functions. This is because we intend to take into consideration the different behavior of both economic units.

The estimated production function is a Cobb-Douglas type in which capital and labor are used as arguments. However, in estimating a primary industry production function, land is used as a third factor, in addition to capital and labor, to explain output.

Production Functions:

(1) Primary Industry

$CH\_GDP1 = f(CH\_KF1[-1], CH\_N1, TREND, CH\_LANDDA/CH\_LANDSO)$

    CH_KF1: Capital Stock (Primary Industry)

    CH_N1: Employment (Primary Industry)

    TREND: Time Trend

    CH_LANDDA: Areas Covered by Natural Disaster

    CH_LANDSO: Total Sown Area

(2) Secondary Industry

$CH\_GDP2 = f(CH\_GVINSE + CH\_GVINNSE)$

    CH_GVINSE: Gross Output Value (State-Owned)

    CH_GVINNSE: Gross Output Value (Non State-Owned)

(3) Tertiary Industry

$CH\_GDP3 = f(CH\_KF3[-1], CH\_N3, TREND)$

    CH_KF3: Capital Stock (Tertiary Industry)

    CH_N3: Employment (Tertiary Industry)

Our specific concern about China's economy is the role of non state-owned economic units in the manufacturing industry. What factor is mainly responsible for the high growth in non state-owned economic unit? The first and most important factor, we believe, is Foreign Direct Investment (FDI). FDI inflow has been increasing in the form of joint ventures or technology cooperation. We assume that technology diffusion to Chinese firms in the form of joint ventures or technology cooperation contributes to the enhancement of productivity in non state-owned economic units. In Figure 3, we show the growth of FDI, output and employment in non state-owned manufacturing industry. These variables seem to be highly correlated. We can easily understand that an increase in FDI inflow affects output growth in non state-owned economic units.

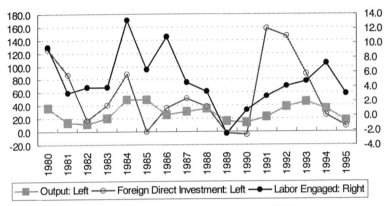

**Figure 3 Growth of Output, Employment and FDI
in Non State-Owned Industry (%)**

In order to take explicit consideration of FDI's effect on the output of non state-owned economic units, we tried to divide capital stock into domestic and foreign capital (stock of FDI[7]). In estimating a production function of non state-owned manufacturing industry, we treat two types of capital as different production factors. In the estimation, we reduce the number of parameters, so as to avoid multicolinearity. We assume that the average share of the wage bill of staff and workers in total value added of manufacturing as an estimate of the parameter for labor. As noted before, we also assume that the production function is of the Cobb-Douglas type. As a LHS variable, we subtract the employment-domestic capital ratio from the manufacturing output-domestic capital ratio, multiplied by the parameter of labor. A RHS variable is the foreign capital stock-domestic capital ratio. All variables are expressed as logarithms.

(4) Industry (Sate-Owned)
  CH_GVINSE = f(CH_KFINSE[-1], CH_NWINSE)
    CH_KFINSE: Capital Stock (Industry: State-Owned)
    CH_NWINSE: Employment (Industry: State-Owned)

---

7 We create data series for FDI stock as follows. (1) First of all, we deflate the FDI series at current prices by the fixed investment deflator mentioned in footnote 13. (2) By using FDI flow at constant prices and proper depreciation rate, we generate the FDI stock series. We assume bench-mark stock as zero. (3) FDI stock is allocated into industrial base by using the same ratio as in domestic capital.

(5) Industry (Non State-Owned)
$$CH\_GVINNSE = f(CH\_KFINNSED[-1], CH\_KFINNSEF[-1], CH\_NINNSE)$$
        CH_KFINNSED: Capital Stock (Industry: Non State-Owned: Domestic Company)
        CH_KFINNSEF: Capital Stock (Industry: Non State-Owned: Foreign Company)
        CH_NWINSE: Employment (Industry: Non State-Owned)

The estimation results of the production function, based on the above procedure, are presented in Table 1. The estimated results are in line with those that we expected. The parameters for labor share become lower in order: primary industry (0.52), tertiary industry (0.51) and manufacturing (state-owned: 0.29, non state-owned: 0.18). The parameters for capital stock become lower in reverse order. The shares of employment, domestic capital and foreign capital in non state-owned manufacturing production function are 0.18, 0.38 and 0.45 respectively. Foreign capital makes a higher contribution to output increase. The coefficients of time-trend, which corresponds to the rate of technological progress, are estimated to be 0.0113 in the primary industry and 0.0193 in tertiary industry. The technological progress rate in tertiary industry seems to be a little bit larger than that in primary industry.

Table 1. Estimation Results of the Production Function

	Labor	Capital			Time –trend
			Domestic	Foreign	
Primary Industry	0.5176	0.4824	—	—	0.0113
Manufacturing (State-Owned)	0.2938	0.7062	—	—	—
Manufacturing (Non State-Owned)	0.1774	—	0.3760	0.4465	—
Tertiary Industry	0.5100	0.4900	—	—	0.0193

3.2.2. Expenditure Bloc

In this bloc, GDE and its components, both at constant and current prices, are determined. First, GDE components at constant prices are determined and then those at current prices by multiplying by corresponding deflators. The expenditure bloc usually plays a central role in the Keynesian model. Regrettably it is quite recent that China's national income statistics based on the principle of SNA have become available, although GDP series are available both in real and nominal terms[8]. However, GDE series are available only at current prices (see, table 2). Thus, how to create series of GDE components at constant prices is an important factor for model building. In this section, we explain how to create series of GDE components in real terms and outline the structure of the expenditure bloc.

Table 2 Gross Domestic Product and Expenditure

GDP (Nominal, Real)	GDE (Nominal)
Primary Industry	Final Consumption Expenditure
Secondary	Residential Consumption (Urban and Rural)
Manufacturing	Public Consumption
Construction	Capital Formation
Tertiary Industry	Fixed Investment
Transportation and Telecom.	Inventory
Commerce	Net Exports

3.2.2.1. Consumption

Final consumption is composed of residential and public consumption. Residential consumption is divided into rural and urban residential consumption[9]. Real residential consumption in rural and urban sectors is explained basically by the corresponding real disposable income with a Koyck-type lag. In the case of rural residential consumption, we add a wealth factor. The wealth parameter in the long run is estimated at 0.3, higher than in developed countries. The urban residential consumption function does not include this direct wealth factor. Instead, we add interest receipts to their income.

Residential consumption at current prices is the product of a real series and a deflator. On the other hand, public consumption at current prices is expressed as a function of sum of corresponding government expenditures (culture and

---

8 Real national income and GDP in China's statistics are not absolute values but indexes at comparable prices (1978=100). We generate real GDP and its components, which satisfy additivity in the following way. First, we transform the real index series into those with base year 1990. Then, we generate absolute values of real GDP components by multiplying the real index series above by their corresponding nominal value in 1990. For the real series, expressed in comparable prices, created by linking different base year indexes directly, real GDP and the sum of GDP components created by the above-mentioned way do not satisfy the adding-up identity. In order for the GDP identity to hold we impose a statistical discrepancy.

9 Correctly, in the *Chinese Statistical Yearbook* (CSY), residential consumption is divided into residential consumption in agriculture and that in non agriculture. For convenience, we call them rural residential consumption and urban residential consumption, respectively.

education, administration, national defense and other items) [10]. Real public consumption is defined by dividing the nominal series by a corresponding deflator[11].

(1) Residential Consumption (Real: Rural)
$$CH\_CPR = f(CH\_CPR[-1], CH\_YHR, CH\_TDPR[-1], CH\_PCPR)$$
   CH_YHR: Household Income (Rural)
   CH_TDPR: Deposits (Rural Household)
   CH_PCPR: Deflator (Residential Consumption: Rural)

(2) Residential Consumption (Real: Urban)
$$CH\_CPU = f(CH\_CPU[-1], CH\_YHU+CH\_INR \times CH\_TDPU[-1], CH\_PCPU)$$
   CH_YHU: Household Income (Urban)
   CH_INR: Interest Rate on Fixed Deposits (1 Year)
   CH_TDPU: Deposits (Urban Household)
   CH_PCPU: Deflator (Residential Consumption: Urban)

(3) Residential Consumption (Real: Total)
$$CH\_CP = CH\_CPR+CH\_CPU$$

(4) Public Consumption (Nominal)
$$CH\_CGN = f(CH\_GESC+CH\_GEAD+CH\_GEND+CH\_GEO)$$
   CH_GESC: Government Expenditure (Culture and Education)
   CH_GEAD: Government Expenditure (Administration)
   CH_GEND: Government Expenditure (National Defense)
   CH_GEO: Government Expenditure (Other)

(5) Public Consumption (Real)
$$CH\_CG = CH\_CGN/CH\_PCP$$
   CH_CGN: Public Consumption (Nominal)
   CH_PCP: Deflator (Residential Consumption)

(6) Total Consumption (Real)
$$CH\_C = CH\_CP+CH\_CG$$

---

10 Residential consumption at constant prices is generated in the following way: In the chapter of "People's Life" in CSY, real and nominal index series of per capita residential consumption, both for rural and urban areas, are available. From real and nominal series, we create a price index series, and we use this index as a proxy for a residential consumption deflator. Finally, we deflate residential consumption at current prices by this deflator. With respect to a consumption-related price index, CPI may be used. However, development of a service price is not well reflected in the CPI. Thus we judge that the CPI is not good for a residential consumption deflator.

11 There is no proper deflator for public consumption. Here we use the residential consumption deflator as a proxy.

3.2.2.2. Investment

As in the case of consumption, how to create a proper investment deflator is also important. In addition, data series for investment by industry are not maintained. Thus, we face difficulty in estimating production functions by industry[12]. First of all, we create an investment deflator by linking two different series of deflators[13]. For the nominal series of investment by industry, we tentatively use the estimates of SIC. Finally, we define the real series of investment by dividing the nominal series by the investment deflator mentioned above. For capital stock, we generate a series by using the initial value of capital stock, investment flow series and an appropriate depreciation rate. We assume the industrial depreciation rate to be the same as in state-owned economy unit, which is available in CSY[14].

Following a two step procedure, we estimate an investment function. At the first step, we estimate total domestic investment and then determine total investment by adding FDI (exogenous variable). At the second step, investment on an industry basis is determined by multiplying industry-base-ratios by total investment.

The domestic investment function is estimated in the following way: For the LHS variable, we subtract government expenditure for economic construction from the domestic investment total. We use firm's cash flow and the real interest rate as RHS variables. As a proxy of cash flow, we subtract wage bills of staff and workers and industrial and commercial taxes from nominal GDP. We also add changes in domestic credit into firm's cash flow. Figure 4 shows fixed investment's source of funds and its share. For fixed investment's source of funds, own fund raising and other sources explain about 60% of the total. In the early 1980s, the share of government funds accounted for more than 20%. Recently its share declined to less than 5%.

---

12 In the chapter on "Fixed Assets Investment" in CSY, investment data by economic agent are available, but investment by industry is available only for state-owned companies.

13 We generate a fixed investment deflator as follows. From the issue of CSY in 1993, a fixed investment deflator is available from 1990. Before 1990, we generate another fixed investment deflator from the investment series in national income used, which is not published now. National income used is composed of consumption and investment. For national income used and consumption, both nominal and real series are available. From these two series, we can generate data series for real fixed investment. Finally we divide nominal investment by a real series, creating a deflator for fixed investment. We link the two different deflators as a fixed investment deflator.

14 For data creation of China's capital stock, Chow (1993) is helpful.

Instead, the share of domestic and foreign loans has been increasing. We paid attention to own fund raising and domestic credit as main sources of funds.

(1) Investment in Fixed Assets (Real: Domestic Enterprise)
$$CH\_IFD = f(CH\_GEEC, CH\_PIF, (CH\_GDEN-CH\_YW-$$
$$CH\_TAXINCM+DIFF(CH\_COS)), CH\_INR)$$
      CH_GEEC: Government Expenditure (Economic Construction)
      CH_PIF: Deflator (Investment in Fixed Assets)
      CH_GDEN: GDE (Nominal)
      CH_TAXINCM: Industrial and Commercial Tax
      CH_YW: Total Wage Bill for Staff and Worker
      CH_COS: Domestic Credit (Claims on Other Sectors)

(2) Investment in Fixed Assets (Real: Total)
$$CH\_IF = CH\_IFD+CH\_IFF$$
      CH_IFF: Investment in Fixed Assets (Real: Foreign Direct
              Investment)

(3) Investment in Fixed Assets (Real: Primary Industry)
$$CH\_IF1 = CH\_RIF1 \times CH\_IF$$
      CH_RIF1: Investment Ratio to Primary Industry

(4) Investment in Fixed Assets (Real: Industry: State-Owned)
$$CH\_IFINSE = CH\_RIFINSE \times CH\_RIFIN \times CH\_IF$$
      CH_RIFIN: Investment Ratio to Industry (Manufacturing)
      CH_RIFINSE: Investment Ratio to Sate-Owned Industry
              (Manufacturing)

(5) Investment in Fixed Assets (Real: Industry: Non State-Owned: Domestic
              Company)
$$CH\_IFINNSED = CH\_RIFINNSED \times CH\_RIFIN \times CH\_IF$$
      CH_RIFINNSED: Investment Ratio to Non State-Owned Industry
              (Manufacturing: Domestic Company)

(6) Investment in Fixed Assets (Real: Industry: Non State-Owned: Foreign
              Company)
$$CH\_IFINNSEF = CH\_RIFINNSEF \times CH\_RIFIN \times CH\_IF$$
      CH_RIFINNSEF: Investment Ratio to Non State-Owned Industry
              (Manufacturing: Foreign Company)

(7) Investment in Fixed Assets (Real: Construction)
$$CH\_IFCT = CH\_RIFCT \times CH\_IF$$
   CH_RIFCT: Investment Ratio to Construction Industry

(8) Investment in Fixed Assets (Real: Tertiary Industry)
$$CH\_IF3 = CH\_RIF3 \times CH\_IF$$
   CH_RIF3: Investment Ratio to Tertiary Industry

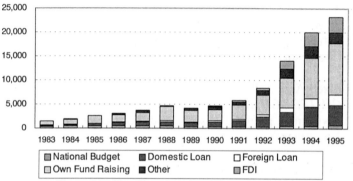

Figure 4-(a) Fixed Investment and Source of Funds
100M yuan: at 1990 price

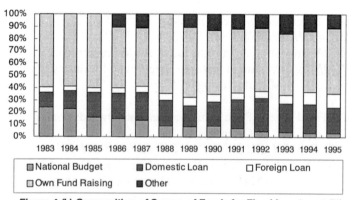

Figure 4-(b) Composition of Source of Funds for Fixed Investment (%)

3.2.2.3. Net Exports

The third item of GDE components is net exports. However, in the national account, exports and imports of goods and services are not separately reported, and only a net export series is available. In the trade bloc of our model, first, we estimate exports and imports functions of goods and services on a BOP basis. Then we explain net exports on a GDE basis by those on a BOP basis. For net exports in real terms, we deflate exports and imports of goods and services on BOP basis by corresponding price indexes and use this as an explanatory variable. The coefficient of the RHS variable should be unity. The coefficient of nominal net exports is almost unity, but it is 0.59, less than one, for *real* net exports. The reason why the coefficient for real net exports is less than unity may be concerned with the deflator. We use only a commodity price index without a service price component.

(1) Net Exports (Real)

$$CH\_NEX = f((CH\_EXMN+CH\_EXSN)/CH\_PEXM-$$
$$(CH\_IMMN+CH\_IMSN)/CH\_PIMM)$$

      CH_EXMN: Merchandise Export (BOP basis)
      CH_EXSN : Receipt of Service (BOP basis)
      CH_PEXM: Export Unit Value ($ basis)
      CH_IMMN: Merchandise Import (BOP basis)
      CH_IMSN : Payment of Service (BOP basis)
      CH_PIMM: Import Unit Value ($ basis)

(2) Net Exports (Nominal)

$$CH\_NEXN = f((CH\_EXMN+CH\_EXSN-CH\_IMMN-CH\_IMSN)/CH\_RATE)$$

      CH_RATE: Exchange Rate

3.2.3. Income Distribution and Related Items

In this bloc, wage bills, household income and capital stock are determined. Total wage bills are defined as the product of wage per worker and the number of staff and workers. There are no proper data for household income. Thus we generate household income data in the following way. In the chapter "People's Life" of the *Chinese Statistical Yearbook*, basic household surveys for urban and rural residents are available. From these surveys, we assume average living cost revenue for an urban family and net revenue for a rural family as corresponding household incomes. From the same survey, we calculate an income-consumption ratio on a household basis for urban and rural households. Then, we multiply these ratios by consumption for urban and rural households on GDE basis. They are household incomes on a GDE basis.

While urban household income is explained by wage bills of staff and other workers, rural household income is determined by primary industry GDP and gross value of output in Town and Village Enterprise. We assume that urban household income consists mainly of a wage bill, and rural household income comes from agriculture and industry in rural areas.

(1) Total Wage Bill for Staff and Other Workers
$$CH\_YW = CH\_WAGE \times CH\_NW$$
     CH_WAGE: Wage per Worker
     CH_NW: Number of Staff and Worker

(2) Household Income (Urban)
$$CH\_YHU = f(CH\_YW)$$

(3) Household Income (Rural)
$$CH\_YHR = f(CH\_GDP1,\ CH\_PFSP,\ CH\_GVINTVEN,\ CH\_RPI)$$
     CH_PFSP: Farm and Sideline Product Purchasing Price
     $CH\_GVINTVEN$: Gross Output Value (Nominal: Industry: Town
                              Village Enterprise)
     CH_RPI: Retail Price Index

3.2.4. Labor Bloc

In this bloc, labor demand by industry and population are determined. In the old CSY, there was no difference in concept between labor force and labor engaged. There were no data for unemployment or the unemployment rate. But recently, the situation has improved, and unemployment data are also available. Here, in line with the classification in the production bloc, employment in primary, secondary and tertiary industry are determined[15]. Employment in the manufacturing sector is divided into those in state-owned and non state-owned economies.

Employment by industry is explained basically by the scale of economic activity and its own lag. We assume that an adjustment process by the movement of the real wage rate does not work well. However, demand in non state-owned manufacturing sector is determined by a more market-oriented mechanism. Thus we assume firm's profit maximization principle and add a

---

15 Labor statistics in CSY, after Census 1990, were revised upward. For example, according to the 1995 Census, labor engaged in 1990 is larger by 100 million than in the old Census. For the transition period, CSY reported two data series based on new and old Census material. For the time being, we use a series based on old Census.

wage factor (unit labor cost) to the explanatory variable other than a scale factor.

(1) Employment (Primary Industry)
  $CH\_N1 = f(CH\_GDE, CH\_N1[-1])$

(2) Employment (Industry: State-Owned)
  $CH\_NWINSE = f(CH\_GVINSE, CH\_NWINSE[-1])$
    CH_GVINSE: Gross Value of Output (Real: Industry: State-Owned)

(3) Employment (Industry: Non State-Owned)
  $CH\_NINNSE = f(CH\_GDE, CH\_YW/CH\_GDE, CH\_NINNSE[-1])$

(4) Employment (Secondary Industry)
  $CH\_N2 = f(CH\_NWINSE+CH\_NINNSE)$

(5) Employment (Tertiary Industry)
  $CH\_N3 = f(CH\_GDE, CH\_N3[-1])$

(6) Employment (Total)
  $CH\_N = CH\_N1+CH\_N2+CH\_N3$

(7) Staff and Other Workers
  $CH\_NW = f(CH\_NU, CH\_NW[-1])$

(8) Employment (Urban)
  $CH\_NU = f(CH\_N, CH\_NU[-1])$

(9) Population (Rural)
  $CH\_POPR = f(CH\_YHU/CH\_YHR, CH\_POP, CH\_POPR[-1])$
    CH_YHU: Household Income (Urban)
    CH_YHR: Household Income (Rural)
    CH_POP: Total Population

(10) Population (Urban)
  $CH\_POPU = CH\_POP-CH\_POPR$

(11) Labor Force
  $CH\_LF = f(DIFF(CH\_POP[-16]), CH\_LF[-1])$

Figure 5 shows the urban population ratio and per capita income differ-ential between rural and urban areas. Amidst a strict family registration system which regulates population inflow, the exodus of rural population into the urban area continues. Figure 5 suggests that population movement is closely related to income differentials between the two areas. Thus, in our model, the population increase in the rural area is explained by relative income between urban and rural areas. Urban population is determined, as a residual, by subtracting rural population from total population. Labor force is explained by the net increase of population over 16 years old and its own lag.

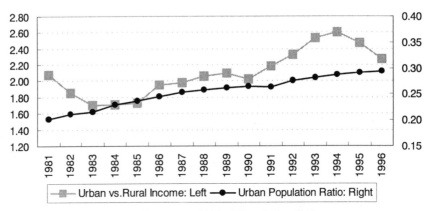

Figure 5 *Income Difference and Urban Population Ratio*

3.2.5. Wage and Price Bloc

In this bloc, wage and prices are determined. A key price variable in the model is the retail price index. Figure 6-(a) and (b) show recent price development, such as, retail price index, farm and sideline product purchasing price index, fixed investment deflator and an import price index. Also inflation related variables such as wage, money supply and exchange rate are shown in the figures. We select unit labor cost, farm and sideline product purchasing price index and money supply as good candidates for explaining the movement of the retail price index.

Figure 6-(a) Inflation Development 1: (%)

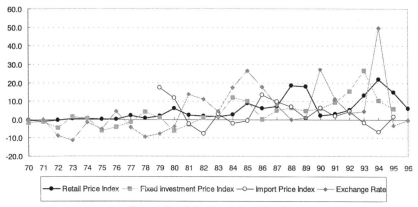

Figure 6-(b) Inflation Development 2: (%)

Figure 6-(c) decomposed inflation factors in the retail price index. Since the start of "Open Door " policies, there have been two waves of inflation in 1988-89 and 1994-95. From this figure, we can point out a policy factor such as a rise in farm and sideline product purchasing price which explains inflation in this period best. Alleged loose monetary control is not the most important factor to explain inflation. However, recently (1995-96), money supply growth explains more of an inflation rate in retail price. This suggests that tight monetary control in China does work. Thus a main explanatory factor of inflation is not a cost-push factor such as a rise in unit labor cost, but a policy factor such as an increase in grain price and in money supply.

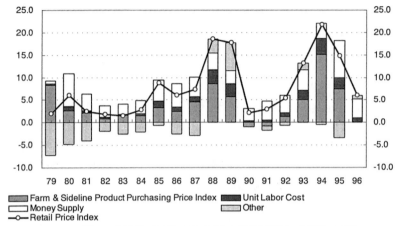

Figure 6-(c) Factor Decomposition of Retail Price Inflation: (%)

Among price variables other than the retail price index, the deflator for investment in fixed assets is explained by the retail price index and investment to GDE ratio as a proxy of the demand pressure. Deflators other than the GDP deflator and deflator for residential consumption are estimated mainly by the retail price index. The GDE deflator is defined by dividing nominal GDE by real GDP. Thus, we can keep the identity relating nominal GDE and nominal GDP. The wage bill per worker is a function of labor productivity in non-agriculture and the consumer price index of residents. On the other hand, the consumer price index of residents is explained by the retail price index and the wage bill per worker.

(1) Retail Price Index
   $CH\_RPI = f(CH\_YW/CH\_GDP, CH\_PFSP, CH\_M2[-1])$
      CH_M2: Money Supply

(2) Consumer Price Index of Residents (Urban)
   $CH\_CPIU = f(CH\_RPI, CH\_WAGE)$
      CH_WAGE: Wage per Worker

(3) Deflator (Residential Consumption: Urban)
   $CH\_PCPU = f(CH\_CPIU)$

(4) Deflator (Residential Consumption: Rural)
  $CH\_PCPR = f(CH\_RPI, CH\_PFSP)$

(5) Deflator (Investment in Fixed Assets)
  $CH\_PIF = f(CH\_RPI, CH\_IF/CH\_GDE)$

(6) Export Unit Value ($ basis)
  $CH\_PEXM = f(CH\_RPI, CH\_RATE, CH\_PEXM[-1])$

(7) Wage per Worker
  $CH\_WAGE = f(CH\_LPNAG, CH\_CPIU)$
    CH_LPNAG: Labor Productivity (Non Agriculture)

3.2.6. Fiscal and Monetary Bloc

So far, fiscal and monetary policies do not function as the government leaders expected. In a relatively short period, economic boom and bust changed places with each other. We build this bloc under the consideration that as a tool of macroeconomic control, fiscal and monetary policies may become important more and more in the future.

3.2.6.1. Fiscal Bloc

Here, in this bloc, main revenue items, government bond and interest payments are endogenous variables. Total government revenue comes from agriculture and an animal husbandry tax, industrial and commercial tax, customs duties and other revenue. Tax revenues, except other tax revenues, are explained by a corresponding tax base. Total government expenditure is the sum of expenditure for economic construction, culture and education, administration, national defense and others. They are exogenous variables in the model. A gap between total expenditure plus interest payment and total revenue determines total new debt incurred. Total new debt incurred is the sum of domestic debt (government bond) and foreign debt. Foreign debt is an exogenous variable. If money transfers, such as ODA, come to China, government can reduce the issue of government bonds by the same amount, equivalent to a money inflow. Interest payments are explained by debt and interest rate.

(1) Total Government Revenue
  $CH\_GTR = CH\_TAXAG + CH\_TAXINCM + CH\_TAXCUS + CH\_TAXO$

(2) Tax Revenue (Agriculture and Animal Husbandry Tax)
   $CH\_TAXAG = f(CH\_GDP1 \times CH\_PFSP)$

(3) Tax Revenue (Industrial and Commercial Tax)
   $CH\_TAXINCM = f(CH\_GDPN\text{-}CH\_GDP1 \times CH\_PFSP)$

(4) Tax Revenue (Custom Duties)
   $CH\_TAXCUS = f(CH\_IMMN, CH\_RATE)$

(5) Tax Revenue (Others)
   $CH\_TAXO = f(CH\_GTR, CH\_IFINSE \times CH\_PIF)$
      CH_IFINSE: Investment in Fixed Assets (Real: Industry: State-Owned)

(6) Total Government Expenditure
   $CH\_GTE = CH\_GEEC+CH\_GESC+CH\_GEAD+CH\_GEND+CH\_GEO$
      CH_GEEC: Government Expenditure (Economic Construction)
      CH_GESC: Government Expenditure (Culture and Education)
      CH_GEAD: Government Expenditure (Administration)
      CH_GEND: Government Expenditure (National Defense)
      CH_GEO: Government Expenditure (Other)

(7) Total Debt Incurred (Domestic Debt)
   $CH\_GBD = f(CH\_GTE+CH\_GEPL\text{-}CH\_GTR, CH\_GBF)$
      CH_GEPL: Interest Payment
      CH_GBF: Total Debt Incurred (Foreign Debt)

(8) Interest Payment
   $CH\_GEPL = f(CH\_INR, CH\_GBD, CH\_GBF)$

3.2.6.2. Finance Bloc

Although it is important to explain the working of financial sector in the Chinese economy, so far there is no clear model framework. The financial system in China is now in transition, full of change; besides there is no good database. The following two tables are helpful to understand the money supply mechanism. Table 3-1 is the balance sheet of national banks. On the other hand, Table 3-2 is a monetary survey table based on IMF standards. It is composed of the three tables of a monetary authority, banking institutions, and a consolidated table of a banking survey. It may be useful for understanding the ripple effect of monetary policy, but the data are available only since 1985. They can provide a very small sample for robust estimation of parameters. On the other hand, data on a national bank basis are available since 1980. However, the definition and coverage of monetary institutions are not clear. This table may correspond to the IMF's banking survey table, but exact comparison is impossible. Figure 7 compares the movement of total loans on a national bank basis and claims on other sectors in IMF's survey table. Except for 1993, movements of both variables are quite similar.

We assume that the monetary authority can control reserve money through changes in net foreign assets, claims on government and claims on banking institutions. If the credit multiplier (reserve money to money supply) is stable, the monetary authority can control money supply. On the other hand, the monetary authority can affect the banking sector's claim on other sectors through change in claims on deposit money institutions. For this reason, we assume the money supply to be an exogenous variable. Then, we explain bank's claims on other sectors (domestic credit) by money supply. Also changes in banks' claims play a role in explaining fixed investment. This is the channel through which a change in monetary policy affects real variables.

Table 3-1 Flow of Funds (National Bank Basis)

Assets	Liabilities
Loan Total	Currency
Industry	Deposits Total
Commerce	Enterprises
Construction	Urban
Agriculture	Rural
Fixed Assets Loan	Profits and Losses
Other Use of Funds	Other Liabilities

Table 3-2 Monetary Survey Table: 1995 （Unit: 100M Yuan）

Monetary Authority

Assets	(a)	(b)	(c)
Foreign Assets	11	CH_FAMA	6669.5
Claims on Central Government	12a	CH_CCGMA	1582.8
Claims on Other Sectors	12d	CH_COSMA	680.1
Claims on Deposit Money Banks	12e	CH_CDMB	11510.3
Claims on Other Banking Institutions	12f	CH_COBIMA	181.6

Liabilities	(a)	(b)	(c)
Reserve Money	14	CH_RM	20759.8
Currency Outside Banking Institutions	14a	CH_CUR	7882.4
Reserves of Deposit Money Banks	14c	CH_RDMB	9319.8
Deposits of Other Sectors	14d	CH_DOS	2513.3
Deposits of Other Banking Institutions	14f	CH_DOBI	1044.3
Bonds	16ab	CH_BONMA	197.1
Foreign Liabilities	16c	CH_FLMA	
Central Government Deposits	16d	CH_CGDP	973.4
Capital Accounts	17a	CH_CAMA	400.4
Other Items (net)	17r	CH_NOIMA	−1706.4

Banking Institutions

Assets	(a)	(b)	(c)
Reserves	20	CH_RMBI	10055.1
Foreign Assets	21	CH_FABI	3905.0
Claims on Central Government	22a	CH_CCGBI	714.0
Claims on Other Sectors	22d	CH_COSBI	50932.5

Liabilities	(a)	(b)	(c)
Demand Deposits	24	CH_DDP	15201.6
Saving Deposits	25a	CH_SDP	28045.5
Time Deposits	25b	CH_TDP	3324.2
Other Deposits	25e	CH_ODP	3777.0
Bonds	26ab	CH_BONBI	189.1
Foreign Liabilities	26c	CH_FLBI	4189.5
Credit from Monetary Authorities	26g	CH_CMA	11197.8
Capital Accounts	27a	CH_CABI	3515.8
Other Items (net)	27r	CH_NOIBI	−3833.9

Banking Survey

Assets	(a)	(b)	(c)
Foreign Assets (Net)	31n	CH_NFA	6385.0
Domestic Credit	32	CH_DC	52936.0
Claims on Central Government	32an	CH_NCCG	1323.4
Claims on Other Sectors	32d	CH_COS	51612.6

Liabilities	(a)	(b)	(c)
Money	34	CH_M1	25597.3
Quasi-Money	35	CH_QM	35146.7
Bonds	36ab	CH_BON	386.2
Capital Accounts	37a	CH_CA	3916.2
Other Items (net)	37r	CH_NOI	−5725.4

Note: (a) *IFS* Code Number. (b) Variable names. (c) Value at year end, 1995.

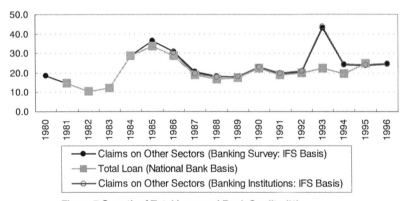

— Claims on Other Sectors (Banking Survey: IFS Basis)
— Total Loan (National Bank Basis)
— Claims on Other Sectors (Banking Institutions: IFS Basis)

Figure 7 Growth of Total Loan and Bank Credits (%)

(1) Domestic Credit (Claims on Other Sector: Banking Survey)

$$CH\_COS = f(CH\_M2)$$

Also in this bloc, deposits of both urban and rural residents are determined. The change in deposits is explained by the sum of corresponding residents' income and interest receipts.

(2) Deposit (Urban Resident: National basis)

$$CH\_TDPU = f(CH\_YHU+CH\_INR \times CH\_TDPU[-1])$$

(3) Deposit (Rural Resident: National basis)
$$CH\_TDPR = f(CH\_GDP1 \times CH\_PFSP + CH\_INR \times CH\_TDPR[-1])$$

3.2.7. Trade Bloc

In this bloc, exports and imports of goods and services are determined. Taking into consideration the promptness of data availability, exports and imports functions are estimated, based on customs clearance data.

We explain merchandise exports by a demand factor (real world GDP) and relative prices (export price to world GDP deflator). For merchandise imports, we estimate import functions by commodity such as machinery import (SITC7) and imports other than machinery (other than SITC7). We assume that machinery imports are induced by real GDE. Other imports are estimated from a conventional import function, with real GDE as an income factor and relative prices (import price ratio to retail price index).

(1) Merchandise Exports (CC basis)
$$CH\_EXMCN/CH\_PEXM = f(WO\_GDP, CH\_PEXM, WO\_PGDP)$$
WO_GDP: World GDP (Real)
CH_PEXM: Export Unit Value ($ basis)
WO_PGDP: World GDP Deflator

(2) Merchandise Exports (BOP basis)
$$CH\_EXMN = f(CH\_EXMCN)$$

(3) Receipt for Services (BOP basis)
$$CH\_EXSN = f(CH\_EXMN)$$

(4) Merchandise Imports (CC basis: Other than Machinery)
$$CH\_IMMC0689N/CH\_PIMM = f(CH\_GDE, CH\_PIMM, CH\_RATE, CH\_RPI)$$
CH_PIMM: Import Unit Value ($ basis)

(5) Merchandise Imports (CC basis: Machinery)
$$CH\_IMMC7N \times CH\_RATE/CH\_PIF = f(CH\_GDE)$$

(6) Merchandise Imports (CC basis: Total)
$$CH\_IMMCN = CH\_IMMC7N + CH\_IMMC0689N$$

(7) Merchandise Imports (BOP basis: Total)
$$CH\_IMMN = f(CH\_IMMCN)$$

(8) Payment for Services (BOP basis)
$$CH\_IMSN = f(CH\_IMMN)$$

4. Some Simulation Analyses

In this section, we examine five simulation results in order to investigate the properties of the model. They are the effects of (1) FDI increase, (2) money supply expansion, (3) government consumption increase, (4) public investment increase and (5) world GDP increase. Simulations were conducted over 11 years, 1985 through 1995.

4.1. Effects of FDI Increase

In the first simulation, we examine the impact of FDI increase by 1% of real GDP from its historical value. An increase in FDI expands investment in fixed assets by 0.6%-5.9% in the simulation period from the baseline solution. As a result, real GDE increases by 0.8%-2.0% from the baseline. An increase in GDE deteriorates the trade balance by $2.96 billion at most. On the other hand, an increase in FDI enhances productivity and leads to the improvement of export price competitiveness, giving a downward pressure on price level. Thus, retail price index declines 0.2% from the baseline. In the private sector, the ratio of saving-investment balance to nominal GDE declines by 1.0-percentage point in the final year of simulation period, as private investment increases. Meanwhile the ratio in the government sector improves 0.5 percentage-point in the same year as tax revenue increases through an economic expansion. Current account balance to nominal GDP deteriorates by 0.5 percentage-point (see, Simulation 1 in **Appendix B**).

4.2. Effects of Money Supply Expansion

The effect of a 5% money supply increase is reviewed in this simulation. A money supply increase leads to an increase in banks lending to the private sector, expanding private investment. An increase in banks lending expands investment in fixed assets by 1.3%-7.9% from the baseline. On the other hand, money expansion accelerates an inflation rate in the retail price index by 0.7%-1.0%. An acceleration of inflation rate pushes down real incomes and private consumption. As a result, real GDE declines somewhat in the seventh year of the simulation period. As banks' lending increases private investment and a decline in real income reduces saving, the ratio of saving-investment balance to nominal GDP declines by 3.8-percentage point in the final year.

Meanwhile the ratio in the government sector improves 2.8 percentage-point in the same year because of tax revenue increase by inflation. Current account balance to nominal GDE deteriorates by 1.0 percentage-point. (See Simulation 2 in **Appendix B**).

4.3. Effects of Increase in Government Consumption

In this simulation, effects of an increase in government consumption by 1% of nominal GDP are investigated. An increase in government consumption (here, national defense) lifts real GDE by 1.2%-1.7% in the simulation period from the baseline solution, while it also expands real GDP by 0.1%-0.8%. A sharp increase in real GDE has a downward pressure on price level through a decline in unit labor cost. As a result, no inflation can be seen in the simulation period. Government expenditure increase requires new issuance of government bonds by 5-30 billion yuan. In the private sector, the ratio of saving-investment balance to nominal GDP improves by 1.7-percentage point in the final year, as saving exceeds investment. The ratio in the government sector deteriorates 2.1 percentage-point in the same year as an increase in government expenditure surpasses tax revenue increases. Current account balance to nominal GDP deteriorates by 0.4 percentage-point. (See Simulation 3 in **Appendix B**). It should be noted that in this simulation, we assume an increase in national defense induces only domestic consumption expenditure such as salaries of soldiers and ammunitions. Instead, if China's government plans to import weapons from foreign countries for arms modernization, trade balance deteriorates further.

4.4. Effects of Increase in Public Investment

This simulation is similar to the previous one. Here, effects of increase in public investment (expenditure for basic economic construction) by the same amount as in simulation 3 are analyzed. Almost the same results are expected. However, results are quite different from those in simulation 3. Investment in fixed assets increases by 0.2%-5.7%, while real GDE increases by 0.2%-1.2% from the baseline. On the other hand, real GDP expands by some 1.5% at a maximum in this simulation. The impact on GDP is twice as much as in simulation 3. An enhancement in production capacity pushes down the price level. As a result, retail price index declines 0.1-0.2% from the baseline. In the private sector, the ratio of saving-investment balance to nominal GDP improves by 3.2-percentage point in the final year of simulation period. On the contrary, the ratio in the government sector deteriorates 3.6 percentage-point in the same year. Current account balance to nominal GDP deteriorates by 0.4 percentage-point. (See Simulation 4 in **Appendix B.**)

4.5. Effects of World GDP Increase

In this simulation, we examine the impact of world GDP increase by 1 percentage point from historical value. An expansion of world GDP increases China's net exports. As a result, real GDE increases by 0.4-0.8% from the baseline. Trade balance ameliorates by $0.7-3.7 billion in the simulation period. The ratio of saving-investment balance to nominal GDP in the private sector improves by 0.3-percentage point in the final year of simulation period, while the ratio in the government sector increases the same percentage-point. Current account balance to nominal GDP lifts by 0.6 percentage-point. (See Simulation 5 in **Appendix B**).

5. Reference

Chow, G.C. (1993), "Capital Formation and Economic Growth in China", *Quarterly Journal of Economics* Vol. 108, August, pp. 809-842.

Ichimura, S. (1993), "Development of Econometric Models in Asian-Pacific Countries." in S. Ichimura and Y. Matsumoto ed., *Econometric Models of Asian-Pacific Countries.* Springer-Verlag.

Inada, Yoshihisa (1992), *Mutual Dependency of Japan-U.S. Economy and LINK Model,* Nihon Hyoron (in Japanese)

Inada, Y. and R.F. Wescott (1993), "The ICSEAD Japan-U.S.-ROW Model", in S. Ichimura and Y. Matsumoto ed., *Econometric Models of Asian-Pacific Countries.* Springer-Verlag.

Inada, Y and K. Fujikawa (1993), "Development and Application of ICSEAD World LINK Model: Empirical Analysis of a Free Trade Area in Dynamic Asian Economies", ICSEAD Working Paper Series (A) No. 93-5.

Inada, Y and Y. Ichino (1995), "Econometric Model Building of the Chinese Economy and Some Simulation Analyses", ICSEAD Working Paper Series (A) No. 95-3.

Inada, Y and Y. Ichino (1996), "The Economic Impact of the Regional Integration with Special Reference to APEC", ICSEAD Working Paper Series (A) No. 95-5.

Krugman, P. (1994), "The Myth of Asia's Miracle", *Foreign Affairs* November/December, pp. 62-78.

Lau, L. J. (1993), "The Chinese Economy in the Twenty-First Century", Asia/Pacific Research Center, Stanford University Working Paper Series No. 103.

Liang, Y. (1994), "A Long Term Econometric Model of the Chinese Economy", Mimeo.

Nogami, K. and Baoliang Zhu (1994) "Quantitative Analysis of Chinese Economy - Macro Econometric Model For China-", ICSEAD Working Paper Series (A) No. 94-1.

Nogami, K. and Baoliang Zhu (1994) "Quantitative Analysis of Chinese Economy - Simulations of Reform Policy and Chinese Economy-", ICSEAD Working Paper Series (A) No. 94-2.

Tang, Guoxing (1993), "Economy of China: I969-1989 A Macro-Econometric Model (CMD90)", in S. Ichimura and Y. Matsumoto ed., *Econometric Models of Asian-Pacific Countries*. Springer-Verlag.

Toida, M and Y. Liang (1990), "Econometric Link Model of China and Japan", Joint Research Program Series No. 81, Institute of Developing Economies.

The World Bank (1992), *China Reform and The Role of The Plan in the 1990's*, The World Bank.

Zhang Shou Yi (1993), "Macroeconomic Model Building", in *China-US-Japan: Macro Econometric LINK Model and Its Application*, Renmin Chubanshe. (in Chinese)

Appendix A

China Macro Econometric Model 1997 Version Equation List

Notation

1	LOG(XX)	Natural logarithms of XX
2	PCH(XX)	Percentage change of XX
3	DIFF(XX)	First difference of XX
4	XX[-n]	N-period(s)-lagged XX
5	SPIKE(yy,1)	Dummy variable for 19yy
6	STEP(yy,1)	Dummy variable for 19yy and forward
7	AR_0 = + 0.86979 * AR_1	First-order autoregressive error term
8	FROM 0 TO 2 DEGREE 1 FAR	Length and degree of polynomial lags. FAR is far-end point restriction
9	(.....)	Figures in parentheses under coefficients are t-values.
10	SUM SQ	Sum of squares of LHS variable
11	STD ERR	Standard error of estimation
12	LHS MEAN	Mean of LHS variable
13	R SQ	Coefficient of determination
14	R BAR SQ	Adjusted coefficient of determination
15	F X, Y	F statistic with degree of freedom X, Y
16	D.W.	Durbin-Watson statistic
17	H	H statistic

ICSEAD China Macro Econometric Model Equation List: 1997 version
BLOC A 8 BLOC B 22 BLOC C 11 BLOC D 14
BLOC E 10 BLOC F 11 BLOC G 10 TOTAL 86 EQUATIONS

A. Production Bloc

[A–01]: CHEQ98: CH_GDP1: GROSS DOMESTIC PRODUCT(REAL: PRIMARY INDUSTRY) ANNUAL DATA FOR 18 PERIODS FROM 1978 TO 1995

LOG (CH_GDP1/CH_KF1[−1])
= 0.51764 * LOG (CH_N1/CH_KF1[−1])
 (5.17591)
 − 0.07348 * LOG (CH_LANDDA/CH_LANDSO) + 0.01131 * (TREND−1977)
 (2.06610)   (2.02445)
 − 0.09058 * SPIKE (80,1)+SPIKE(81,1)+SPIKE(82,1)
 (5.17857)
 + 0.09960 * STEP (94,1) − 0.92356
 (3.87731)   (2.75125)
SUM SQ 0.0069 STD ERR 0.0239 LHS MEAN 0.7803
R SQ   0.9405 R BAR SQ 0.9157 F 5, 12   37.9221 D.W.   2.5366

[A–02]: CHEQ98: CH_GVINSE: GROSS OUTPUT VALUE(REAL: INDUSTRY: STATE-OWNED UNITS) ANNUAL DATA FOR 18 PERIODS FROM 1978 TO 1995

LOG (CH_GVINSE/CH_KFINSE[−1])
= 0.29384 * LOG(CH_NWINSE/CH_KFINSE[−1])
 (27.1162)
 − 0.05222 * SPIKE(81,1)+SPIKE(82,1)+SPIKE(83,1)
 (4.54327)
 − 0.03955 * SPIKE(89,1) − 0.07771 * SPIKE(90,1)+SPIKE(91,1) + 0.43400
 (2.28420)   (5.96372)   (44.4793)
SUM SQ 0.0035 STD ERR 0.0165 LHS MEAN 0.1899
R SQ   0.9873 R BAR SQ 0.9834 F 4, 13 252.310 D.W.   2.0984

[A–03]: CHEQ98: CH_GVINNSE: GROSS OUTPUT VALUE(REAL: INDUSTRY: NON-STATE-OWNED UNITS)   ANNUAL DATA FOR 16 PERIODS FROM 1980 TO 1995

LOG (CH_GVINNSE/CH_KFINNSED[−1]) − .177435*LOG(CH_NINNSE/CH_KFINNSED[−1])
= 0.46541 * LOG(CH_KFINNSEF[−1]/CH_KFINNSED[−1])
 (17.6398)
 − 0.44143 * SPIKE(82,1)+SPIKE(83,1)+SPIKE(84,1)
 (4.43209)
 + 0.23385 * SPIKE(92,1)+SPIKE(93,1)+SPIKE(94,1) + 2.83643
 (2.19768)   (18.8101)

SUM SQ   0.2459   STD ERR   0.1431   LHS MEAN   0.3170
R SQ   0.9816   R BAR SQ   0.9770   F 3, 12   213.163   D.W.   1.7180

[A–04]: CHEQ98: CH_GVIN(IDENTITY): GROSS OUTPUT VALUE(REAL: INDUSTRY)

CH_GVIN = CH_GVINSE+CH_GVINNSE

[A–05]: CHEQ98: CH_GDP2: GROSS DOMESTIC PRODUCT(REAL: SECONDARY INDUSTRY)
COCHRANES-ORCUTT   ANNUAL DATA FOR 18 PERIODS FROM 1979 TO 1996

CH_GDP2
  =   0.23404 * (CH_GVINSE+CH_GVINNSE) + 2572.31
       (18.9817)   (2.17987)
SUM SQ   411822   STD ERR   165.695   LHS MEAN   7967.09
R SQ   0.9991   R BAR SQ   0.9989   F 2, 15   8026.54   D.W.   1.9699
AR_0 = + 0.86979 * AR_1
           (6.60730)

[A–06]: CHEQ98: CH_GDP3: GROSS DOMESTIC PRODUCT(REAL: TERTIARY IN-
DUSTRY) ANNUAL DATA FOR   18 PERIODS FROM 1978 TO 1995

LOG (CH_GDP3/CH_KF3[–1])
  =   0.50998 * LOG (CH_N3/CH_KF3[–1]) + 0.01928 * (TREND–1977)
       (3.68207)   (2.43665)
     + 0.07730 * SPIKE (78,1)+SPIKE(79,1) + 0.07695 * STEP(85,1)–STEP(90,1)
       (3.84397)   (6.75672)
     – 0.08949 * STEP(95,1) – 1.03985
       (3.75144)   (18.8346)
SUM SQ   0.0051   STD ERR   0.0207   LHS MEAN   –0.9045
R SQ   0.9634   R BAR SQ   0.9482   F 5, 12   63.2084   D.W.   2.1774

[A–07]:CHEQ98:CH_GDP(IDENTITY): GROSS DOMESTIC PRODUCT(REAL)
CH_GDP = CH_GDP1+CH_GDP2+CH_GDP3+CH_DSCGDP

[A–08]: CHEQ98: CH_GDPN(IDENTITY): GROSS DOMESTIC PRODUCT(NOMINAL)

CH_GDPN = CH_GDP*CH_PGDP/100

B. Expenditure Bloc

[B–01]: CHEQ98: CH_CPR: RESIDENTIAL CONSUMPTION(REAL: RURAL)
ANNUAL DATA FOR   18 PERIODS FROM 1979 TO 1996
CH_CPR
  =   0.49542 * CH_CPR[–1] + 0.37009 * CH_YHR/CH_PCPR*100
       (10.3029)   (9.6051)

+ 0.16542 * CH_TDPR[–1]/CH_PCPR*100 – 138.671 * SPIKE(93,1) + 266.391
  (2.56499)   (2.40300)   (2.61416)
SUM SQ 35517.1 STD ERR   52.2693 LHS MEAN   4822.18
R SQ   0.9992   R BAR SQ 0.9990 F 4, 13 4047.11   D.W. 2.2906 H   –
0.9578

[B–02]: CHEQ98: CH_CPU: RESIDENTIAL CONSUMPTION(REAL: URBAN)
ANNUAL DATA FOR 16 PERIODS FROM 1981 TO 1996

CH_CPU
 =   0.26212 * CH_CPU[–1]
   (2.35271)
   + 0.59599 * (CH_YHU+CH_INR*CH_TDPU[–1]/100)/CH_PCPU*100
   (7.69284)
   + 231.881 * SPIKE(88,1) + 151.607 * SPIKE(91,1)+SPIKE(92,1) + 266.720
   (3.25631)   (2.76099)   (4.98080)
SUM SQ 51438.3 STD ERR 68.3828   LHS MEAN   4179.02
R SQ   0.9994   R BAR SQ 0.9991   F 4, 11   4348.60
D.W.   1.2418 H   1.6041

[B–03]: CHEQ98: CH_CP(IDENTITY): RESIDENTIAL CONSUMPTION(REAL: TOTAL)

CH_CP = CH_CPR+CH_CPU

[B–04]: CHEQ98: CH_CG(IDENTITY): PUBLIC CONSUMPTION(REAL)

CH_CG = CH_CGN/CH_PCP*100

[B–05]: CHEQ98: CH_C(IDENTITY): TOTAL CONSUMPTION(REAL)

CH_C = CH_CP+CH_CG

[B–06]: CHEQ98: CH_IFD: INVESTMENT IN FIXED ASSETS(REAL: DOMESTIC EN-
TERPRISES)
ANNUAL DATA FOR   18 PERIODS FROM 1978 TO 1995

CH_IFD–CH_GEEC/CH_PIF*100
 =   0.27820 * (CH_GDEN–CH_YW– CH_TAXINCM+DIFF(CH_COS))/CH_PIF*100
    (32.4722)
   – 38.6970 * CH_INR–PCH(CH_PIF)– 602.216 * SPIKE(84,1)+SPIKE(85,1)
    (4.28995)   (3.48433)
   – 608.008 * SPIKE(89,1)+SPIKE(90,1)+SPIKE(91,1)
    (4.34149)
   – 800.898 * SPIKE(94,1) – 441.154
    (3.14191)   (3.56316)
SUM SQ 515412   STD ERR 207.246 LHS MEAN 2949.21
R SQ   0.9934   R BAR SQ 0.9906   F 5, 12   360.364 D.W.   2.2152

[B–07]: CHEQ98: CH_IF(IDENTITY): INVESTMENT IN FIXED ASSETS(REAL: TOTAL)

CH_IF = CH_IFD+CH_IFF

[B–08]: CHEQ98: CH_IF1(IDENTITY): INVESTMENT IN FIXED ASSETS(REAL: PRIMARY INDUSTRY)

CH_IF1 = CH_RIF1*CH_IF/100

[B–09]: CHEQ98: CH_IFINSE(IDENTITY): INVESTMENT IN FIXED ASSETS(REAL: INDUSTRY: STATE-OWNED UNITS)

CH_IFINSE = CH_RIFINSE*CH_RIFIN*CH_IF/10000

[B–10]:CHEQ98:CH_IFINNSED(IDENTITY): INVESTMENT IN FIXED ASSETS(REAL: INDUSTRY: NON STATE-OWNED UNITS: DOMESTIC ENTERPRISES)
CH_IFINNSED = CH_RIFINNSED*CH_RIFIN*CH_IF/10000

[B–11]: CHEQ98: CH_IFINNSEF(IDENTITY): INVESTMENT IN FIXED ASSETS(REAL: INDUSTRY: NON STATE-OWNED UNITS: FOREIGN ENTERPRISES)

CH_IFINNSEF = CH_RIFINNSEF*CH_RIFIN*CH_IF/10000

[B–12]: CHEQ98: CH_IFCT(IDENTITY): INVESTMENT IN FIXED ASSETS(REAL: CONSTRUCTION)

CH_IFCT = CH_RIFCT*CH_IF/100

[B–13]: CHEQ98: CH_IF3(IDENTITY): INVESTMENT IN FIXED ASSETS(REAL: TERTIARY INDUSTRY)

CH_IF3 = CH_RIF3*CH_IF/100

[B–14]: CHEQ98: CH_J: CHANGES IN INVENTORIES(REAL)
ANNUAL DATA FOR 14 PERIODS FROM 1982 TO 1995

CH_J
$=$ 26.6667 * PCH(CH_GDE[–3]) + 0.05364 * CH_GDE
   (2.26312)   (8.70255)
  + 0.03446 * SPIKE(85,1)*CH_GDE
  (2.29725)
  + 0.04577 * (SPIKE(89,1)+SPIKE(90,1))*CH_GDE – 268.605
  (6.57815)   (1.54910)

SUM SQ	233272	STD ERR	160.994	LHS MEAN	1103.58	
R SQ	0.9307	R BAR SQ	0.8999	F 4, 9	30.2332	D.W. 2.4472

[B–15]: CHEQ98: CH_NEX: NET EXPORT(REAL)
ANNUAL DATA FOR 18 PERIODS FROM 1978 TO 1995

CH_NEX=
0.58945*(CH_EXMN+CH_EXSN)/(CH_PEXM/4.7832)(CH_IMMN+CH_IMSN)/(CH_PIMM/4.7832)
(8.16006)
  − 723.732 * SPIKE(82,1) − 286.003 * SPIKE(86,1)
  (8.46102)   (3.38197)
  − 352.282 * SPIKE(91,1)+SPIKE(92,1) + 318.036 * SPIKE(93,1)
  (4.66805)   (3.73029)
  + 799.508 * SPIKE(94,1) + 1114.87 * STEP(95,1) + 239.424
  (8.99618)   (12.3650)   (9.24544)
SUM SQ 64231.4 STD ERR   80.1445   LHS MEAN 255.657
R SQ   0.9834   R BAR SQ 0.9718   F 7, 10   84.7091 D.W.   1.8797

[B–16]: CHEQ98: CH_GDE(IDENTITY): GROSS DOMESTIC EXPENDITURE(REAL)

CH_GDE = CH_CP+CH_CG+CH_IF+CH_J+CH_NEX

[B–17]: CHEQ98: CH_CPN(IDENTITY): RESIDENTIAL CONSUMPTION(NOMINAL)
CH_CPN = CH_CPR*CH_PCPR/100+CH_CPU*CH_PCPU/100

[B–18]: CHEQ98: CH_CGN: PUBLIC CONSUMPTION(NOMINAL)
ANNUAL DATA FOR 18 PERIODS FROM 1978 TO 1995

CH_CGN
  = 1.77156 * (CH_GESC+CH_GEAD+CH_GEND+CH_GEO)
    (69.0332)
   + 142.570 * STEP(79,1)–STEP(85,1)
    (2.71352)
   − 313.604 * SPIKE(89,1)+SPIKE(90,1)+SPIKE(91,1)
    (5.69576)
   + 353.962 * SPIKE(94,1) − 389.161
    (3.66114)   (7.45915)
SUM SQ 85956.5 STD ERR   81.3144   LHS MEAN 2146.54
R SQ   0.9986   R BAR SQ 0.9981   F 4, 13   2252.69 D.W.   1.8038

[B–19]: CHEQ98: CH_IFN(IDENTITY): INVESTMENT IN FIXED ASSETS(NOMINAL)

CH_IFN = CH_IF*CH_PIF/100

[B–20]: CHEQ98: CH_J(IDENTITY): CHANGES IN INVENTORIES(NOMINAL)

CH_JN = CH_J*CH_PIF/100

[B–21]: CHEQ98: CH_NEXN: NET EXPORT (NOMINAL)
ANNUAL DATA FOR 18 PERIODS FROM 1978 TO 1995

CH_NEXN
  = 0.99794 * (CH_EXMN+CH_EXSN–CH_IMMN–CH_IMSN)*CH_RATE/100
  (381.377)
  + 27.8053 * SPIKE(78,1)+SPIKE(79,1)+SPIKE(80,1)
  (10.0497)
  – 20.1676 * SPIKE(93,1)+SPIKE(94,1) + 2.23993
  (6.19283)   (1.82828)
SUM SQ 254.699 STD ERR 4.2653 LHS MEAN 84.3275
R SQ   0.9999 R BAR SQ 0.9999 F 3, 14   NC D.W.   2.6480

[B–22]: CHEQ98: CH_GDEN (IDENTITY): GROSS DOMESTIC EXPENDITURE (NOMINAL)

CH_GDEN = CH_CPN+CH_CGN+CH_IFN+CH_JN+CH_NEXN

C. Income Distribution and Others Bloc

[C–01]: CHEQ98: CH_YW (IDENTITY): TOTAL WAGE BILL FOR STAFF AND WORKERS

CH_YW = CH_WAGE*CH_NW/10000

[C–02]: CHEQ98: CH_YHU: HOUSEHOLD INCOME (URBAN)
ANNUAL DATA FOR 16 PERIODS FROM 1981 TO 1996

CH_YHU
  = 2.01214 * CH_YW + 657.331 * STEP(81,1)–STEP(86,1)
  (54.5575)   (5.17014)
  + 761.061 * SPIKE(95,1) + 1772.93 * STEP(96,1) – 1460.12
  (3.06035)   (6.44042)   (10.7320)
SUM SQ 310018 STD ERR 167.879 LHS MEAN   5518.00
R SQ   0.9993 R BAR SQ 0.9991 F 4, 11   3963.32 D.W.   1.4496

[C–03]: CHEQ98: CH_YHR: HOUSEHOLD INCOME(RURAL)
ANNUAL DATA FOR 18 PERIODS FROM 1978 TO 1995

CH_YHR
  = 1.13813 * CH_GDP1*CH_PFSP/100
  (33.0240)
  + 0.04607 * CH_RGVINTVEN*CH_GVIN*CH_RPI/10000
  (7.13660)
  + 362.679 * STEP(84,1)–STEP(88,1) – 378.404 * SPIKE(89,1)
  (5.00459)   (2.70825)
  + 696.047 * SPIKE(92,1)+SPIKE(93,1) + 207.939
  (7.39781)   (2.51393)

SUM SQ   171274   STD ERR   119.469   LHS MEAN   5296.96
R SQ   0.9994   R BAR SQ 0.9992   F 5, 12   4004.50   D.W.   2.3180

[C–04]: CHEQ98: CH_KF1 (IDENTITY): CAPITAL STOCK (REAL: PRIMARY INDUSTRY)

CH_KF1 = (1–CH_RDEP/100)*CH_KF1[–1]+CH_IF1

[C–05]: CHEQ98: CH_KFINSE(IDENTITY): CAPITAL STOCK(REAL: INDUSTRY: STATE-OWNED UNITS)

CH_KFINSE = (1–CH_RDEP/100)*CH_KFINSE[–1]+CH_IFINSE

[C–06]: CHEQ98: CH_KFINNSED(IDENTITY): CAPITAL STOCK(REAL: INDUSTRY: NON STATE-OWNED UNITS: DOMESTIC ENTERPRISES)

CH_KFINNSED = (1–CH_RDEP/100)*CH_KFINNSED[–1]+CH_IFINNSED

[C–07]: CHEQ98: CH_KFINNSEF(IDENTITY): CAPITAL STOCK(REAL: INDUSTRY: NON STATE-OWNED UNITS: FOREIGN ENTERPRISES)

CH_KFINNSEF = (1–CH_RDEP/100)*CH_KFINNSEF[–1]+CH_IFINNSEF

[C–08]: CHEQ98: CH_KFCT(IDENTITY): CAPITAL STOCK(REAL: CONSTRUCTION)

CH_KFCT = (1–CH_RDEP/100)*CH_KFCT[–1]+CH_IFCT

[C–09]: CHEQ98: CH_KF3(IDENTITY): CAPITAL STOCK(REAL: TERTIARY INDUSTRY)

CH_KF3 = (1–CH_RDEP/100)*CH_KF3[–1]+CH_IF3

[C–10]: CHEQ98: CH_KF(IDENTITY): CAPITAL STOCK(REAL: TOTAL)

CH_KF = CH_KF1+CH_KFINSE+CH_KFINNSED+CH_KFINNSEF+CH_KFCT+CH_KF3

[C–11]: CHEQ98: CH_KFF(IDENTITY): CAPITAL STOCK(REAL: FOREIGN DIRECT INVESTMENT)

CH_KFF = (1–CH_RDEP/100)*CH_KFF[–1]+CH_IFF

D. Labor Bloc

[D–01]: CHEQ98: CH_N1: EMPLOYMENT(PRIMARY INDUSTRY)
ANNUAL DATA FOR 18 PERIODS FROM 1978 TO 1995

LOG (CH_N1)
 = 0.63627 * LOG(CH_N1)[–1] + 0.05552 * LOG(CH_GDE)
     (5.20819)   (2.99541)

+ 0.03630 * SPIKE(82,1) + 0.02226 * SPIKE(89,1) +SPIKE(90,1)+SPIKE(91,1)
(3.05842)   (2.58911)
− 0.03780 * STEP(93,1) + 3.24461
(3.26270)   (2.91591)

SUM SQ	0.0015	STD ERR	0.0111	LHS MEAN	10.3647
R SQ	0.9793	R BAR SQ	0.9707	F 5, 12	113.580
D.W.	1.5195	H	0.0014		

[D–02]: CHEQ98: CH_NWINSE: EMPLOYMENT (INDUSTRY: STATE-OWNED UNITS)
ANNUAL DATA FOR   26 PERIODS FROM 1970 TO 1995
LOG (CH_NWINSE)

=   0.68682 * LOG(CH_NWINSE)[−1] + 0.10926 * LOG(CH_GVINSE)
(13.1189)   (3.95453)
− 0.05294 * STEP(93,1) + 1.60461
(3.23252)   (7.98075)

SUM SQ	0.0083	STD ERR	0.0194	LHS MEAN	8.1327
R SQ	0.9947	R BAR SQ	0.9940	F 3, 22	1372.89
D.W.	1.1790	H	1.9759		

[D–03]: CHEQ98: CH_NINNSE: EMPLOYMENT(INDUSTRY: NON STATE-OWNED UNITS)
ANNUAL DATA FOR   17 PERIODS FROM 1979 TO 1995

LOG (CH_NINNSE)
=   0.51821 * LOG(CH_NINNSE)[−1] + 0.38440 * LOG(CH_GDE)
(5.45079)   (4.94081)
− 0.27215 * LOG(CH_YW/CH_GDE) − 0.06403 * SPIKE(83,1)
(3.62039)   (2.69734)
+ 0.05304 * SPIKE(86,1) − 0.13140
(2.52242)   (0.23423)

SUM SQ	0.0042	STD ERR	0.0196	LHS MEAN	8.4634
R SQ	0.9953	R BAR SQ	0.9931	F 5, 11	464.028
D.W.	2.4689	H	−1.8435		

[D–04]: CHEQ98: CH_N2: EMPLOYMENT(SECONDARY INDUSTRY)
ANNUAL DATA FOR   17 PERIODS FROM 1979 TO 1995

CH_N2
=   1.49145 * (CH_NWINSE+CH_NINNSE) + 233.582 * SPIKE(85,1)
(91.1023)   (2.82865)
+ 173.555 * STEP(93,1) − 2267.73
(2.74420)   (16.1762)

| SUM SQ | 82277.4 | STD ERR | 79.5552 | LHS MEAN | 10981.9 | | |
| R SQ | 0.9990 | R BAR SQ | 0.9988 | F 3, 13 | 4435.44 | D.W. | 0.9233 |

[D–05]: CHEQ98: CH_N3: EMPLOYMENT (TERTIARY INDUSTRY)
ANNUAL DATA FOR 17 PERIODS FROM 1979 TO 1995

LOG (CH_N3)
= 0.50296 * LOG (CH_N3)[–1] + 0.34769 * LOG(CH_GDE)
  (6.88159)   (6.93395)
  + 0.08091 * SPIKE(84,1)
  (6.90857)
  + 0.03068 * SPIKE (85,1)+SPIKE (86,1)+SPIKE(87,1) + 1.20663
  (3.99173)   (6.37711)

SUM SQ	0.0014	STD ERR	0.0107	LHS MEAN	9.0919
R SQ	0.9992	R BAR SQ	0.9989	F 4, 12	3806.25
D.W.	2.5574	H	–2.0672		

[D–06]: CHEQ98: CH_NNAG(IDENTITY): EMPLOYMENT(NON AGRICULTURE)

CH_NNAG = CH_N2+CH_N3

[D–07]: CHEQ98: CH_N(IDENTITY): EMPLOYMENT(TOTAL)
CH_N = CH_NNAG+CH_N1

[D–08]:CHEQ98:CH_NW: STAFF AND WORKERS
ANNUAL DATA FOR 18 PERIODS FROM 1978 TO 1995
LOG(CH_NW)
= 0.72714 * LOG(CH_NW)[–1] + 0.20271 * LOG(CH_NU)
  (6.84949)   (2.05582)
  – 0.02523 * STEP (93,1) + 0.67747
  (3.97746)   (5.42019)

SUM SQ	0.0006	STD ERR	0.0065	LHS MEAN	9.4421
R SQ	0.9984	R BAR SQ	0.9981	F 3, 14	2918.38
D.W.	1.7944	H	0.2549		

[D–09]: CHEQ98: CH_NU: EMPLOYMENT(URBAN)
ANNUAL DATA FOR 18 PERIODS FROM 1978 TO 1995

LOG(CH_NU)
= 0.60814 * LOG (CH_NU)[–1] + 0.43008 * LOG(CH_N)
  (4.45964)   (2.47658)
  + 0.00972 * STEP (85,1)–STEP (89,1) + 0.02811 * STEP (94,1) – 0.92934
  (2.34904)   (4.37235)   (1.53183)

SUM SQ	0.0006	STD ERR	0.0070	LHS MEAN	9.4862
R SQ	0.9988	R BAR SQ	0.9985	F 4, 13	2817.11
D.W.	1.3622	H	0.7319		

[D–10]:CHEQ98:CH_POPR: POPULATION(RURAL)
ANNUAL DATA FOR 13 PERIODS FROM 1984 TO 1996

CH_POPR/CH_POP*100
= 0.64206 * CH_POPR/CH_POP*100[−1]
   (5.75678)
   − 1.89026 * ((CH_YHU/CH_POPU)/(CH_YHR/CH_POPR))
   (2.42489)
   + 0.84006 * SPIKE (91,1) + 29.6038
   (3.11721)   (3.03728)

SUM SQ	0.5372	STD ERR	0.2443	LHS MEAN		73.5255
R SQ	0.9890	R BAR SQ	0.9854	F 3, 9		270.567
D.W.	1.9132	H	−0.0181			

[D–11]: CHEQ98: CH_POPU(IDENTITY): POPULATION (URBAN)
CH_POPU = CH_POP–CH_POPR

[D–12]: CHEQ98: CH_LF: LABOR FORCE
ANNUAL DATA FOR 21 PERIODS FROM 1975 TO 1995
DIFF (CH_LF)
= 0.22738 * DIFF(CH_POP[−16])
   (4.04609)
   + 444.068 * SPIKE(84,1)+SPIKE(85,1)
   (2.96724)
   + 296.832 * SPIKE(87,1)+SPIKE(88,1)
   (1.99673)
   + 369.542 * SPIKE(90,1)+SPIKE(91,1) + 768.784
   (2.58218)   (8.64340)

SUM SQ 571245 STD ERR 188.952 LHS MEAN 1216.12
R SQ   0.7544 R BAR SQ 0.6930 F 4, 16 12.2871 D.W.   3.0560

[D–13]: CHEQ98: CH_U(IDENTITY): UNEMPLOYMENT

CH_U = CH_LF–CH_N

[D–14]: CHEQ98: CH_UR(IDENTITY): UNEMPLOYMENT RATE

CH_UR = CH_U/(CH_NU+CH_U)*100

E. Price and Wage Bloc

[E–01]: CHEQ98: CH_RPI: RETAIL PRICE INDEX
ANNUAL DATA FOR 17 PERIODS FROM 1979 TO 1995

PCH (CH_RPI)
= 0.16555 * PCH (CH_YW/CH_GDP) + 0.14534 * PCH(CH_M2[−1])
   (2.06209)   (4.14404)
   + 0.37843 * PCH(CH_PFSP) − 5.07414 * SPIKE(79,1)+SPIKE(80,1)
   (8.06653)   (4.11480)

+ 7.69253 * SPIKE (88,1)+SPIKE(89,1) + 3.65783 * SPIKE (93,1) – 1.66925
  (5.95429)   (2.19231)   (1.58723)
SUM SQ   24.9460   STD ERR   1.5794 LHS MEAN   7.9467
R SQ   0.9652   R BAR SQ 0.9444 F 6, 10   46.2881 D.W.   2.5425

[E–02]: CHEQ98: CH_CPIU: CONSUMER PRICE INDEX OF RESIDENTS (URBAN)
ANNUAL DATA FOR 18 PERIODS FROM 1978 TO 1995

LOG (CH_CPIU)
  = 0.97900 * LOG (CH_RPI) + 0.09863 * LOG (CH_WAGE)
   (22.0040)   (3.74871)
  – 0.03097 * SPIKE (90,1) – 0.62677
   (3.42563)   (28.0192)
SUM SQ   0.0010   STD ERR   0.0084 LHS MEAN 4.3423
R SQ   0.9997   R BAR SQ 0.9997 F 3, 14   16836.3 D.W.   1.8502

[E–03]: CHEQ98: CH_PCP(IDENTITY): DEFLATOR(RESIDENTIAL CONSUMPTION)

CH_PCP = CH_CPN/(CH_CPR+CH_CPU)*100

[E–04]: CHEQ98: CH_PCPU: DEFLATOR (RESIDENTIAL CONSUMPTION: URBAN)
ANNUAL DATA FOR 19 PERIODS FROM 1978 TO 1996

LOG (CH_PCPU)
  = 0.70222 * LOG (CH_CPIU) – 0.05931 * SPIKE(78,1)
   (136.523)   (7.95070)
  + 0.06813 * SPIKE (94,1) + 0.13234 * STEP (95,1) + 1.35774
   (8.20501)   (17.7900)   (61.6872)
SUM SQ   0.0007   STD ERR   0.0069 LHS MEAN 4.4586
R SQ   0.9998   R BAR SQ 0.9997 F 4, 14   14589.0 D.W.   2.6304

[E–05]: CHEQ98: CH_PCPR: DEFLATOR (RESIDENTIAL CONSUMPTION: RURAL)
ANNUAL DATA FOR 18 PERIODS FROM 1978 TO 1995

LOG (CH_PCPR)
  = 0.83132 * LOG(CH_RPI) + 0.12015 * LOG(CH_PFSP)
   (25.4125)   (4.23953)
  – 0.04726 * STEP(89,1)–STEP(93,1) + 0.05040 * STEP(95,1) + 0.27589
   (8.73332)   (4.90093)   (8.64667)
SUM SQ   0.0008   STD ERR   0.0079 LHS MEAN 4.3978
R SQ   0.9997   R BAR SQ 0.9996 F 4, 13   10230.6   D.W.   2.4884

[E–06]: CHEQ98: CH_PIF: DEFLATOR (INVESTMENT IN FIXED ASSETS)
ANNUAL DATA FOR 17 PERIODS FROM 1979 TO 1995

LOG (CH_PIF)
$$= 0.79872 * LOG (CH\_RPI) + 0.72529 * LOG(CH\_IF/CH\_GDE)$$
    (22.0652)   (4.37085)
    + 0.22752 * SPIKE (78,1)+SPIKE(79,1) + 0.09672 * SPIKE (84,1)+SPIKE (85,1)
    (5.24920)   (3.35088)
    − 0.11562 * SPIKE (88,1)+SPIKE(89,1) + 0.12567 * SPIKE (93,1) + 1.95506
    (4.19114)   (3.18835)   (5.71556)

SUM SQ	0.0128	STD ERR	0.0357	LHS MEAN	4.5333
R SQ	0.9938	R BAR SQ	0.9900	F 6, 10	266.320
D.W.	2.1836				

[E–07]: CHEQ98: CH_PEXM: EXPORT UNIT VALUE(IN TERMS OF US DOLLAR)
ANNUAL DATA FOR 17 PERIODS FROM 1979 TO 1995

LOG (CH_PEXM)
$$= 0.35161 * LOG (CH\_PEXM)[-1] + 0.54635 * LOG (CH\_RPI)$$
    (3.35406)   (5.91070)
    − 0.29104 * LOG (CH_RATE) + 0.12073 * SPIKE (87,1)
    (4.79731)   (3.12163)
    + 0.10304 * SPIKE (90,1)+SPIKE (91,1)+SPIKE(92,1) + 0.84612
    (4.28117)   (1.97443)

SUM SQ	0.0114	STD ERR	0.0322	LHS MEAN	4.4615
R SQ	0.9589	R BAR SQ	0.9402	F 5, 11	51.3458
D.W.	2.2183	H	−0.7846		

[E–08]: CHEQ98: CH_PGDP (IDENTITY): DEFLATOR (GROSS DOMESTIC PRODUCT)

CH_PGDP = (CH_GDEN–CH_DSCN)/(CH_GDE–CH_DSC)*100

[E–09]: CHEQ98: CH_WAGE: WAGE PER WORKER
ANNUAL DATA FOR 16 PERIODS FROM 1980 TO 1995
PCH (CH_WAGE)
$$= 0.55219 * PCH (CH\_LPNAG [-1]) + 0.91896 * PCH (CH\_CPIU)$$
    (6.71058)   (13.0283)
    − 9.13410 * SPIKE (81,1) − 7.35360 * SPIKE (87,1)+SPIKE (88,1)
    (5.34739)   (5.68103)
    − 13.2092 * SPIKE (89,1) − 3.99835 * STEP (95,1) + 4.75416
    (7.57459)   (2.28454)   (6.34967)

| SUM SQ | 22.6232 | STD ERR | 1.5855 | LHS MEAN | 14.4956 | | |
| R SQ | 0.9793 | R BAR SQ | 0.9655 | F 6, 9 | 70.9196 | D.W. | 2.1079 |

[E–10]: CHEQ98: CH_LPNAG (IDENTITY): LABOR PRODUCTIVITY (NON AGRICULTURE)

CH_LPNAG = (CH_GDE–CH_GDP1)/CH_NNAG*100

F. Public Finance and Banking Bloc

[F–01]: CHEQ98: CH_GTR(IDENTITY) : TOTAL GOVERNMENT REVENUE

CH_GTR = CH_TAXINCM+CH_TAXAG+CH_TAXCUS+CH_TAXO

[F–02]: CHEQ98: CH_TAXINCM (IDENTITY): TAX REVENUE(INDUSTRIAL AND COMMERCIAL TAX)

CH_TAXINCM = CH_RTAXINCM*(CH_GDPN–CH_GDP1*CH_PFSP/100)/100

[F–03]: CHEQ98: CH_TAXAG(IDENTITY): TAX REVENUE (AGRICULTURAL AND ANIMAL HUSBANDRY TAX)

CH_TAXAG = CH_RTAXAG*CH_GDP1*CH_PFSP/10000

[F–04]: CHEQ98: CH_TAXCUS (IDENTITY): TAX REVENUE (TARIFFS)

CH_TAXCUS = CH_RTAXCUS*(CH_IMMN*CH_RATE)/10000

[F–05]: CHEQ98: CH_TAXO: TAX REVENUE (OTHERS)
ANNUAL DATA FOR 17 PERIODS FROM 1979 TO 1995

CH_TAXO
  = – 0.16002 * CH_IFINSE [–1]*CH_PIF[–1]/100 + 0.17943 * CH_GTR
     (2.47108)   (3.43307)
     – 88.2882 * SPIKE (82,1) + 74.1462 * SPIKE (87,1) + 157.849 * SPIKE (90,1)
     (2.46017)   (2.12180)   (6.77566)
     +SPIKE (91,1)+SPIKE (92,1) + 151.400 * STEP(95,1) + 440.514
                              (2.81972)   (9.5954)
SUM SQ   11131.1   STD ERR   33.3633   LHS MEAN   718.445
R SQ   0.9685   R BAR SQ   0.9496   F 6, 10   51.2917   D.W.   2.7615

[F–06]: CHEQ98: CH_GTE(IDENTITY): GOVERNMENT TOTAL EXPENDITURE

CH_GTE = CH_GEEC+CH_GESC+CH_GEAD+CH_GEND+CH_GEO

[F–07]: CHEQ98: CH_GBD: TOTAL DEBT INCURRED(DOMESTIC DEBT)
ANNUAL DATA FOR 18 PERIODS FROM 1978 TO 1995

CH_GBD+CH_GBF
  = 1.06048 * (CH_GTE+CH_GEPL–CH_GTR) – 106.112 * SPIKE (79,1)+SPIKE (80,1)
     (61.7598)   (5.05739)
     – 82.6392 * SPIKE (91,1)+SPIKE(92,1) + 21.7836
     (3.90134)   (2.37302)
SUM SQ   10476.4   STD ERR   27.3553   LHS MEAN   350.787
R SQ   0.9967   R BAR SQ   0.9960   F 3, 14   1400.23   D.W.   1.8994

[F–08]: CHEQ98: CH_GEPL: TOTAL RETIREMENT OF DEBT AND INTEREST PAYMENTS
ANNUAL DATA FOR   19 PERIODS FROM 1978 TO 1996

DIFF (CH_GEPL)
$$= 0.03035 * \text{CH\_INR}*(\text{CH\_GBD}[-1]+\text{CH\_GBF}[-1]) - 91.9616 * \text{SPIKE}(89,1)$$
   (14.2053)   (3.43016)
$$+ 91.5282 * \text{SPIKE}(92,1) - 319.872 * \text{SPIKE}(93,1)$$
   (3.39969)   (10.9300)
$$- 77.5524 * \text{SPIKE}(94,1) + 81.7116 * \text{STEP}(96,1) - 5.60729$$
   (2.58708)   (2.40303)   (0.72184)
SUM SQ 7952.43 STD ERR   25.7430 LHS MEAN 69.1737
R SQ   0.9764   R BAR SQ 0.9645   F 6, 12   82.6185   D.W.   1.9852

[F–09]: CHEQ98: CH_TDPU: DEPOSITS(URBAN HOUSEHOLD)
ANNUAL DATA FOR   15 PERIODS FROM 1981 TO 1995

DIFF (CH_TDPU)
$$= 0.41093 * (\text{CH\_YHU}+\text{CH\_INR} * \text{CH\_TDPU}[-1] / 100) - 274.579 * \text{SPIKE}(88,1)$$
   (87.3481)   (4.30768)
$$+\text{SPIKE}(89,1) - 562.422 * \text{SPIKE}(92,1)+\text{SPIKE}(93,1) - 419.605$$
                     (8.55484)   (12.5776)
SUM SQ 75227.7 STD ERR   82.6975 LHS MEAN 1545.61
R SQ   0.9986   R BAR SQ 0.9983   F 3, 11   2667.36   D.W.   1.9042

[F–10]: CHEQ98: CH_TDPR: DEPOSITS(RURAL HOUSEHOLD)
ANNUAL DATA FOR   18 PERIODS FROM 1978 TO 1995

DIFF (CH_TDPR)
$$= 0.12259 * (\text{CH\_GDP1}*\text{CH\_PFSP}/100+\text{CH\_INR}*\text{CH\_TDPR}[-1]/100)$$
   (67.7741)
$$- 210.087 * \text{SPIKE}(88,1)+\text{SPIKE}(89,1) - 58.4640 * \text{SPIKE}(90,1)$$
   (13.5811)   (2.75294)
$$+ 179.621 * \text{SPIKE}(94,1) - 142.030$$
   (7.51443)   (16.9373)
SUM SQ 5369.72 STD ERR   20.3238 LHS MEAN   341.617
R SQ   0.9981   R BAR SQ 0.9975   F 4, 13   1686.22   D.W.   1.2742

[F–11]: CHEQ98: CH_COS: CLAIMS ON OTHER SECTORS (BANKING SURVEY)
ANNUAL DATA FOR   19 PERIODS FROM 1978 TO 1996

DIFF (CH_COS)
$$= 0.16374 * \text{CH\_M2} + 705.142 * \text{SPIKE}(85,1)+\text{SPIKE}(86,1)$$
   (90.2996)   (5.92861)
$$+ 505.412 * \text{SPIKE}(90,1) + 5214.35 * \text{SPIKE}(94,1) + 107.800$$
   (3.14300)   (30.7210)   (2.13380)
SUM SQ 339182 STD ERR   155.651 LHS MEAN 3293.01
R SQ   0.9989   R BAR SQ 0.9985   F 4, 14   3090.30   D.W.   1.9950

G. International Transaction Bloc

[G–01] CH_EXMN (IDENTITY): EXPORTS OF GOODS AND SERVICES (MERCHANDISE: BOP BASIS)

CH_EXMN = CH_REXMN*CH_EXMCN/100

[G–02]: CHEQ98: CH_EXSN: EXPORTS OF GOODS AND SERVICES (NON FACTOR SERVICES: BOP BASIS)
ANNUAL DATA FOR   26 PERIODS FROM 1970 TO 1995

CH_EXSN
  =   0.15190 * CH_EXMN − 1315.57 * SPIKE (89,1)+SPIKE(90,1)+SPIKE (91,1)
    (63.9371)   (6.23361)
  + 1635.79 * SPIKE (94,1) − 712.153
    (4.27957)   (7.61188)
SUM SQ   2379542 STD ERR   328.878   LHS MEAN   4046.96
R Sq 0.9962   R Bar Sq 0.9957 F 3, 22 1910.95 D.W.(1)   1.7457 D.W.(2)   2.0776

[G–03] CH_EXMCN: MERCHANDISE EXPORTS (CC BASIS)
RESTRICTED ANNUAL DATA FOR   16 PERIODS FROM 1980 TO 1995

LOG (CH_EXMCN/CH_PEXM)
  = + 3.93787 * LOG (WO_GDP) − 0.44613 * LOG (CH_PEXM/WO_PGDP)
    (7.66826)   (1.55542)
    − 0.29742 * LOG (CH_PEXM/WO_PGDP)[−1]
    (1.55542)
    − 0.14871 * LOG(CH_PEXM/WO_PGDP)[−2] + 0.19944 * SPIKE(81,1)
    (1.55542)   (3.11754)
    +SPIKE (82,1) + 0.09355 * SPIKE (83,1)+SPIKE(84,1) − 0.16454 * SPIKE(88,1)
                (1.78185)   (4.15180)
    +SPIKE(89,1)+SPIKE(90,1) + 0.28984 * STEP(94,1) − 32.8966
                            (5.50605)   (6.42496)

POLYNOMIAL LAGS: LOG (CH_PEXM/WO_PGDP)
 FROM 0 TO 2 DEGREE 1 FAR
SUM SQ   0.0266 STD ERR   0.0544   LHS MEAN   6.2376
R SQ   0.9945 R BAR SQ   0.9908   F 6, 9 270.213 D.W.(1) 2.1274 D.W.(2)   2.6731

[G–04] CH_IMMN (IDENTITY): IMPORTS OF GOODS AND SERVICES (MERCHANDISE: BOP BASIS)

CH_IMMN = CH_RIMMN*CH_IMMCN/100

[G–05] CH_IMSN: IMPORTS OF GOODS AND SERVICES (NON FACTOR SERVICES: BOP BASIS) ANNUAL DATA FOR   23 PERIODS FROM 1973 TO 1995

CH_IMSN
= 0.14970 * CH_IMMN – 2317.47 * STEP (85,1)–STEP(92,1)
  (35.7108)   (12.3650)
  + 2654.02 * SPIKE (94,1) + 9462.06 * STEP (95,1) – 715.365
  (5.48979)   (18.0316)   (5.28472)
SUM SQ 2365250 STD ERR 362.495 LHS MEAN 4432.39
R SQ 0.9970 R BAR SQ 0.9964 F 4, 18 1504.63 D.W.(1) 2.7862 D.W.(2) 1.9361

[G–06] CH_IMMCN (IDENTITY): IMPORTS (CC BASIS: TOTAL)

CH_IMMCN = CH_IMMC7N+CH_IMMC0689N

[G–07] CH_IMMC7N: IMPORTS (CC BASIS: MACHINERY)
ANNUAL DATA FOR 16 PERIODS FROM 1980 TO 1995

LOG (CH_IMMC7N*CH_RATE/CH_PIF)
= 1.73026 * LOG (CH_IF) – 0.61084 * SPIKE (82,1)+SPIKE (83,1)
  (26.1893)   (6.49045)
  + 0.56976 * SPIKE (85,1)+SPIKE (86,1)
  (6.47399)
  + 0.24277 * STEP (89,1)–STEP(93,1) + 0.20892 * SPIKE(94,1) – 8.23460
  (3.47362)   (1.62716)   (14.8952)
SUM SQ   0.1186 STD ERR   0.1089 LHS MEAN   6.3080
R SQ   0.9931 R BAR SQ 0.9897 F 5, 10   288.078
D.W.(1) 2.5720 D.W.(2) 1.2250

[G–08] CH_IMMC0689N: IMPORTS (CC BASIS: OTHER THAN MACHINERY)
RESTRICTED OLS ANNUAL DATA FOR 16 PERIODS FROM 1980 TO 1995

LOG (CH_IMMC0689N/CH_PIMM)
= 1.19654 * LOG (CH_GDE) – 0.24082 * LOG(CH_PIMM*CH_RATE/CH_RPI)
  (14.3128)   (3.98063)
  – 0.16055 * LOG (CH_PIMM*CH_RATE/CH_RPI)[–1]
  (3.98063)
  – 0.08027 * LOG (CH_PIMM*CH_RATE/CH_RPI)[–2]
  (3.98063)
  + 0.19232 * SPIKE (85,1) + 0.09117 * SPIKE(88,1)+SPIKE(89,1)
  (4.47474)   (2.83364)
  – 0.12362 * SPIKE (90,1) – 5.02326
  (2.86576)   (7.63844)
POLYNOMIAL LAGS: LOG (CH_PIMM*CH_RATE/CH_RPI)
  FROM 0 TO 2 DEGREE 1 FAR
SUM SQ   0.0167 STD ERR   0.0409 LHS MEAN   5.9016
R SQ   0.9932 R BAR SQ 0.9898 F 5, 10   292.699
D.W.(1) 2.2876 D.W.(2) 2.3062

[G–09] CH_TB (IDENTITY): TRADE BALANCE

CH_TB = CH_EXMN–CH_IMMN

[G–10] CH_GSB (IDENTITY): BALANCE ON GOODS AND SERVICES

CH_GSB
= CH_EXMN+CH_EXSN–(CH_IMMN+CH_IMSN)

Variable List
Abbreviations for Data Sources:
CSY: China Statistical Yearbook, IFS: International Financial Statistics
SIC: State Information Center, WEFA: WEFA Group, WT: World Tables
XX/TRN: Transformed data using data in the source of XX

Endogenous Variables

	MNEMONIC	TYPE	DESCRIPTION	UNIT	SOURCE
(01)	CH_C	ID	TOTAL CONSUMPTION (REAL)	Yuan100m	CSY
(02)	CH_CG	ID	PUBLIC CONSUMPTION (REAL)	ditto.	CSY
(03)	CH_CGN	ST	PUBLIC CONSUMPTION (NOMINAL)	ditto.	CSY
(04)	CH_COS	ST	CLAIMS ON OTHER SECTORS (BANKING SURVEY)	ditto.	IFS
(05)	CH_CP	ID	RESIDENTIAL CONSUMPTION (TOTAL: REAL)	ditto.	CSY
(06)	CH_CPIU	ST	CONSUMER PRICE INDEX OF RESIDENTS (URBAN)	1990 =100	CSY
(07)	CH_CPN	ID	RESIDENTIAL CONSUMPTION (NOMINAL)	YUAN 100M	CSY
(08)	CH_CPR	ST	RESIDENTIAL CONSUMPTION (REAL: RURAL)	ditto.	CSY
(09)	CH_CPU	ST	RESIDENTIAL CONSUMPTION (REAL: URBAN)	ditto.	CSY
(10)	CH_EXMCN	ST	EXPORTS (CC BASIS)	$M	CSY
(11)	CH_EXMN	ID	EXPORTS OF GOODS AND SERVICES (MERCHANDISE: BOP BASIS)	ditto.	WT/IFS
(12)	CH_EXSN	ST	EXPORTS OF GOODS & SERVICES (NON FACTOR SERVICES: BOP BASIS)	ditto.	WT/IFS
(13)	CH_GBD	ST	TOTAL DEBT INCURRED (DOMESTIC DEBT)	YUAN 100M	CSY
(14)	CH_GDE	ID	GROSS DOMESTIC EXPENDITURE (REAL)	ditto.	CSY
(15)	CH_GDEN	ID	GROSS DOMESTIC EXPENDITURE (NOMINAL)	ditto.	CSY
(16)	CH_GDP	ID	GROSS DOMESTIC PRODUCT (REAL)	ditto.	CSY
(17)	CH_GDP1	ST	GROSS DOMESTIC PRODUCT	ditto.	CSY

			(REAL: PRIMARY INDUSTRY)		
(18)	CH_GDP2	ST	GROSS DOMESTIC PRODUCT (REAL: SECONDARY INDUSTRY)	ditto.	CSY
(19)	CH_GDP3	ST	GROSS DOMESTIC PRODUCT (REAL: TERTIARY INDUSTRY)	ditto.	CSY
(20)	CH_GDPN	ID	GROSS DOMESTIC PRODUCT (NOMINAL)	ditto.	CSY
(21)	CH_GEPL	ST	TOTAL RETIREMENT OF DEBT AND INTEREST PAYMENTS	ditto.	CSY
(22)	CH_GSB	ID	BALANCE ON GOODS AND SERVICES	$M	
(23)	CH_GTE	ID	GOVERNMENT TOTAL EXPENDI-TURE	YUAN 100M	CSY
(24)	CH_GTR	ID	TOTAL GOVERNMENT REVENUE	ditto.	CSY
(25)	CH_GVIN	ID	GROSS OUTPUT VALUE (REAL: INDUSTRY)	ditto.	CSY
(26)	CH_GVINNSE	ST	GROSS OUTPUT VALUE (REAL: IN-DUSTRY: NON STATE-OWNED UNITS)	ditto.	CSY
(27)	CH_GVINSE	ST	GROSS OUTPUT VALUE (REAL: IN-DUSTRY: STATE-OWNED UNITS)	ditto.	CSY
(28)	CH_IF	ID	INVESTMENT IN FIXED ASSETS (REAL: TOTAL)	ditto.	CSY/TRN
(29)	CH_IF1	ID	INVESTMENT IN FIXED ASSETS (REAL: PRIMARY INDUSTRY)	ditto.	SIC/TRN
(30)	CH_IF3	ID	INVESTMENT IN FIXED ASSETS (REAL: TERTIARY INDUSTRY)	ditto.	SIC/TRN
(31)	CH_IFCT	ID	INVESTMENT IN FIXED ASSETS (REAL: CONSTRUCTION)	ditto.	CSY/ TRN
(32)	CH_IFD	ST	INVESTMENT IN FIXED ASSETS (REAL: DOMESTIC ENTERPRISES)	ditto.	CSY/ TRN
(33)	CH_IFINNSED	ID	INVESTMENT IN FIXED ASSETS (REAL: INDUSTRY: NON STATE-OWNED UNITS: DOMESTIC ENTERPRISES)	ditto.	SIC/TRN
(34)	CH_IFINNSEF	ID	INVESTMENT IN FIXED ASSETS (REAL: INDUSTRY: NON STATE-OWNED UNITS: FOREIGN ENTERPRISES)	ditto.	SIC/TRN
(35)	CH_IFINSE	ID	INVESTMENT IN FIXED ASSETS (REAL: INDUSTRY: STATE-OWNED UNITS)	ditto.	SIC/TRN
(36)	CH_IFN	ID	INVESTMENT IN FIXED ASSETS (NOMINAL)	ditto.	CSY
(37)	CH_IMMC0689N	ST	IMPORTS (CC BASIS: OTHER)	$M	CSY
(38)	CH_IMMC7N	ST	IMPORTS (CC BASIS: MACHINERY)	ditto.	CSY
(39)	CH_IMMCN	ID	IMPORTS (CC BASIS: TOTAL)	ditto.	CSY
(40)	CH_IMMN	ID	IMPORTS OF GOODS AND SERVICES (TOTAL: MERCHANDISE: BOP BASIS)	ditto.	WT/IFS
(41)	CH_IMSN	ST	IMPORTS OF GOODS AND SERVICES (NON FACTOR SERVICES: BOP BASIS)	ditto.	WT/IFS
(42)	CH_J	ST	CHANGES IN INVENTORIES	YUAN	CSY

			(REAL)	100M	
(43)	CH_JN	ID	CHANGES IN INVENTORIES (NOMINAL)	ditto.	CSY
(44)	CH_KF	ID	CAPITAL STOCK (REAL: TOTAL)	ditto.	SIC/TRN
(45)	CH_KF1	ID	CAPITAL STOCK (REAL: PRIMARY INDUSTRY)	ditto.	SIC/TRN
(46)	CH_KF3	ID	CAPITAL STOCK (REAL: TERTI-ARY INDUSTRY)	ditto.	SIC/TRN
(47)	CH_KFCT	ID	CAPITAL STOCK (REAL: CON-STRUCTION)	ditto.	SIC/TRN
(48)	CH_KFF	ID	CAPITAL STOCK (REAL: FOREIGN DIRECT INVESTMENT)	ditto.	CSY/TRN
(49)	CH_KFINNSED	ID	CAPITAL STOCK(REAL: INDUSTRY: NON STATE-OWNED UNITS: DOMES-TIC ENTERPRISES)	ditto.	SIC/TRN
(50)	CH_KFINNSEF	ID	CAPITAL STOCK (REAL: INDUSTRY: NON STATE-OWNED UNITS: FOREIGN ENTERPRISES)	ditto.	SIC/TRN
(51)	CH_KFINSE	ID	CAPITAL STOCK (REAL: INDUS-TRY: STATE-OWNED UNITS)	ditto.	SIC/TRN
(52)	CH_LF	ST	LABOR FORCE	10T	CSY
(53)	CH_LPNAG	ID	LABOR PRODUCTIVITY (NON AG-RICULTURE)	YUAN	CSY/TRN
(54)	CH_N	ID	EMPLOYMENT (TOTAL)	10T	CSY
(55)	CH_N1	ST	EMPLOYMENT (PRIMARY INDUS-TRY)	ditto.	CSY
(56)	CH_N2	ST	EMPLOYMENT (SECONDARY IN-DUSTRY)	ditto.	CSY
(57)	CH_N3	ST	EMPLOYMENT (TERTIARY IN-DUSTRY)	ditto.	CSY
(58)	CH_NEX	ST	NET EXPORT (REAL)	Yuan100m	CSY/TRN
(59)	CH_NEXN	ST	NET EXPORT (NOMINAL)		CSY
(60)	CH_NINNSE	ST	EMPLOYMENT (INDUSTRY: NON STATE-OWNED UNITS)	10T	CSY
(61)	CH_NNAG	ID	EMPLOYMENT (NON AGRICULTURE)	ditto.	CSY/TRN
(62)	CH_NU	ST	EMPLOYMENT (URBAN)	ditto.	CSY
(63)	CH_NW	ST	STAFF AND WORKERS	ditto.	CSY
(64)	CH_NWINSE	ST	EMPLOYMENT(INDUSTRY: STATE-OWNED UNITS)	ditto.	CSY
(65)	CH_PCP	ID	DEFLATOR (RESIDENTIAL CON-SUMP-TION)	1990 =100	CSY/ TRN
(66)	CH_PCPR	ST	DEFLATOR (RESIDENTIAL CON-SUMPTION: RURAL)	ditto.	CSY/ TRN
(67)	CH_PCPU	ST	DEFLATOR (RESIDENTIAL CON-SUMPTION: URBAN)	ditto.	CSY/ TRN
(68)	CH_PEXM	ST	EXPORT UNIT VALUE (IN TERMS OF US DOLLAR)	ditto.	WT

(69)	CH_PGDP	ID	DEFLATOR (GROSS DOMESTIC PRODUCT)	ditto.	CSY/TRN
(70)	CH_PIF	ST	DEFLATOR (INVESTMENT IN FIXED ASSETS)	ditto.	CSY/TRN
(71)	CH_POPR	ST	POPULATION (RURAL)	10T	CSY
(72)	CH_POPU	ID	POPULATION (URBAN)	ditto.	CSY
(73)	CH_RPI	ST	RETAIL PRICE INDEX	1990=100	CSY
(74)	CH_TAXAG	ID	TAX REVENUE (AGRICULTURAL AND ANIMAL HUSBANDRY TAX)	YUAN 100M	CSY
(75)	CH_TAXCUS	ID	TAX REVENUE (TARIFFS)	ditto.	CSY
(76)	CH_TAXINCM	ID	TAX REVENUE (INDUSTRIAL AND COMMERCIAL TAX)	ditto.	CSY
(77)	CH_TAXO	ST	TAX REVENUE(OTHERS)	ditto.	CSY
(78)	CH_TB	ID	TRADE BALANCE	$M	WT/IFS
(79)	CH_TDPR	ST	DEPOSITS (RURAL HOUSEHOLD)	Yuan100m	CSY
(80)	CH_TDPU	ST	DEPOSITS (URBAN HOUSEHOLD)	ditto.	CSY
(81)	CH_U	ID	UNEMPLOYMENT	10T	CSY
(82)	CH_UR	ID	UNEMPLOYMENT RATE	%	CSY
(83)	CH_WAGE	ST	WAGE PER WORKER	YUAN	CSY/TRN
(84)	CH_YHR	ST	HOUSEHOLD INCOME (RURAL)	yuan100m	CSY/TRN
(85)	CH_YHU	ST	HOUSEHOLD INCOME (URBAN)	ditto.	CSY/TRN
(86)	CH_YW	ID	TOTAL WAGE BILL FOR STAFF AND WORKERS	ditto.	CSY

Note) ST: stochastic equations, ID: identities.

Exogenous Variables

	MNEMONIC	Type	DESCRIPTION	UNIT	SOURCE
(1)	CH_DSC	EX	=CH_GDE-CH_GDP	Yuan100m	CSY/TRN
(2)	CH_DSCGDP	EX	=CH_GDP-CH_GDP1-CH_GDP2-CH_GDP3	ditto.	CSY/TRN
(3)	CH_DSCN	EX	=CH_GDEN-CH_GDPN	ditto.	CSY/TRN
(4)	CH_GBF	EX	TOTAL DEBT INCURRED (FOREIGN DEBTS)	ditto.	CSY
(5)	CH_GEAD	EX	ADMINISTRATION (GOV. EXPEND. BY GENERAL CATEGORIES)	ditto.	CSY
(6)	CH_GEEC	EX	ECONOMIC CONSTRUCTION (GOV. EXPEND.BY GENERAL CATEGORIES)	ditto.	CSY
(7)	CH_GEND	EX	NATIONAL DEFENSE (GOV. EXPEND. BY GENERAL CATEGORIES)	ditto.	CSY
(8)	CH_GEO	EX	OTHERS (GOVERNMENT EXPENDI-TURES BY GENERAL CATEGORIES)	ditto.	CSY/TRN
(9)	CH_GESC	EX	CULTURE AND EDUCATION (GOV. EXPEND. BY GENERAL CATEGORIES)	ditto.	CSY
(10)	CH_IFF	EX	INVESTMENT IN FIXED ASSETS (REAL: FOREIGN DIRECT INVESTMENT)		

(11)	CH_INR	EX	INTEREST RATE ON FIXED DEPOSITS (1 YEAR)	%	CSY
(12)	CH_LANDDA	EX	AREAS HIT BY NATURAL DISASTER	1000 ha	CSY
(13)	CH_LANDSO	EX	TOTAL SOWN AREA	ditto.	CSY
(14)	CH_M2	EX	MONEY SUPPLY(M2: BANKING SURVEY)	Yuan 100m	IFS
(15)	CH_PFSP	EX	OVERALL FARM AND SIDELINE PRODUCTS PURCHASING PRICE INDEX	1990= 100	CSY/TRN
(16)	CH_PIMM	EX	IMPORT UNIT VALUE (IN TERMS OF US DOLLAR)	ditto.	WT
(17)	CH_POP	EX	POPULATION (TOTAL)	10T	CSY
(18)	CH_RATE	EX	EXCHANGE RATE	Yuan / $	CSY
(19)	CH_RDEP	EX	BASIC DEPRECIATION RATE OF FIXED ASSETS OF SOE	%	CSY
(20)	CH_REXMN	EX	=CH_EXMN/TR_EXMN_C*100	ditto.	CSY/TRN
(21)	CH_RGVINTVEN	EX	=CH_GVINTVEN / (CH_GVIN*CH_RPI/100) *100	ditto.	ditto.
(22)	CH_RIF1	EX	=CH_IF1/CH_IF*100	ditto.	ditto.
(23)	CH_RIF3	EX	=CH_IF3/CH_IF*100	ditto.	ditto.
(24)	CH_RIFCT	EX	=CH_IFCT/CH_IF*100	ditto.	ditto.
(25)	CH_RIFIN	EX	=CH_IFIN/CH_IF*100	ditto.	ditto.
(26)	CH_RIFINNSED	EX	=CH_IFINNSED/CH_IFIN*100	ditto.	ditto.
(27)	CH_RIFINNSEF	EX	=CH_IFINNSEF/CH_IFIN*100	ditto.	ditto.
(28)	CH_RIFINSE	EX	=CH_IFINSE/CH_IFIN*100	ditto.	ditto.
(29)	CH_RIMMN	EX	=CH_IMMN/TR_IMMN_C*100	ditto.	ditto.
(30)	CH_RTAXAG	EX	=CH_TAXAG/(CH_GDP1*CH_PFSP/ 100)*100	ditto.	ditto.
(31)	CH_RTAXCUS	EX	=CH_TAXCUS/(CH_IMMN*CH_RATE) *10000	ditto.	ditto.
(32)	CH_RTAXINCM	EX	=CH_TAXINCM / (CH_GDPNCH_GDP1*CH_PFSP/100)*100	ditto.	ditto.
(33)	TREND	EX	TIME TREND		
(34)	WO_PGDP	EX	DEFLATOR FOR WORLD GDP	1990=100	WEFA

Note) EX: exogenous variables.

Appendix B: Simulation

Simulation 1: An Increase in FDI by 1% of Real GDP

1–1

Year	1985	1986	1987	1988	1989	1990
Real GDE Component: Yuan 100M						
GDE						
Baseline	12457	13733	15198	16907	17395	18320
% Diff	1.5	0.8	2.0	1.6	1.6	1.8
Private Consumption						
Baseline	6834	7262	7820	8607	8722	9113
% Diff	0.0	0.4	0.3	0.6	0.7	0.7
Fixed Investment						
Baseline	3287	3845	4420	5139	4610	4732
% Diff	5.9	0.6	5.0	2.5	4.2	3.4
Net Exports						
Baseline	−355	−221	318	247	117	510
% Diff	6.7	−21.3	11.4	15.7	23.1	7.4
GDP						
Baseline	12701	13827	15427	17165	17863	18548
% Diff	0.1	0.5	0.6	0.9	1.1	1.3
GDP (Industry)						
Baseline	5022	5537	6296	7210	7481	7717
% Diff	0.0	0.5	0.5	0.9	1.1	1.3
Income Distribution:						
Wage and Salary, Yuan 100M						
Baseline	1383	1660	1881	2316	2619	2951
% Diff	0.0	1.0	0.2	1.0	0.6	0.5
Production and Labor:						
Employment, 10 T						
Baseline	49873	51282	52783	54334	55329	56740
% Diff	0.3	0.3	0.5	0.6	0.6	0.7
Labor Productivity, Yuan						
Baseline	44.6	47.4	50.9	55.9	57.4	58.6
% Diff	1.6	0.4	1.6	0.9	0.8	0.9
Wage and Prices:						
Retail Price Index, 1990=100						
Baseline	61.7	65.4	70.1	83.1	97.9	100
% Diff	0.0	0.1	0.0	0.0	−0.1	−0.1
Inflation Rate, %						
Baseline	8.8	6	7.3	18.5	17.8	2.1
Diff	0.0	0.1	−0.1	0.1	−0.1	0.0

Note: % Diff denotes percentage difference between baseline and simulation. Diff means difference between baseline and simulation.

1–2

Year	1991	1992	1993	1994	1995
Real GDE Component: Yuan 100M					
GDE					
Baseline	19937	22464	26157	29806	33209
% Diff	1.6	1.6	1.5	1.3	1.4
Private Consumption					
Baseline	10063	11519	12762	13794	15222
% Diff	0.8	0.8	0.8	0.9	0.9
Fixed Investment					
Baseline	5425	6588	8121	9552	10863
% Diff	3.6	3.4	3.5	3.0	3.1
Net Exports					
Baseline	249	85	349	1207	1552
% Diff	15.2	20.8	−8.8	−2.5	−2.8
GDP					
Baseline	20253	23137	26258	29583	32691
% Diff	1.4	1.5	1.6	1.8	1.7
GDP (Industry)					
Baseline	8788	10646	12760	15105	17199
% Diff	1.3	1.7	1.9	2.1	1.9
Income Distribution:					
Wage and Salary, Yuan 100M					
Baseline	3324	3939	4916	6656	8100
% Diff	0.6	0.5	0.4	0.3	0.3
Production and Labor:					
Employment, 10 T					
Baseline	58360	59432	60220	61470	62388
% Diff	0.7	0.7	0.7	0.7	0.7
Labor Productivity, Yuan					
Baseline	63	69.3	78.2	85.3	92.1
% Diff	0.5	0.4	0.3	0.2	0.2
Wage and Prices:					
Retail Price Index, 1990=100					
Baseline	102.9	108.4	122.7	149.3	171.4
% Diff	−0.1	−0.2	−0.2	−0.2	−0.2
Inflation Rate, %					
Baseline	2.9	5.4	13.2	21.7	14.8
Diff	0.0	−0.1	0.0	0.0	0.0

1–3

Year	1985	1986	1987	1988	1989	1990
CPI, 1990=100						
Baseline	60.4	64.7	70.4	84.9	98.7	100
% Diff	0.0	0.2	0.0	0.1	0.0	−0.1
GDP deflator, 1990=100						
Baseline	70.6	73.8	77.5	87	94.7	100
% Diff	0.7	−0.6	0.2	−0.3	0.0	−0.3
Wage per Worker, Yuan						
Baseline	1119	1296	1424	1702	1905	2099
% Diff	0.0	1.0	0.1	0.8	0.4	0.2
Budget and Finance:						
Govt. Bond, Yuan 100M						
Baseline	90	138	170	271	283	375
Diff	−25	12	−24	−7	−38	−35
International Trade:						
Trade Balance, $M						
Baseline	−13123	−9140	−1661	−5315	−5620	9165
Diff	−2417	−812	−1355	−1263	−1805	−1514
Merchandise Exports, $M						
Baseline	27350	30942	39437	47516	52538	62091
% Diff	−4.2	−1.5	−0.3	−0.1	−0.7	−0.4
Merchandise Imports, $M						
Baseline	42252	42904	43216	55268	59140	53345
% Diff	3.6	1.2	3.5	2.6	3.1	3.1
Machinery Imports, $M						
Baseline	16239	16781	14607	16697	18207	16845
% Diff	6.4	1.6	5.6	4.3	5.5	5.2
S-I Balance: vs. GDP, %						
Private						
Baseline	−3.2	−1.2	1.5	0.8	0.6	4.8
Diff	−1.1	−0.2	−0.7	−0.4	−0.7	−0.7
Government						
Baseline	−1.0	−1.4	−1.4	−1.8	−1.7	−2.0
Diff	0.3	−0.1	0.2	0.1	0.3	0.2
Current Account						
Baseline	−4.2	−2.6	0.1	−1.0	−1.1	2.8
Diff	−0.8	−0.3	−0.5	−0.3	−0.4	−0.5

1-4

Year	1991	1992	1993	1994	1995
CPI, 1990=100					
Baseline	105.1	114.1	132.5	165.7	193.5
% Diff	−0.1	−0.2	−0.2	−0.2	−0.2
GDP deflator, 1990=100					
Baseline	106.7	115.1	131.9	158.1	178.9
% Diff	−0.2	0.0	0.4	0.1	0.1
Wage per Worker, Yuan					
Baseline	2291	2663	3311	4483	5433
% Diff	0.3	0.1	0.0	−0.1	−0.2
Budget and Finance:					
Govt. Bond, Yuan 100M					
Baseline	461	670	739	1175	1550
Diff	−55	−81	−152	−210	−299
International Trade:					
Trade Balance, $M					
Baseline	8743	5183	−10654	7290	18050
Diff	−1533	−1346	−2367	−2155	−2956
Merchandise Exports, $M					
Baseline	71910	84940	91744	121006	148780
% Diff	−0.1	0.7	0.5	0.2	−0.1
Merchandise Imports, $M					
Baseline	63791	80585	103959	115615	132084
% Diff	2.9	2.8	3.2	2.5	2.6
Machinery Imports, $M					
Baseline	19601	31313	44987	51564	52638
% Diff	5.2	4.3	5.0	3.7	4.2
S-I Balance: vs. GDP, %					
Private					
Baseline	5.1	3.6	0.2	3.9	4.3
Diff	−0.8	−0.7	−0.9	−0.9	−1.0
Government					
Baseline	−2.2	−2.6	−2.1	−2.5	−2.6
Diff	0.3	0.3	0.5	0.5	0.5
Current Account					
Baseline	2.9	1.1	−1.9	1.4	1.7
Diff	−0.5	−0.3	−0.4	−0.5	−0.5

Simulation 2: An Increase in Money Growth by 5%

2–1

Year	1985	1986	1987	1988	1989	1990
Real GDE Component: Yuan 100M						
GDE						
Baseline	12457	13733	15198	16907	17395	18320
% Diff	0.5	0.2	0.4	0.1	0	0.1
Private Consumption						
Baseline	6834	7262	7820	8607	8722	9113
% Diff	0.0	0.1	0.0	0.0	−0.1	−0.2
Fixed Investment						
Baseline	3287	3845	4420	5139	4610	4732
% Diff	2.6	1.3	2.7	1.7	2.8	3.7
Net Exports						
Baseline	−355	−221	318	247	117	510
% Diff	7.2	7.9	−10.2	−17.5	−50.6	−14.5
GDP						
Baseline	12701	13827	15427	17165	17863	18548
% Diff	0.0	0.2	0.3	0.4	0.5	0.6
GDP (Industry)						
Baseline	5022	5537	6296	7210	7481	7717
% Diff	0.0	0.2	0.3	0.5	0.5	0.7
Income Distribution:						
Wage and Salary, Yuan 100M						
Baseline	1383	1660	1881	2316	2619	2951
% Diff	0.0	1.1	1.6	2.5	3.1	3.7
Production and Labor:						
Employment, 10 T						
Baseline	49873	51282	52783	54334	55329	56740
% Diff	0.1	0.1	0.1	0.0	−0.1	−0.2
Labor Productivity, Yuan						
Baseline	44.6	47.4	50.9	55.9	57.4	58.6
% Diff	0.6	0.1	0.4	0.2	0.2	0.4
Wage and Prices:						
Retail Price Index, 1990=100						
Baseline	61.7	65.4	70.1	83.1	97.9	100.0
% Diff	0.0	0.8	1.6	2.3	3.0	3.8
Inflation Rate, %						
Baseline	8.8	6.0	7.3	18.5	17.8	2.1
Diff	0.0	0.9	0.8	0.9	0.8	0.8

2–2

Year	1991	1992	1993	1994	1995
Real GDE Component: Yuan 100M					
GDE					
Baseline	19937	22464	26157	29806	33209
% Diff	−0.1	0	−0.6	0.5	−0.1
Private Consumption					
Baseline	10063	11519	12762	13794	15222
% Diff	−0.2	−0.4	−0.5	−0.6	−0.6
Fixed Investment					
Baseline	5425	6588	8121	9552	10863
% Diff	3.7	4.8	3.3	7.9	5.8
Net Exports					
Baseline	249	85	349	1207	1552
% Diff	−37.8	−168.0	−54.9	−28.2	−24.4
GDP					
Baseline	20253	23137	26258	29583	32691
% Diff	0.7	0.9	1.1	1.3	1.7
GDP (Industry)					
Baseline	8788	10646	12760	15105	17199
% Diff	0.8	1.0	1.4	1.6	2.0
Income Distribution:					
Wage and Salary, Yuan 100M					
Baseline	3324	3939	4916	6656	8100
% Diff	4.7	5.2	6.0	6.2	7.7
Production and Labor:					
Employment, 10 T					
Baseline	58360	59432	60220	61470	62388
% Diff	−0.3	−0.3	−0.5	−0.4	−0.5
Labor Productivity, Yuan					
Baseline	63.0	69.3	78.2	85.3	92.1
% Diff	0.3	0.5	0.2	1.3	0.7
Wage and Prices:					
Retail Price Index, 1990=100					
Baseline	102.9	108.4	122.7	149.3	171.4
% Diff	4.7	5.4	6.2	6.7	7.6
Inflation Rate, %					
Baseline	2.9	5.4	13.2	21.7	14.8
Diff	0.9	0.7	0.8	0.6	1.0

2–3

Year	1985	1986	1987	1988	1989	1990
CPI, 1990=100						
Baseline	60.4	64.7	70.4	84.9	98.7	100.0
% Diff	0.0	0.9	1.7	2.5	3.3	4.1
GDP deflator, 1990=100						
Baseline	70.6	73.8	77.5	87.0	94.7	100.0
% Diff	0.7	1.0	2.0	2.4	3.2	4.1
Wage per Worker, Yuan						
Baseline	1119	1296	1424	1702	1905	2099
% Diff	0.0	1.1	1.5	2.5	3.1	3.7
Budget and Finance:						
Govt. Bond, Yuan 100M						
Baseline	90	138	170	271	283	375
Diff	−18	−24	−57	−85	−161	−235
International Trade:						
Trade Balance, $M						
Baseline	−13123	−9140	−1661	−5315	−5620	9165
Diff	−543	−276	−504	−629	−862	−1037
Merchandise Exports, $M						
Baseline	27350	30942	39437	47516	52538	62091
% Diff	0.0	0.3	0.4	0.4	0.5	0.6
Merchandise Imports, $M						
Baseline	42252	42904	43216	55268	59140	53345
% Diff	1.4	1.0	1.8	1.7	2.2	3.2
Machinery Imports, $M						
Baseline	16239	16781	14607	16697	18207	16845
% Diff	2.7	1.9	3.3	3.3	4.5	6.3
S-I Balance: vs. GDP, %						
Private						
Baseline	−3.2	−1.2	1.5	0.8	0.6	4.8
Diff	−0.4	−0.3	−0.7	−0.8	−1.2	−1.7
Government						
Baseline	−1.0	−1.4	−1.4	−1.8	−1.7	−2.0
Diff	0.2	0.3	0.5	0.6	1.0	1.3
Current Account						
Baseline	−4.2	−2.6	0.1	−1.0	−1.1	2.8
Diff	−0.2	−0.1	−0.2	−0.2	−0.2	−0.4

2–4

Year	1991	1992	1993	1994	1995
CPI, 1990=100					
Baseline	105.1	114.1	132.5	165.7	193.5
% Diff	5.2	5.8	6.6	7.2	8.2
GDP deflator, 1990=100					
Baseline	106.7	115.1	131.9	158.1	178.9
% Diff	4.8	5.7	6.7	7.8	8.4
Wage per Worker, Yuan					
Baseline	2291	2663	3311	4483	5433
% Diff	4.8	5.3	6.1	6.4	7.9
Budget and Finance:					
Govt. Bond, Yuan 100M					
Baseline	461	670	739	1175	1550
Diff	−312	−437	−726	−1161	−1674
International Trade:					
Trade Balance, $M					
Baseline	8743	5183	−10654	7290	18050
Diff	−1246	−2318	−3120	−5849	−5686
Merchandise Exports, $M					
Baseline	71910	84940	91744	121006	148780
% Diff	0.7	0.6	0.7	0.7	0.8
Merchandise Imports, $M					
Baseline	63791	80585	103959	115615	132084
% Diff	3.3	4.2	4.2	6.9	6.1
Machinery Imports, $M					
Baseline	19601	31313	44987	51564	52638
% Diff	6.6	7.1	7.1	11.0	10.6
S–I Balance: vs. GDP, %					
Private					
Baseline	5.1	3.6	0.2	3.9	4.3
Diff	−2.0	−2.3	−2.6	−3.7	−3.8
Government					
Baseline	−2.2	−2.6	−2.1	−2.5	−2.6
Diff	1.5	1.7	2.1	2.5	2.8
Current Account					
Baseline	2.9	1.1	−1.9	1.4	1.7
Diff	−0.5	−0.6	−0.5	−1.2	−1.0

Simulation 3: An Increase in National Defense Expenditure by 1% of Nominal GDP

3–1

Year	1985	1986	1987	1988	1989	1990
Real GDE Component: Yuan 100M						
GDE						
Baseline	12457	13733	15198	16907	17395	18320
% Diff	1.2	1.4	1.4	1.7	1.6	1.7
Private Consumption						
Baseline	6834	7262	7820	8607	8722	9113
% Diff	0.0	0.3	0.4	0.4	0.6	0.6
Fixed Investment						
Baseline	3287	3845	4420	5139	4610	4732
% Diff	1.1	1.2	1.1	1.5	1.6	1.5
Net Exports						
Baseline	−355	−221	318	247	117	510
% Diff	9.3	14.4	−9.2	−17.5	−37.8	−7.2
GDP						
Baseline	12701	13827	15427	17165	17863	18548
% Diff	0.1	0.2	0.3	0.4	0.5	0.6
GDP (Industry)						
Baseline	5022	5537	6296	7210	7481	7717
% Diff	0.0	0.1	0.2	0.3	0.5	0.6
Income Distribution:						
Wage and Salary, Yuan 100M						
Baseline	1383	1660	1881	2316	2619	2951
% Diff	0.0	0.9	0.9	0.8	1.0	0.8
Production and Labor:						
Employment, 10 T						
Baseline	49873	51282	52783	54334	55329	56740
% Diff	0.2	0.3	0.4	0.5	0.6	0.6
Labor Productivity, Yuan						
Baseline	44.6	47.4	50.9	55.9	57.4	58.6
% Diff	1.3	1.2	1.1	1.2	1.0	1.0
Wage and Prices:						
Retail Price Index, 1990=100						
Baseline	61.7	65.4	70.1	83.1	97.9	100.0
% Diff	0.0	0.1	0.1	0.1	0.1	0.0
Inflation Rate, %						
Baseline	8.8	6.0	7.3	18.5	17.8	2.1
Diff	0.0	0.1	0.0	0.0	0.0	0.0

3–2

Year	1991	1992	1993	1994	1995
Real GDE Component: Yuan 100M					
GDE					
Baseline	19937	22464	26157	29806	33209
% Diff	1.7	1.6	1.5	1.5	1.5
Private Consumption					
Baseline	10063	11519	12762	13794	15222
% Diff	0.6	0.7	0.7	0.7	0.7
Fixed Investment					
Baseline	5425	6588	8121	9552	10863
% Diff	1.4	1.2	1.0	1.1	1.1
Net Exports					
Baseline	249	85	349	1207	1552
% Diff	−17.2	−59.7	−20.2	−6.4	−5.4
GDP					
Baseline	20253	23137	26258	29583	32691
% Diff	0.7	0.7	0.8	0.8	0.8
GDP (Industry)					
Baseline	8788	10646	12760	15105	17199
% Diff	0.6	0.7	0.8	0.8	0.8
Income Distribution:					
Wage and Salary, Yuan 100M					
Baseline	3324	3939	4916	6656	8100
% Diff	0.9	0.9	0.9	0.8	0.8
Production and Labor:					
Employment, 10 T					
Baseline	58360	59432	60220	61470	62388
% Diff	0.6	0.6	0.6	0.7	0.7
Labor Productivity, Yuan					
Baseline	63.0	69.3	78.2	85.3	92.1
% Diff	0.9	0.8	0.7	0.6	0.6
Wage and Prices:					
Retail Price Index, 1990=100					
Baseline	102.9	108.4	122.7	149.3	171.4
% Diff	0.0	0.0	0.0	0.0	0.0
Inflation Rate, %					
Baseline	2.9	5.4	13.2	21.7	14.8
Diff	0.0	0.0	0.0	0.0	0.0

3–3

Year	1985	1986	1987	1988	1989	1990
CPI, 1990=100						
Baseline	60.4	64.7	70.4	84.9	98.7	100.0
% Diff	0.0	0.2	0.2	0.1	0.2	0.1
GDP deflator, 1990=100						
Baseline	70.6	73.8	77.5	87.0	94.7	100.0
% Diff	−0.1	0.0	−0.1	0.0	0.0	−0.1
Wage per Worker, Yuan						
Baseline	1119	1296	1424	1702	1905	2099
% Diff	0.0	0.8	0.8	0.7	0.8	0.6
Budget and Finance:						
Govt. Bond, Yuan 100M						
Baseline	90	138	170	271	283	375
Diff	48	66	92	130	184	248
International Trade:						
Trade Balance, $M						
Baseline	−13123	−9140	−1661	−5315	−5620	9165
Diff	−695	−734	−728	−1175	−1213	−1059
Merchandise Exports, $M						
Baseline	27350	30942	39437	47516	52538	62091
% Diff	0.0	0.1	0.0	0.0	0.0	0.0
Merchandise Imports, $M						
Baseline	42252	42904	43216	55268	59140	53345
% Diff	1.8	2.2	2.0	2.5	2.5	2.5
Machinery Imports, $M						
Baseline	16239	16781	14607	16697	18207	16845
% Diff	2.5	3.0	2.5	3.7	3.6	3.6
S-I Balance: vs. GDP, %						
Private						
Baseline	−3.2	−1.2	1.5	0.8	0.6	4.8
Diff	0.3	0.4	0.5	0.5	0.8	0.9
Government						
Baseline	−1.0	−1.4	−1.4	−1.8	−1.7	−2.0
Diff	−0.5	−0.6	−0.8	−0.8	−1.1	−1.3
Current Account						
Baseline	−4.2	−2.6	0.1	−1.0	−1.1	2.8
Diff	−0.2	−0.2	−0.3	−0.3	−0.3	−0.4

3–4

Year	1991	1992	1993	1994	1995
CPI, 1990=100					
Baseline	105.1	114.1	132.5	165.7	193.5
% Diff	0.1	0.1	0.1	0.0	0.0
GDP deflator, 1990=100					
Baseline	106.7	115.1	131.9	158.1	178.9
% Diff	−0.2	−0.3	−0.3	−0.3	−0.2
Wage per Worker, Yuan					
Baseline	2291	2663	3311	4483	5433
% Diff	0.6	0.5	0.5	0.4	0.4
Budget and Finance:					
Govt. Bond, Yuan 100M					
Baseline	461	670	739	1175	1550
Diff	326	434	626	912	1296
International Trade:					
Trade Balance, $M					
Baseline	8743	5183	−10654	7290	18050
Diff	−1260	−1566	−2184	−2206	−2426
Merchandise Exports, $M					
Baseline	71910	84940	91744	121006	148780
% Diff	0.0	0.0	0.0	0.0	0.0
Merchandise Imports, $M					
Baseline	63791	80585	103959	115615	132084
% Diff	2.5	2.4	2.5	2.3	2.2
Machinery Imports, $M					
Baseline	19601	31313	44987	51564	52638
% Diff	3.7	3.1	3.4	2.9	3.0
S-I Balance: vs. GDP, %					
Private					
Baseline	5.1	3.6	0.2	3.9	4.3
Diff	1.1	1.2	1.4	1.4	1.7
Government					
Baseline	−2.2	−2.6	−2.1	−2.5	−2.6
Diff	−1.5	−1.6	−1.8	−1.9	−2.1
Current Account					
Baseline	2.9	1.1	−1.9	1.4	1.7
Diff	−0.4	−0.4	−0.4	−0.5	−0.4

Simulation 4: An Increase in Economic Construction Expenditure by 1% of Nominal GDP

4–1

Year	1985	1986	1987	1988	1989	1990
Real GDE Component: Yuan 100M						
GDE						
Baseline	12457	13733	15198	16907	17395	18320
% Diff	1.2	0.2	1.2	1.0	1.0	1.2
Private Consumption						
Baseline	6834	7262	7820	8607	8722	9113
% Diff	0.0	0.4	0.2	0.4	0.5	0.5
Fixed Investment						
Baseline	3287	3845	4420	5139	4610	4732
% Diff	5.7	0.2	4.4	2.2	3.9	3.0
Net Exports						
Baseline	−355	−221	318	247	117	510
% Diff	15.4	2.6	−10.5	−11.2	−31.2	−5.8
GDP						
Baseline	12701	13827	15427	17165	17863	18548
% Diff	0.1	0.5	0.5	0.8	0.9	1.1
GDP (Industry)						
Baseline	5022	5537	6296	7210	7481	7717
% Diff	0.0	0.5	0.4	0.8	0.9	1.2
Income Distribution:						
Wage and Salary, Yuan 100M						
Baseline	1383	1660	1881	2316	2619	2951
% Diff	0.0	0.8	−0.1	0.5	0.2	0.2
Production and Labor:						
Employment, 10 T						
Baseline	49873	51282	52783	54334	55329	56740
% Diff	0.2	0.1	0.3	0.4	0.4	0.4
Labor Productivity, Yuan						
Baseline	44.6	47.4	50.9	55.9	57.4	58.6
% Diff	1.3	−0.1	0.9	0.4	0.4	0.4
Wage and Prices:						
Retail Price Index, 1990=100						
Baseline	61.7	65.4	70.1	83.1	97.9	100.0
% Diff	0.0	0.1	−0.1	0.0	−0.1	−0.1
Inflation Rate, %						
Baseline	8.8	6.0	7.3	18.5	17.8	2.1
Diff	0.0	0.1	−0.2	0.1	−0.1	0.0

4–2

Year	1991	1992	1993	1994	1995
Real GDE Component: Yuan 100M					
GDE					
Baseline	19937	22464	26157	29806	33209
% Diff	1.1	1.0	1.0	1.0	1.1
Private Consumption					
Baseline	10063	11519	12762	13794	15222
% Diff	0.6	0.6	0.6	0.7	0.7
Fixed Investment					
Baseline	5425	6588	8121	9552	10863
% Diff	3.3	2.8	2.6	2.6	2.9
Net Exports					
Baseline	249	85	349	1207	1552
% Diff	−13.1	−44.4	−16.4	−4.9	−4.8
GDP					
Baseline	20253	23137	26258	29583	32691
% Diff	1.2	1.3	1.4	1.5	1.5
GDP (Industry)					
Baseline	8788	10646	12760	15105	17199
% Diff	1.2	1.5	1.6	1.7	1.6
Income Distribution:					
Wage and Salary, Yuan 100M					
Baseline	3324	3939	4916	6656	8100
% Diff	0.3	0.1	0.1	0.1	0.1
Production and Labor:					
Employment, 10 T					
Baseline	58360	59432	60220	61470	62388
% Diff	0.5	0.5	0.5	0.5	0.5
Labor Productivity, Yuan					
Baseline	63.0	69.3	78.2	85.3	92.1
% Diff	0.2	0.1	0.1	0.1	0.2
Wage and Prices:					
Retail Price Index, 1990=100					
Baseline	102.9	108.4	122.7	149.3	171.4
% Diff	−0.1	−0.2	−0.2	−0.2	−0.2
Inflation Rate, %					
Baseline	2.9	5.4	13.2	21.7	14.8
Simulation	2.9	5.3	13.2	21.7	14.8
Diff	0.0	0.0	0.0	0.0	0.0

4–3

Year	1985	1986	1987	1988	1989	1990
CPI, 1990=100						
Baseline	60.4	64.7	70.4	84.9	98.7	100.0
% Diff	0.0	0.1	−0.1	0.0	−0.1	−0.1
GDP deflator, 1990=100						
Baseline	70.6	73.8	77.5	87.0	94.7	100.0
% Diff	1.4	0.1	0.8	0.3	0.6	0.3
Wage per Worker, Yuan						
Baseline	1119	1296	1424	1702	1905	2099
% Diff	0.0	0.8	−0.2	0.4	0.1	0.0
Budget and Finance:						
Govt. Bond, Yuan 100M						
Baseline	90	138	170	271	283	375
Diff	57	128	139	232	308	425
International Trade:						
Trade Balance, $M						
Baseline	−13123	−9140	−1661	−5315	−5620	9165
Diff	−1165	−128	−888	−779	−1058	−923
Merchandise Exports, $M						
Baseline	27350	30942	39437	47516	52538	62091
% Diff	0.0	0.0	0.0	0.0	0.0	0.0
Merchandise Imports, $M						
Baseline	42252	42904	43216	55268	59140	53345
% Diff	3.1	0.4	2.4	1.7	2.2	2.2
Machinery Imports, $M						
Baseline	16239	16781	14607	16697	18207	16845
% Diff	5.8	0.5	4.3	3.0	4.3	3.9
S-I Balance: vs. GDP, %						
Private						
Baseline	−3.2	−1.2	1.5	0.8	0.6	4.8
Diff	0.3	1.2	0.8	1.3	1.6	1.9
Government						
Baseline	−1.0	−1.4	−1.4	−1.8	−1.7	−2.0
Diff	−0.6	−1.3	−1.1	−1.5	−1.8	−2.3
Current Account						
Baseline	−4.2	−2.6	0.1	−1.0	−1.1	2.8
Diff	−0.3	0.0	−0.3	−0.2	−0.3	−0.3

4–4

Year	1991	1992	1993	1994	1995
CPI, 1990=100					
Baseline	105.1	114.1	132.5	165.7	193.5
% Diff	−0.1	−0.2	−0.2	−0.2	−0.2
GDP deflator, 1990=100					
Baseline	106.7	115.1	131.9	158.1	178.9
% Diff	0.4	0.2	0.4	0.2	0.3
Wage per Worker, Yuan					
Baseline	2291	2663	3311	4483	5433
% Diff	0.0	−0.1	−0.2	−0.2	−0.2
Budget and Finance:					
Govt. Bond, Yuan 100M					
Baseline	461	670	739	1175	1550
Diff	550	736	1047	1534	2184
International Trade:					
Trade Balance, $M					
Baseline	8743	5183	−10654	7290	18050
Diff	−1036	−1266	−1891	−1868	−2335
Merchandise Exports, $M					
Baseline	71910	84940	91744	121006	148780
% Diff	0.0	0.0	0.0	0.0	0.0
Merchandise Imports, $M					
Baseline	63791	80585	103959	115615	132084
% Diff	2.1	1.9	2.2	1.9	2.1
Machinery Imports, $M					
Baseline	19601	31313	44987	51564	52638
% Diff	4.0	3.1	3.6	3.0	3.6
S-I Balance: vs. GDP, %					
Private					
Baseline	5.1	3.6	0.2	3.9	4.3
Diff	2.2	2.5	2.6	2.8	3.2
Government					
Baseline	−2.2	−2.6	−2.1	−2.5	−2.6
Diff	−2.5	−2.8	−3.0	−3.2	−3.6
Current Account					
Baseline	2.9	1.1	−1.9	1.4	1.7
Diff	−0.3	−0.3	−0.3	−0.4	−0.4

Simulation 5: An Increase in World GDP by 1%

5–1

Year	1985	1986	1987	1988	1989	1990
Real GDE Component: Yuan 100M						
GDE						
Baseline	12457	13733	15198	16907	17395	18320
% Diff	0.4	0.5	0.6	0.6	0.6	0.7
Private Consumption						
Baseline	6834	7262	7820	8607	8722	9113
% Diff	0.0	0.1	0.1	0.2	0.2	0.2
Fixed Investment						
Baseline	3287	3845	4420	5139	4610	4732
% Diff	0.4	0.4	0.5	0.5	0.7	0.8
Net Exports						
Baseline	−355	−221	318	247	117	510
% Diff	−9.1	−16.4	14.7	17.4	39.2	10.4
GDP						
Baseline	12701	13827	15427	17165	17863	18548
% Diff	0.0	0.1	0.1	0.2	0.2	0.3
GDP (Industry)						
Baseline	5022	5537	6296	7210	7481	7717
% Diff	0.0	0.0	0.1	0.1	0.2	0.2
Income Distribution:						
Wage and Salary, Yuan 100M						
Baseline	1383	1660	1881	2316	2619	2951
% Diff	0.0	0.3	0.3	0.3	0.3	0.3
Production and Labor:						
Employment, 10 T						
Baseline	49873	51282	52783	54334	55329	56740
% Diff	0.1	0.1	0.2	0.2	0.2	0.2
Labor Productivity, Yuan						
Baseline	44.6	47.4	50.9	55.9	57.4	58.6
% Diff	0.4	0.4	0.4	0.4	0.4	0.4
Wage and Prices:						
Retail Price Index, 1990=100						
Baseline	61.7	65.4	70.1	83.1	97.9	100.0
% Diff	0.0	0.0	0.0	0.0	0.0	0.0
Inflation Rate, %						
Baseline	8.8	6.0	7.3	18.5	17.8	2.1
Diff	0.0	0.0	0.0	0.0	0.0	0.0

5–2

Year	1991	1992	1993	1994	1995
Real GDE Component: Yuan 100M					
GDE					
Baseline	19937	22464	26157	29806	33209
% Diff	0.7	0.6	0.6	0.8	0.8
Private Consumption					
Baseline	10063	11519	12762	13794	15222
% Diff	0.3	0.3	0.3	0.3	0.3
Fixed Investment					
Baseline	5425	6588	8121	9552	10863
% Diff	0.8	0.6	0.5	0.8	0.8
Net Exports					
Baseline	249	85	349	1207	1552
% Diff	25.5	76.7	18.2	8.1	7.4
GDP					
Baseline	20253	23137	26258	29583	32691
% Diff	0.3	0.3	0.3	0.4	0.4
GDP (Industry)					
Baseline	8788	10646	12760	15105	17199
% Diff	0.3	0.3	0.4	0.4	0.4
Income Distribution:					
Wage and Salary, Yuan 100M					
Baseline	3324	3939	4916	6656	8100
% Diff	0.4	0.4	0.3	0.3	0.4
Production and Labor:					
Employment, 10 T					
Baseline	58360	59432	60220	61470	62388
% Diff	0.3	0.3	0.2	0.3	0.3
Labor Productivity, Yuan					
Baseline	63.0	69.3	78.2	85.3	92.1
% Diff	0.4	0.3	0.2	0.4	0.3
Wage and Prices:					
Retail Price Index, 1990=100					
Baseline	102.9	108.4	122.7	149.3	171.4
% Diff	0.0	0.0	0.0	0.0	0.0
Inflation Rate, %					
Baseline	2.9	5.4	13.2	21.7	14.8
Diff	0.0	0.0	0.0	0.0	0.0

5–3

Year	1985	1986	1987	1988	1989	1990
CPI, 1990=100						
Baseline	60.4	64.7	70.4	84.9	98.7	100.0
% Diff	0.0	0.1	0.1	0.1	0.0	0.0
GDP deflator, 1990=100						
Baseline	70.6	73.8	77.5	87.0	94.7	100.0
% Diff	0.0	0.1	0.2	0.1	0.1	0.2
Wage per Worker, Yuan						
Baseline	1119	1296	1424	1702	1905	2099
% Diff	0.0	0.3	0.3	0.3	0.3	0.2
Budget and Finance:						
Govt. Bond, Yuan 100M						
Baseline	90	138	170	271	283	375
Diff	−3	−5	−8	−11	−17	−28
International Trade:						
Trade Balance, $M						
Baseline	−13123	−9140	−1661	−5315	−5620	9165
Diff	737	807	1195	1153	1287	1664
Merchandise Exports, $M						
Baseline	27350	30942	39437	47516	52538	62091
% Diff	3.9	4.1	4.3	3.8	4.0	4.1
Merchandise Imports, $M						
Baseline	42252	42904	43216	55268	59140	53345
% Diff	0.6	0.7	0.8	0.9	0.9	1.1
Machinery Imports, $M						
Baseline	16239	16781	14607	16697	18207	16845
% Diff	0.9	1.0	1.1	1.3	1.4	1.7
S–I Balance: vs. GDP, %						
Private						
Baseline	−3.2	−1.2	1.5	0.8	0.6	4.8
Diff	0.3	0.3	0.4	0.3	0.2	0.3
Government						
Baseline	−1.0	−1.4	−1.4	−1.8	−1.7	−2.0
Diff	0.0	0.1	0.1	0.1	0.1	0.2
Current Account						
Baseline	−4.2	−2.6	0.1	−1.0	−1.1	2.8
Diff	0.3	0.3	0.4	0.3	0.3	0.5

5–4

Year	1991	1992	1993	1994	1995
CPI, 1990=100					
Baseline	105.1	114.1	132.5	165.7	193.5
% Diff	0.0	0.0	0.0	0.0	0.0
GDP deflator, 1990=100					
Baseline	106.7	115.1	131.9	158.1	178.9
% Diff	0.3	0.2	0.1	0.3	0.3
Wage per Worker, Yuan					
Baseline	2291	2663	3311	4483	5433
% Diff	0.3	0.2	0.2	0.1	0.2
Budget and Finance:					
Govt. Bond, Yuan 100M					
Baseline	461	670	739	1175	1550
Diff	−37	−46	−67	−114	−154
International Trade:					
Trade Balance, $M					
Baseline	8743	5183	−10654	7290	18050
Diff	2002	2042	1953	3043	3719
Merchandise Exports, $M					
Baseline	71910	84940	91744	121006	148780
% Diff	4.3	3.9	3.7	4.1	3.9
Merchandise Imports, $M					
Baseline	63791	80585	103959	115615	132084
% Diff	1.1	1.0	0.9	1.2	1.2
Machinery Imports, $M					
Baseline	19601	31313	44987	51564	52638
% Diff	1.7	1.3	1.3	1.6	1.7
S-I Balance: vs. GDP, %					
Private					
Baseline	5.1	3.6	0.2	3.9	4.3
Diff	0.4	0.3	0.2	0.4	0.3
Government					
Baseline	-2.2	-2.6	-2.1	-2.5	-2.6
Diff	0.2	0.2	0.2	0.3	0.3
Current Account					
Baseline	2.9	1.1	-1.9	1.4	1.7
Diff	0.5	0.5	0.4	0.6	0.6

Appendix C: Statistical Data

Endogenous Variables

	CH_C	CH_CG	CH_CGN	CH_COS	CH_CP	CH_CPIU	CH_CPN
1970	NA	NA	NA	NA	NA	42.8	NA
1971	NA	NA	NA	NA	NA	42.8	NA
1972	NA	NA	NA	NA	NA	42.9	NA
1973	NA	NA	NA	NA	NA	42.9	NA
1974	NA	NA	NA	NA	NA	43.2	NA
1975	NA	NA	NA	NA	NA	43.4	NA
1976	NA	NA	NA	NA	NA	43.5	NA
1977	NA	NA	NA	1663.3	NA	44.7	NA
1978	4345.5	931.6	480.0	1850.0	3414.0	45.0	1759.1
1979	4766.7	1117.3	614.0	2039.6	3649.3	45.8	2005.4
1980	5186.8	1148.5	659.0	2414.3	4038.3	49.3	2317.1
1981	5616.6	1196.6	705.0	2764.7	4420.0	50.5	2604.1
1982	6072.4	1285.3	770.0	3052.3	4787.1	51.5	2867.9
1983	6627.8	1381.5	838.0	3431.1	5246.4	52.6	3182.5
1984	7590.8	1649.3	1020.0	4419.6	5941.5	54.0	3674.5
1985	8597.4	1763.3	1184.0	6022.8	6834.1	60.4	4589.0
1986	9180.1	1918.3	1367.0	7883.2	7261.8	64.7	5175.0
1987	9774.1	1954.5	1490.0	9500.7	7819.6	70.4	5961.2
1988	10553.7	1947.2	1727.0	11231.0	8606.5	84.9	7633.1
1989	10802.8	2080.4	2033.0	13251.3	8722.4	98.7	8523.5
1990	11365.2	2252.0	2252.0	16268.5	9113.2	100.0	9113.2
1991	12823.4	2760.6	2830.0	19444.7	10062.8	105.1	10315.9
1992	14747.5	3228.6	3492.3	23488.7	11518.9	114.1	12459.8
1993	16423.9	3661.8	4499.7	28766.3	12762.1	132.5	15682.4
1994	17684.0	3889.6	5986.2	41771.1	13794.4	165.7	21230.0
1995	18880.1	3658.3	6690.5	51612.6	15221.8	193.5	27838.9
1996	20527.8	3876.5	7583.0	64230.5	16651.2	210.5	32572.0

	CH_CPR	CH_CPU	CH_EXMCN	CH_EXMNN	CH_EXSN	CH_GBD	CH_GDE
1970	NA	NA	2260	2309	128	0.0	NA
1971	NA	NA	2640	2803	81	0.0	NA
1972	NA	NA	3440	3652	132	0.0	NA
1973	NA	NA	5820	5677	103	0.0	NA
1974	NA	NA	6950	7108	128	0.0	NA
1975	NA	NA	7260	7689	139	0.0	NA
1976	NA	NA	6850	6943	440	0.0	NA

1977	NA	NA	7590	8050	500	0.0	NA
1978	2157.2	1256.8	9750	9437	763	0.0	6550.7
1979	2354.9	1294.5	13660	13658	1388	0.0	7147.5
1980	2544.7	1493.6	18119	18492	1897	0.0	7694.4
1981	2827.1	1592.9	22007	22027	2403	0.0	8103.9
1982	3112.6	1674.5	22321	21125	2512	43.8	8403.0
1983	3461.8	1784.6	22226	20707	2479	41.6	9950.6
1984	3922.8	2018.7	26139	23905	2811	42.5	11183.0
1985	4404.0	2430.2	27350	25108	3055	60.6	12456.9
1986	4552.4	2709.5	30942	25756	3827	62.5	13732.9
1987	4796.3	3023.3	39437	34734	4386	63.1	15197.7
1988	5040.2	3566.3	47516	41054	4823	132.2	16907.3
1989	5013.3	3709.1	52538	43220	4550	138.9	17394.9
1990	5129.1	3984.1	62091	51519	5803	197.2	18319.5
1991	5475.2	4587.6	71910	58919	6905	281.3	19937.1
1992	6031.9	5487.0	84940	69568	9189	460.8	22464.4
1993	6275.5	6486.6	91744	75659	11146	381.3	26156.6
1994	6660.8	7133.6	121006	102561	16503	1028.6	29805.5
1995	7278.3	7943.5	148780	128110	19130	1510.9	33209.0
1996	7918.3	8732.9	151066	NA	NA	NA	36906.2

	CH_GDE N	CH_GDP	CH_GDP1	CH_GDP2	CH_GD P3	CH_GDPI N	CH_GEPL
1970	NA	NA	NA	NA	NA	NA	0
1971	NA	NA	NA	NA	NA	NA	0
1972	NA	NA	NA	NA	NA	NA	0.5
1973	NA	NA	NA	NA	NA	NA	0.5
1974	NA	NA	NA	NA	NA	NA	0.5
1975	NA	NA	NA	NA	NA	NA	0
1976	NA	NA	NA	NA	NA	NA	0
1977	NA	NA	NA	NA	NA	NA	0
1978	3605.6	6584.27	2630.83	2537.78	1601.52	2249.26	0
1979	4074.0	7084.68	2791.32	2745.88	1726.43	2444.95	0
1980	4551.3	7637.76	2751.85	3118.94	1828.93	2753.1	28.58
1981	4901.4	8039.4	2943.9	3177.31	2021.11	2800.33	62.89
1982	5489.2	8105.24	3283.28	3352.41	2283.76	2962.28	55.52
1983	6076.3	9718.39	3554.26	3700.09	2631.29	3250.18	42.47
1984	7164.4	11193.27	4014.65	4235.56	3140.57	3733.78	28.91
1985	8792.1	12701.06	4088.32	5022.27	3713.91	4413.05	39.56
1986	10132.8	13826.98	4222.49	5537.44	4163.94	4840.41	50.16
1987	11784.7	15426.95	4422.43	6296.24	4762.91	5479.2	79.83
1988	14704.0	17165.2	4532.93	7209.84	5392.3	6315.93	76.75
1989	16466.0	17863.13	4672.36	7481.39	5682.18	6635.32	72.36
1990	18319.5	18547.9	5017	7717.4	5813.5	6858	190.4

1991	21280.4	20253.23	5135.39	8788.35	6325.99	7845.43	246.8
1992	25863.6	23137.14	5377.42	10646	7110.73	9505.38	438.57
1993	34500.6	26258.08	5629.98	12759.98	7868.24	11415	336.22
1994	47110.9	29583.14	5856.24	15104.89	8620.96	13574.3	499.36
1995	59404.9	32690.92	6148.26	17198.56	9343.24	15479.42	886.9
1996	69764.0	35864.54	6461.33	19315.07	10091.15	17445.28	1314.3

	CH_GSB	CH_GTE	CH_GTR	CH_GVIN	CH_GVINNSE	CH_GVINSE	CH_IF
1970	-81	649.41	662.9	2954.39	59.87	2894.53	NA
1971	-122	732.2	744.73	3388.1	87.76	3300.34	NA
1972	-134	765.9	766.56	3621.2	136.37	3484.83	NA
1973	529	808.8	809.67	3964.49	187.63	3776.86	NA
1974	-723	790.3	783.14	3988.67	261.67	3727	NA
1975	-269	820.88	815.61	4606.52	368.54	4237.97	NA
1976	258	806.2	776.58	4718.92	527.98	4190.93	NA
1977	402	843.53	874.46	5407.88	684.7	4723.18	NA
1978	-2170	1122.09	1132.26	6140.64	735.44	5405.21	1570.26
1979	-2796	1281.79	1146.38	6681.64	796.45	5885.19	1665.03
1980	-3751	1228.83	1159.93	7301.02	1085.67	6215.35	2024.27
1981	871	1138.41	1175.79	7614.24	1241.64	6372.6	1976.34
1982	4737	1229.98	1212.33	8209.67	1387.8	6821.87	2330.58
1983	2475	1409.52	1366.95	9128.33	1665.89	7462.44	2619.96
1984	-32	1701.02	1642.86	10614.42	2486.34	8128.09	2909.39
1985	-12592	2004.25	2004.82	12884.85	3704.99	9179.86	3287.28
1986	-7589	2204.91	2122.01	14388.51	4641.33	9747.18	3845.1
1987	240	2262.18	2199.35	16933.84	6085.23	10848.61	4420.03
1988	-4095	2491.21	2357.24	20454.38	8237.77	12216.62	5138.92
1989	-4980	2823.78	2664.9	22201.19	9513.01	12688.18	4609.58
1990	10616	3083.59	2937.1	23924	10860.25	13063.75	4732
1991	11527	3386.62	3149.48	27457.57	13267.73	14189.85	5424.66
1992	4958	3742.2	3483.37	34239.6	18290.21	15949.39	6587.54
1993	-11522	4642.3	4348.95	43587	26728.5	16858.5	8120.78
1994	7592	5792.62	5218.1	54135.06	36180.76	17954.3	9552.48
1995	11957	6823.72	6242.2	61876.38	42449.82	19426.56	10863.37
1996	NA	7914.4	7366.6	72024.1	51412.52	20611.58	NA

	CH_IF1	CH_IF3	CH_IFCT	CH_IFD	CH_IFINNSED	CH_IFINNSEF	CH_IFINSE
1970	NA	NA	NA	NA	NA	NA	NA
1971	NA	NA	NA	NA	NA	NA	NA
1972	NA	NA	NA	NA	NA	NA	NA
1973	NA	NA	NA	NA	NA	NA	NA

1974	NA	NA	NA	NA	NA	NA	NA
1975	NA	NA	NA	NA	NA	NA	NA
1976	NA	NA	NA	NA	NA	NA	NA
1977	NA	NA	NA	NA	NA	NA	NA
1978	170.56	538.97	60.1	1570.3	222.3	0.0	578.4
1979	188.68	680.07	54.5	1662.1	218.6	0.4	522.8
1980	206.69	876.9	46.8	2018.5	306.3	0.9	586.7
1981	135.28	888.82	34.8	1967.1	349.6	1.6	566.2
1982	153.9	1067.88	40.9	2317.9	349.8	1.9	716.2
1983	200.87	1213.44	39.8	2600.7	362.6	2.7	800.6
1984	266.74	1355.87	40.5	2869.4	362.6	5.1	878.6
1985	234.72	1583.17	58.3	3226.6	268.8	5.1	1137.2
1986	157.45	1865.1	53.3	3764.8	322.9	6.9	1439.5
1987	194.44	2060.55	50.1	4318.3	442.4	10.4	1662.1
1988	232.7	2377.87	47.4	5006.8	547.7	14.5	1918.8
1989	193.85	2199.93	36.7	4473.9	468.3	14.2	1696.6
1990	306.62	2200.33	29.3	4565.2	372.3	13.6	1809.9
1991	230.45	2332.75	34.5	5212.4	862.0	35.1	1929.9
1992	170.13	2873.88	173.9	6106.8	1097.6	86.4	2185.7
1993	122.69	4327.03	102.6	7128.9	1171.0	162.9	2234.5
1994	184.36	5682.23	269.1	7903.2	982.8	205.1	2228.9
1995	245.51	6454.29	304.3	9186.5	1215.3	221.8	2422.1
1996	NA	NA	NA	NA	NA	NA	NA

	CH_IFN	CH_IMM C0689N	CH_IMM C7N	CH_IMMC N	CH_IM MN	CH_IMSN	CH_J
1970	NA	NA	NA	2330	2280	238	NA
1971	NA	NA	NA	2200	2144	862	NA
1972	NA	NA	NA	2860	2819	1099	NA
1973	NA	NA	NA	5160	5031	220	NA
1974	NA	NA	NA	7620	7791	168	NA
1975	NA	NA	NA	7490	7926	171	NA
1976	NA	NA	NA	6580	6660	465	NA
1977	NA	NA	NA	7210	7627	521	NA
1978	1073.9	NA	NA	10890	11201	1169	631.4
1979	1151.2	NA	NA	15670	16212	1630	657.7
1980	1318.0	14898	5119	20017	22049	2091	522.6
1981	1253.0	16149	5866	22015	21047	2512	615.4
1982	1493.2	16081	3204	19285	16876	2024	491.6
1983	1709.0	17402	3988	21390	18717	1994	536.9
1984	2125.6	20165	7245	27410	23891	2857	605.3
1985	2641.0	26013	16239	42252	38231	2524	1207.9
1986	3098.0	26123	16781	42904	34896	2276	1144.0
1987	3742.0	28609	14607	43216	36395	2485	826.8

1988	4624.0	38571	16697	55268	46369	3603	1047.5
1989	4339.0	40933	18207	59140	48840	3910	1793.1
1990	4732.0	36500	16845	53345	42354	4352	1712.0
1991	5940.0	44190	19601	63791	50176	4121	1532.7
1992	8317.0	49272	31313	80585	64385	9414	1216.5
1993	12980.0	58972	44987	103959	86313	12014	1644.3
1994	16856.3	64051	51564	115615	95271	16201	1609.8
1995	20300.5	79446	52638	132084	110060	25223	2086.0
1996	24148.0	84067	54771	138838	NA	NA	2523.8

	CH_JN	CH_KF	CH_KF1	CH_KF3	CH_KFCT	CH_KFF	CH_KFINNSE
1970	NA	NA	NA	NA	NA	NA	NA
1971	NA	NA	NA	NA	NA	NA	NA
1972	NA	NA	NA	NA	NA	NA	NA
1973	NA	NA	NA	NA	NA	NA	NA
1974	NA	NA	NA	NA	NA	NA	NA
1975	NA	NA	NA	NA	NA	NA	NA
1976	NA	NA	NA	NA	NA	NA	NA
1977	NA	10953.9	966.0	3345.3	245.4	0.0	NA
1978	304.0	12118.8	1100.9	3760.5	296.4	0.0	2880.4
1979	323.0	13335.5	1248.8	4301.4	339.9	3.0	2992.8
1980	272.0	14813.0	1404.3	5002.0	372.7	8.6	3177.3
1981	328.0	16182.0	1482.0	5685.7	392.3	17.5	3398.2
1982	267.0	17849.1	1575.1	6520.5	417.1	29.5	3610.6
1983	296.0	19719.4	1709.9	7460.0	439.3	47.5	3824.2
1984	343.0	21761.1	1901.4	8487.7	460.5	85.4	4023.6
1985	745.0	24025.6	2046.7	9671.9	497.2	142.1	4108.4
1986	748.0	26693.5	2103.9	11063.1	526.1	215.4	4236.8
1987	580.0	29805.5	2195.2	12581.5	550.4	306.6	4482.0
1988	871.0	33454.2	2318.2	14330.3	570.3	423.4	4820.1
1989	1756.0	36391.1	2396.1	15813.7	578.5	537.9	5061.5
1990	1712.0	39376.3	2587.7	17255.0	580.0	678.9	5204.5
1991	1577.0	42635.3	2675.8	18638.7	582.5	853.8	5815.4
1992	1319.0	46877.9	2698.8	20487.5	724.4	1287.6	6679.6
1993	2018.0	52420.3	2673.1	23687.7	787.1	2208.7	7646.1
1994	2404.3	59089.7	2710.4	28067.1	1013.0	3736.5	8413.5
1995	3576.5	66703.1	2806.8	32977.7	1261.6	5207.8	9387.9
1996	4591.0	NA	NA	NA	NA	NA	NA

	CH_KFINNSED	CH_KFINSE	CH_LF	CH_LPNAG	CH_N	CH_N1	CH_N2
1970	NA	NA	34432	NA	34432	27786	3479
1971	NA	NA	35620	NA	35620	28365	3941

1972	NA	NA	35854	NA	35854	28248	4225
1973	NA	NA	36652	NA	36652	28820	4436
1974	NA	NA	37369	NA	37369	29180	4646
1975	NA	NA	38168	NA	38168	29415	5075
1976	NA	NA	38834	NA	38834	29398	5529
1977	NA	3636.9	39377	NA	39377	29294	5736
1978	2880.4	4080.8	40682	33.11	40152	28313	6970
1979	2992.4	4452.6	41592	35.14	41024	28629	7241
1980	3176.0	4856.7	42903	37.32	42361	29117	7736
1981	3395.4	5223.8	44165	36.98	43725	29771	8033
1982	3605.9	5725.9	45674	35.45	45295	30853	8377
1983	3817.1	6286.0	46707	41.83	46436	31145	8711
1984	4011.7	6888.0	48433	41.35	48197	30862	9622
1985	4092.0	7701.5	50112	44.59	49873	31105	10418
1986	4214.4	8763.7	51547	47.38	51283	31212	11251
1987	4450.3	9996.4	53060	50.90	52783	31614	11762
1988	4775.4	11415.3	54630	55.90	54334	32197	12188
1989	5004.9	12541.2	55707	57.41	55329	33170	12012
1990	5137.0	13749.1	57123	58.62	56740	34049	12158
1991	5716.5	14922.8	58713	63.03	58361	34876	12469
1992	6499.7	16287.7	59796	69.28	59432	34769	12921
1993	7313.2	17626.3	60640	78.18	60220	33966	13517
1994	7893.8	18885.8	61946	85.28	61470	33386	13961
1995	8675.0	20269.1	62908	92.14	62388	33018	14315
1996	NA	NA	NA	NA	NA	NA	NA

	CH_N3	CH_NEX	CH_NEXN	CH_NINNSE	CH_NNAG	CH_NU	CH_NW
1970	3167	NA	NA	NA	6646	6312	6216
1971	3315	NA	NA	NA	7255	6868	6787
1972	3381	NA	NA	NA	7606	7200	7134
1973	3396	NA	NA	NA	7832	7388	7337
1974	3543	NA	NA	NA	8189	7687	7651
1975	3678	NA	NA	NA	8753	8222	8198
1976	3907	NA	NA	NA	9436	8692	8673
1977	4347	NA	NA	NA	10083	9127	9112
1978	4869	190.4	-11.4	2952	11839	9514	9499
1979	5154	248.6	-19.6	3090	12395	9999	9967
1980	5508	65.6	-14.8	3380	13244	10525	10444
1981	5921	-6.4	11.3	3487	13954	11053	10940
1982	6065	-416.7	91.1	3622	14442	11428	11281
1983	6580	249.0	50.8	3765	15291	11746	11515
1984	7713	213.3	1.3	4261	17335	12229	11890
1985	8350	-355.1	-366.9	4534	18768	12808	12358

1986	8819	-220.7	-255.2	5025	20071	13293	12810
1987	9407	318.4	11.5	5256	21169	13783	13214
1988	9949	246.6	-151.1	5432	22137	14267	13608
1989	10147	117.0	-185.5	5296	22159	14390	13742
1990	10533	510.3	510.3	5334	22691	14730	14059
1991	11015	248.9	617.5	5475	23485	15268	14508
1992	11742	84.7	275.5	5698	24663	15630	14792
1993	12737	349.4	-679.5	5969	26254	15964	14849
1994	14123	1206.6	634.1	6403	28084	16816	14849
1995	15055	1551.7	998.5	6596	29370	17346	14908
1996	NA	NA	870.0	NA	NA	NA	NA

	CH_NWINSE	CH_PCP	CH_PCPR	CH_PCPU	CH_PEXM	CH_PGDP	CH_PIF
1970	1959	NA	NA	NA	NA	NA	76.47
1971	2233	NA	NA	NA	NA	NA	75.55
1972	2350	NA	NA	NA	NA	NA	72.01
1973	2397	NA	NA	NA	NA	NA	73.1
1974	2494	NA	NA	NA	NA	NA	73.67
1975	2691	NA	NA	NA	NA	NA	69.3
1976	2866	NA	NA	NA	NA	NA	66.49
1977	3013	NA	NA	NA	NA	NA	65.61
1978	3139	51.5	50.6	53.1	60.6	55.0	68.4
1979	3208	55.0	53.5	57.6	71.1	57.0	69.1
1980	3334	57.4	56.1	59.6	84.8	59.2	65.1
1981	3488	58.9	57.7	61.1	85.7	60.5	63.4
1982	3582	59.9	58.7	62.2	80.3	65.3	64.1
1983	3632	60.7	59.6	62.7	76.2	61.1	65.2
1984	3669	61.8	60.8	63.8	76.3	64.1	73.1
1985	3815	67.2	66.3	68.6	72.7	70.6	80.3
1986	3955	71.3	70.5	72.5	73.0	73.8	80.6
1987	4086	76.2	75.7	77.1	82.7	77.5	84.7
1988	4229	88.7	88.8	88.6	87.3	87.0	90.0
1989	4273	97.7	98.1	97.2	90.6	94.7	94.1
1990	4364	100.0	100.0	100.0	100.0	100.0	100.0
1991	4472	102.5	103.0	101.9	100.9	106.7	109.5
1992	4521	108.2	109.0	107.3	101.8	115.1	126.3
1993	4498	122.9	125.4	120.5	100.0	131.9	159.8
1994	4371	153.9	157.5	150.5	98.8	158.1	176.5
1995	4397	182.9	187.7	178.5	102.4	178.9	186.9
1996	NA	195.6	201.2	190.5	NA	189.0	NA

	CH_POPR	CH_POPU	CH_RPI	CH_TAX AG	CH_TAX CUS	CH_TAXI NCM	CH_TAX O
1970	68568	14424	46.6	32.0	7.0	242.2	381.7
1971	70518	14711	46.2	30.9	5.0	276.7	432.2
1972	72242	14935	46.1	28.4	5.0	283.7	449.5
1973	73866	15345	46.4	30.5	9.0	309.4	460.7
1974	75264	15595	46.7	30.1	14.0	316.3	422.7
1975	76390	16030	46.7	29.5	15.0	358.3	412.8
1976	77376	16341	46.9	29.1	15.0	363.8	368.6
1977	78305	16669	47.8	29.3	26.2	412.7	406.2
1978	79014	17245	48.2	28.4	28.8	462.1	613.0
1979	79047	18495	49.1	29.5	26.0	482.3	608.6
1980	79565	19140	52.1	27.7	33.5	510.5	588.2
1981	79901	20171	53.3	28.4	54.0	547.5	545.9
1982	80174	21480	54.3	29.4	47.5	623.2	512.3
1983	80734	22274	55.1	33.0	53.9	688.8	591.4
1984	80340	24017	56.7	34.8	103.1	809.4	695.5
1985	80757	25094	61.7	42.1	205.2	1097.5	660.1
1986	81141	26366	65.4	44.5	151.6	1202.2	723.7
1987	81626	27674	70.2	50.8	142.4	1282.5	723.7
1988	82365	28661	83.2	73.7	155.0	1485.7	642.8
1989	83164	29540	97.9	84.9	181.5	1760.5	637.9
1990	84142	30191	100.0	87.9	159.0	1859.0	831.2
1991	85280	30543	102.9	90.7	187.3	1981.1	890.4
1992	84799	32372	108.4	119.2	212.8	2244.2	907.2
1993	85166	33351	122.7	125.7	256.5	3194.5	772.3
1994	85549	34301	149.4	231.5	272.7	3914.2	799.7
1995	85947	35174	171.5	278.1	291.8	4589.7	1082.6
1996	86439	35950	181.9	NA	NA	4617.5	NA

	CH_TB	CH_TDPR	CH_TDPU	CH_U	CH_UR	CH_WAG E	CH_YHR
1970	29	15.0	64.5	NA	NA	537.8	NA
1971	659	17.0	73.3	NA	NA	536.3	NA
1972	833	20.1	85.1	NA	NA	574.2	NA
1973	646	27.1	94.1	NA	NA	584.8	NA
1974	-683	30.7	105.8	NA	NA	577.6	NA
1975	-237	35.0	114.6	NA	NA	565.4	NA
1976	283	36.9	122.2	NA	NA	564.1	NA
1977	423	46.5	135.1	NA	NA	565.0	NA
1978	-1764	55.7	154.9	530.0	5.28	598.9	1257.2
1979	-2554	78.4	202.6	567.6	5.37	648.8	1500.0
1980	-3557	117.0	282.5	541.5	4.89	739.6	1683.5
1981	980	169.6	354.1	439.5	3.82	749.5	1909.7

1982	4249	228.1	447.3	379.4	3.21	781.9	2240.2
1983	1990	319.9	572.6	271.4	2.26	811.6	2574.3
1984	14	438.1	776.6	235.7	1.89	953.2	3096.1
1985	-13123	564.8	1057.8	238.5	1.83	1119.1	3659.5
1986	-9140	766.1	1471.5	264.4	1.95	1295.6	3810.8
1987	-1661	1005.7	2067.6	276.6	1.97	1423.6	4215.8
1988	-5315	1142.3	2659.2	296.2	2.03	1702.1	5114.0
1989	-5620	1412.1	3734.8	377.9	2.56	1905.5	5527.6
1990	9165	1841.6	5192.6	383.2	2.54	2099.1	6021.2
1991	8743	2319.4	6790.9	352.2	2.25	2291.1	6447.5
1992	5183	2867.3	8678.1	363.9	2.28	2663.1	7817.9
1993	-10654	3576.2	11627.3	420.1	2.56	3310.8	9420.6
1994	7290	4816.0	16702.8	476.4	2.80	4482.7	12597.9
1995	18050	6195.6	23466.7	519.6	2.90	5433.3	16451.7
1996	NA	NA	NA	552.8	3.00	NA	19519.2

	CH_YHU	CH_YW
1970	NA	334.3
1971	NA	364.0
1972	NA	409.6
1973	NA	429.1
1974	NA	441.9
1975	NA	463.5
1976	NA	489.2
1977	NA	514.8
1978	NA	568.9
1979	NA	646.7
1980	NA	772.4
1981	987.9	820.0
1982	1106.1	882.0
1983	1163.4	934.6
1984	1399.7	1133.4
1985	1697.5	1383.0
1986	2036.1	1659.7
1987	2414.3	1881.1
1988	3203.9	2316.2
1989	3751.7	2618.5
1990	4321.7	2951.1
1991	4967.2	3323.9
1992	6431.8	3939.2
1993	8651.0	4916.2
1994	11973.3	6656.4
1995	15599.3	8100.0
1996	18583.1	9080.0

Exogenous Variables

	CH_DSC	CH_DSC GDP	CH_DSC N	CH_GBF	CH_GEA D	CH_GEEC	CH_GEN D
1970	NA	NA	NA	0	32.0	392.6	145.3
1971	NA	NA	NA	0	37.6	418.3	169.5
1972	NA	NA	NA	0	38.9	432.0	159.4
1973	NA	NA	NA	0	38.6	468.3	145.4
1974	NA	NA	NA	0	39.8	460.9	133.4
1975	NA	NA	NA	0	41.8	481.7	142.5
1976	NA	NA	NA	0	43.4	466.2	134.5
1977	NA	NA	NA	0	45.2	493.7	149.0
1978	-33.6	-185.9	-18.5	0.0	52.9	719.0	167.8
1979	62.8	-179.0	35.8	35.3	63.1	769.9	222.6
1980	56.6	-62.0	33.5	43.0	75.5	715.5	193.8
1981	64.5	-102.9	39.0	73.1	82.6	630.8	168.0
1982	297.8	-814.2	194.5	40.0	90.8	675.4	176.4
1983	232.2	-167.3	141.8	37.8	103.1	794.8	177.1
1984	-10.3	-197.5	-6.6	34.8	139.8	968.2	180.8
1985	-244.1	-123.4	-172.3	29.2	171.1	1127.6	191.5
1986	-94.1	-96.9	-69.4	75.7	220.0	1159.0	200.8
1987	-229.3	-54.6	-177.8	106.5	228.2	1153.5	209.6
1988	-257.9	30.1	-224.3	138.6	271.6	1258.4	218.0
1989	-468.2	27.2	-443.2	144.1	386.3	1291.2	251.5
1990	-228.4	0.0	-228.4	178.2	414.6	1368.0	290.3
1991	-316.1	3.5	-337.4	180.1	414.0	1428.5	330.3
1992	-672.7	3.0	-774.5	208.9	463.4	1612.8	377.9
1993	-101.4	-0.1	-133.8	357.9	634.3	1834.8	425.8
1994	222.4	1.1	351.5	146.7	847.7	2393.7	550.7
1995	518.1	0.9	926.8	38.9	996.5	2855.8	636.7
1996	1041.6	-3.0	1969.0	NA	NA	NA	715.0

	CH_GEO	CH_GESC	CH_IFF	CH_INR	CH_LAN DDA	CH_LAN DSO	CH_M2
1970	27.3	52.2	NA	NA	3295	143487	NA
1971	43.0	63.8	NA	3.24	7450	145684	NA
1972	60.3	75.3	NA	3.24	17180	147919	NA
1973	68.0	88.6	NA	3.24	7620	148547	NA
1974	61.2	95.0	NA	3.24	6530	148635	NA
1975	51.4	103.6	NA	3.24	10239	149545	NA
1976	42.1	120.1	NA	3.24	11440	149723	NA
1977	36.2	119.4	NA	3.24	15160	149333	858.4
1978	35.4	147.0	0.0	3.24	21800	150104	889.7
1979	51.0	175.2	3.0	3.96	15120	148477	1327.8

1980	45.0	199.0	5.8	5.4	22317	146379	1671.1
1981	45.6	211.5	9.2	5.4	18743	145157	1977.7
1982	44.4	243.0	12.7	5.76	16120	144755	2265.7
1983	52.1	282.5	19.3	5.76	16209	143993	2712.8
1984	80.2	332.1	40.0	5.76	15264	144221	3598.5
1985	105.7	408.4	60.7	7.2	22705	143626	4874.9
1986	140.1	485.1	80.3	7.2	23656	144204	6348.6
1987	165.1	505.8	101.7	7.2	20393	144957	7957.4
1988	162.0	581.2	132.1	8.64	23945	144869	9602.1
1989	226.4	668.4	135.7	11.34	24449	146554	11393.1
1990	273.1	737.6	166.8	8.64	17819	148362	14681.9
1991	364.2	849.7	212.3	7.56	27814	149586	18598.9
1992	318.0	970.1	480.8	7.56	25895	149007	24327.3
1993	569.2	1178.3	991.9	10.98	23133	147741	30075.7
1994	499.0	1501.5	1649.3	10.98	31380	148241	46920.3
1995	578.0	1756.7	1676.8	10.98	22267	149879	60744.0
1996	NA	1705.1	NA	7.47	NA	152220	76095.3

	CH_PFSP	CH_PIMM	CH_POP	CH_RATE	CH_RDEP	CH_REXMN	CH_RGVINTVEN
1970	32.8	NA	82992	2.46	3.20	100.09	NA
1971	33.3	NA	85229	2.46	3.20	100.72	NA
1972	33.8	NA	87177	2.25	3.20	98.92	NA
1973	34.0	NA	89211	1.99	3.20	96.61	NA
1974	34.3	NA	90859	1.96	3.20	100.00	NA
1975	35.0	NA	92420	1.86	3.60	100.00	NA
1976	35.2	NA	93717	1.94	3.60	100.00	NA
1977	35.1	NA	94974	1.86	3.70	107.05	NA
1978	36.5	59.2	96259	1.68	3.70	94.84	9.09
1979	44.6	69.5	97542	1.56	3.70	100.32	9.05
1980	47.8	77.6	98705	1.50	4.10	102.17	9.88
1981	50.6	75.7	100072	1.70	4.10	102.14	10.73
1982	51.7	69.9	101654	1.89	4.10	96.50	11.12
1983	53.9	72.1	103008	1.98	4.20	93.71	11.72
1984	56.1	70.7	104357	2.32	4.40	96.30	16.35
1985	60.9	70.2	105851	2.94	4.70	91.87	18.81
1986	64.8	79.6	107507	3.45	4.90	82.11	21.56
1987	72.6	87.3	109300	3.72	4.90	88.01	23.48
1988	89.3	93.3	111026	3.72	5.00	86.13	24.85
1989	102.7	94.1	112704	3.77	5.00	81.68	23.82
1990	100.0	100	114333	4.78	4.80	81.94	25.29
1991	98.0	101.8	115823	5.32	5.50	81.90	32.71
1992	101.3	106.3	117171	5.51	5.50	81.37	39.41
1993	114.9	104.4	118517	5.76	5.50	82.59	48.44

1994	160.8	97.3	119850	8.62	5.50	84.89	46.08
1995	192.7	98.9	121121	8.35	5.50	86.04	55.78
1996	NA	NA	122389	8.31	5.50	NA	NA

	CH_RIF1	CH_RIF3	CH_RIFC T	CH_RIFIN	CH_RIFIN NSE	CH_RIFIN NSED	CH_RIFIN SE
1970	9.54	28.97	2.60	58.89	NA	NA	NA
1971	10.15	32.78	2.00	55.07	NA	NA	NA
1972	12.15	33.50	4.28	50.06	NA	NA	NA
1973	12.69	36.14	3.92	47.26	NA	NA	NA
1974	13.73	37.81	3.05	45.41	NA	NA	NA
1975	9.56	34.15	2.10	54.19	NA	NA	NA
1976	11.02	33.42	2.32	53.23	NA	NA	NA
1977	11.04	31.84	2.55	54.57	NA	NA	NA
1978	10.86	34.32	3.82	50.99	27.76	27.76	72.24
1979	11.33	40.84	3.27	44.55	29.52	29.47	70.48
1980	10.21	43.32	2.31	44.16	34.36	34.27	65.64
1981	6.84	44.97	1.76	46.42	38.28	38.1	61.72
1982	6.60	45.82	1.75	45.82	32.93	32.75	67.07
1983	7.67	46.32	1.52	44.50	31.33	31.1	68.67
1984	9.17	46.60	1.39	42.84	29.5	29.1	70.5
1985	7.14	48.16	1.77	42.93	19.41	19.05	80.59
1986	4.09	48.51	1.38	46.01	18.64	18.25	81.36
1987	4.40	46.62	1.13	47.85	21.41	20.92	78.59
1988	4.53	46.27	0.92	48.28	22.66	22.08	77.34
1989	4.21	47.73	0.80	47.27	22.14	21.49	77.86
1990	6.48	46.50	0.62	46.40	17.58	16.96	82.42
1991	4.25	43.00	0.64	52.11	31.73	30.49	68.27
1992	2.58	43.63	2.64	51.15	35.14	32.57	64.86
1993	1.51	53.28	1.26	43.94	37.38	32.82	62.62
1994	1.93	59.48	2.82	35.77	34.77	28.76	65.23
1995	2.26	59.41	2.80	35.53	37.24	31.49	62.76
1996	1.51	53.28	1.26	43.94	NA	NA	NA

	CH_RIM MN	CH_RTA XAG	CH_RTA XCUS	CH_RTA XINCM	TREND	WO_PGD P
1970	109.05	NA	12.47	NA	1970	25.2
1971	109.82	NA	9.47	NA	1971	26.9
1972	107.78	NA	7.90	NA	1972	31.1
1973	105.3	NA	8.99	NA	1973	35.5
1974	109	NA	9.16	NA	1974	39.8
1975	109	NA	10.18	NA	1975	44.1
1976	109	NA	11.60	NA	1976	46.1
1977	116.3	NA	18.51	NA	1977	49.9

1978	109.69	2.96	15.25	17.35	1978	53.0
1979	113.12	2.37	10.31	17.26	1979	59.1
1980	120.52	2.11	10.15	15.93	1980	66.0
1981	106.35	1.9	15.06	16.23	1981	67.6
1982	97.32	1.73	14.86	17.32	1982	67.0
1983	103.3	1.72	14.57	17.14	1983	66.8
1984	97.27	1.55	18.60	16.45	1984	66.8
1985	99.96	1.69	18.28	16.95	1985	67.5
1986	96.53	1.63	12.58	16.10	1986	76.6
1987	92.73	1.58	10.51	14.65	1987	84.6
1988	89.53	1.82	8.98	13.65	1988	90.9
1989	93.88	1.77	9.87	14.53	1989	92.5
1990	86.35	1.75	7.85	13.74	1990	100.0
1991	81.18	1.8	7.01	11.94	1991	104.0
1992	78.39	2.19	5.99	10.59	1992	110.2
1993	79.72	1.94	5.16	11.34	1993	106.6
1994	78.99	2.46	3.32	10.48	1994	110.3
1995	75.31	2.35	3.17	9.84	1995	117.5
1996	NA	NA	NA	NA	1996	115.3

3   OUTLINE OF THE PAIR CHINA-HONG KONG LINK MODEL[1]

So Umezaki

The Institute of Developing Economies

The purpose of this chapter is to present a prototype econometric link model for China and Hong Kong, named PAIR China-Hong Kong Link Model (PLM). For this purpose, we start with a brief introduction on the PAIR project in section 1, and then, in section 2, discuss the data problems confronting model building. In section 3, we make a presentation of the model specification. In the last section, estimation results of the model and some simulation analyses are shown.

In order to guarantee the ability to reproduce the model and discussion in this paper to the reader, much space is devoted to a detailed explanation of data sources and data-processing procedures.

1. PAIR Project[2]

The Institute of Developing Economies (IDE) had released its economic forecasts for Asian NIEs and ASEAN every December from 1985 to 1990 in conjunction with IDE's project "Econometric Link System for ASEAN (ELSA)".

---

[1] This paper is prepared for the workshop on econometric models for China held by ICSEAD, on March 30th-31st, 1998. The basic idea for building a PAIR China model and a PAIR Hong Kong model is heavily dependent on Ms Mariko Watanabe, who is the author's predecessor on the PAIR project. The author is very grateful also to Dr Mitsuru Toida (chief of the PAIR Project), other members of the PAIR project, including Prof Yoshihisa Inada, Mr Youcai Liang, Dr Tzong Biau Lin, and participants of the workshop including Dr Shinichi Ichimura, Ms Li Shantong, Prof Shen Lisheng, Prof Zhou Fang, for their helpful comments. Possible errors in this paper are solely the responsibility of the author. For enquiries about this paper, please contact the author via e-mail at umezaki@ide.go.jp.

[2] Quoted from "Preface", Toida, M and D Hiratsuka, eds., *1998 Economic Forecasts for Asian Industrializing Region*, PAIR Economic Forecasting Report No 7, Institute of Developing Economies: Tokyo, 1998.

Asian NIEs, ASEAN, and China attained rapid economic growth in the latter half of the 1980s while succeeding in industrialization of their economies. Although levels of industrialization differ economy by economy, we believe that they will all continue their industrialization in the 1990s. Hence, we call them the Asian Industrializing Region.

The IDE realized the increasing importance of studying this region in a world-wide perspective, and started a project: *Projections for Asian Industrializing Region* (PAIR) in the 1991 fiscal year, by expanding the previous ELSA project. We have invited overseas research institutions to join the project not only from each economy in the Asian industrializing region but from developed economies, including Australia, Canada, New Zealand, and the United Kingdom. Since the 1992 fiscal year we have also invited research institutions from France and the United States of America.

One of the major objectives of the PAIR Project is to conduct economic forecasts for the Asian NIEs, ASEAN and China. These economic forecasts can be conducted with more confidence because our overseas partners have sent us their forecasts one month before the press-release of our forecasts.

2. Data Problems

2.1 China[3]

The State Statistical Bureau of PRC (SSB) has published the data series for the expenditure-side of GDP (GDE) in *China Statistical Yearbook (CSY)*, since its 1995 edition. However, those data series are not complete enough to build a demand-oriented econometric model. Therefore, we need to estimate some data series from appropriate proxies, or to resort to other statistical sources. In practice, we depend primarily on the data published in *CSY*, and supplement these from *International Financial Statistics (IFS)*, published by IMF.

2.1.1 Decomposition of Net Exports

The most obvious shortcoming of China's GDE statistics is the lack of export/import data series based on the SNA system. Data for only "net exports"

---

[3] Measures to cope with data limitations presented in this sub-section are heavily dependent on helpful advice made by Mr Zhu Baoling of the State Information Center of PRC, IDE's counterpart within the PAIR-China project, and by Prof Yoshihisa Inada of Konan University.

in nominal Renminbi Yuan (RMB) terms are available. The SSB has published the balance of payment statistics in *CSY* since its 1990 edition. However, those data for the period before 1984 and between 1986 and 1989 are not available in *CSY*. In order to decompose "net exports" into exports and imports of goods and services, therefore, we refer to the balance of payment (BOP) statistics published in *IFS*. The treatment of exports/imports of goods and services in the SNA system is generally identical with that in the BOP accounts as described in the *Balance of Payment Manual (BMP)*.[4]

On the other hand, in order to analyze detailed international trade in goods, say, by country or by commodity, it is necessary for us to refer to customs statistics. Figure 1 shows China's merchandise exports/imports in nominal US dollar terms based on customs clearance and on BOP. Differences between the two export data series are basically a result of the time of recording and the procedure of data compilation.

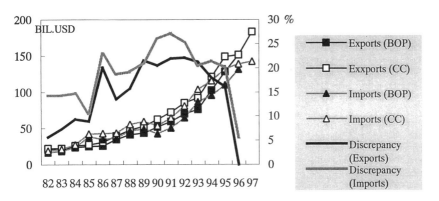

Figure1. China's Trade Statistics

Sources: For customs clearance basis, General Administration of Customs of PRC, China's Customs Statistics (Monthly Exports & Imports), Economic Information & Agency: Hong Kong, various issues; for balance of payment basis, IMF, *International Financial Statistics Yearbook 1997*, Washington, D. C.
Note: "Discrepancy" = 100*(CC – BOP)/BOP.

---

[4] IMF, *Balance of Payment Manual: 4th edition (BPM4)*, Washington, DC, 1977 (reprinted in 1978); IMF, *Balance of Payment Manual: 5th edition (BPM5)*, Washington, DC, 1993.

As a matter of course, China's merchandise trade statistics on a BOP basis are compiled from customs statistics. Prior to 1996, China's BOP statistics had presented "goods for processing" in accordance with the *BPM4* guidelines (*i.e.* processing fees were recorded under "business service") rather than according to the *BPM5* treatment.[5] *BPM5* recommends that such transactions be recorded as gross values of imports and subsequent exports, under goods. This resulted in a substantial difference between the value of goods reported in the BOP and that reported in the trade data produced by customs authority, as shown in Figure 1. In 1996, when *BMP5* treatment had been adopted, discrepancies between the two trade statistics decreased sharply.

2.1.2 Deflators for Merchandise Trade

SSB has not published the data for price deflators of its exports/imports. In our forecasting work, therefore, we utilize the World Bank's estimates of exports/imports unit values as exports/imports deflators for the period between 1978 to 1993.[6] For the period after 1994, we estimated those two series of deflators based on *China's Customs Statistics (CCS)*.

Quantity and value of major export/import commodities on customs clearance basis, and annual percentage change of them, are available in monthly editions of *CCS*. We can define the link index of export/import price deflators as follows;

$$P_t = \frac{100 * \sum_i NV_{it}}{\varphi_i NV_{iAt-1} * (100 + QC_{iAt})}$$

where P_t is the price index for a year t compared to the previous year, NV_{it}, NV_{it-1} are nominal values of exports/imports of commodity i in respective periods, and QC_{it} is the percentage change in export/import quantity of commodity i in period t. We estimated those price deflators as link indices in

---

[5] IMF, *Balance of Payment Statistics Yearbook: Park 3 Methodologies, Compilation Practices and Data Sources,* Washington, DC, 1997, p. 157. Refer also to *BPM4*, pp. 75-86, and *BPM5*, pp. 54-60.

[6] World Bank, *World Development Indictors 1997; CD-ROM edition*, Washington DC, 1997. Those data series are calculated based on COMTRADE, which is maintained by UNCTAD.

order to maximize the coverage of base data for calculation. Not only some data are missing, but also grouping and units of quantity are changed.[7]

Table 1. Estimates of Export/Import Deflators

	1993	1994	1995
Export Price Link Index (Previous Year = 100)	93.9	107.9	108.1
Nominal Value of Exports Compiled (Mil. US$)	57553	71613	90344
Real Value of Exports Compiled (Mil. US$)	61303	66350	83549
Nominal Value of Total Exports (Mil. US$)	91744	12100	148780
Coverage Ratio (%)	62.7	59.2	60.7
	1996	1997	
Export Price Link Index (Previous Year = 100)	103.3	100.2	
Nominal Value of Exports Compiled (Mil. US$)	87675	75998	
Real Value of Exports Compiled (Mil. US$)	84902	75828	
Nominal Value of Total Exports (Mil. US$)	151066	182697	
Coverage Ratio (%)	58.0	41.6	
	1993	1994	1995
Import Price Link Index (Previous Year = 100)	91.6	95.3	112.9
Nominal Value of Imports Compiled (Mil. US$)	59338	63515	77330
Real Value of Imports Compiled (Mil. US$)	64803	66627	68506
Nominal Value of Total Imports (Mil. US$)	103959	115615	132084
Coverage Ratio (%)	57.1	54.9	58.5
	1996	1997	
Import Price Link Index (Previous Year = 100)	93.3	101.9	
Nominal Value of Imports Compiled (Mil. US$)	78342	84409	
Real Value of Imports Compiled (Mil. US$)	83930	82867	
Nominal Value of Total Imports (Mil. US$)	138838	142361	
Coverage Ratio (%)	56.4	59.3	

Sources: Author's estimates. Original data sources are General Administration of Customs of PRC, *China's Customs Statistics (Monthly Exports & Imports)*, Economic Information Agency: Hong Kong, various issues; State Statistical Bureau of PRC, *China Foreign Economic Statistical Yearbook 1996*, China Statistical Publishing House: Beijing, 1997, Table 2-23, 2-24, 2-25, 2-26; State Statistical Bureau of PRC, *China Statistical Yearbook 1997*, China Statistical Publishing House: Beijing, 1997, Table 16-8, 16-9.

Note: "Coverage Ratio" of the export/import deflator estimate is defined as the ratio of "Nominal Value of Exports/Imports Compiled" to "Nominal Value of Total Exports/Imports", respectively.

---

[7] For example, quantity of textile garments exported in 1997, which shared 14.4% of total export value in the year, is not available. This reflects the sharp drop in the coverage ratio for export deflator estimates (see Table 1). Changes in the unit of quantity are often shown between 1993 and 1994.

Table 1 shows the estimated link indices of export/import price deflators, coverage ratio of estimation, and some background data. As we can see in Table 1, the coverage ratios of calculation are around 50-60% of total trade value. Obviously, the best way to estimate export/import price deflators is to refer to original customs statistics. However, we adopt the above method despite its incomplete coverage of commodities traded so far, because of prompt availability of data series.[8] This point is to be considered as important, especially for short-term economic forecasts, as in the PAIR project.

The government consumption deflator can be estimated only up to 1993 because of the lack of data series for a government consumption index at comparable prices. Therefore, we use the household consumption deflator as a proxy for the government consumption deflator for the period after 1994.

2.1.3 Investment Deflator

Since the data for the investment price is available only for the period after 1990, we use the accumulation deflator as the proxy for the former period. According to the *China Statistical Yearbook 1994 edition (CSY94)*, accumulation is defined as follows:

Accumulation = National income used–Consumption
= National income produced+Imports–Exports-Consumption

Nominal values of accumulation are shown in Table 2-19 of *CSY94*. Data for accumulation in real terms are not published directly. Using the data series for nominal values and real indices of national income produced in Table 2-12 and Table 2-13 of *CSY94*, we can calculate national income produced in real terms. Similarly, based on the data series for nominal values and real indices of consumption (on a national income basis) in Table 2-19 and Table 2-21 of *CSY94*, we can calculate real values of consumption. Based on the data sources explained in sub-sections above (2.1.1 and 2.1.2), the data series for exports/imports in real terms became available. We can calculate the data series for accumulations in real terms. Dividing nominal accumulation by real accumulation, we get estimates of accumulation deflators. For the period after

---

[8] The author plans to calculate export/import price deflators based on original customs statistics, after electric materials become available at IDE. Since 1992, the Commodity Classification for China Customs Statistics (CCCCS) has switched to a base on the Harmonized Commodity Description and Coding System (HS), rather the standard International Trade Classification: Revision 2 (SITC Rev. 2), which had been used from 1980 until 1991. The HS-based CCCCS contains over 6000 8-digit commodity subdivisions.

1990, we simply link the price deflator of fixed asset investment, published in *CSY* since its 1993 edition, with the estimated accumulation deflator.

2.2 Hong Kong

Compared with the statistical data of China, those of Hong Kong are more suited for building a demand-oriented econometric model. To reflect the nature of the Hong Kong economy, however, we introduce some special treatment for building the external block of an econometric model for Hong Kong.

2.2.1 Definition of Re-exports

Needless to say, Hong Kong is one of the most trade-dependent economies in the world. In 1997, export and import ratios to GDE were 109.7% and 122.0%, respectively. If we add trade in services, those ratios become 131.6% and 135.4%, respectively.

This feature is a consequence of the role of Hong Kong as an entrepôt which has connected China to the rest of the world. Therefore, a large portion of Hong Kong's exports takes the form of re-exports. They accounted for 85.5% of Hong Kong's total exports of goods, and 93.8% of its GDE in 1997. According to the definition of re-exports set by the United Nations, the re-export value is equal to the original imported value; that is, re-exports have little direct effect on GDE, because they are offset by imports.

However, the definition set by the Hong Kong authority allows a re-export margin around 25% the import value.[9] Thus, the re-exported value can be regarded as the sum of its prior import value and the value added within the territory. RRXM is defined as the re-export margin valued as a percentage of re-exports.[10]

2.2.2 Estimation of the Re-export Margin (RRXM)

The Government of Hong Kong has estimated RRXM in order to calculate the consumption deflator and published the estimates in *Estimate of Gross*

---

[9] This figure, 25% is approximate. For example, RRXM of China origin was estimated at 26.1% in 1993, and 25.6% in 1997. See Figure 2.

[10] For further explanation of RRXM, refer to Census & Statistics Department, "Chapter 5 Technical Notes", in *Gross Domestic Product: Quarterly Estimates and Revised Annual Estimates*, Hong Kong, 1991, pp. 32-34; *ibid.*

Domestic Product (HKGDP), regularly since its 1993 edition. Those data series are disaggregated by broad commodity groups (i.e. consumer goods, capital goods, foodstuffs, fuels, and raw materials and semi-manufactures),[11] and by origin of re-exported goods; China and the rest of the world.

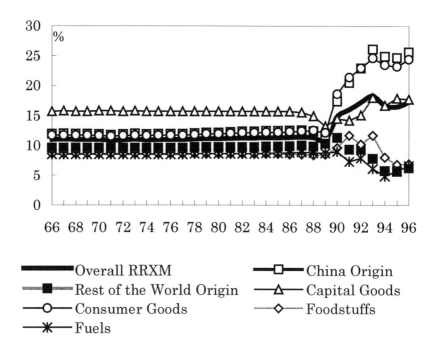

Figure2. Estimates of RRXM

Sources: For 1989 to 1996, Census & Statistics Department, "Analysis of Hong Kong's Retained Imports" Hong Kong Monthly Digest of Statistics, Hong Kong February 1996, pp. F1-F18; Goernment of Hong Kong SAR, *Estimate of Gross DomesticProduct 1961 to 1997.* Hong Kong, 1998, pp. 76-77. Before 1998. for RRXM by commodity group, data provided by C&SD; for overall RRXM and RRXM by origin, author's estimates.

However, we cannot go back to the years before 1989 from published data. We, therefore, need to estimate RRXM for the period between 1966 and

---

[11] Since RRXM for "fuels" and "raw materials and semi-manufactures" are exactly the same figures, the discussion below neglects the latter.

1988, estimating RRXM by broad commodity groups provided by the Census & Statistics Department of Hong Kong (C&SD).[12]

Appendix 1 shows the regression results using the overall RRXM, RRXM originating from China, and RRXM originating from the rest of the world as dependent variables; those by commodity group as explanatory variables. For the RRXM of China origin, regression coefficients for RRXM of foodstuffs and fuels is negative and statistically insignificant. On the other hand, the RRXM of the rest of the world origin shows similar results for RRXM of consumer and capital goods. Those results would imply that a large part of re-exported goods originating from China have been shared by consumer and capital goods. A large part of imported foodstuffs and fuels from China have been consumed within Hong Kong. Re-exported goods originating from China bring about higher RRXM than do those from the rest of the world. Of course, the observed data set is small, only 8 years, and must be interpreted as merely indicative. Figure 2 shows the estimated RRXM series.

2.3 Merchandise Trade Statistics

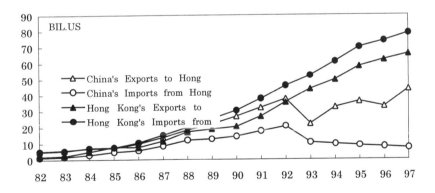

Figure3. Trade between China and Hong Kong

Figure 3 shows four data series; China's exports to Hong Kong, China's imports from Hong Kong, Hong Kong's exports to China, and Hong Kong's imports from China. Every data series is obtained from customs statistics of both economies and expressed in terms of nominal US dollars. Apart from

---

[12] Because those data series are very crude estimates, cautious treatment is called for.

the CIF/FOB factor, by definition, China's exports to Hong Kong must be equal to Hong Kong's imports from China, and China's imports from Hong Kong must be equal to Hong Kong's exports to China. However, we find extraordinary discrepancies between those series after 1993. The cause of those discrepancies has not been explained clearly. We can guess that some portion of China's trade with Hong Kong has been counted as trade with industrial countries, since the beginning of 1993, as a result of a conceivable change in the standard of classification.[13] Based on *Direction of Trade Statistics,* which is compiled by the IMF on the basis of customs statistics of each reporting country/region, Figures 4-1 and 4-2 show the share in China's exports/imports by destination/supplier, respectively. We can see an extraordinary decrease in Hong Kong's share of China's exports, and a corresponding increase in the share of industrial countries.

With respect to the data consistency, we should use the data from Hong Kong's customs statistics to explain the development of trade between China and Hong Kong.

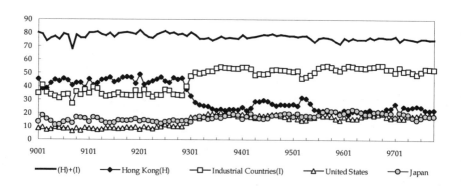

Figure4-1. Share of Main Destination in China's Export (%)

---

[13] According to IMF, *Direction of Trade Statistics Yearbook 1997*, Washington, DC, p. 159 (footnote), "Discrepancies in bilateral trade statistics as reported by China and its trading partners exist, particularly with industrial countries. Trade with these countries is classified by China as trade with Hong Kong if it passes through Hong Kong ports".

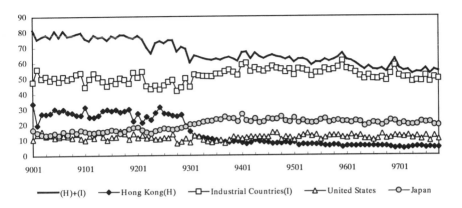

Figure4-2. Share of Main Origin in China's Imports(%)

3. Model Specification

3.1 Background

PAIR China-Hong Kong Link Model (PLM) is a trade link model of PAIR China Model (PCM) and PAIR Hong Kong Model (PHM), which have been developed within the PAIR project.[14]

PCM and PHM are small, demand-oriented macroeconometric models. The main purpose of those two models is to make an economic forecast for a short-term period. Taking the purpose into account, we have assumed that supply-side factors do not have immediate crucial effects on their GDP levels. As for PCM, regarding the fact that China recently has suffered from excess production capacity,[15] we could justify our procedure. For PHM, we believe

---

[14] M. Watanabe, "Macroeconometric Model for Hong Kong: A Simulation Analysis on an Increase of Interest Rates", in M. Toida *et.al.* eds., *Projections for Asian Industrializing Region (III)*, IDE: Tokyo, 1994 (in Japanese).

[15] See, Liang, Y., and Tao, L., "China's Current Economic Situation and Outlook for 1998", in Toida *et al.* eds., *op sit.*, p. 238. In 1995, capacity utilization rates of some industries were

that we are able to treat Hong Kong's economy as a sufficiently developed one; that is, the bottleneck of its economic growth is not on the supply-side, but on the demand-side of the economy.

So far, we have basically used in our forecasting work for an individual economy an econometric model for the respective economy. Growing economic interdependence within East Asian economies, however, has brought us to consider the interactions among economies within econometric models. Such treatment is especially necessary for China and Hong Kong.

Needless to say, trade between China and Hong Kong has been growing considerably after the opening up of the Chinese economy in the late 1970s. According to China's customs statistics, China's exports to Hong Kong amounted to 27.4% of China's total exports in 1978; the share increased to more than 40% by the end of the 1980s. Within the same decade, the share of Hong Kong in China's total imports has expanded rapidly from 0.7% in 1978 to 27.4% in 1991. Similarly, according to Hong Kong's customs statistics, the share of China in Hong Kong's total exports and imports has increased rapidly from 0.5% and 16.7% in 1978, to 34.9% and 37.7% in 1997, respectively.

Thus, it has become more and more important to develop a trade-link model of China and Hong Kong for further investigation into the economic interdependence between them. The rest of this section illustrates the basic structure PLM.

3.2 Trade Link

Appendix 2 highlights the structure of the trade block of PLM. Here, we have 8 variables (in the shaded box) to be determined through behavioral equations (causalities are shown by thin arrows), and 11 through identities (thick arrows), other than GDE of both economies. Circles denote world GDP as an explanatory variable.

We decompose Hong Kong's exports of goods (HK_EXM) into domestic exports (HK_DXM) and re-exports (HK_RXM). Here, we divide both types of exports by destination; China (HK_DXM_C,HK_RXM_C) and the rest of the world (HK_DXM_W, HK_RXM_W). Both types of exports are basically assumed to be determined by demand conditions, price conditions, and inertia effects. We use the real index of world GDP (WD_GDPX), compiled by IMF,

---

lower than 80%. In 1997, capacity utilization rates of most industries were lower than those in 1995.

to denote demand conditions for exports to the rest of the world. Reflecting the movement of Hong Kong's manufacturers to China to utilize cheaper production resources, Hong Kong's domestic exports have peaked out in the late 1980s. To illustrate this phenomenon, a downward time trend (TREND89) is assumed.

On the other hand, Hong Kong's imports (HK_IMM) are distinguished by final demand; imports for domestic use (HK_IMD) and those for re-exports (HK_IMX).[16] We assume that imports for re-exports are determined by demand conditions for Hong Kong's re-exports through the identity with the rate of re-export margins (HK_RRXM). As for retained imports, that is, total imports of goods less those for re-exports, domestic demand (HK_DD) and import price (HK_PIMM) relative to general price (HK_PGDE), measured by the GDE deflator, are regarded as explanatory variables. For Hong Kong's imports from China, an explicit demand variable is replaced by Hong Kong's total imports (HK_IMM). This is derived from the structure of the model. As shown in Appendix 3-1, Hong Kong's total imports are assumed to be determined as the sum of retained imports and imports for re-exports, not as the sum of imports decomposed by origin. Because of data limitations, it is impossible to classify Hong Kong's imports by final demand *and* their origin.

China's exports-imports (CH_EXMC, CH_IMMC) can be divided only by destination/origin; Hong Kong (CH_EXMC_H, CH_IMMC_H) and the rest of the world (CH_EXMC_W, CH_IMMC_W). As mentioned in Section 2.3, regarding the data consistency as important, China's exports/imports to/from Hong Kong are formulated to be determined by Hong Kong's imports/exports from/to China through identities. Following the *IFS*, CIF/FOB factors are assumed to be 10%.

3.3 Domestic Block

3.3.1 China

When we discuss on the economic development of China after its opening to the rest of the world, it is necessary to consider the macroeconomic impact of FDI inflows. We assume that FDI actually used (CH_FDIACN), as determined by FDI agreements (CH_FDIAGN) made within the last two years, FDI actually used in the previous year, and the GDE deflator of China

---

[16] Calculating with the C&SD estimates of RRXM, 65.0% of Hong Kong's imports were re-exported in 1997.

(CH_PGDE) relative to that of the world (WD_PGDP). There is usually some lag between the time FDI is agreed upon and actually used. In addition, in case inflation in China were much higher than the world average, FDI might not be realized because of the consequent higher operating costs in China. FDI is assumed to have positive effects on total investment (CH_IF) through providing funds and reinvestment.[17]

Even though China has transformed from a directly planned economy toward a socialist market economy, the price level cannot stay free from political intervention. In PCM, the price level is assumed to be determined as illustrated in Appendix 3. As we can see, the price index of farm and sideline products (CH_PFSP), money supply (CH_M2), and exchange rate (CH_RATE) are left as policy variables which influence the overall price level in China. Import price (CH_PIMM) is assumed to be determined by export price of the world (WD_PEXM) and that of Hong Kong (HK_PEXM).

3.3.2 Hong Kong Block

Within the private consumption (HK_CP) function, an income effect, real interest rate, and inertia effect are taken into account. We use real GDE as the proxy for real disposable income. The real interest rate is defined as the difference between the best lending rate (HK_HSPR), quoted by the Hong Kong Shanghai Banking Corporation Limited, less the annual percentage change in the private consumption deflator (HK_PCP).

Private investment (HK_IFP) is assumed to be determined by the acceleration principle, wealth effect, and inertia effect. Here, we use an annual average of the Hang Seng Index (HK_HSIDX), the most widely quoted stock price index in Hong Kong, to represent the wealth effect.

---

[17] In the original PCM, the share of capital stock of FDI relative to that of total capital stock in the previous year is introduced in the goods exports function to capture the export-oriented nature of FDI. As for the goods import function, FDI in the current year is introduced to represent the fact that some portion of FDI tends to take the form of imported machinery and/or equipment. In PLM, however, as a result of the decomposition of China's trade by its trading partners, such specification does not prove to be statistically significant so far. We need further investigation on this point.

4. Estimation Results and Simulation Analysis

4.1 Estimation Results

Appendices 4 to 7 show the list of equations in PLM, the list of the data used in estimation, estimation results of behavioral equations, and results of a final test for all endogenous variables, respectively.

Notations used in Appendices above are as follows; LOG denotes the natural logarithm of the variable; DLOG is the first difference of LOG variable; Dxx is a dummy variable which takes 1 for the year 19xx, and 0 for the other years; Dxxyy is a dummy variable, which takes 1 for the years from 19xx to 19yy, and 0 for the other years; TRENDxx denotes a time-trend dummy variable, which takes 0 for the years before 19xx, 1 for the year 19xx, 2 for the next year, and so on; STEPxx is a variant of the dummy variable, which takes 0 for the years before 19xx (excluding 19xx), and 1 for the years after 19xx; @PCH means the annual percentage change of the variable; (-x) denotes the x-term lagged variable; AR(x) is the x-term autoregressive coefficient in simulation error.

We tested the estimated model through dynamic simulation for the period from 1985 to 1996, a period for which all exogenous variables are available. Root mean squared error (RMSE), root mean squared percent error (RMSPE), mean simulation error (MSE), and mean percent error (MSPE) are calculated as follows:

$$RMSE = \sqrt{\frac{1}{T}\sum_{t=1}^{T}(Y_t^s - Y_t^a)^2} \ ,$$

$$RMSPE = 100 * \sqrt{\frac{1}{T}\sum_{t=1}^{T}\left(\frac{Y_t^s - Y_t^a}{Y_t^s}\right)^2} \ ,$$

$$MSE = \frac{1}{T}\sum_{t=1}^{T}(Y_t^s - Y_t^a)^2 \ ,$$

$$MSPE = \frac{1}{T}\sum_{t=1}^{T}\frac{Y_t^s - Y_t^a}{Y_t^a}$$

where Y_t^s is the simulated value of Y_t, Y_t^a is the actual value of Y_t, and T is the number of periods in the simulation $(=12)$[18].

4.2 Simulation Analyses of Exchange Rate Policy

4.2.1 Simulation settings

Using the estimated PLM, we conducted some simulation analyses regarding exchange rate policies of China and Hong Kong, which recently have been drawing attention. The focus of their concern is especially on the effect of possible depreciation of the RMB yuan by the Chinese government. Another concern is the effect of possible amendment of the linked exchange rate system of Hong Kong, which could result in depreciation of the Hong Kong dollar. The East Asian financial crisis, which began in the middle of 1997, has brought about sharp depreciation in Asian currencies, and consequently relative appreciation of RMB yuan and the Hong Kong dollar, which have been fixed to the US dollar, by strict rules in the case of Hong Kong. Note, however, that only an income and price effect on merchandise trade between China and Hong Kong, and a price effect on the FDI inflow to China are taken into account within the model.

We simulated 10 cases as shock simulations. That is, we manipulated the exchange rate of RMB yuan and the Hong Kong dollar for the year 1996, and solved the model for the period from 1985 to 1996. Since PLM was developed for short term forecasts, it is difficult to conduct a dynamic simulation over several years.

Table 2 shows the simulation settings. F1—F3 simulate the impact of depreciation in RMB yuan by 10%—30%, respectively. F4—F6 simulate depreciation of 10%—30% in the Hong Kong dollar. F7 simulates the impact of Hong Kong dollar depreciation on the actual exchange rate of RMB yuan. F8—F10 simulate the same depreciation of both currencies; 10%—30%, simultaneously.

Tables 3 to 6 show the summaries of simulation results, simulated impacts on merchandise trade in US dollar terms in 1990 prices, and impacts on the trade prices in local currencies and US dollar terms, respectively.

---

[18] See, for example, R S Pindyck and D L Rubinfeld, *Econometric Models and Economic Forecasts*, 3rd *edition*, McGraw-Hill: New York, pp. 336-338.

Figures are presented in percentage change compared to the base case, except for net exports of goods and services (in Table 3) and merchandise trade balance (in Table 4) which are indicated by asterisks (*) and shown as percentage differences between simulation results and the base case.

Table 2. Assumptions for Simulation

		RMB/US$	HK$/US$
F	Base Case	8.31420	7.73400
F1	10% depreciation in RMB	9.14562	7.73400
F2	20% depreciation in RMB	9.97704	7.73400
F3	30% depreciation in RMB	10.80846	7.73400
F4	10% depreciation in HK$	8.31420	8.50740
F5	20% depreciation in HK$	8.31420	9.28080
F6	30% depreciation in HK$	8.31420	10.05420
F7	Depreciation in HK$ to the same rate as RMB	8.31420	8.31420
F8	10% depreciation in RMB, and depreciation in HK$ to the same rate as RMB	9.14562	9.14562
F9	20% depreciation in RMB, and depreciation in HK$ to the same rate as RMB	9.97704	9.97704
F10	30% depreciation in RMB, and depreciation in HK$ to the same rate as RMB	10.80846	10.80846

Table 3. Summary of Simulation Results

China	F1	F2	F3	F4	F5	F6	F7	F8	F9	F10
GDE	2.6	5.2	7.9	-0.2	-0.3	-0.4	-0.1	2.2	4.4	6.7
Household Cons.	2.5	5.1	7.8	-0.2	-0.3	-0.4	-0.1	2.1	4.4	6.6
Fixed Assets Inv.	2.2	4.3	6.2	0.4	0.7	1.0	0.3	2.8	5.3	7.6
Exports	13.4	27.3	41.7	-3.0	-5.6	-7.7	-2.3	7.4	17.2	27.2
Imports	10.6	21.5	32.7	-2.2	-4.0	-5.6	-1.7	6.3	14.3	22.4
Net Exports*	0.7	1.5	2.2	-0.2	-0.4	-0.6	-0.2	0.3	0.7	1.2
GDE Deflator	0.0	0.1	0.0	-0.1	-0.2	-0.2	-0.1	-0.1	-0.1	-0.2
Household Cons.	-0.6	-1.2	-1.8	0.0	0.1	0.1	0.0	-0.5	-1.0	-1.6
Investment Price	3.0	5.7	8.2	-0.7	-1.3	-1.8	-0.5	1.8	3.8	5.8
Hong Kong	F1	F2	F3	F4	F5	F6	F7	F8	F9	F10
GDE	0.5	1.1	1.6	5.2	10.0	14.5	4.0	9.8	15.1	20.2
Private Consump.	0.2	0.3	0.5	1.7	3.3	4.6	1.3	3.2	4.8	6.3
Private Investment	0.4	0.9	1.4	4.5	8.6	12.3	3.4	8.3	12.9	17.1
Exports	1.2	2.4	3.6	2.0	3.9	5.7	1.5	4.8	7.9	11.1
Imports	1.0	2.0	3.1	0.6	1.1	1.7	0.4	2.0	3.7	5.4

Net Exports*	*0.3*	*0.6*	*1.0*	*3.1*	*5.7*	*7.9*	*2.4*	*5.5*	*8.2*	*10.5*
GDE Deflator	**-0.4**	**-0.9**	**-1.3**	**-0.2**	**-0.3**	**-0.3**	**-0.2**	**-0.7**	**-1.1**	**-1.5**
Private Consump.	-0.5	-1.0	-1.5	-1.9	-3.5	-4.8	-1.5	-3.7	-5.6	-7.2
Investment Price	-0.2	-0.4	-0.7	4.0	7.7	11.3	3.0	6.8	10.4	13.7

Table 4. Impacts on Merchandise Trade(US dollar term : 1990 prices)

China	F1	F2	F3	F4	F5	F6	F7	F8	F9	F10
Balance of Merchandise Trade*	*0.6*	*1.1*	*1.7*	*0.1*	*0.2*	*0.3*	*0.1*	*0.8*	*1.5*	*2.2*
Total Exp. of Goods	3.3	6.5	9.7	-3.2	-5.8	-8.1	-2.4	-2.4	-2.2	-2.0
to Hong Kong	5.1	10.2	15.1	-7.0	-13.0	-18.1	-5.4	-7.5	-9.3	-10.7
To ROW	1.5	2.9	4.2	0.7	1.3	1.9	0.5	2.7	4.7	6.7
Total Imp. of Goods	0.8	1.8	2.9	-3.3	-6.0	-8.3	-2.5	-5.1	-7.2	-8.9
from HK	3.3	6.8	10.3	-7.4	-13.6	-18.9	-5.7	-9.8	-13.2	-16.0
from ROW	-1.5	-2.8	-3.9	0.5	1.0	1.4	0.4	-0.7	-1.6	-2.4
Hong Kong	**F1**	**F2**	**F3**	**F4**	**F5**	**F6**	**F7**	**F8**	**F9**	**F10**
Balance of Merchandise Trade*	*0.4*	*0.8*	*1.2*	*3.5*	*6.4*	*8.8*	*2.7*	*6.2*	*9.2*	*11.8*
Total Exp. of Goods	1.3	2.7	4.1	-7.2	-13.3	-18.6	-5.5	-11.2	-15.9	-19.9
to China	3.3	6.8	10.3	-7.4	-13.6	-18.9	-5.7	-9.8	-13.2	-16.0
to ROW	0.3	0.6	0.9	-7.1	-13.2	-18.4	-5.4	-11.9	-17.3	-22.0
Domestic Exp.	0.4	0.9	1.3	-7.0	-13.0	-18.1	-5.4	-11.6	-16.8	-21.3
to China	1.4	2.7	4.1	-4.3	-8.1	-11.4	-3.3	-6.2	-8.7	-10.7
to ROW	0.1	0.3	0.4	-7.9	-14.6	-20.3	-6.1	-13.4	-19.6	-24.8
Re-exports	1.5	3.0	4.6	-7.2	-13.4	-18.6	-5.5	-11.1	-15.8	-19.7
to China	3.6	7.3	11.1	-7.8	-14.3	-19.9	-6.0	-10.2	-13.7	-16.6
to ROW	0.3	0.7	1.0	-6.9	-12.9	-18.0	-5.3	-11.6	-16.9	-21.4
Total Imp. of Goods	1.0	2.1	3.2	-8.7	-15.9	-22.0	-6.7	-13.8	-19.7	-24.7
from China	5.1	10.2	15.1	-7.0	-13.0	-18.1	-5.4	-7.5	-9.3	-10.7
from ROW	-1.1	-2.2	-3.1	-9.5	-17.4	-24.0	-7.3	-17.2	-25.3	-32.2
Retained Imp.	0.3	0.6	0.9	-11.2	-20.3	-27.9	-8.6	-18.6	-26.7	-33.5
Imp.for Reexp.	1.5	3.0	4.6	-7.2	-13.4	-18.6	-5.5	-11.1	-15.8	-19.7

Table 5. Impacts on Trade Prices(Local Currency Term)

China	F1	F2	F3	F4	F5	F6	F7	F8	F9	F10
Exports	7.3	14.4	21.3	-1.1	-2.1	-3.0	-0.8	5.2	11.1	16.7
Imports	9.8	19.5	29.2	-2.0	-3.7	-5.3	-1.5	6.0	13.3	20.4
Hong Kong	**F1**	**F2**	**F3**	**F4**	**F5**	**F6**	**F7**	**F8**	**F9**	**F10**
Exports	-0.3	-0.7	-1.0	6.2	12.3	18.1	4.7	10.8	16.6	22.1

	F1	F2	F3	F4	F5	F6	F7	F8	F9	F10
Domestic exports	-0.4	-0.7	-1.1	6.4	12.5	18.5	4.8	11.0	17.0	22.7
Re-exports	-0.4	-0.8	-1.2	7.1	14.0	20.8	5.3	12.3	19.0	25.5
Imports	-0.5	-1.1	-1.6	9.7	19.5	29.1	7.3	17.1	26.7	36.0

Table 6. Impacts on Trade Prices(US Dollar Term)

China	F1	F2	F3	F4	F5	F6	F7	F8	F9	F10
Exports	-2.5	-4.7	-6.7	-1.1	-2.1	-3.0	-0.8	-4.3	-7.4	-10.3
Imports	-0.2	-0.4	-0.6	-2.0	-3.7	-5.3	-1.5	-3.6	-5.6	-7.4
Hong Kong	F1	F2	F3	F4	F5	F6	F7	F8	F9	F10
Exports	-0.3	-0.7	-1.0	-3.4	-6.4	-9.2	-2.6	-6.3	-9.6	-12.6
Domestic exports	-0.4	-0.7	-1.1	-3.3	-6.2	-8.8	-2.5	-6.1	-9.3	-12.2
Re-exports	-0.4	-0.8	-1.2	-2.6	-5.0	-7.1	-2.0	-5.0	-7.7	-10.2
Imports	-0.5	-1.1	-1.6	-0.2	-0.5	-0.7	-0.2	-1.0	-1.8	-2.7

4.2.2 Impacts of Depreciation of RMB Yuan[19]

Depreciation of RMB yuan has positive impacts on both economies through expanding domestic demand and net exports. Although depreciation in RMB yuan has an upward pressure on the investment price (3.0%) through rising import prices in RMB terms (9.8%), the general price level in China, compared to the rest of the world, is lowered. Such a favorable change in relative prices accelerates an FDI inflow to China (19.4%); as a consequence, China's investment in fixed assets is forecast to increase (2.2%).

Depreciation of RMB yuan accelerates not only China's merchandise exports (3.3%), but also imports (0.8%) in US dollar terms, through increasing imports from Hong Kong (3.3%). The reason why imports from Hong Kong increase; whereas those from the rest of the world decrease, is attributable mainly to the different property of the income effect and to a variant of the trade diversion effect. Of course, China's import prices in RMB terms are expected to rise. However, expected increasing ratios of China's import price from Hong Kong in RMB terms, that is, the export prices of Hong Kong in RMB terms (9.6%) are lower than China's overall import price (9.8%). The merchandise trade balance and net exports of goods and services in China are forecast to be improved (0.6 and 0.7 point, respectively).

---

[19] Figures in parentheses in this sub-section are results of simulation F1.

The impacts on the Hong Kong economy are also positive. Decreasing prices of imports from China are expected to have downward pressures on Hong Kong's overall price level, including export prices (–0.3%). Lower price levels accelerate both domestic demand and net exports of Hong Kong (0.3 point) and thus, the GDE level (0.5%).

4.2.3 Impacts of Depreciation of the Hong Kong Dollar[20]

Depreciation of the Hong Kong dollar has positive impacts on Hong Kong's GDE (5.2% in F4) but negative impacts on China's GDE (–0.2%). This asymmetry is attributable to the impact on net exports of both economies. Depreciation of the Hong Kong dollar increases import prices in Hong Kong dollar terms (9.4%), which is expected to result in decreases in Hong Kong's export prices in US dollar terms (–3.4%). Such price changes have positive impacts on Hong Kong's merchandise trade balance in real terms (3.5 points). This results in the acceleration of Hong Kong's GDE.

On the other hand, depreciation of the Hong Kong dollar decreases China's merchandise trade with Hong Kong, accompanying a little improvement in the merchandise trade balance (0.1 point). However, expected deterioration in the balance of trade in services makes net exports of goods and services worse (–0.2%) and decelerates China's GDE.

4.2.4 Impacts of Depreciation in Both Currencies[21]

As explained in the previous two sub-sections, depreciation of each currency has asymmetric impacts on China and Hong Kong. Here, let us consider what will be caused by depreciation in both currencies.

The simulation results show that depreciation in both currencies can have positive impact on GDE levels of both China and Hong Kong (2.2% and 9.8% respectively). As shown above, depreciation of RMB yuan has positive impacts on both economies; whereas depreciation of the Hong Kong dollar has positive impacts on Hong Kong but negative impacts on China. Moreover, the extent of such impacts are expected to become larger in proportion to the depreciation rate of each currency. In order to accelerate both economies, at least, depreciation of the RMB yuan is called for. In case the Hong Kong

---

[20] Figures in parentheses in this sub-section are results of simulation F4.

[21] Figures in parentheses in this sub-section are results of simulation F8.

dollar is depreciated, it is necessary to depreciate the RMB yuan to an extent sufficient to offset the negative impact of Hong Kong dollar depreciation.

Appendix 1. Estimation Results of RRXM

Dependent Variable: LOG (HK_RRXM)
Method: Least Squares : Sample: 1989—1996
Included Observations: 8

Variable	Coefficient	Std. Error	t-Statistic	Prob.
C	−0.05703	0.23341	−0.24433	0.82273
LOG (HK_RRXMCSG)	0.64253	0.03617	17.76186	0.00039
LOG (HK_RRXMCPG)	0.18622	0.08312	2.24026	0.11093
LOG (HK_RRXMFOD)	0.09594	0.02603	3.68512	0.03463
LOG (HK_RRXMOIL)	0.07233	0.03234	2.23636	0.11134
R-squared	0.99779	Mean dependent var		2.75966
Adjusted R-squared	0.99485	S D dependent var		0.16222
S E of regression	0.01164	Akaike info criterion		−5.79990
Sum squared resid	0.00041	Schwarz criterion		−5.75025
Log likelihood	28.19959	F-statistic		339.26975
Durbin-Watson stat	2.78441	Prob (F-statistic)		0.00026

Dependent Variable: LOG(HK_RRXM_C)
Method: Least Squares: Sample (adjusted): 1989—1996
Included Observations: 8 After Adjusting Endpoints

Variable	Coefficient	Std. Error	t-Statistic	Prob.
C	−1.20742	0.21325	−5.66188	0.00239
LOG (HK_RRXMCSG)	0.97543	0.06015	16.21595	0.00002
LOG (HK_RRXMCPG)	0.46743	0.11877	3.93561	0.01101
R-squared	0.99522	Mean dependent var		3.04707
Adjusted R-squared	0.99331	S D dependent var		0.27976
S E of regression	0.02288	Akaike info criterion		−4.43694
Sum squared resid	0.00262	Schwarz criterion		-4.40715
Log likelihood	20.74777	F-statistic		520.68663
Durbin-Watson stat	2.44283	Prob (F-statistic)		0.00000

Dependent Variable: LOG(HK_RRXM_W)
Method: Least Squares: Sample (adjusted): 1989—1996
Included Observations: 8 After Adjusting Endpoints

Variable	Coefficient	Std Error	t-Statistic	Prob.
C	−0.91357	0.29859	−3.05962	0.02811
LOG(HK_RRXMFOD)	0.48113	0.12567	3.82853	0.01227
LOG (HK_RRXMOIL)	0.99959	0.12429	8.04265	0.00048
R-squared	0.95778	Mean dependent var		2.06986
Adjusted R-squared	0.94089	S D dependent var		0.27658

S E of regression	0.06725	Akaike info criterion	−2.28091
Sum of squared resid	0.02261	Schwarz criterion	−2.25112
Log likelihood	12.12365	F-statistic	56.70682
Durbin-Watson stat	1.49765	Prob(F-statistic)	0.00037

Appendix 2. Structure of Trade Block in PCHLM

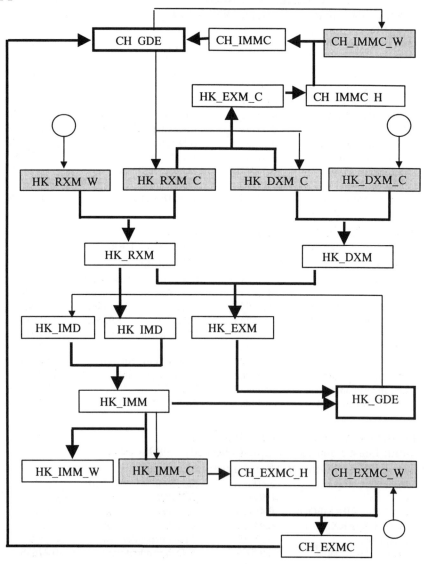

Appendix 3. Price Determination Structure of China Block

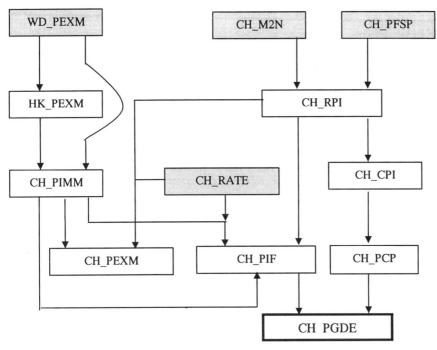

Appendix 4. List of Equation (PLM ver.98.1)

Note: Constants, dummy variables, including time-trend, and autoregressive terms are excluded from this list of equations for simplicity. See Appendix 6 for exact formulation.

[China Block]

$CH\_CP = f[CH\_GDE, CH\_PCP, CH\_INRD]$

$CH\_IF = f[D\{CH\_CREDITN/CH\_PIF\}, CH\_FDI, CH\_INRD, \\ \quad CH\_IF(-1)]$

$CH\_EXMC\_W = f[WD\_GDPX, CH\_PEXM, CH\text{-}EXMC(-1)]$

$CH\_EXM = f[CH\_EXMC]$

$CH\_EXS = f[CH\_EXMC+CH\_IMMC, CH\_EXS(-1)]$

CH_IMMC_W = f[CH_GDE, CH_PIMM*CH_RATE/CH_PGDE, CH_IMMC_W(–1)]
CH_IMM = f[CH_IMMC-CH_IMS]
CH_FDIACN = f[CH_FDIAGN(–1)+CH_FDIAGN(–2),
        CH_PGDE/CH _RATE/WD _PDGP]
CH_CREDITN = f[CH_M2N]
CH_PGDE = f[CH_PCP, CH_PIF]
CH_RPI = f[CH_PFSP, CH_M2N/CH_GDE]
CH_CPI = f[CH_CPI(–1), CH_RPI]
CH_PCP = f[CH_CPI]
CH_PIF = f[CH,RPI, CH_RATE*CH-PIMM]
CH_PEXM = f[CH_RPI, CH_RATE, CH_PIMM, CH_PEXM(–1)]
CH_PIMM = f[WD_PEXM, HK_PEXM/HK_RATE]
CH_GDE ≡ CH_CP+CH_CG+CH_IF+CH_J+CH_SD+CH_X-
        CH_M
CH_GDENPC ≡ 100*CH_GDE*CH_PGDE/CH_RATE/CH_POP
CH_EXMC ≡ CH_EXMC_H+CH_EXMC_W
CH_EXMC_H ≡ HK_IMM_C/1.1/HK_RATE
CH_EX ≡ CH_EXM+CH_EXS
CH_X ≡ CH_EX*CH_RATE/100
CH_IMMC ≡ CH_IMMC_H+CH_IMMC_W
CH_IMMC_H ≡ HK_EXM_C*1.1/HK_RATE
CH_IM ≡ CH_IMM+CH_IMS
CH_M ≡ CH_IM*CH_RATE/100
CH_FDI ≡ 100*CH_FDIACN*CH_RATE/CH_PIF
CH_KIF ≡ (CH_KIF(–1)*(100–CH_RDEP))/100+CH_IF
CH_KFDI ≡ (CH_KFDI(–1)*(100–CH_RDEP))/100+CH_FDI

[Hong Kong Block]

HK_CP = f[HK_GDE, HK_HSPR-@PCH(HK_PCP), HK_CP(–1)]
HK_IFP = f[D(HK_GDE), HK_HSIDX, HK_IFP(–1)]
HK_DXM_C = f[CH_GDE, HK_PDXM/HK_RATE/CH_PIMM,
        HK_DXM,C(–1)]
HK_DXM_W = f[WD_GDP_X, HK_PDXM/HK_RATE/WD/PIMM,
        HK_DXM,W(–1)]
HK_RXM_C = f[CH_GDE, HK_PRXM/HK_RATE/CH_PIMM,
        HK_RXM_C(–1)]
HK_RXM_W = f[WD_GDPX, HK_PRXM/HK_RATE/WD_PGDP]
HK_EXS = f[WD_GDPX, HK_PEXS/HK_RATE/WD_PGDP,
        HK_EXM]
HK_IMM_C = f[HK_IMM, CH_PEXM/WD_PEXM, HK_IMM_C(–1)]

$HK\_IMD = f[HK\_DD, HK\_PIMM/HK\_PGDE]$

$HK\_IMS = f[HK\_GDE, HK\_PIMS/HK\_PEXS, HK\_IMS(-1)]$

$HK\_PGDE = f[HK\_PCP, HK\_PIF, HK\_M2N/HK\_GDE]$

$HK\_PCP = f[HK\_CP/HK\_GDE, HK\_PIMM, HK\_PCP(-1)]$

$HK\_PIF = f[HK\_PIMM, HK\_PIF(-1)]$

$HK\_PDXM = f[HK,PIMM]$

$HK\_PRXM = f[HK\_PIMM, HK\_PRXM(-1)]$

$HK\_PEXM = f[HK\_PDXM, HK\_PRXM]$

$HK\_PEXS = f[HK\_PEXM, HK\_PEXS(-1)]$

$HK\_PIMM/HK\_RATE = f[WD\_PEXM*HK\_IMM\_W/HK\_IMM,$
$\qquad CH\_PEXM*HK\_IMM\_C/HK\_IMM]$

$HK\_PIMS = f[HK\_PIMM, HK\_PIMS(-1)]$

$HK\_GDE \equiv HK\_CP+HK\_CG+HK\_IFP+HK\_IFG+HK\_J+HK\_X-$
$\qquad HK\_M$

$HK\_GDENPC \equiv (10*HK\_GDE*HK\_PGDE)/(HK\_RATE*HK\_POP)$

$HK\_DD \equiv HK\_CP+HK\_CG+HK\_IFP+HK\_IFG+HK\_J$

$HK\_DXM \equiv HK\_DXM\_C+HK\_DXM\_W$

$HK\_RXM \equiv HK\_RXM\_C+HK\_RXM\_W$

$HK\_EXM\_C \equiv HK\_DXM\_C+HK\_RXM\_C$

$HK\_EXM \equiv HK\_DXM+HK\_RXM$

$HK\_X \equiv HK\_EXM+HK\_EXS$

$HK\_IMM\_W \equiv HK\_IMM-HK\_IMM\_C$

$HK\_IMX \equiv HK\_RXM*(100-HK\_RRRXM)/100$

$HK\_IMM \equiv HK\_IMD+HK\_IMX$

$HK\_M \equiv HK\_IMM+HK\_IMS$

Appendix 5-1-1. List of Variables for China

Variable	Description	Unit	Sources & Definitions
CH_CAN	Current Account (BOP: Nominal)	US$M	EXN+EXFN-IMN-IMFN
CH_CG	Public Consumption (1990 Price)	RMB100M	100*CGN/PCG
CH_CGN	Public Consumption (Nominal)	RMB100M	SYC97:2-13
CH_CP	Residents Consumption (1990 Price)	RMB100M	100*CPN/PCP
CH_CPI	Consumer Price Index	1990=100	SYC97:8-1 (Prior to 83, CPI for Urban Area)
CH_CPN	Residents Consumption (Nominal)	RMB100M	SYC97:2-13
CH_CREDIT	Domestic Credit (IFS:32)	RMB100M	IFS: 32
CH_EX	Exports of Goods and Services (BOP: 1990 Pr.)	US$M	EXM+EXS
CH_EXFN	Exports of Factor Services (BOP: Nominal)	US$M	EXIN+EXTN
CH_EXIN	Income: Credit (BOP: Nominal)	US$M	IFS: 78agd
CH_EXM	Exports of Goods (BOP: 1990 Price)	US$M	100*EXMN/PEXM
CH_EXMC	Exports of Goods (Total, FOB: CC)	US$M	100*EXMCN/PEXM
CH_EXMCN	Exports of Goods (Total, FOB: CC)	US$M	CCS, SYC97:16-5

CH_EXMN	Exports of Goods (BOP: Nominal)	US$M	IFS:78aad
CH_EXN	Exports of Goods and Services (BOP: Nominal)	US$M	EXMN+EXSN
CH_EXS	Exports of Services (BOP: 90 Price)	US$M	100*EXSN/PEXM
CH_EXSN	Exports of Services (BOP: Nominal)	US$M	IFS:78add
CH_EXTN	Current Transfer: Credit (BOP: Nominal)	US$M	IFS: 78ajd
CH_FDI	FDI Actually Used (1990 Price)	RMB100M	100*FDIACN*RATE/PIF
CH_FDIACN	FDI Actually Used (Nominal)	US$100M	SYC97:16-13
CH_FDIAGN	FDI Agreed (Nominal)	US$100M	SYC97:16-13
CH_FOREX	Foreign Exchange Reserves	US$M	IFS: 1l.d
CH_GDE	Gross Domestic Expend. (90 Price)	RMB100M	GDEN90*GDPXPY
CH_GDEN	Gross Domestic Expend. (Nominal)	RMB100M	SYC97:2-12
CH_GDPXPY	Real GDP Index	PY=100	SYC97:2-9
CH_IF	Investment in Fixed Assets (90Price)	RMB100M	100*IFN/PIF
CH_IFFUSN	Foreign Investment(Source of Investment)	RMB100M	SYC97:5-3
CH_IM	Imports of Goods and Services (BOP 1990 Pr.)	US$M	IMM+IMS
CH_IMFN	Imports of Factor Services (BOP: Nominal)	US$M	IMIN+IMTN
CH_IMIN	Income: Debit (BOP: Nominal)	US$M	IFS: 78ahd
CH_IMM	Imports of Goods (BOP: 1990 Price)	US$M	100*IMMN/PIMM
CH_IMMC	Imports (Total, CIF: CC)	US$M	100*IMMCN/PIMM
CH_IMMCN	Imports (Total, CIF: CC)	US$M	CCS, SYC97:16-5
CH_IMMN	Imports of Goods (BOP: Nominal)	US$M	IFS:78abd
CH_IMN	Imports of Goods and Services (BOP: Nominal)	US$M	IMMN+IMSN
CH_IMS	Imports of Services (BOP: 90 Price)	US$M	100*IMSN/PIMM
CH_IMSN	Imports of Services (BOP: Nominal)	US$M	IFS:78aed
CH_IMTN	Current Transfer: Debit (BOP: Nominal)	US$M	IFS: 78akd
CH_INRD	Time Deposit Interest Rate (1 Year)	%	SYC97: 17-8
CH_J	Change in Inventories (1990 Price)	RMB100M	100*JN/PIF
CH_JN	Change in Inventories (Nominal)	RMB100M	SYC97:2-13
CH_M2	Money Supply (Nominal)	RMB100M	100*M2N/PGDE
CH_M2N	Money Supply (1990 Price)	RMB100M	MONEY+QMONEY
CH_MONEY	Money	RMB100M	IFS: 34
CH_PCG	Deflator for Public Consumption	1990=100	See text 2.1.3
CH_PCP	Deflator for Residents Consumption	1990=100	See text 2.1.3
CH_PEXM	Deflator for Exports	1990=100	See text 2.1.2
CH_PFSP	Price Index for Overall Farm and Sideline Products Purchase	1990=100	SYC97:8-1
CH_PGDE	Deflator for GDE	1990=100	100*GDEN/GDE
CH_PIF	Deflator for Fixed Asset Investment	1990=100	See text 2.1.4
CH_PIMM	Deflator for Import	1990=100	See text 2.1.2
CH_POP	Population	10T	SYC97:3-1
CH_QMONEY	Quasi-Money	RMB100M	IFS: 35
CH_RATE	Exchange Rate	Yuan/$	IFS: rf
CH_RPI	Retail Price Index	1990=100	SYC97:8-1
CH_SD	Statistical Discrepancy (1990 Price)	RMB100M	GDE-CG-CP-IF-J-(EX-IM)*RATE/100
CH_SDN	Statistical Discrepancy (Nominal)	RMB100M	GDEN-CGN-CPN-IFN-JN-(EXN-IMN)*RATE/100

Appendix 5-1-2. Data Set for China

Year	CH_CA N	CH_CG	CH_CG N	CH_CP	CH_CPI	CH_CP N	CH_CRE DIT	CH_EX	CH_EX FN
1978	NA	686.3	480.0	3471.7	46.2	1759.1	1393.1	16823.7	NA
1979	NA	870.3	614.0	3739.7	47.1	2005.4	1981.1	21151.9	NA
1980	NA	893.1	659.0	4122.4	50.6	2317.1	2422.5	24038.6	NA
1981	NA	950.7	705.0	4502.5	51.8	2604.1	2739.9	28489.6	NA
1982	5674.0	1043.4	770.0	4828.8	52.9	2867.9	3046.7	29396.6	1764.0
1983	4240.0	1137.6	838.0	5262.4	53.9	3182.5	3437.0	30407.4	2169.0
1984	2030.0	1378.9	1020.0	5971.5	55.4	3674.5	4514.5	35036.9	2604.0
1985	-11417.0	1561.7	1184.0	6921.5	60.5	4589.0	5929.5	38699.5	1917.0
1986	-7034.0	1757.4	1367.0	7331.9	64.5	5175.0	7941.8	40462.1	1616.0
1987	300.0	1872.9	1490.0	7884.2	69.2	5961.2	9708.7	47256.6	1416.0
1988	-3802.0	1967.7	1727.0	8605.3	82.2	7633.1	11536.4	52513.6	2072.0
1989	-4317.0	2048.6	2033.0	8690.7	97.0	8523.5	13497.9	52685.5	2424.0
1990	11997.0	2252.0	2252.0	9113.2	100.0	9113.2	16689.2	57374.0	3393.0
1991	13272.0	2790.2	2830.0	10000.6	103.4	10315.9	20026.7	66235.1	4609.0
1992	6401.0	3402.8	3492.3	11422.8	110.0	12459.8	24499.2	76607.8	6801.0
1993	-11609.0	4079.8	4499.7	12490.2	126.2	15682.4	34810.9	86778.4	5680.0
1994	6908.0	4318.0	5986.2	13451.9	156.6	21230.0	43103.7	110328.3	7006.0
1995	1618.0	4049.2	6690.5	14800.3	183.4	27838.9	53333.8	126051.2	7018.0
1996	7243.0	4235.2	7583.0	15988.1	198.6	32588.7	66410.9	142324.6	9686.0
1997	NA	NA	NA	NA	204.2	NA	79502.7	NA	NA

Year	CH_EX IN	CH_EX M	CH_EX MC	CH_EXM CN	CH_EX MN	CH_EX N	CH_EXS N	CH_EXS N	CH_EX TN
1978	236.0	15565.3	16419.6	9955.0	9437.0	10200.0	1258.5	763.0	NA
1979	305.0	19200.6	19138.8	13614.0	13658.0	15046.0	1951.3	1388.0	NA
1980	512.0	21802.1	21362.3	18119.0	18492.0	20389.0	2236.6	1897.0	NA
1981	697.0	25687.3	25663.9	22007.0	22027.0	24430.0	2802.3	2403.0	NA
1982	1092.0	26272.5	27760.0	22321.0	21125.0	23637.0	3124.1	2512.0	672.0
1983	1549.0	27156.3	29148.4	22226.0	20707.0	23186.0	3251.1	2479.0	620.0
1984	2008.0	31350.4	34280.2	26139.0	23905.0	26716.0	3686.5	2811.0	596.0
1985	1478.0	34501.6	37582.3	27350.0	25108.0	28163.0	4198.0	3055.0	439.0
1986	1100.0	35227.8	42320.9	30942.0	25756.0	29583.0	5234.4	3827.0	516.0
1987	1027.0	41958.4	47639.6	39437.0	34734.0	39120.0	5298.3	4386.0	389.0
1988	1504.0	46992.9	54389.7	47516.0	41054.0	45877.0	5520.7	4823.0	568.0
1989	1947.0	47667.3	57944.2	52538.0	43220.0	47770.0	5018.2	4550.0	477.0
1990	3017.0	51519.0	62091.0	62091.0	51519.0	57374.0	5855.0	5855.0	376.0
1991	3719.0	59220.4	72210.5	71843.0	58919.0	65898.0	7014.7	6979.0	890.0
1992	5595.0	67618.0	82559.2	84940.0	69568.0	78817.0	8989.8	9249.0	1206.0
1993	4390.0	75594.9	91666.3	91744.0	75659.0	86852.0	11183.5	11193.0	1290.0
1994	5737.0	94942.8	112017.7	121006.0	102561.0	119181.0	15385.5	16620.0	1269.0
1995	5191.0	109674.2	127369.6	148780.0	128110.0	147240.0	16377.1	19130.0	1827.0
1996	7318.0	125246.0	125236.6	151065.7	151077.0	171678.0	17078.7	20601.0	2368.0
1997	NA	NA	151121.3	182696.6	NA	NA	NA	NA	NA

Year	CH_F DI	CH_FDIA CN	CH_FDIA GN	CH_FOR EX	CH_GD E	CH_GD EN	CH_GDPX PY	CH_IF	CH_IF FUSN
1978	0.0	0.0	NA	1557.0	6498.7	3605.6	111.7	2255.4	NA
1979	4.1	1.3	NA	2154.0	6992.6	4074.0	107.6	2315.4	NA
1980	8.1	2.5	NA	2545.0	7538.0	4551.3	107.8	2848.2	NA
1981	11.2	3.4	NA	5058.0	7930.0	4901.4	105.2	2430.3	36.4
1982	13.8	4.4	NA	11349.0	8651.6	5489.2	109.1	2480.5	60.5
1983	21.1	6.4	17.3	14987.0	9594.6	6076.3	110.9	2869.8	66.6
1984	47.2	12.6	26.5	17366.0	11053.0	7164.4	115.2	3434.6	70.7
1985	68.5	16.6	59.3	12728.0	12545.2	8792.1	113.5	3710.0	91.5
1986	75.1	18.7	28.3	11453.0	13649.2	10132.8	108.8	3596.8	137.3
1987	95.6	23.1	37.1	16305.0	15232.5	11784.7	111.6	4151.6	182.0
1988	125.1	31.9	53.0	18541.0	16953.7	14704.0	111.3	4865.3	275.3
1989	135.8	33.9	56.0	17960.0	17648.8	16466.0	104.1	4613.2	291.1
1990	166.8	34.9	66.0	29586.0	18319.5	18319.5	103.8	4732.0	284.6
1991	212.3	43.7	119.8	43674.0	20004.9	21280.4	109.2	5424.7	318.9
1992	480.8	110.1	581.2	20620.0	22845.6	25863.7	114.2	6587.5	468.7
1993	991.9	275.2	1114.4	22387.0	25929.7	34500.6	113.5	8120.8	954.3
1994	1649.3	337.7	826.8	52914.0	29196.9	47110.9	112.6	9552.5	1769.0
1995	1676.8	375.2	912.8	75377.0	32262.6	59404.9	110.5	10863.4	2295.9
1996	1785.1	417.3	732.8	107039.0	35359.8	68498.2	109.6	12007.5	2747.4
1997	NA	452.6	510.0	142762.0	NA	NA	108.8	NA	NA

Year	CH_IFN	CH_IM	CH_IMF N	CH_IMI N	CH_IM M	CH_IM MC	CH_IM MCN	CH_IM MN	CH_IMN
1978	1073.9	20890.3	NA	0.0	18916.1	18390.9	10890.0	11201.0	12370.0
1979	1151.2	25664.7	NA	624.0	23320.0	22540.4	15670.0	16212.0	17842.0
1980	1318.0	31116.5	NA	612.0	28421.2	25801.9	20017.0	22049.0	24140.0
1981	1253.0	31114.3	NA	821.0	27796.7	29075.1	22015.0	21047.0	23559.0
1982	1493.2	27039.0	827.0	641.0	24143.4	27589.8	19285.0	16876.0	18900.0
1983	1709.0	28736.8	404.0	295.0	25970.1	29678.9	21390.0	18717.0	20711.0
1984	2125.6	37805.0	542.0	388.0	33767.0	38740.7	27410.0	23891.0	26748.0
1985	2641.0	57983.7	742.0	546.0	54392.7	60113.5	42252.0	38231.0	40755.0
1986	3098.0	46655.0	1061.0	924.0	43798.4	53849.3	42904.0	34896.0	37172.0
1987	3742.0	44508.3	1356.0	1191.0	41663.5	49472.0	43216.0	36395.0	38880.0
1988	4624.0	53588.9	1779.0	1630.0	49725.2	59275.8	55275.0	46369.0	49972.0
1989	4339.0	56101.3	1761.0	1665.0	51942.9	62897.2	59140.0	48840.0	52750.0
1990	4732.0	46706.0	2064.0	1962.0	42354.0	53345.0	53345.0	42354.0	46706.0
1991	5940.0	54381.4	2938.0	2879.0	50254.0	63890.1	63791.0	50176.0	54297.0
1992	8317.0	71436.0	5398.0	5347.0	62306.5	78007.9	80610.1	64385.0	73819.0
1993	12980.0	97441.9	5792.0	5674.0	85516.9	102991.6	103950.5	86313.0	98349.0
1994	16856.3	115957.0	7709.0	6775.0	99017.1	120241.9	115692.8	95271.0	111570.0
1995	20300.5	124559.0	17357.0	16965.0	101335.4	121608.2	132078.2	110060.0	135283.0
1996	23336.1	152030.7	19994.0	19755.0	129752.9	136949.6	138837.9	131542.0	154127.0
1997	NA	NA	NA	NA	NA	137859.6	142360.8	NA	NA

Year	CH_RA TE	CH_R PI	CH_S D	CH_SD N
1978	1.6836	48.2	-529.1	1.5
1979	1.5550	49.1	-553.5	-1.6

1980	1.4984	52.1	-866.3	10.2
1981	1.7045	53.3	-574.2	6.2
1982	1.8925	54.3	-157.0	66.1
1983	1.9757	55.2	-180.7	38.3
1984	2.3200	56.7	-274.3	1.4
1985	2.9367	61.7	-628.9	-324.0
1986	3.4528	65.4	112.6	-233.2
1987	3.7221	70.2	672.9	10.9
1988	3.7221	83.1	601.9	-140.1
1989	3.7651	97.9	438.6	-172.3
1990	4.7832	100.0	488.0	488.0
1991	5.3234	102.9	327.0	595.7
1992	5.5146	108.5	378.4	266.5
1993	5.7620	122.8	-5.0	-659.5
1994	8.6187	149.4	518.5	625.3
1995	8.3514	171.5	634.0	984.2
1996	8.3142	182.0	1323.7	1438.2
1997	8.2898	183.4	NA	NA

Appendix 5-2-1. List of Variable for Hong Kong

Variable	Description	Unit	Sources & Definitions
HK_CG	Government Consumption(1990 Price)	MIL HK$	HKGDP/TRN
HK_CGN	Government Consumption (Nominal)	MIL HK$	HKGDP
HK_CIFFOB	CIF/FOB Factor	%	IFS
HK_CP	Private Consumption (1990 Price)	MIL HK$	HKGDP/TRN
HK_CPN	Private Consumption (Nominal)	MIL HK$	HKGDP
HK_DD	Domestic Demand	MIL HK$	CP+CG+IF+J
HK_DDN	Domestic Demand (Nominal)	MIL HK$	CPN+CGN+IFN+JN
HK_DXM	Domestic Exports (1990 Price)	MIL HK$	100*DXMN/PDXM
HK_DXM_C	Domestic Exports to China (1990 Pr)	MIL HK$	100*DXMN_C/PDXM
HK_DXM_W	Domestic Exports to ROW (1990 Pr)	MIL HK$	DXM-DXM_C
HK_DXMN	Domestic Exports (Nominal)	MIL HK$	HKMDS
HK_DXMN_C	Domestic Exports to China (Nominal)	MIL HK$	HKMDS
HK_DXMN_W	Domestic Exports to ROW (Nominal)	MIL HK$	DXMN-DXMN_C
HK_EXM	Total Exports (1990 Price)	MIL HK$	DXM+RXM
HK_EXM_C	Total Exports to China (1990 Price)	MIL HK$	DXM_C+RXM_C
HK_EXM_W	Total Exports to the ROW (1990 Pr.)	MIL HK$	EXM-EXM_C
HK_EXMN	Total Exports (Nominal)	MIL HK$	DXMN+RXMN
HK_EXMN_C	Total Exports to China (Nominal)	MIL HK$	DXMN_C+RXMN_C
HK_EXMN_W	Total Exports to the ROW (Nominal)	MIL HK$	EXMN-EXMN_C
HK_EXS	Exports of Services (1990 Price)	MIL HK$	HKGDP
HK_EXSN	Exports of Services (Nominal)	MIL HK$	HKGDP
HK_GDE	GD Expenditure (1990 Price)	MIL HK$	HKGDP/TRN

HK_GDEN	GD Expenditure (Nominal)	MIL HK$	HKGDP
HK_HSIDX	Hang Seng Index	64/7/31=100	HKMDS
HK_HSPR	HK Shanghai Bank Prime Rate	% per annum	HKMDS
HK_IF	Investment (1990 Price)	MIL HK$	HKGDP/TRN
HK_IFG	Government Investment (1990 Price)	MIL HK$	HKGDP/TRN
HK_IFGN	Government Investment (Nominal)	MIL HK$	HKGDP
HK_IFN	Investment (Nominal)	MIL HK$	HKGDP
HK_IFP	Private Investment (1990 Price)	MIL HK$	HKGDP/TRN
HK_IFPN	Private Investment (Nominal)	MIL HK$	HKGDP
HK_IMD	Imports for Domestic Use (1990 Price)	MIL HK$	IMMC-IMX
HK_IMD_C	Imports for Domestic Use from China (1990 Price)	MIL HK$	IMMC_C-IMX_C
HK_IMD_W	Imports for Domestic Use from the Rest of the World (1990 Price)	MIL HK$	IMD-IMD_C
HK_IMDN	Imports for Domestic Use (Nominal)	MIL HK$	IMMCN-IMXN
HK_IMDN_C	Imports for Domestic Use from China (Nominal)	MIL HK$	IMMCN_C-IMXN_C
HK_IMDN_W	Imp. for Domestic Use from ROW (Nominal)	MIL HK$	IMDN-IMDN_C
HK_IMM	Total Imports (1990 Price)	MIL HK$	100*IMMCN/PIMM
HK_IMM_C	Total Imports from China (1990 Price)	MIL HK$	100*IMMCN_C/PIMM
HK_IMM_W	Total Imports from the Rest of the World (1990 Price)	MIL HK$	IMMC-IMMC_C
HK_IMMN	Total Imports (Nominal)	MIL HK$	HKMDS
HK_IMMN_C	Total Imports from China (Nominal)	MIL HK$	HKMDS
HK_IMMN_W	Total Imp. from the ROW (Nominal)	MIL HK$	IMMCN-IMMCN_C
HK_IMS	Imports of Services (1990 Price)	MIL HK$	HKGDP
HK_IMSN	Imports of Services (Nominal)	MIL HK$	HKGDP
HK_IMX	Imports for Re-exports (90 Price)	MIL HK$	RXM*(100-RRXM)/100
HK_IMX_C	Imports for Re-exports from China (1990 Price)	MIL HK$	RXMO_C*(100-RRXM_C)/100
HK_IMX_W	Imports for Re-exports from the Rest of the World (1990 Price)	MIL HK$	IMX-IMX_C
HK_IMXN	Imports for Re-exports (Nominal)	MIL HK$	RXMN*(100-RRXM)/100
HK_IMXN_C	Imports for Re-exports from China (Nominal)	MIL HK$	RXMON_C*(100-RRXM_C)/100
HK_IMXN_W	Imports for Re-exports from the Rest of the World (Nominal)	MIL HK$	IMXN-IMXN_C
HK_J	Changes in Inventories (90 Price)	MIL HK$	HKGDP/TRN
HK_JN	Changes in Inventories (Nominal)	MIL HK$	HKGDP
HK_M2N	Money Supply (M2)	MIL HK$	HKMDS

HK_PCG	Deflator for Government Consumption	1990=100	HKGDP/TRN
HK_PCP	Deflator for Private Consumption	1990=100	HKGDP/TRN
HK_PDD	Deflator for Domestic Demand	1990=100	100*DDN/DD
HK_PDXM	Deflator for Domestic Exports	1990=100	HKMDS
HK_PEXS	Deflator for Exports of Services	1990=100	HKGDP/TRN
HK_PGDE	Deflator for GDE	1990=100	HKGDP/TRN
HK_PIF	Deflator for Investment	1990=100	HKGDP/TRN
HK_PIFP	Deflator for Private Investment	1990=100	HKGDP/TRN
HK_PIMM	Deflator for Imports of Goods	1990=100	HKGDP/TRN
HK_PIMS	Deflator for Imports of Services	1990=100	HKGDP/TRN
HK_PJ	Deflator for Changes in Inventories	1990=100	HKGDP/TRN
HK_POP	Population	1000	HKMDS
HK_PRXM	Price Deflator for Re-exports	1990=100	HKMDS
HK_RATE	Exch. Rate to US$ (Annual Average)	Eq. to 1$	HKMDS
HK_RRXM	Rate of Re-exports Margin (RRM)	%	See text 2.2.2.
HK_RRXM_C	RRM for China Origin	%	See text 2.2.2.
HK_RRXM_W	RRM for the Rest of the World Origin	%	See text 2.2.2.
HK_RRXMCPG	RRM (Capital Goods)	%	C&SD ESTIMATES
HK_RRXMCSG	RRM (Consumer Goods)	%	C&SD ESTIMATES
HK_RRXMFOD	RRM (Foodstuffs)	%	C&SD ESTIMATES
HK_RRXMOIL	Rate of Re-exports Margin (Fuels)	%	C&SD ESTIMATES
HK_RRXMRAW	RRM(Raw Materials & Semi-Manuf.)	%	C&SD ESTIMATES
HK_RXM	Re-exports (1990 Price)	MIL HK$	100*RXMN/PRXM
HK_RXM_C	Re-exports to China (1990 Price)	MIL HK$	100*RXMN_C/PRXM
HK_RXM_W	Re-exports to the Rest of the World (1990 Price)	MIL HK$	RXM-RXM_C
HK_RXMN	Re-exports (Nominal)	MIL HK$	HKMDS
HK_RXMN_C	Re-exports to China (Nominal)	MIL HK$	HKMDS
HK_RXMN_W	Re-exports to the Rest of the World (Nominal)	MIL HK$	RXMN-RXMN_C
WD_GDPX	World GDP Index (1990 Price)	1990=100	IFS97Y
WD_PEXM	Exp. Price Deflator of the World	1990=100	IFS97Y
WD_PGDP	World GDP Deflator	1990=100	IFS97Y
WD_PIMM	Imports Price Deflator of the World	1990=100	IFS97Y

Appendix 5-2-2. Data Set for Hong Kong

Year	HK_CG	HK_CGN	HK_CIFFOB	HK_CP
1961	5323.8	619.0	110.0	31063.1
1962	5583.5	654.0	110.0	34367.7
1963	6189.5	746.0	110.0	37672.3
1964	6795.4	847.0	110.0	40976.9
1965	7358.1	949.0	110.0	46264.3
1966	8180.5	1070.0	110.0	51882.1
1967	9046.1	1199.0	110.0	52543.0

1968	9565.5	1300.0	110.0	57830.3
1969	10387.9	1412.0	110.0	62787.2
1970	10993.9	1630.0	110.0	69396.4
1971	11253.6	1741.0	110.0	78318.8
1972	11946.1	2078.0	110.0	83936.6
1973	13158.0	2558.0	110.0	95172.2
1974	14370.0	3171.0	110.0	93189.4
1975	15278.9	3493.0	110.0	96494.0
1976	16317.7	4007.0	110.0	103764.1
1977	17832.6	4655.0	110.0	121278.5
1978	19607.2	5436.0	110.0	142758.3
1979	21684.8	6755.0	110.0	156307.1
1980	23329.5	8720.0	110.0	174812.8
1981	28436.9	12226.0	110.0	188031.2
1982	29995.1	14566.0	110.0	197944.9
1983	31813.0	16359.0	110.0	213146.1
1984	33068.2	18056.0	110.0	225373.0
1985	33977.2	19787.0	110.0	234956.3
1986	36184.6	22887.0	110.0	253462.1
1987	37612.9	25722.0	110.0	279237.9
1988	38998.0	30008.0	110.0	302370.0
1989	41032.3	36253.0	110.0	312614.2
1990	43283.0	43283.0	110.0	330459.0
1991	46615.8	51470.0	110.0	358878.5
1992	52805.3	64070.0	110.0	386637.0
1993	53930.6	72620.0	110.0	415717.4
1994	56051.5	83658.0	110.0	443476.0
1995	57869.4	94236.0	110.0	450415.6
1996	60206.7	104385.0	110.0	472225.9
1997	61894.7	114567.0	110.0	506924.1

Year	HK_CPN	HK_DD	HK_DDN	HK_DXM
1961	5596.0	54426.3	8003.0	13778.4
1962	6256.0	64198.9	9381.0	15811.3
1963	6900.0	76482.1	11138.0	17392.4
1964	7611.0	84129.1	12767.0	19877.0
1965	8578.0	94217.0	14396.0	23039.3
1966	9728.0	95434.6	14746.0	26879.1
1967	10403.0	90975.3	14714.0	30493.1
1968	11547.0	94190.8	15594.0	36365.9
1969	13064.0	101120.9	17655.0	42916.3
1970	14904.0	112249.2	21249.0	47207.9
1971	17194.0	128869.8	25430.0	49466.6
1972	19819.0	138808.7	29441.0	52177.1
1973	26457.0	156297.3	38472.0	56920.5
1974	30104.0	155496.5	44699.0	55113.5
1975	31696.0	160277.6	46568.0	55339.4
1976	36080.0	180543.9	56117.0	71376.5
1977	43994.0	210285.5	68085.0	74764.6

1978	54466.0	241026.9	84547.0	82444.4
1979	67172.0	269329.1	110704.0	97126.3
1980	84660.0	306275.5	143136.0	108871.8
1981	101829.0	334067.5	174308.0	117680.9
1982	117902.0	343334.2	192691.0	114744.5
1983	136840.0	354095.5	210494.0	131233.4
1984	156223.0	371452.0	237414.0	153820.9
1985	167483.0	377001.9	246019.0	145463.5
1986	189159.0	409769.0	285987.0	168954.5
1987	219315.0	456333.9	346495.0	208030.9
1988	254682.0	493158.0	414951.0	226778.5
1989	287677.0	499263.1	463597.0	227004.4
1990	330459.0	533246.0	533246.0	225875.0
1991	391098.0	577649.8	624395.0	227004.4
1992	451670.0	631351.6	737735.0	227456.1
1993	514239.0	662091.4	834340.0	217065.9
1994	592665.0	739794.2	998698.0	212096.6
1995	654496.0	792121.7	1123966.0	216388.3
1996	722328.0	819070.5	1212353.0	198092.4
1997	806030.0	887899.9	1378020.0	202158.1

Year	HK_DXM_C	HK_DXM_W	HK_DXMN	HK_DXMN_C
1961	36.9	13741.5	2939.0	7.9
1962	40.4	15770.9	3317.0	8.5
1963	37.6	17354.8	3831.0	8.3
1964	58.4	19818.6	4428.0	13.0
1965	81.2	22958.0	5027.0	17.7
1966	71.6	26807.5	5730.0	15.3
1967	28.3	30464.8	6700.0	6.2
1968	37.3	36328.6	8428.0	8.7
1969	27.7	42888.5	10518.0	6.8
1970	114.7	47093.2	12347.0	30.0
1971	68.4	49398.3	13750.0	19.0
1972	71.9	52105.3	15245.0	21.0
1973	143.2	56777.3	19474.0	49.0
1974	238.1	54875.4	22911.0	99.0
1975	67.8	55271.6	22859.0	28.0
1976	52.5	71324.0	32629.0	24.0
1977	66.2	74698.4	35004.0	31.0
1978	164.0	82280.3	40711.0	81.0
1979	1047.5	96078.8	55912.0	603.0
1980	2563.2	106308.5	68171.0	1605.0
1981	4278.6	113402.3	80423.0	2924.0
1982	5259.6	109484.9	83032.0	3806.0
1983	7822.1	123411.3	104405.0	6223.0
1984	12582.4	141238.5	137936.0	11283.0
1985	17011.2	128452.3	129882.0	15189.0
1986	19774.2	149180.3	153983.0	18022.0
1987	29694.8	178336.1	195254.0	27871.0

1988	39636.0	187142.5	217664.0	38043.0
1989	43832.2	183172.1	224104.0	43272.2
1990	47469.6	178405.4	225875.0	47469.6
1991	53452.4	173552.0	231045.0	54403.9
1992	60194.1	167262.0	234124.0	61958.7
1993	61673.1	155392.7	223027.0	63366.8
1994	58263.3	153833.4	222092.0	61009.0
1995	59366.0	157022.2	231657.0	63555.0
1996	57534.2	140558.2	212160.0	61620.0
1997	61072.0	141086.1	211410.0	63867.0

Year	HK_DXMN_W	HK_EXM	HK_EXM_C	HK_EXM_W
1961	2931.1	19160.4	535.0	18625.3
1962	3308.5	21607.2	457.0	21150.2
1963	3822.7	23602.4	368.5	23233.8
1964	4415.0	26501.0	286.6	26214.4
1965	5009.3	30491.2	348.2	30143.0
1966	5714.7	35987.1	340.0	35647.1
1967	6693.8	40843.1	235.7	40607.4
1968	8419.4	46301.9	204.0	46097.9
1969	10511.2	54508.2	159.5	54348.8
1970	12317.0	59213.8	255.9	58958.0
1971	13731.0	63542.6	245.6	63296.9
1972	15224.0	68323.1	390.6	67932.5
1973	19425.0	77620.5	847.5	76773.0
1974	22812.0	74157.5	764.8	73392.7
1975	22831.0	74383.3	441.9	73941.4
1976	32605.0	95802.4	389.0	95413.4
1977	34973.0	100018.6	515.8	99502.7
1978	40630.0	113080.3	660.8	112419.5
1979	55309.0	136042.2	3603.4	132438.8
1980	66566.0	162277.6	10807.1	151470.5
1981	77499.0	185990.7	17443.4	168547.3
1982	79226.0	180984.3	17195.4	163788.9
1983	98182.0	207823.2	24397.5	183425.7
1984	126653.0	253594.6	46114.3	207480.3
1985	114693.0	269663.2	71310.0	198353.2
1986	135961.0	310542.2	67022.5	243519.6
1987	167383.0	414616.4	97701.4	316915.0
1988	179621.0	527755.8	143342.5	384413.3
1989	180831.8	583871.5	150449.6	433421.9
1990	178405.4	639874.0	158377.5	481496.5
1991	176641.1	750713.1	203579.3	547133.8
1992	172165.3	899376.5	266494.0	632882.5
1993	159660.2	1021051.9	329818.4	691233.5
1994	161083.0	1127034.4	369865.1	757169.3
1995	168102.0	1262563.7	420523.1	842040.7
1996	150540.0	1322927.7	453822.6	869105.0
1997	147543.0	1403997.2	489720.6	914276.6

Appendix 6. Estimation Results of Equations

Dependent Variable: LOG (CH_CP)
Method: Two-Stage Least Squares; Sample (adjusted): 1980—1996
Included observations: 17 after adjusting endpoints
Instruments: CH_INRD D8586 CH_GDE(–1) CH_PFSP

Variable	Coefficient	Std. Error	t-Statistic	Prob.
C	0.235	0.146	1.614	0.133
LOG (CH_GDE)	0.960	0.032	30.315	0.000
LOG (CH_PCP)	–0.093	0.036	–2.591	0.024
LOG (CH_INRD)	–0.052	0.021	–2.430	0.032
D8586	0.028	0.010	2.753	0.018
R-squared	0.999	Mean dependent var		9.013
Adjusted R-squared	0.999	S.D. dependent var		0.421
S.E. of regression	0.012	Sum squared resid		0.002
F-statistic	5174.917	Durbin-Watson stat		2.178
Prob (F-statistic)	0.000			

Dependent Variable: LOG(CH_CPI)
Method: Two-Stage Least Squares; Sample (adjusted): 1979—1996
Included Observations: 18 after adjusting endpoints
Instruments: CH_CPI(–1) CH_PFSP D8992

Variable	Coefficient	Std. Error	t-Statistic	Prob.
C	–0.367	0.013	–28.737	0.000
LOG (CH_CPI(–1))	0.109	0.027	4.078	0.001
LOG (CH_RPI)	0.977	0.027	36.443	0.000
D8992	–0.022	0.003	–7.647	0.000
R-squared	1.000	Mean dependent var		4.418
Adjusted R-squared	1.000	S.D. dependent var		0.466
S.E. of regression	0.005	Sum squared resid		0.00
F-statistic	5384.460	Durbin-Watson stat		2.275
Prob (F-statistic)	0.000			

Dependent Variable: LOG (CH_CREDITN)
Method: Two-Stage Least Squares; Sample (adjusted): 1979—1997
Included Observations: 19 after adjusting endpoints
Convergence achieved after 8 iterations
Instruments: CH_M2N CH_INRD

Variable	Coefficient	Std. Error	t-Statistic	Prob.
C 1.336	0.122	10.913	0.000	
LOG (CH_M2N)	0.870	0.012	69.765	0.000
AR(1)	0.677	0.187	3.557	0.003
R-squared	1.000	Mean dependent var		9.534
Adjusted R-squared	1.000	S.D. dependent var		1.189
S.E. of regression	0.026	Sum squared resid		0.011

F-statistic	16622.010	Durbin-Watson stat	1.825
Prob (F-statistic)	0.000	Inverted AR Roots	0.670

Dependent Variable: LOG (CH_EXM)

Method: Two-Stage Lease Squares; Sample (adjusted): 1981—1996
Included Observations: 16 after adjusting endpoints
Convergence achieved after 7 iterations
Instruments: C D86 Step96 WD_GDPX

Variable	Coefficient	Std. Error	t-Statistic	Prob.
C	–0.11415	1.190	–0.349	0.734
LOG (CH_EXMC)	1.020	0.099	10.299	0.000
D86	–0.076	0.015	–5.025	0.000
STEP96	0.155	0.021	7.523	0.000
R(1)	0.838	0.119	7.067	0.000
R-squared	0.999	Mean dependent var		10.811
Adjusted R-squared	0.999	S.D. dependent var		0.510
S.E. of regression	0.020	Sum squared resid		0.004
F-statistic	2525.127	Durbin-Watson stat		1.968
Prob (F-statistic)	0.000	Inverted AR Roots		0.840

Dependent Variable: LOG (CH_EXMC_W)

Method: Two-Stage Least Squares; Sample (adjusted): 1980—1996
Included Observations: 17 after adjusting endpoints
Instruments; WD_PEXM WD_GDPX CH_EXMC_W(–1) D9495

Variable	Coefficient	Std. Error	t-Statistic	Prob.
C 1.293	0.515	2.513	0.027	
LOG (WD_GDPX)	1.330	0.642	2.072	0.061
LOG (CH_PEXM)	–0.599	0.264	–2.267	0.043
LOG	0.558	0.187	2.982	0.012
D9495	0.229	0.051	4.462	0.001
Adjusted R-squared	0.982	S.D. dependent var		0.430
S.E. of regression	0.058	Sum squared resid		0.041
F-statistic	213.627	Durbin-Watson stat		1.912
Prob (F-statistic)	0.000			

Dependent Variable: LOG (CH_EXS)

Method: Two-Stage Least Squares; Sample (adjusted): 1980—1996
Included Observations: 17 after adjusting endpoints
Instruments: CH_EXS(–1), WD_GDPX, D89, D94

Variable	Coefficient	Std. Error	t-Statistic	Prob.
C	–1.738	0.826	–2.104	0.057
LOG (CH_EXS(–1)	0.580	0.162	3.582	0.004
LOG (CH_EXMC_CH_IMMC)				
	0.471	0.187	2.521	0.027

D89	−0.245	0.059	−4.133	0.001
D94	0.159	0.064	2.475	0.029
R-squared	0.994	Mean dependent var	8.686
Adjusted R-squared	0.992	S.D. dependent var	0.630
S.E. of regression	0.057	Sum squared resid	0.038
F-statistic	484.777	Durbin-Watson stat	1.874
Prob (F-statistic)	0.000		

Dependent Variable: LOG (CH_FDIACN)

Method: Two-Stage Least Squares; Sample (adjusted): 1985—1996
Included Observations: 12 after adjusting endpoints
Instruments: CH_FDIAGN(−1), CH_FDIAGN(−2), WD_PGDP, CH_RATE
D9091, D93

Variable	Coefficient	Std. Error	t-Statistic	Prob.
C	0.729	0.297	2.450	0.044
LOG (CH_FDIAGN(−1) +CH_FDIAGN(−2))				
	0.332	0.111	2.975	0.021
LOG (CH_PGDE/CH_RATE /WD_PGDP)				
	−1.173	0.240	−4.894	0.002
D9091	−0.590	0.171	−3.448	0.011
D930.413	0.164	2.514	0.040	
R-squared	0.991	Mean dependent var	4.275
Adjusted R-squared	0.986	S.D. dependent var	1.259
S.E. of regression	0.152	Sum squared resid	0.161
F-statistic	188.486	Durbin-Watson stat	2.228
Prob (F-statistic)	0.000		

Dependent Variable: LOG (CH_IF)

Method: Two-Stage Least Squares; Sample (adjusted): 1979—1996
Included Observations: 18 after adjusting endpoints

Variable	Coefficient	Std. Error	t-Statistic	Prob.
C	3.641	0.719	5.066	0.000
DLOG (CH_CREDITN/CH_PIF)				
	0.351	0.161	2.176	0.050
LOG (CH_FDI)	0.179	0.028	6.504	0.000
LOG (CH_INRD)	−0.236	0.080	−2.951	0.012
LOG (CH_IF(−1))	0.524	0.100	5.216	0.000
D80	0.183	0.059	3.075	0.010
R-squared	0.993	Mean dependent var	8.433
Adjusted R-squared	0.991	S.D. dependent var	0.520
S.E. of regression	0.050	Akaike info criterion	−2.893
Sum squared resid	0.030	Schwarz criterion	−2.596
Log likelihood	32.035	F-statistic	365.035
Durbin-Watson stat	1.955	Prob (F-statistic)	0.000

Dependent Variable: LOG (CH_IMM)
Method: Two-Stage Least Squares; Sample (adjusted): 1979—1996
Included Observations: 18 after adjusting endpoints
Instruments: CH_GDE(–1) WD_PEXM TREND93

Variable	Coefficient	Std. Error	t-Statistic	Prob.
C	8480.093	1938.397	4.375	0.001
CH_IMMC-CH_IMS	0.733	0.040	18.168	0.000
TREND93	8379.072	972.399	8.617	0.000
R-squared	0.993	Mean dependent var		54193.210
Adjusted R-squared	0.992	S.D. dependent var		30548.440
S.E. of regression	2658.372	Sum squared resid		1.060E+08
F-statistic	1087.807	Durbin-Watson stat		2.072
Prob (F-statistic)	0.000			

Dependent Variable: LOG (CH_IMMC_W)
Method: Two-Stage Least Squares
Sample (adjusted): 1979—1996
Included Observations: 18 after adjusting endpoints
Instruments: CH_RATE CH_PFSP CH_IMMC_W(–1) WD_PEXM CH_GDE(–1) D85 D90 D9394

Variable	Coefficient	Std. Error	t-Statistic	Prob.
C	0.703	0.930	0.756	0.466
LOG (CH_GDE)	0.526	0.114	4.601	0.001
LOG(CH_PIMM*CH_RATE/CH_PGDE)	–0.311	0.140	–2.229	0.048
LOG (CH_IMMC_W(–1))	0.490	0.099	4.934	0.000
D85	0.408	0.072	5.696	0.000
D90	–0.246	0.079	–3.115	0.010
D9394	0.161	0.059	2.751	0.019
R-squared	0.978	Mean dependent var		10.542
Adjusted R-squared	0.966	S.D. dependent var		0.373
S.E. of regression	0.069	Sum squared resid		0.052
F-statistic	80.591	Durbin-Watson stat		2.620
Prob (F-statistic)	0.000			

Dependent Variable: CH_IMS
Method: Two-Stage Least Squares; Sample (adjusted): 1979—1996
Included Observations: 18 after adjusting endpoints
Instruments: CH_IMS(–1) CH_GDE(–1) D9495

Variable	Coefficient	Std. Error	t-Statistic	Prob.
C	–909.522	864.665	–1.052	0.311
CH_GDE	0.167	0.076	2.193	0.046
CH_IMS(–1)	0.767	0.113	6.807	0.000
D9495	4792.391	1179.095	4.064	0.001

R-squared	0.971	Mean dependent var	7074.861
Adjusted R-squared	0.964	S.D. dependent var	6862.679
S.E. of regression	1297.480	Sum squared resid	2.357E+07
F-statistic	153.498	Durbin-Watson stat	1.845
Prob (F-statistic)	0.000		

Dependent Variable: LOG (CH_PCP)

Method: Two-Stage Least Squares; Sample (adjusted): 1978—1996
Included Observations: 19 after adjusting endpoints
Instruments: CH_PFSP D8993

Variable	Coefficient	Std. Error	t-Statistic	Prob.
C	0.378	0.025	14.920	0.000
LOG (CH_CPI)	0.931	0.006	158.574	0.000
D8993	−0.059	0.006	−9.640	0.000
R-squared	0.999	Mean dependent var		4.449
Adjusted R-squared	0.999	S.D. dependent var		0.431
S.E. of regression	0.011	Sum squared resid		0.002
F-statistic	13983.470	Durbin-Watson stat		2.273
Prob (F-statistic)	0.000			

Dependent Variable: LOG (CH_PEXM)

Method: Two-Stage Least Squares; Sample (adjusted): 1979—1996
Included Observations: 18 after adjusting endpoints
Instruments: CH_RATE CH_PEXM(−1) CH_PFSP WD_PEXM D8889 D93

Variable	Coefficient	Std. Error	t-Statistic	Prob.
C	−0.563	0.506	−1.112	0.290
LOG (CH_RPI)	0.379	0.102	3.730	0.003
LOG (CH_RATE)	−0.222	0.060	−3.676	0.004
LOG (CH_PIMM)	0.569	0.119	4.762	0.001
LOG (CH_PEXM(−1))	0.256	0.101	2.538	0.028
D8889	−0.083	0.025	−3.290	0.007
D93	−0.079	0.033	−2.412	0.035
R-squared	0.978	Mean dependent var		4.492
Adjusted R-squared	0.967	S.D. dependent var		0.165
S.E. of regression	0.030	Sum squared resid		0.010
F-statistic	83.173	Durbin-Watson stat		2.310
Prob (F-statistic)	0.000			

Dependent Variable: CH_PGDE

Method: Two-Stage Least Squares; Sample (adjusted): 1980—1996
Included Observations: 17 after adjusting endpoints
Instruments: CH_PFSP CH_PGDE(−1) CH_RATE WD_PEXM

Variable	Coefficient	Std. Error	t-Statistic	Prob.
C	7.937	2.592	3.062	0.010
CH_PCP	0.744	0.060	12.468	0.000
CH_PIF	0.178	0.058	3.081	0.010

AR(1)	1.269	0.296	4.279	0.001
AR(2)	−0.672	0.304	−2.210	0.047
R-squared	0.999	Mean dependent var		100.432
Adjusted R-squared	0.999	S.D. dependent var		43.423
S.E. of regression	1.559	Sum squared resid		9.174
F-statistic	3086.220	Durbin-Watson stat		1.822
Prob (F-statistic)	0.000			
Inverted AR Roots	.63 −52I	.63+.52i		

Dependent Variable: LOG (CH_PIF)

Method: Two-Stage Least Squares; Sample (adjusted): 1978-1996
Included Observations: 19 after adjusting endpoints
Instruments: CH_PFSP CH_RATE WD_PEXM D8991 D93

Variable	Coefficient	Std. Error	t-Statistic	Prob.
C	0.499	0.127	3.937	0.002
LOG (CH_RPI)	0.467	0.099	4.734	0.000
LOG (CH_RATE*CH_PIMM)				
	0.345	0.059	5.826	0.000
D8081	−0.121	0.030	−4.052	0.001
D8991	−0.143	0.023	−6.115	0.000
D93	0.132	0.038	3.507	0.004
R-squared	0.996	Mean dependent var		4.477
Adjusted R-squared	0.995	S.D. dependent var		0.478
S.E. of regression	0.035	Sum squared resid		0.016
F-statistic	660.579	Durbin-Watson stat		1.841
Prob (F-statistic)	0.000			

Dependent Variable: LOG (CH_PIMM)

Method: Two-Stage Least Squares; Sample (adjusted): 1979—1996
Included Observations: 18 after adjusting endpoints
Instruments: WD_PEXM, HK_RATE, HK_REXM(−1), CH_PIMM(−1),
    D8082, D94, STEP96

Variable	Coefficient	Std. Error	t-Statistic	Prob.
C	−0.536	0.191	−2.802	0.016
LOG (WD_PEXM)	0.803	0.154	5.204	0.000
LOG (HK_PEXM/HK_RATE)	0.568	0.275	2.063	0.061
D8082	−0.096	0.015	−6.590	0.000
D94	−0.062	0.025	−2.457	0.030
STEP96	−0.114	0.025	−4.528	0.001
R-squared	0.987	Mean dependent var		4.457
Adjusted R-squared	0.982	S.D. dependent var		0.162
S.E. of regression	0.022	Sum squared resid		0.006
F-statistic	181.795	Durbin-Watson stat		1.560
Prob (F-statistic)	0.000			

Dependent Variable: LOG (CH_RPI)
Method: Two-Stage Least Squares; Sample (adjusted): 1979—1996
Included Observations: 18 after adjusting endpoints
Convergence achieved after 3 iterations
Instruments: CH_PFSP CH_GDE(–1) D8687

Variable	Coefficient	Std. Error	t-Statistic	Prob.
C	2.360	0.337	6.994	0.000
LOG (CH_PFSP)	0.498	0.071	7.020	0.000
LOG (CH_M2N/CH_GDE)	0.266	0.045	5.901	0.000
D8687	–0.048	0.019	–2.456	0.029
AR(1)	0.381	0.092	4.157	0.001
R-squared	0.998	Mean dependent var		4.418
Adjusted R-squared	0.998	S.D. dependent var		0.432
S.E. of regression	0.022	Sum squared resid		0.006
F-statistic	1704.181	Durbin-Watson stat		2.009
Prob (F-statistic)	0.000	Inverted AR Roots		0.380

Dependent Variable: LOG (HK_CP)
Method: Two-Stage Least Squares; Sample (adjusted): 1966—1997
Included Observations: 32 after adjusting endpoints
Instruments: HK_CP(–1) HK_HSPR HK_GDE(–1) HK_PCP(–1) D67 D7476

Variable	Coefficient	Std. Error	t-Statistic	Prob.
C	–0.084	0.337	–0.250	0.804
LOG (HK_GDE)	0.336	0.183	.833	0.078
LOG (HK_HSPR-@PCH(HK_PCP))	–0.030	0.016	–1.918	0.066
LOG (HK_CP(–1))	0.665	0.168	3.968	0.001
D67	–0.086	0.024	–3.551	0.002
D7476	–0.065	0.014	–4.721	0.000
R-squared	0.999	Mean dependent var		12.066
Adjusted R-squared	0.999	S.D. dependent var		0.723
S.E. of regression	0.020	Sum squared resid		0.010
F-statistic	8168.525	Durbin-Watson stat		1.678
Prob (F-statistic)	0.000			

Dependent Variable: LOG (HK_DXM_C)
Method: Two-Stage Least Squares; Sample (adjusted): 1979—1996
Included Observations: 18 after adjusting endpoints
Instruments: HK_DXM_C(–1) HK_RATE CH_PIMM(–1) CH_GDE(–1),
           HK_PDXM(–1), D8485, D95

Variable	Coefficient	Std. Error	t-Statistic	Prob.
C	–4.949	1.447	–3.420	0.005
LOG (CH_GDE)	0.299	0.101	2.955	0.012
LOG (HK_PDXM/HK_RATE/CH_PIMM)				

	−3.736	0.902	−4.142	0.001
LOG (HK_DXM_C(−1))	0.490	0.052	9.334	0.000
D8485	0.438	0.116	3.770	0.003
D95	−0.241	0.098	−2.452	0.030
R-squared	0.997	Mean dependent var		9.887
Adjusted R-squared	0.996	S.D. dependent var		1.262
S.E. of regression	0.079	Sum squared resid		0.076
F-statistic	856.863	Durbin-Watson stat		2.204
Prob (F-statistic)	0.000			

Dependent Variable: LOG (HK_DXM_W)

Method: Two-Stage Least Squares; Sample (adjusted): 1968—1996
Included Observations: 29 after adjusting endpoints
Instruments: WD_GDPX   HK_DXM_W(−1)   HK_RATE   WD_PIMM
HK_PDXM(−1) D7475 D85 TREND89

Variable	Coefficient	Std. Error	t-Statistic	Prob.
C	1.455	0.270	5.389	0.000
LOG (WD_GDPX)	1.449	0.304	4.758	0.000
LOG (HK_PDXM/HK_RATE/WD_PIMM)				
	−0.377	0.151	−2.497	0.021
LOG (HK_DXM_W(−1))	0.277	0.143	1.933	0.066
D7475	−0.165	0.031	−5.251	0.000
D85	−0.112	0.044	−2.544	0.019
TREND89	−0.073	0.012	−6.144	0.000
R-squared	0.995	Mean dependent var		11.513
Adjusted R-squared	0.994	S.D. dependent var		0.521
S.E. of regression	0.040	Sum squared resid		0.035
F-statistic	788.500	Durbin-Watson stat		1.804
Prob (F-statistic)	0.000			

Dependent Variable: LOG (HK_EXS)

Method: Two-Stage Least Squares; Sample (adjusted): 1968—1996
Included Observations: 29 after adjusting endpoints
Instruments: WD_GDPX HK_RATE WD_PGDP D7475 D8788 HK_PEXS
    HK_EXM(−1)

Variable	Coefficient	Std. Error	t-Statistic	Prob.
C	4.243	0.168	25.224	0.000
LOG (WD_GDPX)	1.148	0.168	6.933	0.000
LOG (HK_PEXS/HK_RATE/WD_PGDP)				
	−0.145	0.047	−3.068	0.005
LOG (HK_EXM)	0.152	0.069	2.189	0.039
D7475	−0.062	0.017	−3.716	0.001
D8788	0.084	0.017	5.051	0.000
R-squared	0.999	Mean dependent var		11.293

Adjusted R-squared	0.999	S.D. dependent var	0.593
S.E. of regression	0.021	Sum squared resid	0.010
F-statistic	4436.422	Durbin-Watson stat	2.351
Prob (F-statistic)	0.000		

Dependent Variable: LOG (HK_IFP)

Method: Two-Stage Least Squares; Sample (adjusted): 1967—1997
Included Observations: 31 after adjusting endpoints
Instruments: D(HK_GDE(–1) HK_HSIDX HK_IFP(–1) D7374 D93

Variable	Coefficient	Std. Error	t-Statistic	Prob.
C	1.801	1.002	1.798	0.084
DLOG (HK_GDE)	0.860	0.415	2.074	0.049
LOG (HK_IFP(–1))	0.756	0.125	6.062	0.000
LOG (HK_HSIDX)	0.135	0.059	2.274	0.032
D7374	–0.104	0.050	–2.078	0.048
D93	–0.139	0.062	–2.251	0.033
R-squared	0.995	Mean dependent var		11.245
Adjusted R-squared	0.994	S.D. dependent var		0.717
S.E. of regression	0.057	Sum squared resid		0.082
F-statistic	907.942	Durbin-Watson stat		1.642
Prob (F-statistic)	0.000			

Dependent Variable: LOG (HK_IMD)

Method: Two-Stage Least Squares; Sample (adjusted): 1972—1996
Included Observations: 25 after adjusting endpoints
Instruments: HK_IMD(–1) HK_DD(–1) WD_PEXM

Variable	Coefficient	Std. Error	t-Statistic	Prob.
C	–0.781	0.399	–1.958	0.063
LOG (HK_DD)	1.012	0.031	33.167	0.000
LOG (HK_PIMM/HK_PGDE)				
	–0.481	0.074	–6.478	0.000
R-squared	0.997	Mean dependent var		12.097
Adjusted R-squared	0.997	S.D. dependent var		0.652
S.E. of regression	0.038	Sum squared resid		0.032
F-statistic	3437.083	Durbin-Watson stat		1.738
Prob (F-statistic)	0.000			

Dependent Variable: LOG (HK_IMM_C)

Method: Two-Stage Least Squares; Sample (adjusted): 1978—1996
Included Observations: 19 after adjusting endpoints
Instruments: HK_IMM_C WD_PEXM HK_RATE CH_PFSP

Variable	Coefficient	Std. Error	t-Statistic	Prob.
C	–2.498	1.665	–1.501	0.154

LOG (HK_IMM)	0.582	0.344	1.692	0.111
LOG (CH_PEXM/WD_PEXM)				
	−1.770	0.585	−3.028	0.009
LOG (HK_IMM_C(−1))	0.579	0.243	2.385	0.031
R-squared	0.999	Mean dependent var		11.732
Adjusted R-squared	0.998	S.D. dependent var		1.034
S.E. of regression	0.040	Sum squared resid		0.024
F-statistic	3880.287	Durbin-Watson stat		2.338
Prob (F-statistic)	0.000			

Dependent Variable: LOG (HK_IMS)

Method: Two-Stage Least Squares; Sample (adjusted): 1964—1997
Included Observations: 34 after adjusting endpoints
Instruments: HK_IMS(−1) HK_GDE(−1) HK_PIMS(−1) HK_PEXM(−1)
   D74, D79

Variable	Coefficient	Std. Error	t-Statistic	Prob.
C	−2.153	0.602	−3.577	0.001
LOG (HK_GDE)	0.656	0.183	3.592	0.001
LOG (HK_PIMS_HK_PEXS)				
	−0.679	0.335	−2.027	0.052
LOG (HK_IMS(−1))	0.426	0.179	2.373	0.025
D74	−0.090	0.030	−2.988	0.006
D79	0.074	0.034	2.186	0.037
R-squared	0.999	Mean dependent var		10.275
Adjusted R-squared	0.999	S.D. dependent var		1.069
S.E. of regression	0.028	Sum squared resid		0.022
F-statistic	9476.772	Durbin-Watson stat		2.097
Prob (F-statistic)	0.000			

Dependent Variable: LOG (HK_PCP)

Method: Two-Stage Least Squares; Sample (adjusted): 1968—1996
Included Observations: 29 after adjusting endpoints
Instruments: HK_PCP(−1) WD_PEXM HK_RATE HK_CP(−1) HK_GDE(−1) D7374 D76 D85

Variable	Coefficient	Std. Error	t-Statistic	Prob.
C	0.732	0.350	2.093	0.048
LOG (HK_PIMM)	0.208	0.057	3.637	0.002
LOG (HK_CP/HK_GDE)	1.135	0.462	2.455	0.023
LOG (HK_PCP(−1))	0.783	0.066	11.836	0.000
D7374	0.097	0.023	4.181	0.000
D76	0.105	0.052	2.004	0.058
D85	−0.080	0.032	−2.485	0.021
R-squared	0.998	Mean dependent var		4.008
Adjusted R-squared	0.998	S.D. dependent var		0.646
S.E. of regression	0.029	Sum squared resid		0.019

F-statistic	2222.925	Durbin-Watson stat	2.218
Prob (F-statistic)	0.000		

Dependent Variable: LOG (HK_PDXM)
Method: Two-Stage Least Squares: Sample (adjusted): 1967—1996
Included Observations: 30 after adjusting endpoints
Convergence achieved after 23 iterations
Instruments: WD_PEXM HK_PIF(–1)

Variable	Coefficient	Std. Error	t-Statistic	Prob.
C	1.687	0.154	10.987	0.000
LOG (HK_PIMM)	0.664	0.025	27.043	0.000
AR(1)	0.940	0.017	53.972	0.000
R-squared	0.999	Mean dependent var		4.090
Adjusted R-squared	0.999	S.D. dependent var		0.547
S.E. of regression	0.017	Sum squared resid		0.008
F-statistic	14126.560	Durbin-Watson stat		1.977
Prob (F-statistic)	0.000	Inverted AR Roots		0.940

Dependent Variable: LOG (HK_PEXM)
Method: Two-Stage Least Squares; Sample (adjusted): 1967—1996
Included Observations: 30 after adjusting endpoints
Convergence achieved after 10 iterations
Instruments: WD_PEXM HK_PDXM(–1) HK_PRXM(–1)

Variable	Coefficient	Std. Error	t-Statistic	Prob.
C	0.211	0.085	2.479	0.020
LOG (HK_PDXM)	0.757	0.045	16.698	0.000
LOG (HK_PRXM)	0.200	0.040	4.986	0.000
AR(1)	0.955	0.036	26.588	0.000
R-squared	1.000	Mean dependent var		4.068
Adjusted R-squared	1.000	S.D. dependent var		0.552
S.E. of regression	0.004	Sum squared resid		0.000
F-statistic	187561.873	Durbin-Watson stat		1.703
Prob (F-statistic)	0.000	Inverted AR Roots		0.960

Dependent Variable: LOG (HK_PEXS)
Method: Two-Stage Least Squares; Sample (adjusted): 1967—1996
Included Observations: 30 after adjusting endpoints
Instruments: WD_PEXM HK_PEXS(–1) D7374 D7980 D8586

Variable	Coefficient	Std. Error	t-Statistic	Prob.
C	–0.127	0.041	–3.093	0.005
LOG (HK_PEXM)	0.143	0.029	4.987	0.000
LOG (HK_PEXS(–1))	0.899	0.021	43.509	0.000
D7374	0.078	0.011	7.383	0.000

D7980	0.056	0.011	5.189	0.000
D8586	−0.059	0.011	−5.483	0.000
R-squared	1.000	Mean dependent var	3.844
Adjusted R-squared	1.000	S.D. dependent var	0.752
S.E. of regression	0.013	Sum squared resid	0.004
F-statistic	18267.240	Durbin-Watson stat	1.731
Prob (F-statistic)	0.000		

Dependent Variable: LOG (HK_PGDE)

Method: Two-Stage Least Squares; Sample (adjusted): 1967—1996
Included Observations: 30 after adjusting endpoints
Instruments: HK_M2N D74 WD_PEXM HK_ GDE(−1) HK_RATE D85

Variable	Coefficient	Std. Error	t-Statistic	Prob.
C	0.071	0.157	0.452	0.655
LOG (HK_PCP)	0.660	0.066	10.035	0.000
LOG (HK_PIF)	0.321	0.036	8.903	0.000
LOG (HK_M2N/HK_GDE)	0.037	0.017	2.191	0.038
D74	−0.047	0.013	−3.565	0.002
D85	0.037	0.014	2.666	0.014
R-squared	1.000	Mean dependent var	3.877
Adjusted R-squared	1.000	S.D. dependent var	0.749
S.E. of regression	0.013	Sum squared resid	0.004
F-statistic	20501.450	Durbin-Watson stat	1.776
Prob (F-statistic)	0.000		

Dependent Variable: LOG (HK_PIF)

Method: Two-Stage Least Squares; Sample (adjusted): 1967—1996
Included Observations: 30 after adjusting endpoints
Instruments: HK_PIF(−1) WD_PEXM D7071 D79 D8385

Variable	Coefficient	Std. Error	t-Statistic	Prob.
C	−0.651	0.215	−3.035	0.006
LOG (HK_PIMM)	0.418	0.124	3.362	0.003
LOG (HK_PIF(−1))	0.740	0.080	9.237	0.000
D7071	0.156	0.041	3.811	0.001
D79	0.133	0.054	2.486	0.020
D8385	−0.144	0.039	−3.704	0.001
R-squared	0.997	Mean dependent var	3.758
Adjusted R-squared	0.996	S.D. dependent var	0.837
S.E. of regression	0.050	Sum squared resid	0.061
F-statistic	1567.560	Durbin-Watson stat	1.734
Prob (F-statistic)	0.000		

Dependent Variable: LOG (HK_PIMM/HK-RATE)
Method: Two-Stage Least Squares; Sample (adjusted): 1979—1996
Included Observations: 18 after adjusting endpoints
Convergence achieved after 6 iterations
Instruments: HK_PIMM(−1) HK_RATE WD_PEXM D83

Variable	Coefficient	Std. Error	t-Statistic	Prob.
C	0.351	0.340	1.032	0.321
LOG (WD_PEXM*HK_IMM_W/HK_IMM)				
	0.371	0.094	3.970	0.002
LOG (CH_PEXM*HK_IMMC/HK_IMM)				
	0.187	0.028	6.706	0.000
D83	−0.041	0.013	−3.081	0.009
AR(1)	0.575	0.260	2.208	0.046
R-squared	0.982	Mean dependent var		2.491
Adjusted R-squared	0.976	S.D. dependent var		0.097
S.E. of regression	0.015	Sum squared resid		0.003
F-statistic	174.099	Durbin-Watson stat		2.193
Prob (F-statistic)	0.000	Inverted AR Roots		0.580

Dependent Variable: LOG (HK_PIMS)
Method: Two-Stage Least Squares; Sample (adjusted): 1967—1996
Included Observations: 30 after adjusting endpoints
Instruments: WD_PEXM HK_PIMS(−1) D8388

Variable	Coefficient	Std. Error	t-Statistic	Prob.
C	−0.001	0.031	−0.042	0.967
LOG (HK_PIMM)	0.347	0.087	4.002	0.001
LOG (HK_PIMS(−1))	0.667	0.084	7.943	0.000
D74	0.075	0.029	2.639	0.014
D8388	−0.066	0.014	−4.625	0.000
R-squared	0.999	Mean dependent var		4.056
Adjusted R-squared	0.999	S.D. dependent var		0.563
S.E. of regression	0.020	Sum squared resid		0.010
F-statistic	5622.240	Durbin-Watson stat		1.240
Prob (F-statistic)	0.000			

Dependent Variable: LOG (HK_PRXM)
Method: Two-Stage Least Squares; Sample (adjusted): 1968—1996
Included Observations: 29 after adjusting endpoints
Instruments: WD_PEXM HK_PRXM(−1) D73 D7477 STEP95

Variable	Coefficient	Std. Error	t-Statistic	Prob.
C	−0.046	0.032	−1.429	0.166
LOG (HK_PIMM)	0.738	0.077	9.635	0.000
LOG (HK_PRXM(−1))	0.274	0.073	3.772	0.001
D73	0.053	0.017	3.083	0.005

D7477	−0.045	0.009	−5.015	0.000
STEP95	−0.021	0.011	−1.805	0.084
R-squared	0.999	Mean dependent var	4.051
Adjusted R-squared	0.999	S.D. dependent var	0.560
S.E. of regression	0.015	Sum squared resid	0.005
F-statistic	7857.884	Durbin-Watson stat	2.015
Prob (F-statistic)	0.000		

Dependent Variable: LOG (HK_RXM_C)

Method: Two-Stage Least Squares; Sample (adjusted): 1979—1996
Included Observations: 18 after adjusting endpoints
Instruments:HK_RXM_C(−1) HK_RATE WD_RATE
WD_PEXM CH_GDE(−1) CH_RATE CH_PIMM(−1) D8485 D9194

Variable	Coefficient	Std. Error	t-Statistic	Prob.
C	−9.664	1.599	−6.043	0.000
LOG (CH_GDE)	1.196	0.173	6.917	0.000
LOG (HK_PRXM/HK_RATE/CH_PIMM)				
	−2.395	0.742	−3.229	0.007
LOG (HK_RXM_C(−1))	0.405	0.051	7.998	0.000
D8485	0.540	0.111	4.879	0.000
D9194	0.187	0.071	2.641	0.022
R-squared	0.996	Mean dependent var	11.022
Adjusted R-squared	0.995	S.D. dependent var	1.455
S.E. of regression	0.106	Sum squared resid	0.136
F-statistic	623.417	Durbin-Watson stat	2.006
Prob (F-statistic)	0.000		

Dependent Variable: LOG (HK_RXM_W)

Method: Two-Stage Least Squares; Sample (adjusted): 1967—1996
Included Observations: 30 after adjusting endpoints
Instruments: WD_GDPX HK_RATE WD_PGDP D7374 D8386 TREND93

Variable	Coefficient	Std. Error	t-Statistic	Prob.
C	−1.037	0.474	−2.188	0.039
LOG (WD_GDPX)	2.582	0.121	21.255	0.000
LOG (HK_PRXM/HK_RATE/WD_PGDP)				
	−0.872	0.049	−17.953	0.000
D7374	0.188	0.058	3.243	0.004
D8386	−0.283	0.041	−6.931	0.000
TREND93	−0.084	0.020	−4.222	0.000
R-squared	0.998	Mean dependent var	11.086
Adjusted R-squared	0.997	S.D. dependent var	1.423
S.E. of regression	0.073	Sum squared resid	0.127
F-statistic	2212.158	Durbin-Watson stat	1.598
Prob (F-statistic)	0.000		

Appendix 7. Final Test (1985—1996)

Variables	RMSE	RMSPE	MSE	MPE
CH_CP	590.09	5.6	−119.5	0.3
CH_CPI	2.6	2.5	0.6	0.0
CH_CREDITN	749.5	3.5	−75.6	−1.8
CH_EX	4153.9	5.3	−252.7	1.2
CH_EXM	3835.7	5.4	−199.1	1.2
CH_EXMC	3560.9	4.3	−760.5	0.0
CH_EXMC_H	1699.6	4.1	−710.2	−1.0
CH_EXMC_W	2029.8	4.8	−50.2	0.7
CH_EXS	506.8	6.5	−53.6	1.0
CH_FDI	116.0	15.6	−6.2	1.8
CH_FDIACN	23.1	12.8	−0.5	1.6
CH_GDE	1208.8	5.3	−274.6	0.2
CH_GDENPC	22.5	5.3	−3.1	0.8
CH_IF	348.3	6.8	9.5	1.1
CH_IM	4733.7	6.5	−192.8	1.1
CH_IMM	4688.5	6.7	−1213.2	−1.2
CH_IMMC	3662.0	4.8	−488.2	−0.3
CH_IMMC_H	2590.8	9.8	197.1	−0.7
CH_IMMC_W	2056.9	4.1	−685.3	−0.6
CH_IMS	2090.4	52.9	1020.4	34.2
CH_KFDI	380.4	13.8	221.6	11.1
CH_KIF	329.5	1.1	144.7	0.6
CH_M	989.8	15.4	−783.3	−13.4
CH_PCP	2.7	2.5	0.7	0.1
CH_PEXM	3.0	2.9	1.5	1.2
CH_KFDI	3.0	3.3	0.6	0.6
CH_PIF	4.3	3.7	0.8	0.1
CH_PIMM	2.3	2.2	1.2	1.0
H_RPI	2.6	2.5	0.4	−0.1
CH_X	1568.9	15.7	−1047.0	−13.7
Variables	RMSE	RMSPE	MSE	MPE
HK_CP	6409.1	1.7	−165.8	0.1
HK_DD	9638.0	1.6	1582.8	0.5
HK_DXM	13954.4	6.5	−12134.1	−5.6
HK_DXM_C	8367.6	18.2	−7524.4	−16.3
HK_DXM_W	6705.5	4.0	−4609.7	−2.7
HK_EXM	22043.6	3.6	−1359.2	−0.8
HK_EXM_C	18298.2	9.8	1357.4	−0.7

HK_EXS	2659.1	1.9	−90.2	−0.4
HK_GDE	17926.0	2.7	−11143.3	−1.7
HK_GDENPC	772.7	6.2	462.6	4.1
HK_IFP	4471.3	3.4	1740.4	1.6
HK_IMD	11689.4	4.3	7740.3	2.2
HK_IMM	25481.2	3.8	16609.2	1.8
HK_IMM_C	14479.4	4.1	−6033.9	−1.0
HK_IMM_W	32967.3	6.5	22643.6	3.4
HK_IMS	6957.9	7.2	−5103.6	−5.6
HK_IMX	21168.7	4.9	8868.9	1.2
HK_M	21907.4	2.9	11505.6	0.9
HK_PCP	9.2	9.3	8.8	8.4
HK_PDXM	4.1	4.0	3.7	3.7
HK_PEXM	3.0	3.0	2.6	2.6
HK_PEXS	1.9	1.7	−0.8	−0.8
HK_PGDE	6.6	7.3	5.8	5.9
HK_PIF	5.3	5.1	0.1	1.0
HK_PIMM	1.6	1.7	0.0	−0.1
HK_PIMS	4.5	4.1	1.6	1.9
HK_PRXM	1.7	1.8	0.1	0.2
HK_RXM	25077.5	4.9	10774.9	1.2
HK_RXM_C	19583.7	11.7	8881.8	4.0
HK_RXM_W	14168.1	5.5	1893.0	0.1
HK_X	23410.2	3.1	−1449.5	−0.7

4   CHINA'S ECONOMETRIC MODEL FOR PROJECT PAIR

Youcai Liang

The State Information Center, Beijing

1. Introduction

In constructing an econometric model of China, special features of the Chinese economy should be taken into consideration. Before 1979 the Chinese economic system was a highly centralized planned economy, characterized by centralized decision-making, few independent managerial rights of enterprises, and an insignificant role of market, in the whole process of resource allocation, production and distribution. As a result, the economy suffered from a lack of vigor and vitality, and the economic development of China was not satisfactory in that period. After 1979, however, China has begun to transform the centralized planned economy into a socialist market economy, and to implement restructuring reforms and policies of opening to the outside world. Since then, changes in the economic structure have given tremendous impetus to the development of the country.

To model the Chinese economy, therefore, we must divide the development after 1949 into two different periods, *before* 1979 and *after* 1979. The Chinese economy has been increasingly open and growing more rapidly in the second period than in the first one, and remarkable changes have taken place in the economy. The economic structure and institutions have changed not only substantially but also frequently. Consequently, we face many difficulties in building a Chinese econometric model, because even the definition of some statistical data changed in different periods. In consideration of the statistical degrees of freedom, a longer time series is obviously preferred, but it cannot be guaranteed only with the data from 1979 to a recent year to have stable and correct estimates for the parameters. We have made a compromise that the stochastic behavior equations are estimated from annual data over the period of 1970 ~1992.

The shortage of natural resources, infrastructure and funds has imposed restrictions on Chinese economic development. Therefore, most of China's econometric models are supply-oriented. Agriculture is still one of the most important sectors in China's national economy, and the labor force in this sector is the most important part of the total labor force. The impact of the agricultural sector on the whole economy comes in two ways. On one hand, agricultural output determines, to a certain extent, the level of aggregate supply. On the other hand, agricultural output influences, to a great extent, the level and structure of aggregate demand. Therefore, most Chinese economic models include agriculture as a separate sector.

The supply-oriented models seem to give a good description of the Chinese economy in the period before 1988. After 1988, however, some new problems arose in the economy. Supply capacities of most sectors grew faster than demands. Since 1989, the sluggish market and weak demand for some manufactured products led to the result that outputs of some manufacturing sectors are not determined by their productive capacities any longer but by the demand for their products. Broadly speaking, however, it may be said that China's Gross Domestic Product is determined by productive capacity. The shortages of energy, raw materials and transportation facilities have been the bottlenecks of the economy, however, which restrict economic development. At the same time, demand is becoming an important factor pulling up the growth of the Chinese economy. For instance, in the past few years, the expansion of consumption directly promoted light industrial development, and the change in fixed investment induced the fluctuation of heavy industrial output. By the same token, weak demand in 1989 and 1990 caused a very slow growth of the economy. According to the requirement of project PAIR, this model is a demand-oriented model.

2. Data

In dealing with the data, we have annual series for population, labor force, output of agriculture, industry, transportation and telecommunication, commerce and construction, capital stocks for agriculture, industry, commerce, transportation and telecommunication and construction, GDP and its main components, foreign trade, major price indices, public finance, per capita cash income for households, and so on. We have no suitable data for the wage rate of each sector, no data for private and public consumption of services, and a price index of fixed investment. Some data follow the MPS accounting system. Therefore, the data have to be adjusted, because we want to construct a Chinese model under the SNA accounting system. Some data, which we could not get from the *Statistical Yearbook of China*, are estimated.

We assume that the identity of GDP at current prices holds. Then we have:

$$\text{GDPC} = \text{CIC} + \text{CSC} + \text{GDIC} + \text{FDIC} + (\text{XXCD} - \text{MMCD}) * \text{EXR} \qquad (1)$$

    GDPC: Gross domestic product at current prices,
    CIC :   Private consumption at current prices,
    CSC :   Public consumption at current prices,
    GDIC :   Gross fixed investment at current prices,
    FDIC :   Change in stocks at current prices,
    XXCD: Exports of goods and services at current US dollars,
    MMCD: Imports of goods and services at current US dollars,
    EXR :   Exchange rate (RMB Yuan/US dollar).

The data for GDPC are available from the *Statistical Yearbook of China* only for the period 1978~1992. The time series data of GDPC in the period 1970~1977 are estimated. The gross fixed investment (GDIC) and change in stocks (FDIC) in the MPS accounting system have the same meaning as those in the SNA accounting system. They are also available from the *Statistical Yearbook of China*. For foreign trade,

$$\text{XXCD} = \text{XX1CD} + \text{XX2CD} \qquad (2)$$

    XXCD: Exports of goods and services at current US dollars,
    XX1CD: Exports of goods at current US dollars,
    XX2CD: Exports of services at current US dollars.

$$\text{MMCD} = \text{MM1CD} + \text{MM2CD} \qquad (3)$$

    MMCD: Imports of goods and services at current US dollars,
    MM1CD: Imports of goods at current US dollars,
    MM2CD: Imports of services at current US dollars.

The time series data of XX1CD, XX2CD, MM1CD, MM2CD and exchange rate (EXR) are available from the *Statistical Yearbook of China*. The data for public consumption of goods at current prices (CS1C) are available from the *Statistical Yearbook of China*. The data for public consumption of services (CS2C) are estimated in the light of the information from the *Statistical Yearbook of China* and the input-output tables (1985, 1987 and 1990).

Private consumption (CIC) is classified in two parts, private consumption of goods (CI1C) and services (CI2C). The former (CI1C) is further divided into rural household consumption of goods (CRI1) and urban household consumption of goods (CUI1). Considering China's situation, we divide rural household consumption of goods (CRI1) into consumption of self-produced goods (CFSSC) and consumption of purchased goods (CFNSSC). Therefore, we have

$$
\begin{aligned}
CIC &= CI1C + CI2C \\
&= CRI1C + CUI1C + CI2C \\
&= CFSSC + CFNSSC + CUI1C + CI2C
\end{aligned} \tag{4}
$$

    CFSSC: Rural household consumption of self-produced goods at current prices,

    CFNSSC: Rural household consumption of purchased goods at current prices,

    CUI1C: Urban household consumption of goods at current prices,

    CRI1C: Rural Household consumption of goods at current prices,

    C12C: Private consumption of services at current prices.

From the *Statistical Yearbook of China*, we have data for CFSSC, CFN-SSC, CRI1C, CUI1C. The remaining problem is how to estimate the time series data for private consumption of services at current prices (CI2C). From (1) and (4), we have the following formula,

$$
CI2C = GDPC - (GDIC+FDIC + CSC + CI1C)- (XXCD–MMCD) * EXR \tag{5}
$$

The data for each variable on the right hand side are available from the *Statistical Yearbook of China*, or calculated and estimated. Therefore, from (5) we can calculate CI2C. Clearly, the data of CI2C include the statistical discrepancy.

Similarly, we assume the identity of GDP at constant prices holds. Then we have,

$$
GDP90 = CI+CS+GDI90+FDI90+((XXCD–MMCD)*EXR/PGDP)*100 \tag{6}
$$

    GDP90:   Gross domestic product at 1990 prices,

    CI: Private consumption of goods and services at 1990 prices,

    CS: Public consumption of goods and services at 1990 prices,

    GDI90:   Gross investment in fixed assets at 1990 prices,

    FDI90:   Change in stocks at 1990 prices,

    PGDP: GDP deflator (1990 = 100).

By definition,

$$
GDP90 = (GDPC/PGDP) * 100 \tag{7}
$$

$$
CI = (CIC/CPI) * 100 \tag{8}
$$

$$
CS = (CSC/PCS) * 100 \tag{9}
$$

$$
GDI90 = (GDIC/PGDI) * 100 \tag{10}
$$

$$\text{FDI90} = (\text{FGDIC/PGDP}) * 100 \tag{11}$$

CPI: Price index of private consumption (1990 = 100),
PCS: Price index of public consumption (1990 = 100),
PGDI: Price index of fixed investments (1990 = 100).

We have calculated the time series data for PGDP, CPI and PCS in the light of the information from the *Statistical Yearbook of China*. Then we calculated the data of GDP90, CI, CS and FDI90. We have no information for directly calculating PGDI. But from (6) and (10), we get the following formula:

$$\text{PGDI} = (\text{GDIC/(((GDP90}-(\text{CI+CS+FDI90} + ((\text{XXCD}-\text{MMCD}) * \text{EXR/PGDP}) * 100))/100)) \tag{12}$$

From (12), we calculate time series data for PDGI, which include the statistical discrepancy. Then, we calculate the data for GDI90.

The data of per capita cash income for rural and urban inhabitants are available from the "Special Survey on Households" in the *Statistical Yearbook of China*. The data are multiplied by the population of rural and urban inhabitants respectively to get cash income data for the rural and urban households.

3. Structure of the Model

The revised version of the model consists of 53 equations, of which 36 are stochastic and 17 are identities. It contains 75 variables (excluding dummy variables), of which 53 are endogenous and 22 exogenous. This model includes 5 blocks. They are domestic demand, production and gross domestic product, fiscal and private cash income, price index and foreign trade blocks.

3.1 Private Consumption Expenditures

In China, about 80 percent of population live in rural areas. Generally speaking, the income level of rural households is much lower than that of urban households, and the living standard of rural households is also much lower than that of urban households. Therefore rural households and urban households have different consumption patterns. As we know, rural household consumption on goods is further divided into two parts: rural household consumption of self-produced goods and purchased goods. The former are assumed to be dependent on real value added in agriculture, and the latter on real disposable cash income, the interest rate on savings deposits and the previous year's consumption of purchased goods. The function for urban household consumption of goods has the same form as that of rural household consumption of purchased goods. Real disposable cash income, interest rate on savings deposits and the previous year's consumption of goods are explanatory variables

$$CUI1 = a0 + a1 * (MIUI/RPI) + a2 * IRSD + a3 * CUI1(-1) \qquad (13)$$

    CUI1:   Urban household consumption of goods (real),
    MIUI: Urban household disposable cash income (nominal),
    RPI: Retail price index,
    IRSD: Interest rate on savings deposits,
    CUI(-1): CUI1 in the previous year.

The combined variable MIUI/RPI represents urban household cash income corrected for changes in prices, i.e., real disposable income. It is clear that the parameter a2 is minus. That means that the higher the interest rate is, the more savings deposits are, and the lower consumption would be. Lagged one year's consumption is used to represent general habit formation of consumers. We also assume that people spend on consumption, to some extent, the amount that they spent in the previous year, but are willing to revise their expenditures in the light of the real income level this year. Some dummy variables are introduced into the private consumption equations, accounting for the impacts of policy adjustments and economic fluctuations.

3.2 Investment Function

In developed economies, gross fixed investment is usually classified as private fixed investment and government investment. The former is further divided into private investment in building and in machinery and equipment. In China, there are no such detailed data for fixed investment. China's gross fixed investment is classified only as domestic gross fixed investment and foreign direct investment. The latter is determined exogenously. In the model, domestic gross fixed investment is assumed to be a function of real gross domestic product, real fixed investment credit provided by the state, and the fixed investment deflator.

$$logGDI90 = a1 * logGDP90 + a2 * log((FECC+GDLC)/PGDI)$$
$$+ a3 * logPGDI \qquad (14)$$

    GDI90:   Real gross fixed investment (at 1990 prices),
    GDP90: Real gross domestic product (at 1990 prices),

FECC: Fiscal allocation of fixed investment at current prices,
GDLC: Loan on fixed investment at current prices,
PGDI: Price index of fixed investment.

Since the economic reform, the State government has gradually changed the fiscal funds allocated for fixed investment (FECC) into fixed investment loans (GDLC). The proportion of fixed investment loans in total credits for fixed investment is getting bigger and bigger, and the ratio of allocated funds to total credits getting smaller and smaller. The two variables FECC and GDLC have the same role. The combined variable ((FECC+GDLC)/PGDI) represents the real fixed investment credit provided by the State and banks. At the beginning, we introduced a real interest rate in the equation, but it was positively related to the dependent variable. In China, for local governments and the state-owned enterprises, the most important thing is how to get the allocated fiscal funds and fixed investment loans from the central government and banks. They do not consider whether the interest rate is high or low. This is a very important feature of decision making for the local governments and state-owned enterprises. The price index of fixed investment (PGDI) is negatively related to the dependent variable, indicating that the higher the price for fixed investment is, the lower is fixed investment.

3.3 Production Functions

China's agriculture includes 5 sectors, *i.e.*, crop planting, husbandry, fisheries, forestry and sideline occupations. If we could set up a production function for each sub-sector separately, then total agricultural output is determined by an identity. That might be more suitable. But we want to keep the model as small as possible; so that only a highly aggregate agricultural production function of the Cobb-Douglas form is included in our model.

$$\log GVA90 = a0 + a1 * \log LFA + a2 * \log KA(-1)$$
$$+ a3 * \log (MIRI/PGDI) + a4 * \log (DAREA/PAREA) \qquad (15)$$

GVA90:   Gross output value of agriculture at 1990 prices,
LFA: Labor force in agriculture,
KA(−1):   Capital stock of agriculture in the previous year at constant prices,
MIRI: Rural household cash income at current prices,
PGDI: Price index of gross fixed investment,
DAREA: Crop areas affected by natural disaster,
PAREA: Sown areas.

The combined variable (MIRI/PGDI) is farmer real disposable cash income, representing farmers' capacity to invest in agricultural intermediate input. The ratio of crop areas affected by natural disaster to total sown areas is an explanatory variable, reflecting an impact of natural disaster on agricultural gross output. The equation of value added in agriculture is a regression estimate of the gross output value of agriculture.

Light industrial gross output is determined by the demand for its products. It is a linear function of household consumption of purchased goods and the exports of manufactured goods. The heavy industrial production function takes the simple linear form.

$$GVHI90 = a0 + a1 * GDI90 + a2 * GVHI90(-1)$$
$$+ a3 * (XX5990) * EXR \qquad (16)$$

GVHI90: Gross output value of heavy industry at 1990 prices,
GDI90: Gross domestic fixed investment at 1990 prices,
GVHI90(−1): GVHI90 in the previous year,
XX5990: Exports of manufactured goods at constant US dollars,
EXR: Exchange rate (RMB yuan/US dollar).

It is assumed that gross fixed investment and exports of manufactured goods increase the demand for heavy industry output.

3.4 Export and Import Functions

Total exports consist of two parts, i.e., exports of goods and services.

$$XXD = XX1D + XX2D \qquad (17)$$

XXD: Total exports of goods and services at constant US dollars,
XX1D: Exports of goods at constant US dollars,
XX2D: Exports of services at constant US dollars.

Exports of goods (XX1D) are a function of world imports of goods and a relative price. It takes a logarithmic form,

$$Log\ XX1D = a0 + a1 * log\ WM90 + a2 * log\ (PWX90/(PXX90/EXR)) \qquad (18)$$

WM90: World imports of goods at constant US dollars,
PWX90: General price index of world exports of goods,
PXX90: Chinese general exports price index,
EXR: Exchange rate (RMB yuan/US dollar).

It is assumed that the exports of goods (XX1D) are determined basically by demand. The variable WM90 is a proxy for demand. Here, the supply of goods exports are assumed to be perfectly elastic. The combined variable

PWX90/(PXX90/EXR) represents the relative price of general world exports to the Chinese general export price. It should be positively related to the dependent variable XX1D. The lower PXX90 is, the higher exports would be. It is clear that the exchange rate plays an important role in determining exports. The higher the exchange rate is, the lower the export price is, and thus the more exports would be. The service export equation is an identity.

$$XX2D = (XX2CD/(PXX90/100)) \tag{19}$$

The variable XX2CD is service exports at current US dollars, and is determined exogenously. The equation of manufactured goods exports has the same form as that of total goods exports. But world exports and the relative price of manufactured goods are explanatory variables.

In the model, total imports are classified as imports of goods and services. The equation of import demand for goods is written as,

$$MM1D = a1*(CONS + GDI90) + a2*(XXCD/(PMM90)) + a3*((PMM90*EXR)/PGDP) \tag{20}$$

MM1D:	Imports of goods at constant US dollars,
CONS:	Total consumption demand at constant prices,
GDI90:	Gross domestic fixed investment at constant prices,
PMM90:	General import price index,
PGDP:	Gross domestic product deflator,
EXR:	Exchange rate (RMB yuan/US dollar),
XXCD:	Total exports at current US dollars.

The combined variable (CONS+GDI90) represents total domestic demand, and the combined variable ((PMM90*EXR)/PGDP) is a relative price, *i.e.*, the ratio of the general import price to the gross domestic product deflator. China is a developing country, and experiences a shortage of foreign exchange. Foreign currency available plays a key role in determining imports. The combined variable XXCD /PMM90 is a proxy for foreign exchange available. During the period of our sample observations, imports and the exchange rate are strictly controlled by the central government. It is difficult to determine import demand endogenously. We introduce some dummy variables to reflect the impacts of policy changes on imports. Imports of services is a function of imports of goods. The import equation of manufactured goods has the same form as that of total goods, but the demand variable is gross fixed investment.

3.5 The Price Index Equations

In the model, there are 13 price index equations, including 4 import and export price index equations. The purchasing prices of farm and sideline products are generally determined by the State government. Therefore, the price index equation of agricultural gross output has the form as follows:

$$PIA = a0 + a1 * PIA(-1) + a2 * PIPFS \tag{21}$$

PIA: Price index of agricultural gross output,
PIA(-1):   PIA in the previous year,
PIPFS: Price index of farm and sideline products for the State.

PIA(-1) represents an effect of the agricultural gross output price in the previous year on this year's price. The price index for value added in agriculture is a function of the price index of agricultural gross output.

At the beginning, it is assumed the price index of light industrial gross output is a function of the price index of agricultural gross output and wage rate within light industry. But the wage rate is negatively related to the dependent variable. Finally, the price index of light industrial gross output (PLI) is a function of the price index of agricultural gross output and lagged (by one year) dependent variable.

$$PLI = a1 * PLI(-1) + a2 * PIA \tag{22}$$

PLI: Price index of light industrial gross output,
PLI(-1):   PLI in the previous year,
PLA: Price index of agricultural gross output,

The price index of heavy industrial gross output has the following form:

$$PHI = a0 + a1 * PHI(-1) + a2 * (WAGE/LHI) \tag{23}$$

PHI: Price index of heavy industrial gross output
PHI(-1):   PHI in the previous year,
WAGE: Wages in the sector of heavy industry,
LHI: Labor force in the heavy industrial sector.

Similarly, PHI(-1) is introduced into the equation to explain an effect of the price of heavy industrial gross output and the import price index for manufactured goods. At the same time, we introduce the growth rate of gross fixed investment at current prices ((GDIC/GDIC(-1)-1) * 100) to catch the effect of gross fixed investment demand on price.

$$PGDI = a1 * PHI + a2 * (PMM59*EXR) + a3 * (GDIC/GDIC(-1)-1) * 100 \tag{24}$$

PGDI: Price index of gross fixed investment,
PHI: Price index of heavy industrial gross output,
PMM59:   Import price index of manufactured goods,
EXR: Exchange rate (RMB yuan/US dollar),
GDIC: Gross fixed investment (nominal),
GDIC(-1): GDIC in the previous year.

As we explained in Section 2, the time series data of PGDI include statistical discrepancy, so we introduce one more dummy variables in the equation. The equation for the retail price index of social commodities is as follows,

$$RPI = a0 + a1 * PLI + s2 * PIA + a4 * (M0/GDP90) \qquad (25)$$

    RPI: Retail price index,
    PLI: Price index of light industrial gross output,
    PIA: Price index of agricultural gross output,
    M0:   Currency in circulation (nominal),
    GDP90: Gross domestic product (real).

The variable PLI represents the cost of light industrial products, and the variable PIA stands for the cost of agricultural products. The combined variable (M0/GDP90) is to set up a linkage between the general retail price and currency in circulation. M1 is better than M0, so that we have used M1 instead of M0 in our new model.

The price index of private consumption (CPI) is a simple linear function of the retail price index (RPI) and CPI(−1). The public consumption price index is a linear function of the retail price index (RPI) in logarithmic form. The gross domestic product deflator is linked directly with consumer price index and gross fixed investment price index.

$$PGDP = a0 + a1 * PGDI + a2 * CPI \qquad (26)$$

    PGDP: Gross domestic product deflator,
    PGDI: Price index of gross fixed investment,
    CPI: Price index of private consumption.

At present, China's trade share in the world market is very small. In general, the export prices of China should be basically determined by the world market prices. They are also influenced by domestic prices and the exchange rate. The export price of manufactured goods (PXX59) is a linear function of the world general export price of manufactured goods in logarithmic form.

$$\log PXX59 = a1 * \log PWX59 + a2 * \log (PGDP/EXR) \qquad (27)$$

    PXX59: Export price index of manufactured goods,
    PWX59: World export price index of manufactured goods,
    PGDP: Gross domestic product deflator,
    EXR: Exchange rate (RMB yuan/US dollar).

For the general export price index (PXX90), it is assumed to be a linear function of the world general export price index, because the domestic prices are insignificant. According to the same reasoning, the general import price index and import price index of manufactured goods are determined by world export prices. The former is a simple linear function of the world general export price, while the latter is a linear function of the world export price of manufactured goods.

3.6 Fiscal and Private Income Equations

Government revenue is mainly from tax revenue. The tax revenue is classified as tax revenue from industry and commerce, tax revenue on agriculture, tariff and other tax revenues. The first one is a linear function of the gross domestic product *minus* agricultural value added. The tax revenue for agriculture is determined by value added in agriculture. It is clear that the tariff is determined by imports, because tariff rates on exports are very low. In all the tax revenue equations, the dependent variables lagged one year are introduced in the equations as explanatory variables.

The government revenue equation is written as:

$$REVE = a1 * TAX + a2 * REVE(-1) \tag{28}$$

    REVE: Government revenue (nominal),
    TAX: Total tax revenues (nominal),
    REVE(-1): REVE of the previous year.

The equation for rural household cash income is as follows:

$$MIRI = a1 * (AVAC-TAX2) + a2 * GDIC + a3 * MIUI \tag{29}$$

    MIRI: Cash income of rural households (nominal),
    AVAC: Agricultural value added (nominal),
    TAX2:   Tax revenue on agriculture (nominal),
    GDIC: Gross fixed investment (nominal),
    MIUI: Cash income of urban households (nominal).

The rural household cash income is mainly from agricultural production activities. The variable GDIC describes the contribution of construction activities to rural household cash income. At present, quite a large part of construction activities are completed by farmers. The variable MIUI represents transfers from urban households.

The urban household cash income equation takes the form:

$$MIUI = a0 + a1 * (GDPC-AVAC-TAX1) + a2 * MIUI(-1) \tag{30}$$

    MIUI: Cash income of urban households (nominal),
    GDPC: Gross domestic product (nominal),
    AVAC: Agricultural value added (nominal),
    TAX1:   Tax revenue on industry and commerce (nominal),
    MIUI(-1): MIUI in the previous year.

In the model, the financial sector is weak with only one money demand equation. Currency in circulation (M0) is explained by the gross domestic demand and foreign demand. M0 is determined as a log-linear function.

$$\log M0 = a0 + a1 * \log (GDIC+CIC+CSC)$$
$$+ a2 * \log(XX1CD*EXR) \tag{31}$$

M0:	Currency in circulation (nominal),
GDIC:	Gross fixed investment (nominal),
CIC:	Private consumption (nominal),
CSC:	Public consumption (nominal),
XX1CD:	Exports of goods (nominal, US dollars),
EXR:	Exchange rate (RMB yuan/US dollar).

4. List of the Equations

4.1 Domestic Demand Block

1. Rural Household Consumption of Self-Produced Goods, Real
    CFSS/AP = 43.3440 + 0.2704 * AVA90/AP
             (11.566) (30.740)
              –13.6766 * D87 – 29.3683 * D88 – 36.2407 * D89
               (–3.124)   (–6.673)   (–8.180)
    DW = 1.2215 Rsq(adj) = 0.9778
    (Sample Period: 1970—1992)

2. Rural Household Consumption of Purchased Goods, Real
    CFNSS = 0.1250 * ((MIRI/RPI) * 100) – 45.8655 * IRSD
            (4.438)   (–2.157)
             + 0.9619 * CFNSS(–1) – 499.6850 * D90
             (14.179)   (–5.470)
    DW = 2.1360   Rsq(adj) = 0.9947
    (Sample Period: 1971—1992)

3. Total Consumption by Rural Households of Goods, Real
    CRI1 = CFSS + CFNSS

4. Urban Household Consumption of Goods, Real
    CUI1 = 84.3222 + 0.3622 * (MIUI/CPI/100)) – 45.6135 + IRSD
            (4.383)   (7.955)   (–5.968)
             + 0.6772 * CUI1(–1) + 142.4698 * D805 + 157.6192 * D88
             (8.649)   (6.598)   (5.348)
    DW = 1.6384   Rsq(adj) = 0.9944
    (Sample Period: 1971—1992)

5. Private consumption of Goods, Real
    CI1 = CRI1 + CUI1

6. Total Private Consumption of Goods and Services, Real
    CI = CI1 + CI2

7. Public Consumption of Goods and Services, Real
    CS = CSC/(PCS/100)

8. Total Consumption of Goods and Services, Real
    CONS = CI + CS

9. Gross Domestic Investment in Fixed Assets, Real
    log (GDI90D) = 0.9566 * log(GDP90) – 0.8639 * log(PGDI)
    $\qquad\qquad$ (7.7577) $\qquad\qquad\qquad$ (–6.1735)
    $\qquad\qquad\quad$ + 0.3708*log(FECC+GDLC)/(PGDI/100)+0.0622*D87
    $\qquad\qquad\quad$ (4.599) $\qquad\qquad\qquad\qquad\qquad\qquad$ (1.231)
    $\qquad\qquad\quad$ + 0.1480*(D889)
    $\qquad\qquad\quad$ (3.656)
    DW = 1.5164 $\qquad\qquad$ Rsq(adj) = 0.9922 $\qquad$ RHO = 0.6368
    $\qquad\qquad\qquad\qquad\qquad\qquad\qquad\qquad\qquad\qquad\qquad$ (3.614)

    (Sample Period: 1970—1992)

10. Foreign Direct Investment, Real
    $\qquad\qquad$ GDI90F = (GDICF * EXR)/(PGDI/100)
11. Gross Domestic Investments in Fixed Assets, Real
    $\qquad\qquad$ GDI90 = GDI90D + GDI90F
12. Gross Domestic Investments in Fixed Assets, Nominal
    $\qquad\qquad$ GDIC = GDI90 * (PGDI/100)

4.2 Production and Gross Domestic Product Block

13. Gross Output of Agriculture, Real
    log GVA90 $\quad$ = 1.3537 + 0.5593 * log KA(–1) + 0.9699 $\,$ * log LFA
    $\qquad\qquad\quad$ (2.596) $\quad$ (3.896) $\qquad\qquad\qquad$ (2.973)
    $\qquad\qquad$ +0.2094*log(MIRI/(PGDI/100))–0.1259*log (DAREA/PAREA)
    $\qquad\qquad$ (4.679) $\qquad\qquad\qquad\qquad\qquad$ (–3.957)
    $\qquad\qquad\quad$ + 0.1031 * D712 + 0.06689 * D78 – 0.0697 * (D8123 + D90)
    $\qquad\qquad\quad$ (3.605) $\qquad\qquad$ (2.368) $\qquad\qquad$ (–4.334)
    DW = 1.8170 $\qquad\qquad\qquad$ Rsq(adj) = 0.9952
    (Sample Period: 1971—1992)

14. Value Added in Agriculture, Real
    log AVA90 = 0.3702 + 0.9185 * log GVA90 − 0.0236 * log T
        (1.1521)(21.8826)   (−1.2596)
    DW = 1.1935   Rsq(adj) = 0.9996
    (Sample Period: 1970—1992)

15. Value Added in Agriculture, Nominal
    AVAC = AVA90 * (PAVA/100)

16. Gross Output of Light Industry, Real
    GVLI90 = −1269.3921 + 0.8273 * (CONS−CFSS) + 0.2457 * GVLI(−1)
        (−6.036)   (8.016)   (2.458)
        + 1.2821 * (XX5990*EXR) − 447.9321 * D84
        (8.441)   (−2.213)
    DW = 1.8924   Rsq(adj) = 0.9984
    (Sample Period: 1970—1992)

17. Gross Output of Heavy Industry, Real
    GVHI90 = 645.1223 + 0.6937 * GDI90 + 0.4530 * GVHI90(−1)
        (5.8841)   (9.904)   (8.082)
        + 438.6788 * D7789 + 1.5349 * (XX5990*EXR)
        (4.214)   (12.191)
        + 330.7835 + D80 + 525.7076 * D85
        (1.967)   (3.130)
    DW = 2.0052   Rsq(adj) = 0.9987
    (Sample Period: 1971—1992)

18. Gross Domestic Product, Real
    GDP90 = GDI90 + FDIC/(PGDP/100) + CI + CS
        + ((XXCD − MMCD)*EXR)/(PGDP/100)
19. Gross Domestic Product, Nominal
    GDPC = GDP90 * (PGDP/100)

20. Labor Force in Agriculture
    LFA = 1.0011 * LFA(−1) + 0.00002 * (TP(−16) − TP(−17))
        (202.626)   (2.458)
        − 0.0823 * (D78 + D84) + 0.00616 * D82 + 0.0523 * D89
        (−3.667)   (2.071)   (1.766)
    DW = 1.8116   Rsq(adj) = 0.9817   (Sample Period: 1970—1992)

4.3 Finance and Private Income Block

21. Tax Revenue from Industry and Commerce, Nominal
    $$TAX1 = 0.0192 * (GDPC{-}AVAC) + 0.9375 * TAX1(-1)$$
    $$\quad\ \ (0.324) \qquad\qquad\qquad (20.806)$$
    $$+ 80.9376 * D8488 + 310.2499 * D85 + 143.0015 * D89$$
    $$\quad (4.294) \qquad\qquad (12.096) \qquad\quad (5.302)$$
    DW = 1.7177   Rsq(adj) = 0.9985   (Sample Period: 1971—1992)

22. Tax Revenue from Agriculture, Nominal
    $$TAX2 = 0.0020 * AVAC + 0.9239 * TAX2(-1) + 4.6314 * D857$$
    $$\quad\ \ (3.002) \qquad\qquad (26.099) \qquad\qquad (15.048)$$
    $$+ 21.2250 * (D88{+}D92) + 8.5604 * D89$$
    $$\quad (5.176) \qquad\qquad\qquad (3.756)$$
    DW = 2.2057   Rsq(adj) = 0.9968   (Sample Period: 1971—1992)

23. Tariff, Nominal
    $$TARIF = 10.9298 + 0.0241 * (MM1CD * EXR) + 0.5600 * TARIF(-1)$$
    $$\quad\ \ (2.469) \quad (4.453) \qquad\qquad\qquad\qquad (6.037)$$
    $$+ 108.0960 * D85 + 30.1508 * D89$$
    $$\quad (7.412) \qquad\qquad (2.019)$$
    DW = 1.7117   Rsq(adj) = 0.9649   (Sample Period: 1970—1992)

24. Total Tax Revenue, Nominal
    $$TAX = TAX1 + TAX2 + TARIF + TAX0$$

25. Government Revenue, Nominal
    $$REVE = 0.2287 * TAX + 0.9071 * REVE(-1) - 113.6757 * (D76{+}D87)$$
    $$\quad\ \ (5.559) \qquad\qquad (23.554) \qquad\qquad (-2.514)$$
    $$+ 180.7135 * (D78 + D84)$$
    $$\quad (4.006)$$
    DW = 1.5908   Rsq(adj) = 0.9966   (Sample Period: 1971—1992)

26. Rural Household Cash Income, Nominal
    $$MIRI = -1.8649 + 0.9755 *(AVAC{-}TAX2){+}0.01015*GDIC{+}0.1572*MIUI$$
    $$\quad\ \ (-0.008) \ (8.5466) \qquad\qquad\qquad (0.1846) \qquad (1.245)$$
    DW = 1.240   Rsq(adj) = 0.9362   RHO = 0.9324
    $$\qquad\qquad\qquad\qquad\qquad\qquad\qquad (15.694)$$
    (Sample Period: 1970—1992)

27. Urban Household Cash Income, Nominal
    $$MIUI = -100.2547 + 0.2420 * (GDPC - AVAC - TAX1)$$
    $$\quad\ \ (-8.224) \quad (10.465)$$

$$+ 0.503 * \text{MIUI}(-1) + 152.036 * \text{D86}$$
$$\qquad (7.547) \qquad\qquad (3.902)$$

DW = 1.8084   Rsq(adj) = 0.9995   (Sample Period: 1971—1992)

28. Total Private Cash Income, Nominal
    MII = MIRI + MIUI

29. Currency in Circulation (M0), Nominal
    log M0 = −6.050 + 1.3481 * log(GDIC + CIC + CSC)
    $\qquad$ (−12.478) (14.928)
    $\qquad\qquad$ + 0.0886 * D848 + 0.1133 * log((XXICD) * EXR)
    $\qquad\qquad$ (2.584) $\qquad\qquad$ (2.298)

    DW = 1.3379   Rsq(adj) = 0.9985   (Sample Period: 1970—1992)

4.4 Price Block

30. Price Index of Agricultural Gross Output
    PIA = −1.0333 + 0.7110 * PIA(−1) + 0.3417 * PIPFS + 5.4281 * D88
    $\qquad$ (−1.646) $\quad$ (12.366) $\qquad\qquad$ (6.461) $\qquad\qquad$ (3.914)

    DW = 1.9517   Rsq(adj) = 0.9980   (Sample Period: 1971—1992)

31. Price Index of Value Added in Agriculture
    PAVA = 2.8706 + 0.9741 * PIA + 1.0773 * D79 − 1.8072 * D889
    $\qquad$ (3.427) $\quad$ (82.914) $\qquad$ (3.611) $\qquad\qquad$ (−6.026)

    DW = 1.9125 $\qquad\qquad$ Rsq(adj) = 0.9958 $\qquad\qquad$ RHO = 0.8642
    $\qquad\qquad\qquad\qquad\qquad\qquad\qquad\qquad\qquad\qquad\qquad$ (8.166)

    (Sample Period: 1971—1992)

32. Price Index of Light Industrial Gross Output
    PLI=0.0237* PIA + 0.9852 * PLI(−1) + 2.8239 * D857 + 8.2721 * D889
    $\qquad$ (2.113) $\qquad\quad$ (121.170) $\qquad$ (4.367) $\qquad\qquad$ (11.580)

    DW = 1.7369   Rsq(adj) = 0.9934   (Sample Period: 1971—1992)

33. Price Index of Heavy Industrial Gross Output
    PHI = 8.2000 + 0.8114 * PHI(−1) + 0.0131 * WAGE/LHI
    $\qquad$ (3.230) $\quad$ (16.566) $\qquad\qquad$ (6.148)
    $\qquad\qquad$ + 2.5032 * D85 + 3.0598 * D88 + 7.0571 * D89
    $\qquad\qquad$ (3.628) $\qquad\qquad$ (4.320) $\qquad\qquad$ (10.327)

    DW = 1.6082   Rsq(adj) = 0.9981   (Sample Period: 1971—1992)

34. Price Index of Fixed Investment
    PGDI = 0.9257 * PHI + 0.0216 * (PMM59*EXR) + 7.1100 * D7047
    $\qquad$ (18.7540) $\qquad$ (1.7026) $\qquad\qquad\qquad$ (4.7066)

$$+ 0.0752 * ((GDIC/GDIC(-1)-1) * 100 - 3.9976 * D823$$
$$(1.6236) \qquad\qquad\qquad (-1.9374)$$
$$- 4.8557 * D88 - 10.7282 * D89$$
$$(-2.0325) \qquad (-4.0804)$$
DW = 1.4995   Rsq(adj) = 0.9762   RHO = 0.7277
$$(4.354)$$

(Sample Period: 1971—1992)

35. Retail Price Index for Social Commodities
RPI = −17.2351 + 0.6216 * PLI + 0.3922 * PIA + 3.4072 * D89
     (−8.517)   (20.818)   (12.016)   (5.699)
DW = 1.6883   Rsq(adj) = 0.9994   (Sample Period: 1970—1992)

36. Price Index of Private Consumption
CPI = 94.8797 + 0.5618 * RPI + 30.2760 * CPI(−1)
    (−22.917)   (34.094)   (24.397)
   + 1.3326 * D88 − 0.7898 * (D89 + D90)
      (4.000)   (−3.364)
DW = 1.9766   Rsq(adj) = 0.9998   (Sample Period: 1970—1992)

37. Price Index of Public Consumption
PCS = 32.0678 + 0.3933 * RPI + 0.2474 * PCS(−1) + 4.5328 * D89
      (9.029)   (9.519)   (3.530)   (4.035)
   + 4.4081 * D91
     (4.347)
DW = 1.5252   Rsq(adj) = 0.9949   (Sample Period: 1971—1992)

38. Gross Domestic Product Deflator
PGDP = 2.0708 + 0.2265 * PGDI + 0.7519 * CPI
     (1.6126) (9.3628)   (31.2226)
DW = 1.6693   Rsq(adj) = 0.9942   RHO = 0.6808
(Sample Period: 1970—1992)

4.5 Foreign Trade Block

39. Exports of Manufactured Goods (Real, US Dollars)
logXX5990= −12.7793 + 1.7574 * log WX5990 − 0.1697 * (D76 + D90)
           (−14.202) (18.120)   (−2.786)
         + 0.1175 * D89 − 7796 * log((PXX59/EXR)/PWX59)
         (1.368)   (−12.699)
        − 0.2095 * D77 + 0.3251 * D8123
        (−2.416)   (5.999)
DW = 1.9389   Rsq(adj) = 0.9943   (Sample Period: 1971—1992)

40. Total Exports of Goods (Real, US Dollars)
    log XX1D = –13.0486 + 1.8002 * log WM90
            (–5.2608) (7.0114)
            + 0.4790 * log(PWX90 * EXR/PXX90)
            (2.9829)
    DW = 1.8308   Rsq(adj) = 0.90646   RHO = 0.7076
                                              (4.935)
           (Sample Period: 1971—1992)

41. Total Exports of Goods (Nominal, US Dollars)
        XX1CD = XX1D * (PXX90/100)

42. Exports of Services (Real, US Dollars)
        XX2D = XX2CD/(PXX90/100)

43. Total Exports of Goods and Services (Nominal, US Dollars)
        XXCD = XX1CD + XX2CD

44. Export Price Index of Manufactured Goods
    log PXX59 = 0.6926 * log PWX59 + 0.4851 * log PGDP/EXR
            (11.4385)   (6.2398)
             – 0.1491 * D82389 + 0.0938 * D73 + 0.1835 * D74
             (–5.1209)   (2.0100)   (3.9739)
    Dw = 1.8340 Rsq(adj) = 0.9688   RHO = 0.7592
                                                (5.203)
       (Sample Period: 1970—1992)

45. General Export Price Index
    PXX90 = 19.3287 +0.8096 * PWX90+12.1433*(D74+D81) + 6.7724 * D88
          (7.940) (20.7695)   (6.8346)   (2.6794)
    DW = 1.8393   Rsq(adj) = 0.9370   RHO = 0.4867
                                              (2.356)
       (Sample Period: 1970—1992)

46. Imports of Manufactured Goods (Real, US Dollars)
    MM5990 = 2.330042 + 0.066859 * GDI90
            (0.2612)   (15.2869)
         + 0.333123 * (XXCD/(PMM59/100)) –17.267766*(PMM59*EXR/PGDP)
         (10.2134)   (–2.334)
         + 38.242712 * (D74+D84)–45.4736 * D823 + 149.82798 * D856
         (44.288)   (–6.4863)   (20.253)
    DW = 2.0333   Rsq(adj) = 0.9985   RHO = 0.6002
                                              (2.989)
       (Sample Period: 1973—1992)

47. Total Imports of Goods (Real, US Dollars)

MM1D = 0.0470 * (CONS + GDI90) + 0.4519 * (XXCD/(PGDP/100))
       (14.452)   (8.892)
    +92.8276 * (D74 + D856) − 103.4402 * (PMM90 * EXR/PGDP)
     (8.892)   (−13.465)
    −54.4046 * D823
    (−4.252)
    DW = 1.9361   Rsq(adj) = 0.9949   (Sample Period: 1970—1992)

48. Total Imports of Goods (Nominal, US Dollars)
    MM1CD = MM1D * (PMM90/100)

49. Imports of Services (Real, US Dollars)
    MM2D=0.0979*MM1D − 11.8975 * D85 + 8.9464 * D90 + 71.4265 * D92
         (19.7998)   (−2.6552)   (2.0483)   (12.7633)
    DW = 1.7092   Rsq(adj) = 0.9663   RHO = 0.4436
                                                          (2.237)

    (Sample Period: 1970—1992)

50. Imports of Services (Nominal, US Dollars)
    MM2CD = MM2D * (PMM90/100)

51. Total Imports of Goods and Services (Current US Dollars)
    MMCD = MM1CD + MM2CD

52. Import Price Index of Manufactured Goods
    PMM59 = 6.5281 + 1.0077 * PWX59 − 6.9619 * (D87 + D90) − 15.5947 * D92
            (3.403)   (36.127)   (−4.280)   (−6.925)
    DW = 1.7678   Rsq(adj) = 0.9869   (Sample Period: 1973—1992)

53. General Import Price Index
    PMM90 = 13.1540+0.8913 * PWX90−5.9058 * (D87+D90)+10.1072 * D89
            (5.452) (25.748)   (−3.964)   (5.270)
    DW = 1.7530   Rsq(adj) = 0.9504   RHO = 0.5368
                                                          (2.892)

    (Sample Period: 1970—1992)

5. Explanation of Variables

5.1 Endogenous Variable

AVAC	Value added in agriculture (nominal);
AVA90	Value added in agriculture (real);
CFNSS	Rural household consumption on purchased goods (real);
CFSS	Rural household consumption on self-purchased goods (real);

CI	Total private consumption of goods and services (real);
CI1	Private consumption of goods (real);
CONS	Total consumption of goods and services (real);
CPI	Consumer price index;
CRI1	Rural household consumption goods (real);
CS	Public consumption of goods and services (real);
CUI1	Urban household consumption of goods (real);
GDIC	Gross domestic investment in fixed assets (nominal);
GDI90	Gross domestic investment in fixed assets (real);
GDI90D	Domestic gross investment in fixed assets (real);
GDI90F	Foreign direct investment (real);
GDPC	Gross domestic product (nominal);
GDP90	Gross domestic product (real);
GVA90	Agricultural gross output (real);
GVHI90	Gross output of heavy industry (real);
GVLI90	Gross output of light industry (real);
LFA	Labor force in agriculture (100 million);
MII	Private cash income (nominal);
MIRI	Rural household cash income (nominal);
MIUI	Urban household cash income (nominal);
MMCD	Total imports of goods and services (nominal, US dollars);
MM1CD	Total imports of goods (nominal, US dollars);
MM1D	Total imports of goods (real, US dollars);
MM2CD	Imports of services (nominal, US dollars);
MM2D	Imports of services (real, US dollars);
MM5990	Imports of manufactured goods (real, US dollars);
M0	Currency in circulation (nominal);
PAVA	Price index of value added in agriculture;
PCS	Price index of public consumption;
PGDI	Price index of fixed investment;
PGDP	Gross domestic product deflator;
PHI	Price index of heavy industrial gross output;
PIA	Price index of agricultural gross output;
PLI	Price index of light industrial gross output;
PMM59	Import price index of manufactured goods;
PMM90	General import price;
PXX59	Export price index of manufactured goods;
PXX90	General export price index;
REVE	Government revenue (nominal);
RPI	Retail price index of social commodities;
TARIF	Tariff (nominal);
TAX	Total tax revenues (nominal);

TAX1	tax revenue of industry and commerce (nominal);
TAX2	Tax revenue of agriculture (nominal);
XXCD	Total exports of goods and services (nominal, US dollars);
XX1CD	Total exports of goods (nominal, US dollars);
XX1D	Total exports of goods (real, US dollars);
XX2D	Exports of services (real, US dollars);
XX5990	Exports of manufactured goods (real, US dollars).

5.2 Exogenous Variables

AP	Rural population (100 million);
CI2	Private consumption of services (real);
CSC	Public consumption of goods and services (nominal);
DAREA	Crop area affected by natural disasters (1000 hectares);
EXR	Exchange rate (RMB yuan/US dollar);
FDIC	Change in stocks (nominal);
FECC	Fiscal allocation for fixed investment (nominal);
GDICF	Foreign direct investment (nominal, US dollars);
GDLIC	Fixed investment loans (nominal);
IRSD	Interest rate of savings deposits (one year);
KA	Capital stock in agriculture (real);
LHI	Labor force in heavy industry;
PAREA	Sown area of farm crops (1000 hectares);
PIPFS	Price index for purchase of farm and sideline products by the state;
PWX59	World export price index of manufactured goods;
PWX90	General world export price index;
TAX	Other tax revenues (nominal);
UP	Urban population (100 million);
WAGE	Total wages and bonus in heaving industrial sector (nominal);
WM90	World imports of goods (real, US dollars);
WX5990	World exports of manufactured goods (real, US dollars);
XX2CD	Exports of services (nominal, US dollars);
Dij	Dummy variables (19ij=1, others 0);
Dijk	Dummy variables (19ij=1, 19ik=1, others 0);
Dijkm	Dummy variables (19ij=1, 19ik=1, 19im=1, others 0).

Notes: 1. The units of all variables are 100 million RMB yuan unless otherwise stated.

2. All price variables are in index form, 1990=100.

3. Lags are indicated by the brackets "(-i)", where "i" is the number of years lagged.

6. Dynamic Simulation Test

The performance of the model has been examined by a dynamic simulation covering the period 1987—1992. Such a test is rather stringent, since both current and lagged endogenous variables are generated by the model, which may result in an accumulation of prediction errors. The simulation results are listed in Table 1. Generally speaking, the model performs quite well. The RMSPEs of all the endogenous variables are less than 10%; more than 90 percent of RMSPEs are less than 5%; and about 65 percent of RMSPEs less than 3%. The predictions for real GDP and its components are fairly good, expect for import and export variables, which are difficult to predict in China. Especially, the course of real private consumption and gross domestic product follows the observed values very closely, and the model performs very well with regard to the price variables. Bigger errors occur in variables such as TARIF (nominal tariff) and XX1D (exports of manufactured goods at constant US dollars); their RMSPEs are 8.19% and 7.27%, respectively. The RMSPEs of most import and export variables lie between 3% and 6%. The reason why some foreign trade variables have quite big errors is that their observed values fluctuated widely during the simulation period.

7. Policy Simulations

Four policy simulations are conducted to study the impacts of the changes in one or two exogenous variables on the Chinese economy over the period 1987—1992. (1) An increase of 10% in nominal public consumption; (2) An increase of 10% in fixed investment loans; (3) An increase of 10% in tax revenues; (4) An increase of 10% in exports. In each policy simulation, an external shock is given to one or two exogenous variables in 1987 and thereafter. The model is solved over the period 1987—1992. In the policy simulations, the model is successfully solved. The four dynamic simulation results of major endogenous variables are respectively presented in Tables 2—5.

7.1 Impacts of an Increase of 10% in Nominal Public Consumption.

The simulation results of a 10% increase in public consumption are listed in Table 2. Table 2 shows that the direct impacts of the increase of 10% in public consumption on China's economy are that the gross domestic product and its major components would increase. The gross domestic product (GDP90) would increase by 1.54% annually, gross fixed investment (GDI90) and urban household consumption (CUI1) increase 1.36% and 1.76%, respectively. The impacts become stronger and stronger year after year. However rural household consumption (CRI1) would remain almost unchanged; it would decrease only by 0.01% annually on average, because of decreasing real disposable cash income of rural households. The real imports of goods (MMID) and total imports of goods and services at current prices (MMCD) would increase by 2.69% and 2.66% annually. Key price indexes rise little; the retail price index (RPI), private consumption price index (CPI) and GDP deflator (PGDP) rise respectively by 0.15%, 0.11% and 0.09% annually.

7.2 Impacts of a 10% Increase in Fixed Investment Loans.

The simulation results are listed in Table 3. It indicates that the direct impacts of an increase of 10% in fixed investment loans are that gross fixed investment (GDI90) would increase annually by 3.39%. Then the gross domestic product (GDP90) and private consumption (CI) would increase by 0.94% and 0.52%, respectively. The impact on private consumption expenditure shows a strong increase in trend, from 0.14% in 1987 to 0.80% in 1992. The increase of domestic demand would induce an annual increase of 1.47% in currency in circulation. But the impacts on prices are very weak. The indexes for general retail prices (RPI), private consumption prices (CPI) and the GDP deflator (PGDP) increase, respectively, only by 0.08%, 0.07% and 0.07% annually on average. For 1990, the price index of fixed investment decreases by 0.01%, indicating that austerity in 1990 was too strong. The greater gross domestic demand increases imports The imports of manufactured goods (MM5990) increases by 1.65%, while the total nominal imports of goods and services in US dollars (MMCD) increases by 1.63%.

7.3 Impacts of an Increase of 10% in Tax Revenues on Agriculture, Industry and Commerce

In the policy simulation, we assumed that the extra tax revenues were spent on increasing fixed investment. That means that the real fixed investment would increase by 3.88% annually over the period 1987—1992. The simulation results are presented in Table 4. The higher tax rates would reduce real disposable income of households, which adversely affects private consumption expenditures. This, in turn, induces a decrease of gross domestic product. At the same time, the increase in fixed investment promotes economic growth. In the end, gross domestic product increases by 0.788% annually over the simulation period. Private consumption (CI) decreases by 0.142% annually, which shows an increase in growth trend from 0.06% in 1987 to 0.24% in 1992. Currency in circulation (M0) increases by 1.337%, annually on average. Table 4 also indicates that key price indexes annually on average, increase by 0.108% for the general retail price index, 0.09% for the private consumption price index, and 0.08% for the GDP deflator. Accordingly, the increase of the gross domestic product results in an increase of imports. The real imports of manufactured goods (MM5990) and the total real imports of goods (MMID), respectively, increase by 2.567% and 1.388% annually over the simulation period.

7.4 Impacts of an Increase of 10% in Exports

In the simulation, it is assumed that the demand for China's goods and services in the world market increase by 10 percent annually over the period 1987—1992. The simulation results are listed in Table 5. Because of a 10% sustained increase in exports, China's available foreign exchange increases, and then the imports increase too. The increases of both exports and imports promote China's economic expansion. The simulation results indicate that gross domestic product (GDP90), annually on average, increases by 1.43%; private consumption (CI) and gross fixed investment (GDI90) increase annually by 0.64% and 1.25%, respectively. Similarly, the increase of gross domestic demand induces a 1.64% increase of currency in circulation. All the impacts show a strong growth trend. Due to the economic expansion, the real imports of manufactured goods (MM5990) increase annually by 5.3%, and total imports of goods in current US dollars (MM1CD) increase by 6.01%. The impacts on foreign trade also show a strong growth trend.

8. Concluding Remarks

The model is developed for project PAIR (Projections for Asian Industrializing Region) directed by IDE in 1994. It is a demand-oriented model, emphasizing the demand side. At the same time, the production functions for agriculture, heavy industry and light industry are included in the model. The simulation results indicate that the model's performance and dynamic stability are very good. The RMSPEs of the major endogenous variables, such as real gross domestic product (GDP90) and its main components (CI, GDI90), GDP deflator (PGDP), the general retail price index (RPI) and private consumption price index (CPI) are quite low. It could be used for short-run economic analysis and forecasting.

The financial sector in the model is weak. Gross fixed capital formation is too aggregative to express the different natures of various fixed capital formation. In the future, when more detailed data are available, we will disaggregate gross fixed investment into several categories, and set up an equation for each category.

We have developed an econometric model for Project LINK, which is revised, based on the newly published data, every year. The model is demand-oriented. We are still not very satisfied with our models. The poor data are the main reason why we cannot construct a Chinese model of very high quality. When high quality of data are available, we will develop a better model for the Chinese economy.

Table 1 Simulation Results

Variable	RMPSE	Variable	RMPSE
CFSS	2.165	CFNSS	1.163
CRI1	0.963	CUI1	2.078
CI1	1.150	CS	1.188
CI	1.079	CONS	0.922
GDI90D	1.895	GDI90	1.868
GDI90F	3.221	GDIC	2.610
MIRI	2.960	MIUI	1.991
MII	1.946	GUA90	1.540
AUA90	1.859	AVAC	2.883
GVLI90	2.918	GVHI90	1.707
GDP90	0.817	GDOC	1.536
REVE	1.975	TAX	1.809
TAXI	2.132	TAX2	3.002
TARIF	8.185	PLA	1.230
PAVA	1.619	PGDI	3.230
PIRSSC	0.555	M0	2.418
CPI	0.544	PCS	1.195
PGDP	1.607	PLI	0.277
PHI	0.721	MM5990	3.872

PMM59	0.480	PXX59	4.177
XX5990	5.709	XX1D	7.270
XXICD	5.898	XX2D	2.249
XXCD	5.156	MM1D	3.954
MM1CD	4.710	MM2D	3.816
MM2CD	4.438	MMCD	4.400
PMM90	0.940	PXX90	2.318

Table 2 Impacts of 10% Increase in Public Consumption
on Major Endogenous Variables

CRI1:						
YEAR	SHOCK	CASE	BASE	CASE	EFFECT	%
1987	4474.675	5.96	4475.282	5.98	−.607	−.01
1988	4618.801	3.22	4619.621	3.23	−.820	−.02
1989	4691.548	1.58	4692.099	1.57	−.551	−.01
1990	4725.070	.71	4725.504	.71	−.433	−.01
1991	5108.756	8.12	5109.453	8.13	−.698	−.01
1992	5504.223	7.74	5504.068	7.72	.155	.00
CUI1:						
YEAR	SHOCK	CASE	BASE	CASE	EFFECT	%
1987	2856.766	13.85	2841.085	13.23	15.681	.55
1988	3289.487	15.15	3252.306	14.47	37.181	1.14
1989	3410.784	3.69	3353.568	3.11	57.215	1.71
1990	3655.837	7.18	3578.668	6.71	77.168	2.16
1991	4106.756	12.33	4011.070	12.08	95.686	2.39
1992	4660.688	13.49	4541.323	13.22	119.365	2.63
CI:						
YEAR	SHOCK	CASE	BASE	CASE	EFFECT	%
1987	7705.155	8.05	7690.080	7.84	15.074	.22
1988	8286.776	7.05	8250.416	7.29	36.360	.44
1989	8735.510	5.42	8678.846	5.19	56.664	.65
1990	8886.343	1.73	8809.607	1.51	76.735	.87
1991	9750.225	9.72	9655.237	9.60	94.988	.98
1992	10622.182	8.94	10502.663	8.78	119.519	1.44
CONS:						
YEAR	SHOCK	CASE	BASE	CASE	EFFECT	%
1987	9568.257	10.12	9384.635	8.01	183.623	1.96

1988	10331.551	7.98	10110.432	7.73	221.119	2.19
1989	10880.685	5.32	10630.188	5.14	250.497	2.36
1990	11426.972	5.02	11121.063	4.62	305.909	2.75
1991	12584.153	10.13	12233.582	10.00	350.571	2.87
1992	14178.322	12.67	13738.583	12.30	439.739	3.20

GDI90:

YEAR	SHOCK	CASE	BASE	CASE	EFFECT	%
1987	4582.374	15.65	4537.206	14.51	45.169	1.00
1988	5454.127	19.02	5384.088	18.67	70.039	1.30
1989	4882.325	−10.48	4817.902	−10.52	64.423	1.34
1990	4435.828	−9.15	4374.803	−9.20	61.025	1.39
1991	4912.387	10.74	4841.593	10.67	70.793	1.46
1992	6625.755	34.88	6515.789	34.58	109.966	1.69

GDP90:

YEAR	SHOCK	CASE	BASE	CASE	EFFECT	%
1987	14794.647	12.11	14612.317	10.73	182.330	1.25
1988	16405.471	10.89	16172.396	10.68	233.075	1.44
1989	17267.688	5.26	17019.192	5.24	248.496	1.46
1990	18054.050	4.55	17780.799	4.47	273.251	1.54
1991	19684.726	9.03	19376.281	8.97	308.445	1.59
1992	21852.329	11.01	21434.839	10.62	417.490	1.95

PIRSSC						
YEAR	SHOCK	CASE	BASE	CASE	EFFECT	%
1987	70.571	7.94	70.472	7.78	.099	.14
1988	83.676	18.57	83.569	18.58	.107	.13
1989	98.281	17.46	98.165	17.47	.117	.12
1990	99.329	1.07	99.178	1.03	.150	.15
1991	10.3375	4.07	103.199	4.05	.176	.17
1992	109.465	5.89	109.285	5.90	.180	.17

MO:

YEAR	SHOCK	CASE	BASE	CASE	EFFECT	%
1987	1504.230	23.46	1471.385	20.77	32.844	2.23
1988	2256.243	49.99	2207.073	50.00	49.171	2.23
1989	2318.347	2.75	2265.617	2.65	52.733	2.33
1990	2695.969	16.29	2629.271	16.05	66.698	2.54
1991	3334.304	23.68	3248.714	23.56	85.590	2.63
1992	4563.205	36.86	4437.979	36.61	125.226	2.82

CPI:

YEAR	SHOCK	CASE	BASE	CASE	EFFECT	%
1987	75.811	6.92	75.721	6.79	.091	.12

1988	89.547	18.12	89.456	18.14	.091	.10
1989	98.527	10.03	98.436	10.04	.091	.09
1990	99.369	.86	99.252	.83	.117	.12
1991	103.717	4.37	103.592	4.37	.125	.12
1992	108.523	4.63	108.383	4.63	.141	.13

PGDP:

YEAR	SHOCK	CASE	BASE	CASE	EFFECT	%
1987	77.880	6.09	77.789	5.96	.091	.12
1988	88.769	13.98	88.697	14.02	.072	.08
1989	96.041	8.19	95.972	8.20	.069	.07
1990	100.369	4.51	100.280	4.49	.089	.09
1991	104.963	4.58	104.867	4.57	.095	.09
1992	109.768	4.58	109.657	4.57	.111	.10

MM1D:

YEAR	SHOCK	CASE	BASE	CASE	EFFECT	%
1987	513.644	−6.54	502.716	−8.53	10.929	2.17
1988	606.064	17.99	592.272	17.81	13.792	2.33
1989	593.482	−2.08	578.579	−2.31	14.904	2.58
1990	589.637	−.65	572.255	−1.09	17.381	3.04
1991	669.710	13.58	649.771	13.55	19.939	3.07
1992	899.333	34.29	873.422	34.42	25.911	2.97

MMCD:

YEAR	SHOCK	CASE	BASE	CASE	EFFECT	%
1987	453.177	−1.69	443.437	−3.81	9.741	2.20
1988	609.958	34.60	596.024	34.41	13.934	2.34
1989	673.580	10.43	656.636	10.17	16.944	2.58
1990	668.607	−.74	649.151	−1.14	19.455	3.00
1991	745.301	11.47	723.105	11.39	22.196	3.07
1992	978.589	31.30	952.294	31.70	26.295	2.76

Table 3 Impacts of 10% Increase in Fixed Investment Loan

on Major Endogenous Variables

CRI1:

YEAR	SHOCK	CASE	BASE	CASE	EFFECT	%
1987	4476.342	6.00	4475.282	5.98	1.060	.02

1988	4622.994	3.28	4619.621	3.23	3.373	.07
1989	4698.130	1.63	4692.099	1.57	6.031	.13
1990	4734.322	.77	4725.504	.71	8.819	.19
1991	5121.023	8.17	5109.453	8.13	11.569	.23
1992	5520.051	7.79	5504.068	7.72	15.983	.29

CUI1:

YEAR	SHOCK	CASE	BASE	CASE	EFFECT	%
1987	2850.420	13.60	2841.085	13.23	9.335	.33
1988	3276.722	14.96	3252.306	14.47	24.416	.75
1989	3391.296	3.50	3353.568	3.11	37.728	1.12
1990	3626.406	6.93	3578.668	6.71	47.738	1.33
1991	4067.359	12.16	4011.070	12.08	56.289	1.40
1992	4609.700	13.33	4541.323	13.22	68.376	1.51

CI:

YEAR	SHOCK	CASE	BASE	CASE	EFFECT	%
1987	7700.476	7.99	7690.080	7.84	10.395	.14
1988	8278.205	7.50	8250.416	7.29	27.789	.34
1989	8722.605	5.37	8678.846	5.19	43.759	.50
1990	8866.164	1.65	8809.607	1.51	56.557	.64
1991	9723.095	9.67	9655.237	9.60	67.858	.70
1992	10587.022	8.89	10502.663	8.78	84.359	.80

CONS:

YEAR	SHOCK	CASE	BASE	CASE	EFFECT	%
1987	9394.489	8.12	9384.635	8.01	9.854	.11
1988	10137.466	7.91	10110.432	7.73	27.034	.27
1989	10673.364	5.29	10630.188	5.14	43.175	.41
1990	11176.735	4.72	11121.063	4.62	55.672	.50
1991	12300.508	10.05	12233.582	10.00	66.926	.55
1992	13821.043	12.36	13738.583	12.30	82.460	.60

GDI90:

YEAR	SHOCK	CASE	BASE	CASE	EFFECT	%
1987	4655.061	17.49	4537.206	14.51	117.855	2.60
1988	5567.159	19.59	5384.088	18.67	183.071	3.40
1989	4986.031	−10.44	4817.902	−10.52	168.129	3.49
1990	4524.386	−9.26	4374.803	−9.20	149.583	3.42
1991	5016.651	10.88	4841.593	10.67	175.058	3.62

1992	6763.783	34.83	6515.789	34.58	247.995	3.81

GDP90:

YEAR	SHOCK	CASE	BASE	CASE	EFFECT	%
1987	14713.719	11.50	14612.317	10.73	101.402	.69
1988	16340.577	11.06	16172.396	10.68	168.181	1.04
1989	17186.018	5.17	17019.192	5.24	166.826	.98
1990	17933.754	4.35	17780.799	4.47	152.955	.86
1991	19554.176	9.04	19376.281	8.97	177.895	.92
1992	21685.726	10.90	21434.839	10.62	250.886	1.17

PGDI:

YEAR	SHOCK	CASE	BASE	CASE	EFFECT	%
1987	80.890	6.14	80.622	5.79	.268	.33
1988	83.963	3.80	83.916	4.09	.047	.06
1989	86.734	3.30	86.731	3.35	.002	.00
1990	103.372	19.18	103.378	19.19	−.006	−.0.1
1991	109.476	5.90	109.457	5.88	.019	.02
1992	114.874	4.93	114.855	4.93	.020	.02

PIRSSC:

YEAR	SHOCK	CASE	BASE	CASE	EFFECT	%
1987	70.537	7.88	70.472	7.78	.65	.09
1988	83.641	18.58	83.569	18.58	.072	.09
1989	98.216	17.43	98.165	17.47	.051	.05
1990	99.252	1.05	99.178	1.03	.074	.07
1991	103.291	4.07	103.199	4.05	.091	.09
1992	109.403	5.92	109.285	5.90	.119	.11

MO:

YEAR	SHOCK	CASE	BASE	CASE	EFFECT	%
1987	1491.124	22.39	1471.385	20.77	19.739	1.34
1988	2241.646	50.33	2207.073	50.00	34.573	1.57
1989	2296.425	2.44	2265.614	2.65	30.812	1.36
1990	2664.649	16.03	2629.271	16.05	35.378	1.35
1991	3296.240	23.70	3248.714	23.56	47.526	1.46
1992	4515.215	36.98	4437.979	36.61	77.236	1.74

CPI:

YEAR	SHOCK	CASE	BASE	CASE	EFFECT	%
1987	75.781	6.88	75.721	6.79	.060	.08
1988	89.517	18.13	89.456	18.14	.061	.07
1989	98.475	10.01	98.436	10.04	.039	.04

1990	99.309	.85	99.252	.83	.057	.06
1991	103.651	4.37	103.592	4.37	.059	.06
1992	108.475	4.65	108.383	4.63	.092	.09

PGDP:

YEAR	SHOCK	CASE	BASE	CASE	EFFECT	%
1987	77.895	6.11	77.789	5.96	.106	.14
1988	88.753	13.94	88.697	14.02	.056	.06
1989	96.003	8.17	95.972	8.20	.030	.03
1990	100.322	4.50	100.280	4.49	.042	.04
1991	104.916	4.58	104.867	4.57	.049	.05
1992	109.731	4.59	109.657	4.57	.074	.07

MM5990:

YEAR	SHOCK	CASE	BASE	CASE	EFFECT	%
1987	436.313	−10.32	428.520	−11.92	7.793	1.83
1988	477.122	9.35	465.096	8.54	12.026	2.59
1989	458.017	−4.00	446.987	−3.89	11.030	2.47
1990	475.575	3.83	465.750	4.20	9.825	2.11
1991	525.137	10.42	513.636	10.28	11.500	2.24
1992	717.839	36.70	701.552	36.59	16.286	2.32

MM1D:

YEAR	SHOCK	CASE	BASE	CASE	EFFECT	%
1987	508.923	−7.40	502.716	−8.53	6.207	1.23
1988	602.231	18.33	592.272	17.81	9.959	1.68
1989	588.554	−2.27	578.579	−2.31	9.976	1.72
1990	581.965	−1.12	572.255	−1.09	9.710	1.70
1991	661.213	13.62	649.771	13.55	11.442	1.76
1992	889.003	34.45	873.422	34.42	15.581	1.78

MM2D:

YEAR	SHOCK	CASE	BASE	CASE	EFFECT	%
1987	44.143	7.71	43.535	6.23	.608	1.40
1988	56.449	27.88	55.474	27.42	.975	1.76
1989	56.515	−12	55.539	.12	.977	1.76
1990	65.440	15.79	64.489	16.12	.951	1.47
1991	64.531	−1.39	63.410	−1.67	1.120	1.77
1992	158.387	145.44	156.861	147.37	1.526	.97

MMCD:

YEAR	SHOCK	CASE	BASE	CASE	EFFECT	%
1987	448.969	−2.61	443.437	−3.81	5.532	1.25
1988	606.086	35.00	596.024	34.41	10.061	1.69
1989	667.978	10.21	656.636	10.17	11.342	1.73

1990	660.020	−1.19	649.151	−1.14	10.869	1.67
1991	735.842	11.49	723.105	11.39	12.737	1.76
1992	968.106	31.56	952.294	31.70	15.812	1.66

Table 4 Impacts of a Sustained Increase of 10% in Tax Revenues
on Agriculture, Industry and Commerce
over the Period 1987–1992 on Major Endogenous Variables.

CRI1:

YEAR	SHOCK	CASE	BASE	CASE	EFFECT	%
1987	4476.484	6.01	4477.135	6.02	−.657	−.01
1988	4619.831	3.20	4621.059	3.21	−1.228	−.03
1989	4682.810	1.36	4684.683	1.38	−1.873	−.04
1990	4715.747	.70	4718.913	.73	−3.166	−.07
1991	5122.325	8.62	5125.550	8.62	−3.225	−.06
1992	5501.631	7.40	5505.668	7.42	−4.037	−.07

CUI1:

YEAR	SHOCK	CASE	BASE	CASE	EFFECT	%
1987	2832.617	12.89	2836.770	13.06	−4.153	−.05
1988	3233.062	14.14	3239.547	14.20	−6.485	−.20
1989	3321.512	2.74	3329.173	2.77	−7.661	−.23
1990	3539.499	6.56	3550.102	6.64	−10.603	−.30
1991	3988.576	12.69	4004.111	12.79	−15.535	−.39
1992	4568.448	14.54	4589.558	14.62	−21.110	−.46

CI:

YEAR	SHOCK	CASE	BASE	CASE	EFFECT	%
1987	7682.813	7.74	7687.618	7.81	−4.805	−.06
1988	8231.382	7.14	8239.095	7.17	−7.713	−.09
1989	8637.501	4.93	8647.035	4.95	−9.534	−.11
1990	8760.682	1.43	8774.451	1.47	−13.769	−.16
1991	9645.614	10.10	9664.374	10.14	−18.760	−.19
1992	10527.351	9.14	10552.497	9.19	−25.146	−.24

CONS:

YEAR	SHOCK	CASE	BASE	CASE	EFFECT	%
1987	4670.182	17.87	4518.354	14.04	151.828	3.36
1988	5551.979	18.88	5358.181	18.59	193.799	3.62
1989	4987.850	−10.16	4772.541	−10.93	215.309	4.51

1990	4498.875	−9.80	4306.551	−9.76	192.324	4.47
1991	5203.937	15.67	5009.193	16.32	194.744	3.89
1992	7045.842	35.39	6832.312	36.40	213.530	3.13

GDP90:

YEAR	SHOCK	CASE	BASE	CASE	EFFECT	%
1987	14708.514	11.46	14592.393	10.58	116.121	.80
1988	16260.290	10.55	16112.068	10.41	148.221	.92
1989	17103.918	5.19	16942.039	5.15	161.879	.96
1990	17822.413	4.20	17691.365	4.42	131.048	.74
1991	19622.780	10.10	19494.910	10.19	127.869	.66
1992	21885.692	11.53	21744.463	11.54	141.230	.65

PGDI:

YEAR	SHOCK	CASE	BASE	CASE	EFFECT	%
1987	80.925	6.18	80.580	5.73	.345	.43
1988	83.896	3.67	83.914	4.14	−.019	.02
1989	86.764	3.42	86.697	3.32	.067	.08
1990	103.315	19.08	103.325	19.18	−.010	−.01
1991	109.899	6.37	109.955	6.42	−.056	−.05
1992	114.878	4.53	114.959	4.55	−.081	−.07

PIRSSC:

YEAR	SHOCK	CASE	BASE	CASE	EFFECT	%
1987	70.741	8.20	70.667	8.08	.074	.10
1988	84.245	19.09	84.151	19.08	.094	.11
1989	100.260	19.01	100.147	19.01	.113	.11
1990	100.698	.44	100.578	.43	.121	.12
1991	103.985	3.26	103.882	3.29	.103	.10
1992	107.840	3.71	107.717	3.69	.123	.11

MO:

YEAR	SHOCK	CASE	BASE	CASE	EFFECT	%
1987	1505.719	23.59	1483.763	21.78	21.956	1.48
1988	2327.772	54.60	2293.011	54.54	34.761	1.52
1989	2564.610	10.17	2523.975	10.07	40.634	1.61
1990	2891.367	12.74	2855.253	13.13	36.114	1.26
1991	3558.001	23.06	3519.959	23.28	38.042	1.08
1992	4415.311	24.10	4368.366	24.10	46.945	1.07

CPI:

YEAR	SHOCK	CASE	BASE	CASE	EFFECT	%
1987	75.965	7.14	75.899	7.05	.66	.09
1988	90.024	18.51	89.945	18.51	.079	.09
1989	100.031	11.12	99.940	11.11	.091	.09
1990	100.553	.52	100.453	.51	.099	.10

1991	104.207	3.63	104.126	3.66	.081	.08
1992	107.260	2.93	107.165	2.92	.095	.09

PGDP:

YEAR	SHOCK	CASE	BASE	CASE	EFFECT	%
1987	78.041	6.31	77.914	6.13	.128	.16
1988	89.119	14.19	89.064	14.31	.055	.06
1989	97.179	9.04	97.096	9.02	.083	.09
1990	101.243	4.18	101.171	4.20	.072	.07
1991	105.430	4.13	105.382	4.16	.048	.05
1992	108.817	3.21	108.765	3.21	.053	.05

MM5990:

YEAR	SHOCK	CASE	BASE	CASE	EFFECT	%
1987	437.405	−10.10	427.372	−12.16	10.033	2.35
1988	476.353	8.90	463.626	8.48	12.727	2.75
1989	458.816	−3.68	444.667	−4.09	14.150	3.18
1990	474.506	3.42	461.863	3.87	12.644	2.74
1991	537.767	13.33	524.978	13.67	12.789	2.44
1992	735.772	36.82	721.754	37.48	14.017	1.94

MM1D:

YEAR	SHOCK	CASE	BASE	CASE	EFFECT	%
1987	509.014	−7.39	501.894	−8.68	7.119	1.42
1988	598.138	17.51	589.359	17.43	8.779	1.49
1989	585.756	−2.07	576.018	−2.26	9.738	1.69
1990	577.109	−1.48	568.680	−1.27	8.429	1.48
1991	666.882	15.56	658.610	15.81	8.273	1.26
1992	900.425	35.02	891.630	35.38	8.794	.99

Table 5 Impacts of 10% Increase in Exports of Goods and Services
on Endogenous Variables

CRI1:

YEAR	SHOCK	CASE	BASE	CASE	EFFECT	%
1987	4475.066	5.97	4475.146	5.98	−.080	.00
1988	4619.395	3.23	4619.338	3.22	.057	.00
1989	4692.812	1.59	4692.441	1.58	.370	.01
1990	4727.247	.73	4725.609	.71	1.638	.03
1991	5112.792	8.16	5108.226	8.10	4.566	.09
1992	5511.251	7.79	5501.841	7.71	9.410	.17

CUI1:

YEAR	SHOCK	CASE	BASE	CASE	EFFECT	%

1987	2858.012	13.90	2845.913	13.42	12.099	.43
1988	3291.383	15.16	3263.447	14.67	27.936	.86
1989	3410.842	3.63	3368.582	3.22	42.260	1.25
1990	3639.851	6.71	3577.985	6.22	61.866	1.73
1991	4074.127	11.93	3988.797	11.48	85.330	2.14
1992	4639.248	13.87	4522.190	13.37	117.058	2.59

CI:

YEAR	SHOCK	CASE	BASE	CASE	EFFECT	%
1987	7706.791	8.07	7694.772	7.91	12.019	.16
1988	8289.266	7.56	8261.273	7.36	27.993	.34
1989	8736.833	5.40	8694.203	5.24	42.631	.49
1990	8872.533	1.55	8809.029	1.32	63.504	.72
1991	9721.633	9.57	9631.736	9.34	89.897	.93
1992	10607.771	9.12	10481.303	8.82	126.468	1.21

GDI90:

YEAR	SHOCK	CASE	BASE	CASE	EFFECT	%
1987	4586.057	15.75	4551.193	14.87	34.863	.77
1988	5457.342	19.00	5404.865	18.76	52.477	.97
1989	4874.892	−10.67	4828.473	−10.66	46.419	.96
1990	4398.444	−9.77	4342.069	−10.07	56.375	1.30
1991	4872.669	10.78	4797.069	10.48	75.600	1.58
1992	6648.638	36.45	6522.977	35.98	125.662	1.93

MII:

YEAR	SHOCK	CASE	BASE	CASE	EFFECT	%
1987	6569.613	13.83	6540.161	13.32	29.452	.45
1988	8045.617	22.47	7991.083	22.18	54.534	.68
1989	9283.850	15.39	9214.235	15.31	69.614	.76
1990	10457.320	12.64	10357.773	12.41	99.547	.96
1991	11681.864	11.71	11541.924	11.43	139.940	1.21
1992	13366.442	14.42	13160.270	14.02	206.172	1.57

GDP90:

YEAR	SHOCK	CASE	BASE	CASE	EFFECT	%
1987	14809.182	12.22	14668.799	11.16	140.383	.96
1988	16414.601	10.84	16241.181	10.72	173.420	1.07
1989	17233.922	4.99	17056.271	5.02	177.651	1.04
1990	17872.829	3.71	17616.450	3.28	256.379	1.46
1991	19515.806	9.19	19176.938	8.86	338.867	1.77
1992	21974.861	12.60	21490.475	12.06	484.386	2.25

PGDI:

YEAR	SHOCK	CASE	BASE	CASE	EFFECT	%
1987	80.733	5.93	80.654	5.83	.079	.10

1988	83.931	3.96	83.920	4.05	.011	.01
1989	86.717	3.32	86.719	3.33	−.002	.00
1990	103.323	19.15	103.293	19.11	.029	.03
1991	109.472	5.95	109.449	5.96	.024	.02
1992	115.016	5.06	114.978	5.05	.038	.03

PIRSSC:

YEAR	SHOCK	CASE	BASE	CASE	EFFECT	%
1987	70.557	7.91	70.503	7.83	.053	.08
1988	83.672	18.59	83.607	18.59	.065	.08
1989	98.235	17.41	98.179	17.43	.056	.06
1990	99.134	.91	99.110	.95	.023	.02
1991	103.158	4.06	103.163	4.09	−.005	.00
1992	109.264	5.92	109.322	5.97	−.058	−.05

MO:

YEAR	SHOCK	CASE	BASE	CASE	EFFECT	%
1987	1503.645	23.42	1481.635	21.61	22.010	1.49
1988	2256.793	50.09	2222.621	50.01	34.172	1.54
1989	2305.506	2.16	2272.248	2.23	33.258	1.46
1990	2635.241	14.30	2593.455	14.14	41.786	1.61
1991	3264.239	23.87	3208.665	23.72	55.573	1.73
1992	4544.801	39.23	4456.282	38.88	88.520	1.99

CPI:

YEAR	SHOCK	CASE	BASE	CASE	EFFECT	%
1987	75.795	6.90	75.749	6.83	.047	.06
1988	89.543	18.14	89.489	18.14	.054	.06
1989	98.485	9.99	98.441	10.00	.044	.04
1990	99.218	.74	99.199	.77	.019	.02
1991	103.559	4.37	103.560	4.40	−.002	.00
1992	108.360	4.64	108.401	4.67	−.042	−.04

PGDP:

YEAR	SHOCK	CASE	BASE	CASE	EFFECT	%
1987	77.870	6.07	77.818	6.00	.053	.07
1988	88.765	13.99	88.722	14.01	.043	.05
1989	96.006	8.16	95.973	8.17	.033	.03
1990	100.242	4.41	100.221	4.43	.021	.02
1991	104.846	4.59	104.842	4.61	.004	.00
1992	109.676	4.61	109.699	4.63	−.023	−.02

MM5990:

YEAR	SHOCK	CASE	BASE	CASE	EFFECT	%
1987	456.712	−6.13	436.651	−10.25	20.061	4.95

1988	495.708	8.54	473.835	8.52	21.873	4.62
1989	472.279	-4.73	450.708	-4.88	21.571	4.79
1990	470.845	-.30	444.204	-1.44	26.641	6.00
1991	523.420	11.17	493.283	11.05	30.137	6.11
1992	753.133	43.89	710.060	43.95	43.073	6.07

MM1D:

YEAR	SHOCK	CASE	BASE	CASE	EFFECT	%
1987	542.521	-1.29	514.204	-6.44	28.317	5.51
1988	635.969	17.22	604.746	17.61	31.223	5.16
1989	616.327	-3.09	584.334	-3.38	31.993	5.48
1990	581.252	-5.69	543.615	-6.97	37.637	6.92
1991	665.309	14.46	621.958	14.41	43.351	6.97
1992	935.236	40.57	882.238	41.85	52.998	6.01

MM1CD:

YEAR	SHOCK	CASE	BASE	CASE	EFFECT	%
1987	440.409	2.66	417.422	-2.70	22.987	5.51
1988	585.188	32.87	556.458	33.31	28.730	5.16
1989	638.214	9.06	605.085	8.74	33.129	5.48
1990	592.578	-7.15	554.208	-8.41	38.370	6.92
1991	674.566	13.84	630.612	13.79	43.954	6.97
1992	864.442	28.15	815.455	29.31	48.986	6.01

MM2D:

YEAR	SHOCK	CASE	BASE	CASE	EFFECT	%
1987	47.433	15.74	44.660	8.97	2.773	6.21
1988	59.753	25.97	56.695	26.95	3.058	5.39
1989	59.235	-.87	56.102	-1.05	3.133	5.58
1990	65.370	10.36	61.685	9.95	3.686	5.98
1991	64.932	-.67	60.687	-1.62	4.245	7.00
1992	162.915	150.90	157.725	159.90	5.190	3.29

MMCD:

YEAR	SHOCK	CASE	BASE	CASE	EFFECT	%
1987	478.914	3.89	453.676	-1.59	25.238	5.56
1988	640.170	33.67	608.627	34.15	31.543	5.18
1989	699.553	9.28	663.180	8.96	36.373	5.48
1990	659.222	-5.77	617.094	-6.95	42.128	6.83
1991	740.402	12.31	692.143	12.16	48.259	6.97
1992	1015.024	37.09	961.241	38.88	53.783	5.60

APPENDIX: China's Econometric Model for Project LINK

1. List of Equations

(1) Total consumption (real)
$$C = CH + CG$$

(2) Public consumption (real)
$$log(CG) = 0.45820 * log(CG)[-1] + 0.68077 * log(GTEB/PGDP)$$
$$\quad\quad (6.29667) \quad\quad\quad\quad\quad (5.14378)$$
$$\quad - 0.15344 * spike(89,1) - 0.13759 * spike(88,1) + 1.95028$$
$$\quad (1.83045) \quad\quad\quad (1.65159) \quad\quad\quad (6.70556)$$
$DW(1) = 1.4077 \quad\quad\quad DW(2) = 2.2044 \quad\quad\quad Rsq(adj) = 0.9600$
ANNUAL data for 19 periods from 1978 to 1996

(3) Public consumption (nominal)
$$CGN = CG * CPI/100$$

(4) Household consumption (real)
$$CH = CHR + CHU$$

(5) Household consumption (nominal)
$$CHN = CHRN + CHUN$$

(6) Rural household consumption (real)
$$CHR = 0.78355 * CHR[-1] + 0.26432 * WHR/CPIR * 100$$
$$\quad\quad (6.85609) \quad\quad\quad\quad (2.64562)$$
$$\quad -6.41603*(INRD-PCH(CPIR))-668.247*spike(89,1)-402.035*spike(90,1)$$
$$\quad (0.79103) \quad\quad\quad\quad\quad (3.07416) \quad\quad\quad (4.48635)$$
$DW(1) = 2.2926 \quad\quad\quad DW(2) = 1.4648 \quad\quad\quad Rsq(adj) = 0.9947$
ANNUAL data for 18 periods from 1979 to 1996

(7) Rural household consumption (nominal)
$$CHRN = CHR * CPIR/100$$

(8) Urban household consumption (real)
$$CHU = 0.77268 * CHU[-1] + 0.28515 * (WHU/CPIU * 100)$$
$$\quad\quad (6.86342) \quad\quad\quad\quad (2.97208)$$
$$\quad -5.11095 * (INRD - PCH(CPIU)) - 383.630 * spike(89,1) - 57.8420$$
$$\quad (1.15439) \quad\quad\quad\quad (3.63899) \quad\quad\quad (1.04323)$$
$DW(1) = 2.2817 \quad\quad\quad DW(2) = 2.0954 \quad\quad\quad Rsq(adj) = 0.9979$
ANNUAL data for 18 periods from 1979 to 1996

(9) Urban household consumption (nominal)
$$CHUN = CHU * CPIU/100$$

(10) Total consumption (nominal)
$$CN = CHN + CGN$$

(11) Consumer price index (1990=100)
$$CPI = 0.40065 * CPIU + 0.60009 * CPIR$$
$$\quad (170.726) \quad\quad\quad (240.267)$$

$DW(1) = 1.4998$ $\qquad$ $DW(2) = 2.6701$ $\qquad$ $Rsq(adj) = 1.0000$

ANNUAL data for 19 periods from 1978 to 1996

(12) Rural consumer price index (1990=100)

$$log(CPIR) = 0.94833 * log(CPI) + 0.10219 * log(PNVNM) - 0.24566$$
$\qquad$ (35.0204) $\qquad$ (3.16205) $\qquad$ (5.98810)

$DW(1) = 0.9803$ $\qquad$ $DW(2) = 2.2490$ $\qquad$ $Rsq(adj) = 0.9994$

ANNUAL data for 19 periods from 1978 to 1996

(13) Urban consumer price index (1990=100)

$$log(CPIU) = 1.06396 * log(CPI) + 0.09694 * log(PNVNM) - 0.71196$$
$\qquad$ (25.3912) $\qquad$ (2.02500) $\qquad$ (12.7740)

$DW(1) = 1.0141$ $\qquad$ $DW(2) = 2.2367$ $\qquad$ $Rsq(adj) = 0.9990$

ANNUAL data for 16 periods from 1981 to 1996

(14) Total exports (goods + services, nominal US $)

$$EX = EXM + EXS$$

(15) Total exports for goods (real, US $)

$$log(EXM) = 0.94738 * log(WEX) + 0.59851 * log(PEXM/(PNVIND/RATE))$$
$\qquad$ (5.11516) $\qquad$ (3.42787)

$$-0.29676 * spike(90,1) - 0.22464 * spike(91,1)$$
$\qquad$ (2.84262) $\qquad$ (3.2020)

$$-0.32021 * spike(80,1) - 6.51098$$
$\qquad$ (5.1636)

$DW(1) = 1.2798$ $\qquad$ $DW(2) = 1.5172$ $\qquad$ $Rsq(adj) = 0.9790$

ANNUAL data for 17 periods from 1978 to 1996

(16) Total exports for goods (nominal, US $)

$$EXMN = EXM * PEXM/100$$

(17) Exports for services (real, US $)

$$EXS = EXSN/PEXM * 100$$

(18) Exports for services (nominal, US $)

$$EXSN - EXSTM = 0.06313 * (EXMN+IMMN) - 6.99868$$
$\qquad$ (18.9662) $\qquad$ (1.51143)

$DW(1) = 1.8917$ $\qquad$ $DW(2) = 1.0751$ $\qquad$ $Rsq(adj) = 0.9522$

ANNUAL data for 19 periods from 1978 to 1996

(19) Repaid capital and interest (nominal, US $)

$$GBE = 0.31149 * GB + 0.23361 * GB[-1] + 0.15574 * GB[2]$$
$\qquad$ (21.5382) $\qquad$ (21.5382) $\qquad$ (21.5382)

$$+ 0.07787 * GB[-3] - 33.5857$$
$\qquad$ (21.5382) $\qquad$ (1.70340)

$DW(1) = 1.2677$ $\qquad$ $DW(2) = 2.3157$ $\qquad$ $Rsq(adj) = 0.9626$

ANNUAL data for 19 periods from 1978 to 1996

(20) Fiscal balance

$$GDEF = GTEB - GTRB$$

(21) GDP (real)
$$GDP = I + C + J + (EX–IM) * RATE$$
(22) GDP (nominal)
$$GDPN = GDP * PGDP/100$$
(23) Total fiscal expenditure (including debt, nominal)
$$GTE = GTEB + GBE$$
(24) Fiscal expenditure (excluding debt, nominal)
$$GTEB=1.07522*GTEB.1*PGDP/PGDP[–1]–528.337 * spike(94,1) – 62.0986$$
      (49.2023)   (2.90462)   (0.85410)

DW(1) = 1.7464   *DW(2) = 1.9929*   *Rsq(adj) = 0.9938*

ANNUAL data for 18 periods from 1979 to 1996

(25) Total fiscal revenue (including debt, nominal)
$$GTR = GTRB + GB$$
(26) Fiscal revenue (excluding debt, nominal)
$$GTRB = 0.99239 * TAX + 217.098$$
        (20.9464)   (1.25627)

DW(1) = 2.0622   *DW(2) = 1.9421*   *Rsq(adj) = 0.9891*

ANNUAL data for 18 periods from 1979 to 1996

$$AR\_0 = +0.51699 * AR\_1$$
       (2.28475)

(27) Fixed investment (real)
$$I = IFD + IFF$$
(28) Domestic fixed investment (real)
$$IFD=0.78024*IFD[–1]+0.33745*(IFGN+LOANF–LOANF[–1])/PIF*100$$
     (4.93819)   (1.27647)
$$+0.18643*(GDPN–WH–GTRB)/PIF*100–24.8477*(INDR–PCH(PIF))$$
     (2.22686)   (1.70239)

DW(1) = 0.9838   *DW(2) = 1.9815 Rsq(adj) = 0.9810*

ANNUAL data for 19 periods from 1978 to 1996

(29) FDI (real)
$$IFF = IFFUS * RATE/PIF * 100$$
(30) Fixed investment (nominal)
$$IFN = I * PIF/100$$
(31) Total imports (goods + services, real US $)
$$IM = IMM + IMS$$
(32) Imports of goods (real, US $)
$$log(IMM) = 0.36106 * log (IMM)[–1] + 0.96729 * log (GDP)$$
        (2.29787)   (4.95828)
$$+ 0.53331 * log (PIF/((rate[–1] + rate)/2)/PIMM) – 3.88035$$
        (3.34277)   (4.33046)

DW(1) = 1.8715   *DW(2) = 2.9319*   *Rsq(adj) = 0.9751*

ANNUAL data for 19 periods from 1978 to 1996

(33) Imports of goods (nominal, US $)
$$IMMN = IMM * PIMM/100$$
(34) Service imports (real, US $)
$$IMS = IMSN/PIMM * 100$$
(35) Service imports (nominal, US $)

$IMSN=0.12656 * IFFUS + 0.30098 * IFFUS[-1] + 0.47539 * IFFUS[-2]$
   (1.14555)   (7.20327)   (4.64413)
   $+ 0.03807 * (IMMN+EXMN) + 0.66572$
   (1.97432)   (0.04842)

DW(1) = 2.4927   DW(2) = 1.9191   Rsq(adj) = 0.9752
ANNUAL data for 18 periods from 1979 to 1996

(36) Urban labor force supply

$LFU = 1.00003 * LFU[-1] + 0.36476 * (POPU[-16] - POPU[-17])$
   (57.5631)   (2.45742)
   $+ 1841.04 * spike(90,1) + 371.054 * spike(94,1) + 298.691$
   (8.88961)   (1.72657)   (1.26093)

DW(1) = 1.8304   DW(2) = 2.4578   Rsq(adj) = 0.9961
ANNUAL data for 18 periods from 1979 to 1996

(37) Urban labor force demand

$LFUE= 0.85368 * LFUE[-1] + 0.06484 * (GDP-NVA)$
   (13.4525)   (2.58415)
   $+ 1789.91 * spike(90,1) + 1664.22$
   (8.77556)   (2.90535)

DW(1) = 2.0714   DW(2) = 2.6669   Rsq(adj) = 0.9961
ANNUAL data for 18 periods from 1979 to 1996

(38) Loans (nominal)
$$LOAN = LOANOT + LOANF$$
(39) Loans for fixed investment (nominal)

$log(LOANF)= 0.29223 * log(LOANF)[-1]$
        (1.27960)
        $+ 0.82891 * log((TSD+M0)/(1+INRD/100)) - 2.39909$
        (3.24100)   (3.11277)

DW(1) = 0.7690   DW(2) = 1.5897   Rsq(adj) = 0.9962
ANNUAL data for 10 periods from 1986 to 1995

(40) Other loan (nominal)

$log(LOANOT) = 0.66272* log(LOANOT)[-1] + 0.68440 * log(GDP)$
         (5.76505)   (2.98179)
         $- 0.04335 * log (INRD) - 3.33450$
         (0.44281)   (2.90412)

DW(1) = 1.8249   DW(2) = 2.4045   Rsq(adj) = 0.9962
ANNUAL data for 17 periods from 1979 to 1995

(41) M0 Currency in circulation (nominal)

$$M0 = 0.17098 * M0[-1] + 0.15909 * LOAN + 44.4832 * INRD$$
$$\quad\ (0.47442) \qquad\qquad (2.66363) \qquad\qquad (0.63442)$$
$$\quad - 387,165 * spike(90,1) - 381.007 * spike(91,1) - 389.346$$
$$\quad\ (1.24843) \qquad\qquad (1.13464) \qquad\qquad (0.93893)$$

DW(1) = 1.8585   *DW(2) = 1.5649*   *Rsq(adj) = 0.9859*
ANNUAL data for 17 periods from 1979 to 1995

(42) Agricultural value added (nominal)

$$NVAN = NVA * PNVA/100$$

(43) General price index of export (1990=100)

$$log(PEXM) = 0.54388 * log(PWM) + 0.14192 * log(PGDP)$$
$$\qquad\qquad (4.94536) \qquad\qquad (2.46443)$$
$$\qquad - 0.19500 * spike(96,1) + 1.40126$$
$$\qquad\quad (4.29553) \qquad\qquad (2.92648)$$

DW(1) = 1.0457   *DW(2) = 1.4914*   *Rsq(adj) = 0.9310*
ANNUAL data for 19 periods from 1978 to 1996

$$AR\_0 = + 0.51169 * AR\_1$$
$$\qquad\qquad (3.39793)$$

(44) GDP deflator (1990=100)

$$PGDP = 0.25431 * PIF + 0.63672 * CPI + 12.9321$$
$$\qquad\quad (7.44297) \qquad (17.8540) \qquad (19.1308)$$

DW(1) = 1.2447   *DW(2) = 2.2078*   *Rsq(adj) = 0.9990*
ANNUAL data for 19 periods from 1978 to 1996

(45) Price index for fixed investment (1990=100)

$$log(PIF) = 0.79732 * log(PNVIND) + 0.15839 * log(WAGEA)$$
$$\qquad\qquad (3.61989) \qquad\qquad (1.17727)$$
$$\qquad + 0.17489 * log(PIMM * RATE) + 0.15076 * spike(93,1) - 1.32435$$
$$\qquad\quad (2.62131) \qquad\qquad\qquad (4.06089) \qquad\qquad (3.80814)$$

DW(1) = 1.7060   *DW(2) = 2.0111*   *Rsq(adj) = 0.9944*
ANNUAL data for 19 periods from 1978 to 1996

(46) General price index for imports (1990=100)

$$log(PIMM) = 0.60367 * log(PIMM)[-1] + 0.28260 * log(PWM) + 0.50452$$
$$\qquad\qquad\quad (3.16438) \qquad\qquad\qquad (1.01865) \qquad\qquad (0.80793)$$

DW(1) = 1.0876   *DW(2) = 1.1481*   *Rsq(adj) = 0.8132*
ANNUAL data for 19 periods from 1978 to 1996

(47) Deflator for agricultural value added (1990=100)

$$log(PNVA) = 0.83442 * log(PPAS) + 0.29483 * log(PNVIND)$$
$$\qquad\qquad\quad (15.2546) \qquad\qquad\quad (3.01896)$$
$$\qquad - 0.11868 * spike(89,1) - 0.59247$$
$$\qquad\quad (4.43494) \qquad\qquad (2.74748)$$

DW(1) = 1.2900   *DW(2) = 1.9739*   *Rsq(adj) = 0.9977*
ANNUAL data for 19 periods from 1978 to 1996

(48) Deflator for industrial value added (1990=100)

$$log(PNVIND) = 0.86415 * log(PNVIND)[-1] + 0.08879 * log(WAGEA)$$
$$\quad\quad (25.0423) \quad\quad\quad\quad\quad\quad\quad (4.24312)$$

$DW(1) = 1.3087 \quad\quad\quad DW(2) = 2.2907 \quad\quad\quad Rsq(adj) = 0.9879$
ANNUAL data for 19 periods from 1978 to 1996

(49) Deflator for value added of other service sector (1990=100)

$$log(PNVNM)=0.79063* log(PNVNM)[-1]+ 0.15736 * log(WAGEA) - 0.17172$$
$$\quad\quad (6.60710) \quad\quad\quad\quad\quad\quad (2.86911) \quad\quad\quad\quad\quad (0.92175)$$

$DW(1) = 1.6608 \quad\quad\quad DW(2) = 2.1678 \quad\quad\quad Rsq(adj) = 0.9848$
ANNUAL data for 18 periods from 1979 to 1996

(50) Retail price index (1990=100)

$$log(CPI) = 0.50420 * log(PNVA) + 0.43915 * log(PNVIND)$$
$$\quad\quad (4.29070) \quad\quad\quad\quad\quad (2.63027)$$
$$\quad + 0.10416 * log(PIMM * RATE) + 0.10489 * spike(89,1) - 0.41558$$
$$\quad\quad (3.72892) \quad\quad\quad\quad\quad\quad\quad (4.38860) \quad\quad\quad\quad\quad (1.25141)$$

$DW(1) = 1.0172 \quad\quad\quad DW(2) = 1.5947 \quad\quad\quad Rsq(adj) = 0.9971$
ANNUAL data for 18 periods from 1979 to 1996

(51) Total taxes (nominal)

$$TAX= 1.25085 * (TAXA + TAXCUS + TAXIC) - 32.1851$$
$$\quad\quad (24.2059) \quad\quad\quad\quad\quad\quad\quad\quad\quad (0.23439)$$

$DW(1) = 1.4181 \quad\quad\quad DW(2) = 1.8506 \quad\quad\quad Rsq(adj) = 0.9893$
ANNUAL data for 19 periods from 1978 to 1996

$$AR\_0 = + 0.43408 * AR\_1$$
$$\quad\quad (1.64282)$$

(52) Tax on agriculture (nominal)

$$TAXA= 0.02981 * NVAN - 4.15745 * (TREND-1977) - 0.35004$$
$$\quad\quad (25.2977) \quad\quad\quad (5.43712) \quad\quad\quad\quad\quad (0.08568)$$

$DW(1) = 2.9789 \quad\quad\quad DW(2) = 1.8144 \quad\quad\quad Rsq(adj) = 0.9921$
ANNUAL data for 19 periods from 1978 to 1996

(53) Tariff (nominal)

$$TAXCUS = 0.00794 * RATE * IMMN + 96.7238 * spike(85,1)$$
$$\quad\quad (3.69585) \quad\quad\quad\quad\quad\quad (5.49120)$$
$$\quad + 12.2194 * (TREND-1977) + 0.86701$$
$$\quad\quad (8.55414) \quad\quad\quad\quad\quad\quad (0.08748)$$

$DW(1) = 1.8525 \quad\quad\quad DW(2) = 1.9367 \quad\quad\quad Rsq(adj) = 0.9695$
ANNUAL data for 19 periods from 1978 to 1996

(54) Tax on industry and commerce (nominal)

$$TAXIC = 0.06354 * (GDPN - NVAN) + 72.9956 * (TREND-1977)$$
$$\quad\quad (13.2358) \quad\quad\quad\quad\quad\quad (5.50091)$$
$$\quad + 100.924$$
$$\quad\quad (1.18356)$$

$DW(1) = 1.6473 \quad\quad\quad DW(2) = 2.2493 \quad\quad\quad Rsq(adj) = 0.9874$
ANNUAL data for 19 periods from 1978 to 1996

(55) Remaining savings deposits (nominal)

$$TSD = 1.05091 * (TSDF + TSDU + TSDR) + 1389.51$$
$$(47.5566) \qquad\qquad (4.01766)$$

$DW(1) = 0.7754 \qquad\qquad DW(2) = 1.5656 \qquad Rsq(adj) = 0.9925$

ANNUAL data for 18 periods from 1978 to 1995

(56) Remaining savings deposits of enterprise (nominal)

$$TSDF = 0.54452 * TSDF[-1] + 0.36093 * (GDPN - WH - GTRB)$$
$$(3.12676) \qquad\qquad (4.63024)$$
$$- 1243.87 * spike(93,1)$$
$$(3.28620)$$

$DW(1) = 1.5007 \qquad\qquad DW(2) = 2.0634 \qquad Rsq(adj) = 0.9921$

ANNUAL data for 18 periods from 1978 to 1995H

(57) Remaining savings deposits for rural household (nominal)

$$TSDR - TSDR[-1] = 0.10489 * WHR + 3.91041 * (INRD - PCH(CPIR))$$
$$(24.6886) \qquad\qquad (0.99165)$$
$$+ 364.166 * spike(94,1) - 171.518$$
$$(4.16469) \qquad\qquad (6.13977)$$

$DW(1) = 1.9307 \qquad\qquad DW(2) = 1.0448 \qquad Rsq(adj) = 0.9783$

ANNUAL data for 18 periods from 1979 to 1996

(58) Remaining savings deposits for urban household (nominal)

$$TSDU = 0.90661 * TSDU[-1] + 0.59567 * WHU$$
$$(7.55538) \qquad\qquad (3.66747)$$
$$+15.7096 * (INRD - PCH(CPIU)) - 883.744$$
$$(0.66275) \qquad\qquad (3.26083)$$

$DW(1) = 1.2878 \qquad\qquad DW(2) = 1.8628 \qquad Rsq(adj) = 0.9983$

ANNUAL data for 16 periods from 1981 to 1996

(59) Urban unemployment

$$UEM = LFU - LFUE$$

(60) Urban unemployment rate

$$UEMR = UEM/LFU * 100$$

(61) Wage rate

$$WAGEA = 0.24428 * WAGEA[-1] + 0.54785 * WHu/LFUE * 10000$$
$$(4.23032) \qquad\qquad (16.7813)$$
$$- 127.960 * spike (89,1) + 75.4299$$
$$(2.92880) \qquad\qquad (3.92285)$$

$DW(1) = 1.8531 \qquad\qquad DW(2) = 2.8085 \qquad Rsq(adj) = 0.9994$

ANNUAL data for 18 periods from 1979 to 1996

(62) Disposable income (nominal)

$$WH = WHU + WHR$$

(63) Net income of rural households (nominal)

$$WHR = 0.54377 * WHR[-1] + 0.54080 * (NVAN - TAXA) + 0.07432 * IFN$$
$$(4.95902) \qquad\qquad (3.88829) \qquad\qquad (2.52360)$$

$DW(1) = 0.6939 \qquad\qquad DW(2) = 1.3314 \qquad Rsq(adj) = 0.9979$

ANNUAL data for 19 periods from 1978 to 1996
(64) Disposable income of urban households (nominal)

$$WHU = 0.35335 * (GDPN - NVAN - TAXIC) + 420.452 * spike(90,1)$$
$$(168.110) \qquad\qquad (3.22975)$$
$$+ 92.2322$$
$$(2.24581)$$

$DW(1) = 1.8047$ $DW(2) = 1.7897$ $Rsq(adj) = 0.9994$
ANNUAL data for   19 periods from 1978 to 1996

2. Explanation of Variables
(1) Endogenous Variables

C	Total consumption (real)
CG	Public consumption (real)
CGN	Public consumption (nominal)
CH	Household consumption (real)
CHN	Household consumption (nominal)
CHR	Rural household consumption (real)
CHU	Urban household consumption (real)
CHUN	Urban household consumption (nominal)
CN	Total consumption (nominal)
CPI	Consumer price index (1990=100)
CPIR	Rural consumer price index (1990=100)
CPIU	Urban consumer price index (1990=100)
EX	Total exports (goods + services, nominal US $)
EXM	Total exports for goods (real, US $)
EXMN	Total exports for goods (nominal, US $)
EXS	Exports for services (real, US $)
EXSN	Exports for services (nominal, US $)
GBE	Repaid capital and interest (nominal, US $)
GDEF	Fiscal deficit
GDP	Gross domestic product (real)
GDPN	Gross domestic product (nominal)
GTE	Total fiscal expenditure (including debt, nominal)
GTEB	Fiscal expenditure (excluding debt, nominal)
GTR	Total fiscal revenue (including debt, nominal)
GTRB	Fiscal revenue (excluding debt, nominal)
I	Fixed investment (real)
IFD	Domestic fixed investment (real)
IFF	Foreign direct investment (real)
IFN	Fixed investment (nominal)
IM	Total imports (goods + services, real, US $)
IMM	Imports for goods (real, US $)
IMMN	Imports for goods (nominal, US $)
IMS	Service imports (real, US $)

IMSN	Service imports (nominal, US $)
LFU	Urban labor force supply
LFUE	Urban labor force demand
LOAN	Loans (nominal)
LOANF	Loans for fixed investment (nominal)
LOANOT	Other loans (nominal)
M0	Currency in circulation (nominal)
NVAN	Agricultural value added (nominal)
PEXM	General price index of exports (1990=100)
PGDP	GDP deflator (1990=100)
PIF	Price index for fixed investment (1990=100)
PIMM	General price index for imports (1990=100)
PNVA	Deflator for agricultural value added (1990=100)
PNVIND	Deflator for industrial value added (1990=100)
PNVNM	Deflator for value added in other service sector (1990=100)
CPI	Retail price index (1990=100)
TAX	Total taxes (nominal)
TAXA	Taxes on agriculture (nominal)
TAXCUS	Tariffs (nominal)
TAXIC	Taxes on industry and commerce (nominal)
TSD	Remaining savings deposits (nominal)
TSDF	Remaining savings deposits of enterprise (nominal)
TSDR	Remaining savings deposits for rural household (nominal)
TSDU	Remaining savings deposits for urban household (nominal)
UEM	Urban unemployment
UEMR	Urban unemployment rate
WAGEA	Wage rate
WH	Household disposable income (nominal)
WHR	Rural household net income (nominal)
WHU	Urban household net income (nominal)

(2) Exogenous Variables

EXSTM	International tourism income (nominal, US $)
GB	Income from debts
IFFUS	Foreign direct investment (real, US $)
IFGN	Fiscal allocation for fixed investment (nominal)
IRND	Deposit interest rate for one year (%)
J	Change in stocks (real)
NVA	Agricultural value added (real)
POPU	Urban population
PPAS	Price index for farm and sideline products by state (1990=100)
PWM	World export price index (1990=100)
RATE	Exchange rate (Yuan/US $)
TREND	Time series trend
WEX	Total world exports (real, US $)

References

Cheon, Munkun and Yangwoo Kim (1985), "Korea Model", in Ichimura-Ezaki (ed.) *Econometric Models of Asian LINK,* Springer-Verlag: Tokyo 1985.

Chiu, Yi-chung, (1985) "Taiwan Model", in Ichimura-Ezaki, *op. cit..*

Goldberger, Arthur S. (1959), "Impact Multipliers and Dynamic Properties of the Klein-Goldberger Model" (North-Holland Publishing Company: Amsterdam).

Klein, Lawrence R. and Edwin Burmeister (1976), "Econometric Model Performance", University of Pennsylvania Press.

Klein, Lawrence R. and Richard M. Young (1980), "An Introduciton to Econometric Forecasting and Forecasting Models", Lexington Books: Lexington .

Lin, Tzong-Biau and Win-Lin Chou (1985), "Hong Kong Model", in Ichimura-Ezaki, *op. cit..*

Motamen, Homa (1988), "Economic Modeling in the OECD", Chapman and Hall, London

Toida, Mitsuru and Youcai Liang (1990), "Econometric Link Model of China and Japan", IDE Joint Research Program Series No. 81.

Yu, Tzong-Shian and Yuang-San Lee (1978), "Experience of Econometric Modeling in Taiwan", Taiwan.

_____ (1985), "Econometric LINK System for ASEAN", Final Report of ELSA, Vol. 1, IDE, Japan.

_____ (1984), "Review of National Economies and Econometric Models", Interim Report of ELSA, Vol. 1, IDE, Japan.

5   A Computable General Equilibrium Model for The Chinese Economy[*]

Shantong Li and Fan Zhai

Development Research Center, The State Council

1. Introduction

Since the launching of economic reform and opening to the outside world, both the structure and operational system of the Chinese economy have changed dramatically. Although some structural and institutional rigidities have not been eliminated, market mechanisms are becoming a dominant force in determining economic activities in China. This changing situation poses a challenge to both policy makers and policy analysts. There is a strong need for quantitative analytical models, which can simulate the operation and interactions of the economic system, for analyzing the social-economic impact of policy change and external shocks.

For this purpose, we have developed a computable general equilibrium (CGE) model of the Chinese economy to serve as a quantitative tool for macroeconomic and structural policy analysis. CGE models have been used to analyze a wide variety of economic issues in both developed economies and developing economies since the 1960s, and CGE modeling has become a leading tool in multi-sector, economy-wide modeling for policy analysis.

The Development Research Center (DRC) of the State Council, PRC began development of a CGE model for the Chinese economy in the early 1990s. A ten-sector prototype CGE model of the Chinese economy was constructed in 1993 by DRC in collaboration with The Shanghai Academy of Social Science and The Institute of System Science, Chinese Academy of Science (Wang, 1993). The CGE model described in this paper is the second

[*] We are grateful to Wang Huijiong, David Roland-Holst, Dominique van der Mensbrugghe, Sébastien Dessus and Wang Zhi for their help in developing this Chinese CGE model.

generation of a CGE model of the DRC, which is named as DRCCGE.[1] The development of DRCCGE was initiated in the year 1995. During the period January—May, 1995, DRC compiled a detailed 64-sector Social Accounting Matrix (SAM) for China based upon the 1987 input-output table in collaboration with Huazhong University of Science and Technology. This SAM provided a good data base for the development of a Chinese CGE model. From June to August, 1995, DRC cooperated with the OECD Development Center to formulate a recursive dynamic Chinese CGE model with sixty-four sectors and ten groups of households. The base year of the model is 1987. This model inherited the structure of the prototype CGE model developed for the Trade and Environment Programme of the OECD Development Center (Beghin, *et al.*, 1994). We also utilized the CGE model-ing frame-work developed by Dr. Dominique van der Mensbrugghe of the OECD Development Center. From November, 1995, to April, 1996, DRC compiled a SAM based on a 1992 input-output table and updated the CGE model to the new data set. There was also some revision in the model structure according to the structure of 1992 SAM. This resulted in the model DRCCGE1 (Zhai and Li, 1997). This model has been applied in studies on medium-term economic growth and structural change, environment and structural change, etc. From summer 1996 to spring 1997, the model builders of DRC cooperated with Dr. Zhi Wang of Purdue University to update the tax side of the model. A value-added tax and export rebate mechanism are incorporated into the model to capture the major changes in China's 1994 tax reform. Some simulations on tariff reduction and tax replacement have been conducted with the updated model (Wang and Zhai, 1998). From November, 1997, DRC began the development of DRCCGE2. It includes two major improvements: updating the data set to the year 1995 and differentiating China's two separate trade regimes—the ordinary trade regime and the processing trade regime. DRCCGE2 is already operational, and it has been used in the study of "The Impact of China's Joining the World Trade Organization".

The present paper provides a description of DRCCGE2. It is organized as follows. Section 1 is an introduction. Section 2 describes the main methodology, and briefly introduces the characteristics of the CGE. The detailed structure of DRCCGE is introduced in section 3. Section 4 discusses the numerical specification of the CGE model, i.e. the compilation of the bench-

---

[1] DRCCGE, Dynamic Recursive Chinese CGE, which is developed and maintained by the DRC (Development Research Center of the State Council, P.R.C.).

mark equilibrium data set. The last section introduces some applications of this Chinese CGE model.

2. Methodology—Why a CGE model?

CGE models have been applied to over fifty countries and economic communities in the last thirty years and are making valuable contributions to research on taxation, international trade, income distribution, environment and development strategy. CGE models have the following characteristics (Wilcoxen, 1997):

- Multiple interacting agents
- Behavior derived from optimization
- Multiple markets
- Often highly disaggregated
- Finds a decentralized equilibrium rather than optimizing a planner's objective function
- Designed for policy analysis

The CGE model can be thought of as incorporating particular specifications of production and demand functions in the well-known Arrow-Debreu general equilibrium framework. Through explicit specification of production and demand functions for all agents, together with market clearing, it takes into account the interdependence among all markets. The CGE approach reveals more extensive economic linkages than can be captured by partial equilibrium or macro-econometric models. With their clear microeconomic structure, with links between micro and macro variables, these models are no longer "black boxes", despite their large scale.

A CGE model usually starts from a mapping of the flow of goods and services, factors of production, and payments in an economy (called a social accounting matrix—SAM). SAM provides a closed accounting system which details all the basic identities for the modeled economy. The accounting consistency is imposed in CGE models: there can be no sources of supply other than domestic production, inventories, or imports, and no destination of demand other than consumption, investment, inventories, and exports. Expenditures and income also have to match; budget constraints, public and private, have to be respected. This implies that the cost of any subsidies or transfers has to be financed, and revenue from any taxes or tariffs has to be allocated (Mercenier and Srinivasan, 1994). Therefore, the impact of alternative policies on equilibrium prices and on each element of the SAM can be fully traced.

The counterfactual experiment widely used in CGE simulation is the empirical analogue of the comparative-static analysis that is common in theoretical work. Such experiments begin with an assumption that the economy under study is in equilibrium (not necessarily a Walrasian type) in the presence of an existing policy regime and for the data in a chosen year. Using those data, the researchers chose parameter values so that the model will replicate this benchmark equilibrium through a model solution (called calibration). This "benchmark" or "observed" equilibrium data set serves as the point of comparison for counterfactual-equilibrium analysis of any hypothetical policy change (Whalley, 1985).

3. The Structure of DRCCGE2

DRCCGE2 is a 46-sector, 10-representative household (5 rural and 5 urban) recursive dynamic model with special treatment of China's foreign trade regime. It incorporates a stylized version of China's two separate trade regimes—an ordinary trade regime and a processing trade regime, differentiates production by ordinary production and export processing, and incorporates some other features of China's hybrid economy.

The starting point of the DRCCGE is the prototype CGE model for the Trade and Environment Programme of the OECD Development Centre (Beghin, et al., 1994). Some significant modifications were done in DRCCGE to capture the major features of the tax and trade system in the current Chinese economy. First, a value-added tax and export rebate mechanism are incorporated into the model, to capture the major changes in China's 1994 taxation reform (Wan and Zhai, 1998). Second, two separate trade regimes—an ordinary trade regime and a processing trade regime—are introduced into the model. As pointed out, correctly, by Naughton (1996), China had established two separate trading regimes by 1986—87. One is the export processing or export promotion regime, which is extremely open; most foreign-invested firms and some domestic firms paraticipate in it. The other is the traditional, but increasingly reformed, ordinary trade regime.

Since the 1990s, export processing has grown rapidly, and accounts for more than half of all exports. Obviously, to analyze external trade behavior and the impacts of alternative changes of trade policy in such an economy, it is very important to have an explicit treatment of the dualistic foreign trading regimes in the model. Finally, labor is classified by agricultural labor, industrial or commercial production workers and professionals in this model. We added migration behavior between agricultural labor and production workers in this model in order to specify the partial mobility of labor.

The sector classification of this CGE model and the SSB-IO sector concordance are given in Appendix A, and a detailed equation and variable list is presented in Appendix B. This section provides a brief description of the structure of the model.

3.1 Production and factor market

Forty-six production sectors and ten representative households (low, middle-low, middle, middle-high and high income households in both urban and rural areas) are specified in this model. There are five primary factors of production in the model, namely, agricultural land, capital, agricultural laborers, production workers, and professionals. Production and professional workers have basic education in common, but professionals usually have more advanced training. Agricultural laborers are those who have little or no education and work only in farm sectors.

We suppose that there are two types of competitive firms—*ordinary firms* and *export processing firms*—that produce the same product in the same industry. The products of ordinary firms are assumed to be sold on the domestic market or to be exported to the rest of the world by a constant elasticity of transformation (CET) function, while for the more recent export processing firm, their products are exported only.

The production technology is represented by a set of nested constant elasticity of substitution (CES) and Leontief functions. Technology in all sectors is assumed to exhibit constant returns to scale. At the first level, firms are assumed to use a composite of primary factors plus energy inputs, i.e., value-added plus the energy bundle, and aggregate non-energy intermediate input according to a CES cost function. At the second level, the division of intermediate non-energy demand is assumed to follow a Leontief specification; therefore, there is no substitution among other intermediate inputs. At the same level, the value-added plus energy bundle is divided between aggregate labor and energy-capital bundles, that are further split into energy and capital-land bundles. All composite bundles in each nest are assumed to substitute smoothly in a CES cost function. The degree of substitutability among them depends on their base year share in production and on the elasticity of substitution, which is assumed to be constant. The structure of production is illustrated in Figure 1.

Figure 1 Structure of Production

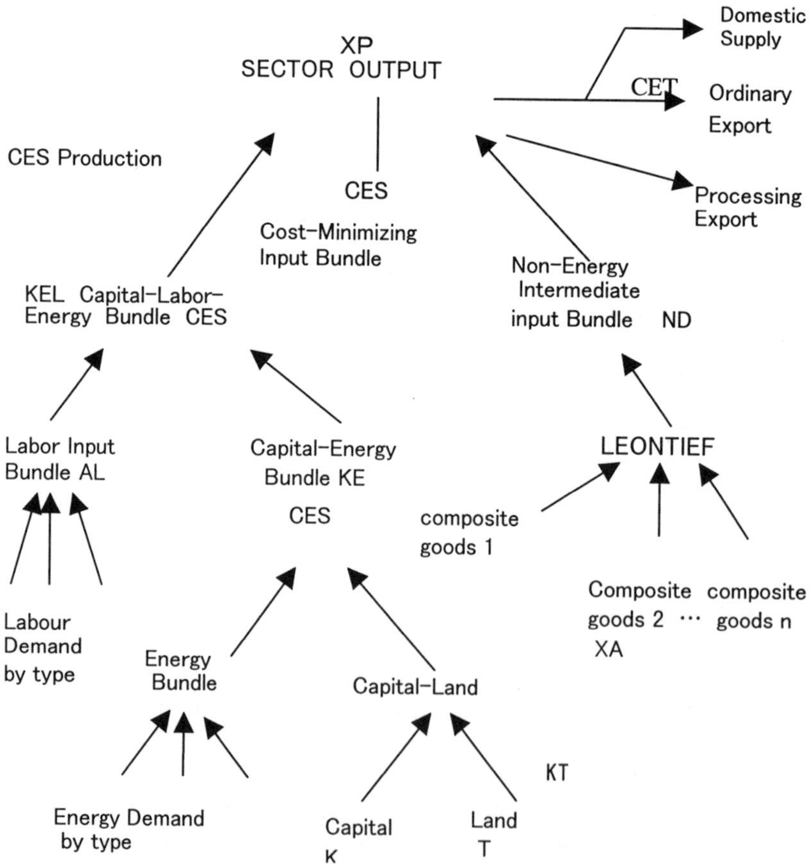

Each type of labor is assumed to be fully mobile across sectors and across the two types of firms. The agricultural laborers work only in farm sectors and production workers work only in non-farm sectors. There is no substitution between agricultural and production workers in production functions. In China, although it is being increasingly reformed, there are still large barriers for rural workers to migrate to urban areas. These barriers include the household registration regime, discrimination in employment, education and social security, *etc.* This segmented labor market is modeled in DRCCGE2 by incorporating partial mobility of agricultural laborers and production workers. We assumed that agricultural laborers and production workers can be converted from one to another. A CET function is used here to capture this specification, i.e., this transfer is determined by the relative wage of agricultural laborers and production workers, as well as the constant elasticity of transformation.

This model distinguishes between old and new capital goods. This assumption of vintage capital allows the substitution elasticity in the production function to differ according to the vintage of capital. The model also includes adjustment rigidities in the capital market. It is assumed that new capital goods are homogeneous and that old capital goods supply second-hand markets. The installed old capital in a sector can disinvest when this sector is in decline The supply curve of old capital is a simple constant elasticity function of relative rental rates. The higher the rental rate on old capital, the higher the supply of old capital. But the rental rate on old capital is not allowed to exceed the rental rate on new capital. Within sectors, capital is fully mobile among ordinary and export processing firms.

3.2 Trade

The rest of the world supplies imports and demands exports. Given China's small trade share in the world, import prices are exogenous in foreign currency (an infinite price-elasticity), i.e. the local consumption of imports does not affect the border price of imports. Exports are demanded according to constant-elasticity demand curves, the price-elasticities of which are high but finite. (Pomfret, 1997)

The ordinary firms allocate their output between export and domestic sales to maximize profits, subject to imperfect transformation between the two alternatives. All the output of export processing firms is sold on overseas markets. We assume that exports by ordinary firms and export processing firms are heterogeneous; a CES aggregation function with relatively high elasticities of substitution is used to form the composite export. In other words, we assume that the buyers from the rest of the world choose a mix between the two types of export in order to minimize their cost.

Three types of imports are differentiated in the model. The first one is ordinary trade import, which operates under an ordinary trade regime, subject to import tariff and nontariff barriers. The second one is duty-free import of raw materials and components for processing trade export. Most of these imports are used as intermediate inputs of export processing firms. But some are transferred to the domestic market. The third one is duty-free import of investment goods for foreign invested enterprises and export processing enterprises.

Agents are assumed to consider products from domestic supply and imports as imperfect substitutes, i.e., the Armington assumption. A two-level nested CES aggregation function is specified for each Armington composite commodity. At the top level, agents choose an optimal combination of the domestic good and an import aggregate, which is determined by a set of relative prices and the degree of substitutability. At the second level of the nest, the import aggregate is further split into ordinary imports, duty-free imports of investment and the imports for processing trade, which is transferred into the domestic market, again as a function of relative import prices and the degree of substitution across different import types. Note that the import prices are specific by import type because of the duty-free nature of the latter two types of imports.

We establish the difference between domestic price and world price in two parts, *i.e.* the tariff rate and non-tariff barriers. NTB is modeled as the tariff equivalent, which creates a pure rent to households. The quantitative restriction on agricultural products is modeled explicitly through a Leontief specification, where imports cannot exceed the quota allocation. The rates of agricultural quota rent are estimated endogenously. In the textile and apparel sectors, China faces the MFA quota in the markets of USA, Canada, EU and other countries. In our model, we treat this VER quota as an export tax equivalent that is added to the domestic export price. The quota premium is assumed to be obtained by households. In the simulations, the MFA quotas are exogenous, with export tax rates adjusted endogenously.

3.3 Demand

The representative households are assumed to maximize a Stone-Geary utility function over the 46 composite (Armington) goods subject to their budget constraints, which leads to an extended linear expenditure system (ELES) of household demand functions. Household savings are treated as demand for future consumption goods with zero subsistence quantity (Howe, 1975). An economy-wide consumer price index is specified as the price of savings. It represents the opportunity cost of giving up current consumption in exchange for future consumption. Other final demands, including social consumption and investment demand, are based on constant-expenditure-share functions for each composite commodity.

Figure 2 Structure of Demand

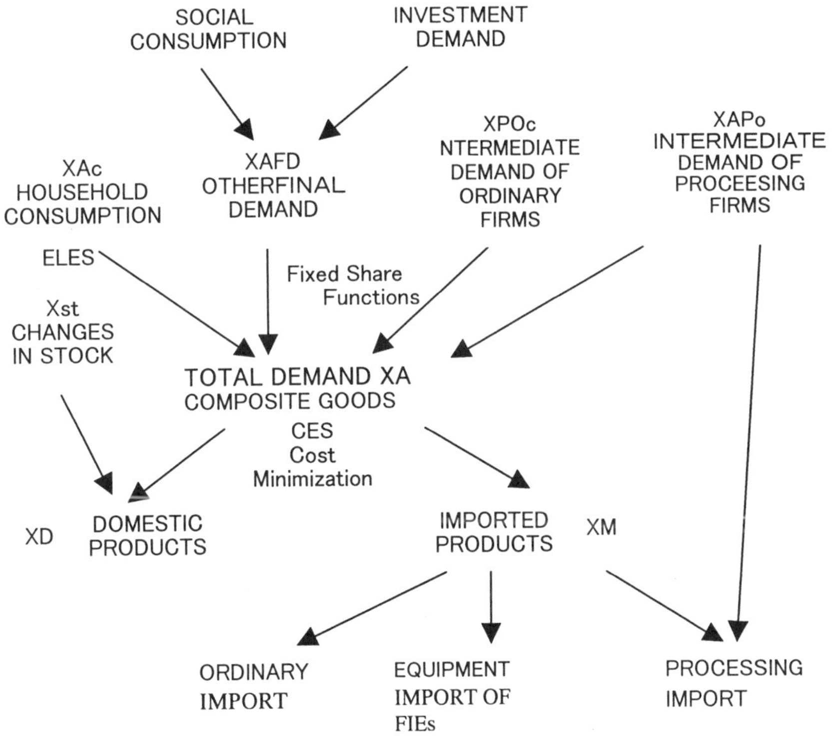

Stock change is assumed to be a demand for domestic products. Intermediate inputs for ordinary firms are provided by the Armington composite goods. While the intermediate inputs for export processing firms are composed of composite goods and duty-free imports of raw materials and components into processing trade export through a CES function. The intermediate inputs for ordinary firms, the domestic part of intermediate input for export processing firms, household consumption, and other final demands constitute the total demand for the same Armington composite of domestic products and imported goods from the rest of the world. The structure of demand is illustrated in Figure 2.

3.4 Income distribution

Production generates income, which is distributed to four major institutions, namely, enterprises, households, the government and an extra-budget public sector. Enterprise earnings equal a share of gross operating surplus, *i.e.* the sum of capital remuneration across all sectors, minus government corporate income taxes. The tax rate is a parameter in the model. However, it can be endogenized to meet government fiscal targets, in which case an adjustment parameter becomes endogenous. A part of net company income is allocated to households as distributed profits, based on fixed shares, which are the assumed shares of capital ownership by households. Another part of net company income is allocated to extra-budget public sectors as fees. Retained earnings, i.e. corporate savings for new investment and depreciation of capital, equals a residual of after-tax company income minus the distributed profits and fees.

Household income consists of labor earnings and the returns from land and capital that they own. Additionally, households receive the distributed corporate profits, transfers and subsidies from the government and remittances from the rest of the world. Households also receive several kinds of import and export quota rents. Assume that the rural households earn all the land returns. Rural households earn their labor income as both agricultural laborers and production workers, while urban households obtain their wages as both production and professional workers. But there is a difference when transformation between agricultural laborer and production worker occurs. If some agricultural laborers transferred to the non-agricultural sector and became production workers, their labor income would be allocated to rural households. On the contrary, if production workers transferred to the agricultural sector and became agricultural labor, their wages are still distributed to urban and rural households according to the distribution share of production workers' wages. The household income tax rate is set as a parameter, but an associated adjustment factor can be endogenous if the government budgets are exogenous. In this case, household tax schedules shift in or out to achieve government budget balance. Household disposable income equals total household income less taxes.

3.5 Government and the extra-budget public sector

The government collects taxes from producers, households and the foreign sector, transfers money to the household sector, and purchases public goods. It derives revenues from direct corporate and household income taxes, import tariffs, and various types of indirect taxes. Subsidies and export tax rebates enter as negative receipts. There are two types of indirect taxes in the model. The value-added tax, which is the most important part of indirect taxation in China after the 1994 tax reform, is treated as a tax levied on production factors; its revenues equal total sector value-added multiplied by a tax rate. The value-added tax is also levied on imports, while firms obtain rebates when they export. The other indirect tax, including various agricultural taxes, and business taxes on construction and services, is treated as a production tax levied on sectoral outputs.

Extra-budget public sectors collect fees from enterprise and households. Their incomes are allocated to consumption and saving. The consumption of extra-budget public sectors and government spending compose a type of final demand, i.e. social consumption.

3.6 Equilibrium and macro closure

Equilibrium is defined as a set of prices and quantities for goods and factors such that (i) demand equals supply for all goods and factors; (ii) each industry earns zero profit; and (iii) gross investment equals aggregate savings, which is the sum of domestic savings plus foreign capital inflows.

Macro closure in a CGE model involves both macroeconomic accounting balances and assumptions about adjustment behavior. It determines the manner in which the following three accounts are brought into balance: (i) the government budget; (ii) aggregate savings and investment; and (iii) the balance of payments.

Two government closure rules are implemented. Under the first rule, government savings is fixed at its base value and one of the taxes, or government transfers to households, is allowed to adjust uniformly to achieve the government fiscal target. Under the second closure rule, all tax levels and transfers are fixed, while real government savings is endogenous. This latter rule has significant consequences for the level of investment, since investment is driven by savings in the model.

The total value of investment expenditure equals total resources allocated to the investment sector; it includes retained corporate earnings, total household savings, government savings, extra-budget savings and foreign capital flows. In this model, aggregate investment is the endogenous sum of the separate saving components, i.e. a "saving driven" model. This specification corresponds to the "neoclassical" macroeconomic closure in CGE literature.

The last macroeconomic identity is the balance of payments. The value of imports, at world prices, must equal the value of exports at border prices, i.e., inclusive of export taxes and subsidies, plus the sum of net transfers and factor payments and net capital inflows. An exchange rate is specified to convert world prices, e.g., in dollars, into domestic prices. Either this exchange rate or total foreign capital inflow can be fixed while the other is allowed to adjust, providing alternative closure rules. With foreign saving set exgenously, the equilibrium would be achieved through changing the relative price of tradables to nontradables, or the real exchange rate.

3.7 Recursive dynamics

The current version of China's CGE model has a simple recursive dynamic structure as agents are assumed to be myopic and to base their decision on static expectations about prices and quantities. Dynamics in the model originate from accumulation of productive factors and productivity changes.

The within-period, static model is solved for several single-period equilibria from 1995—2010. Between the static model solutions, selected parameters are updated in the dynamic (between-period) module, either using lagged endogenous variables (from solutions in previous periods) or exogenously (on the basis of trend).

The growth rate of population, labor force, labor productivity and an autonomous energy efficiency improvement in energy use (known as the AEEI factor) are exogenous. The growth of capital is endogenously determined by the saving/investment relation. In the aggregate, the basic capital accumulation function equates the current capital stock to the depreciated stock inherited from the previous period plus gross investment. At the sectoral level, the specific accumulation functions may differ because the demand for (old and new) capital can be less than the depreciated stock of old capital. We assume that the producer decides the optimal way to divide production of total output across vintages. If sectoral demand exceeds what can be produced with the sectoral installed old capital, the producer will demand new capital. Otherwise, the producer will disinvest some of the installed capital.

In defining the reference simulation, a single economy-wide Hicks neutral efficiency factor (TFP) and sector specific agricultural productivity are determined endogenously to get a pre-specified growth path of real GDP and agricultural output. When alternative scenarios are simulated, the TFP growth rate is exogenous, and the growth rate of real GDP is endogenous.

4. Model Calibration and the Benchmark Equilibrium Data Set

The calibration approach is the most common method for parameterizing the CGE model (Mansur and Whalley, 1984). Its procedure is straightforward. When a benchmark data set consistent with the CGE model under study is ready, the value of model parameters can be computed by calibrating each equation in the model to the benchmark equilibrium data, under extraneous determination of some particular elasticity parameters. The model is solved backward, to generate a benchmark equilibrium as a model solution in the calibration procedure. There is no degree of freedom left in the calibration procedure. The parameters values determined by calib-ration are deterministic in nature, not statistical.

With a large amount of data (for example, a time series of SAMs), statistical estimation techniques could be used to find the parameters of applied general equilibrium models (Jorgenson, 1984). But in many developing countries the lack of time series data makes the application of the econometric approach to determine parameters of CGE models almost impossible.

The shortcoming of the calibration approach is obvious. It may rely on data for a single year, which means that whatever stochastic anomalies were present in that year will strongly influence the model. It also assumes that the benchmark year is a "representative" equilibrium, which sometimes is not the case. However, it is difficult to find a better alternative, especially for developing countries.

DRCCGE2 is calibrated for the 1995 Chinese SAM developed from the most recent I/O table (1995). The SAM provides a consistent framework to organize the relevant flow of value statistics for China's economy to satisfy the requirements of a benchmark data set for CGE modeling, as outlined in Whalley (1985). For each economic agent, there is a row that records incomes and a column that records expenditures. In particular, our SAM includes 46 production sectors (in which there are 13 agricultural and food sectors), 10 groups of household by relative income level. Production and trade are both divided between ordinary trade and processing trade in this SAM.

Table 1 presents the macro 1995 Chinese SAM. The original data for constructing the SAM are mainly from *Input-Output Table of 1995, Statistics Yearbook of China, Chinese Customs Statistics, The Third National Industrial Census of 1995* and *Households Survey*. A general description of the assembling of a Chinese SAM can be found in Zhai (1997), in which the assembling of a 1992 Chinese SAM is discussed. The following introduces some extensions of the 1995 SAM.

4.1 Trade data

The official Chinese input-output table includes only a single vector of "net exports". We aggregated the data of exports and imports from Chinese customs statistics at 8-digits HS classification to 118 SSB input-output sectoral classification for all merchandise. Because the imports and exports were valued at domestic prices when the net exports column in the input-output table was estimated, the imports in. The input-output table include tariff, other import taxes (VAT), rents of NTBs and FTCs' profits (and losses), and the exports in the input-output table includes VAT, rebated for exports, FTCs' profits (and losses) and quota rents in textile and apparel sectors.

We estimated the trade data for 118 input-output sectors by trade styles based upon customs statistics at 2-digits HS classification by different trade styles. Then the sectoral tariff data are estimated, based on actual duty collections, official tariff rates and sectoral import by different trade styles. Other import taxes and taxes rebated for exports by sector are calculated by the assumption of a unified rate. The export tariff equivalent in textiles and apparel is used for the estimation of a GTAP database. According to the above information, we can obtain FTCs' profits (or losses) based upon the difference between the net exports of an input-output table and the net exports of customs statistics. The exports and imports of the "commerce" sector are also adjusted to the values at the border price by taking the FTCs' profits (or losses) into account.

Table 1 Standard Accounting Matrix and Related Sectoral Classification

SAM sector	I/O sector (33)	I/O sector (117)
1. Rice	Agriculture	Grain crop cultivation
2. Wheat	Agriculture	Grain crop cultivation
3. Other grain	Agriculture	Grain crop cultivation
4. Cotton	Agriculture	Other crop cultivation
5. Other non-grain crops	Agriculture	Other crop cultivation
6. Forestry	Agriculture	Forestry
7. Wool	Agriculture	Livestock production
8.Other live-stock production	Agriculture	Livestock production
9. Other agriculture	Agriculture	OTHER AGRICULTURE
10. Fishing	Agriculture	Fishing
15. Grain mill and vegetable oil	Food manufacturing	Grain mill products and vegetable oil manufacturing
16. Sugar	Food manufacturing	Sugar refining
17. Processed food	Food manufacturing	Slaughtering and preparing meat, manufacture of egg and dairy products, fish processing, manufacture of food products not elsewhere classified, wine and spirits industries, beverages, tobacco, forage
19. Apparel	Wearing apparel and leather Products	Wearing apparel
20. Leather	Wearing apparel and leather product	Leather, fur and their products
31. Road vehicles	Transport equipment	Motor vehicles
32. Other transport equipment	Transport equipment	Railroad, ship building, aircraft, transport equip. not elsewhere classified

4.2 Sectoral taxes data

Several kinds of taxes are distinguished in the 1995 SAM. The VAT and other taxes of industrial sectors are estimated, based upon the data of the Industrial Census of 1995, while the taxes from agriculture and services are estimated, based upon some special assumptions.

4.3 Splits of sectors

The 1995 Input-Output table includes only 33 sectors. This SAM includes 46 sectors because of the need for analysis of agricultural trade liberalization. The following sectors are split, based upon other information collected from different sources.

The gross output and value-added of the above manufacturing sectors can be found in *Industrial Census of 1995*. The gross output of grain crops, other crops, livestock, fishing, other agriculture and forestry are from the *Rural Statistical Yearbook*. The output value of rice, wheat, cotton and wool are estimated by their yield and their producer prices from the FAO database. Using all the gross outputs of these sectors as control figures, and based upon the information on input and output structure of these sectors in China's 1992 Input-Output table of 117 sectors and in the GTAP database, the SAM with 46 sectors can be estimated by the "minimizing entropy difference" method (Robinson and El-Said, 1998).

4.4 Estimating the input-output matrix of production for processing exports

The gross output of export processing firms are their processing exports. For the input of production of export processing, we assume that the intermediate input from non-tradable goods (such as services and electricity) and primary goods input (such as agricultural goods, food, and mineral products) are provided by domestic production and imports of the processing trade. Their shares in total cost are the same as those for production by ordinary firms. All the other intermediate input in production for export processing are provided by import of processing trade. The data for exports and imports of processing trade are from Chinese customs statistics. We estimated the production input matrix subject to the above assumed constraints by the "minimizing entropy difference" method.

5. Some Major Applications of DRCCGE Model

The CGE model we described here can be applied to a wide variety of policy issues. On domestic policy, it can be used to analyze domestic taxes and tax reform, employment and human resource development, income growth and distribution, economic growth and structural change, etc. For trade policy, it can be used for the analysis of tariffs, subsidies and other trade distortions, trade-based industrial policy, etc. In addition, DRCCGE can be used for the issue of resource availability, food supply, such as agricultural food policy and trade, energy resources and energy trade, environmental planning and assessment.

The previous application of DRCCGE focused on trade, economic growth and industrial structure, income distribution and environment issues, which are summarized in Table 2.

Table 2 Some Major Applications of DRCCGE

Topics	Period of research	Specification of utilized	Related Publications
Medium-term economic growth and structural change	1996.7—1996.12	DRCCGE1, 22 sectors, 2 households, dynamic	Li and Zhai (1997)
Impact of tariff reduction and taxation on income distribution	1996.7—1997.3	DRCCGE1, 22 sectors, households, static	12 Wang and Zhai (1998)
Growth, structural change, trade policy and their impact on environment	1997.4—1997.6	DRCCGE1, 22 sectors, 2 households, dynamic	Zhai (1997)
Impact of China's WTO accession	1998.1—1998.6	DRCCGE2, 41 sectors, 10 households, dynamic	Unpublished research report

There are many areas in which the present Chinese CGE model should be improved. From our point of view, the following areas are especially worthy for further study in our future work:

1) More detail for the model, *e.g.* disaggregate industry, distinguish between central government and local government, *etc*. This will

improve the capability of the model to analyze real policy issues.

2) Parameter estimation. Estimation of some important elasticity parameters by econometric methods based upon sectoral time series data, or the construction of an econometric CGE model of China based upon SAM time series.

3) Updating of the investment block. Analyze empirical investment behavior of the Chinese economy and update the investment block into a sub-model which will describe the complex Chinese investment system.

Table 3 A marco SAM Chinese Economy, 1995(100Mn Yuan)   (3-1)

	Commodity		Activity		Value-added		
	Ord.	Proc.trade	Ord.	Proc.trade	Labor	Land	Capital
Comm (ordinary)			92066	523			
Comm (proces.)				4509			
Act. (ordinary)	150524						
Act.		6084					
Labor			26641	339			
Land			914				
Capital			26615	585			
Households					**26980**	914	**2319**
Enterprises							*24881*
Government	**666**		2443	40			
Subsidies			**-668**				
Vat			2514	89			
NTBs	353						
VAT rebated							
FTC							
Extra-budget Funds							
Social Consumption							
ROW	7605	4509					
Fixed Invest.							
Stock change							
Total	159147	10593	150524	6084	**26980**	914	27200

(3-2)

	House holds	Enter pries	Govern ment	Subsidies	VAT	NTBs	VAT rebated for export
Comm (ordinary)	**28338**					-93	465
Comm (Proces.)						-92	85
Act. (ordinary)							
Act.							
Labor							
Land							
Capital							
Households		*9908*	**444**	**24**		537	
Enterprises							
Government	**131**	**1237**			**2602**		**-550**
Subsidies			**693**				
Vat							
NTBs							
VAT rebated							
FTC							
Extra-budget funds	900	2375					
Social Consumption			**4490**				
ROW			57				
Fixed Invest.	11876	*11361*	886				
Stock change							
Total	41245	24881	**6570**	**24**	**2602**	353	0

(3-3)

	FTC	Extra-buget funds	Social cons.	ROW	Capital account		Total
					Fixed Assets Invst.	Stoc Change	
Comm (ordinary)	66		**6691**	*7489*	**20301**	*3302*	159147
Comm (Proces.)	-66			6157			10593
Acti .(ordinary)							150524
Acti. (Proces.)							6084
Labor							26980
Land							914
Capital							27200
Households				**120**			41245
Enterprises							24881
Government							6570
Subsidies							24
Vat							2602
NTBs							353
VAT rebated							0
FTC							0
Extra-budget funds							3275
Social Consumption		*2200*					6691
ROW							12170
Fixed Invest.		**1075**		*-1596*			23603
Stock change						*3302*	3302
Total	0	3275	6691	12170	23603	3302	

Notes: Bold type indicates control figures. Bold italic indicate control figures with minor alteration. Normal type indicates estimates. Italic indicate residuals.

References:

Armington, Paul S. (1969), "A Theory of Demand for Products Distinguished by Place of Production". IMF Staff papers, Vol. 16, pp. 159—176.

Beghin, John, Sébastien Dessus, David Roland-Holst and Dominique van der Mensbrugghe (1994), "Prototype CGE Model for the Trade and the Environment Programmes Technical Specification", OECD Development Centre, Paris.

Howe, H. (1975), "Development of the Extended Linear Expenditure System from Simple Savings Assumptions", *European Economic Review*, Volume 6, pp. 305—310.

Jorgenson, D.W. (1984), "Econometric Methods for Applied General Equilibrium Analysis", in H.E. Scarf and J. Shoven eds. *Applied General Equilibrium Analysis* (Cambridge: Cambridge University Press).

Li, Shantong, Fan Zhai (1997), "Medium-Term Economic Growth and Structure Change—Dynamic CGE Analysis", Research Paper No. 166, Developing Research Center of the State Council, PRC (in Chinese).

Mansur, A. and John Whalley (1984), "Numerical Specification of Applied General Equilibrium Models: Estimation, Calibration, and Data", In H.E. Scarf and J. Shoven eds. *Applied General Equilibrium Analysis*, (Cambridge: Cambridge University Press).

Naughton, Barry (1996), "China's Emergence and Prospects as a Trading Nation", *Brookings Papers on Economic Activity* 2: 1996.

Pomfret, Richard (1997), *Is China a "Large Country"?—China's Influence on World Markets*, OECD Development Centre, Paris.

Robinson, Sherman and Mooatax El-Said (1997), "Estimating a Social Accounting Matrix Using Entropy difference Methods", TMD Discussion Paper No. 21, International Food Policy Research Institute, Washington, DC.

Shoven, J.B. and J. Whalley (1992), *Applied General Equilibrium Analysis* (Cambridge: Cambridge University Press.

Wang, Huijiong (1993), "Prototype CGE Model for the Chinese Economy", report prepared for ADB.

Wang, Zhi and Fan Zhai (1998), "Tariff Reduction, Tax Replacement and Implication for Income Distribution in China", *Journal of Comparative Economics*, Vol. 26, June.

Whalley, J. (1985), *Trade Liberalization Among Major World Trading Areas*. The MIT Press.

Wilcoxen, Peter J. (1997), "A Quick Reference Guide to CGE Modeling", http://www.eco.utexas.edu/Homepages/Faculty/Wilcoxen/cge/guide.htm.

Zhai, Fan and Shantong Li (1997), "A Computable General Equilibrium Model for Chinese Economy". *Quantitative and Technical Economics Research*, No. 3 (in Chinese).

Zhai, Fan (1997a), "Computable General Equilibrium Modeling and Simulations for Chinese Economy", Ph.D. Dissertation, Huazhong University of Science and Technology, Wuhan, China (in Chinese).

Zhai, Fan (1997b), "Structural Change and Pollution Discharges", Research Paper No. 122, Developing Research Center of the State Council, PRC (in Chinese).

Appendix A Sector Classification in DRCCGE2 and Their SSB-IO Sector Concordance

Model Sectors	I/O Sectors	SSB Code
1. Rice	Grain crop cultivation (part)	01101
2. Wheat	Grain crop cultivation (part)	01101
3. Other grains	Grain crop cultivation (part)	01101
4. Cotton	Other crop cultivation (part)	01109
5. Other non-grain Crops	Other crop cultivation (part)	01109
6. Forestry	Forestry	01200
7. Wool	Livestock production (part)	01300
8. Other livestock production	Livestock production (part)	01300
9. Other agriculture	Other agricultural production	01400
10. Fishing	Fishing	01500
11. Coal mining	Coal mining, Coal cleaning and screening	02100, 02200
12. Crude oil and natural gas	Crude petroleum production, Natural gas production	03100, 03200
13. Metal mining	Ferrous ore mining, Nonferrous ore mining	04100, 04200
14. Other mining	Quarrying of building materials and nonmetal minerals, Salt mining, Logging and transport of timber and bamboo, Production and supply of water	05100,05200, 05300,05400
15. Grain mill and vegetable oil	Grain mill products and vegetable oil manufacturing	06101
16. Sugar	Sugar refining	06105
17. Processed food	Slaughtering and preparing meat, Manufacturing of egg and dairy products, Fish processing, Manufacturing	06102, 06103, 06104, 06109, 06201, 06209,

	food products not else-where classified, Wine and spirits industries, Beverages, Tobacco, Forage	06300, 06400
18. Textiles	Cotton textiles, Woolen textiles, Hemp textiles, Silk textiles, Knit-ting mills, Textiles not elsewhere classified	07001, 07002, 07003,07004, 07005, 07009
19. Apparel	Wearing apparel	08100
20. Leather	Leather, fur and their products	08200
21. Sawmills and furniture	Sawmills and fire boards, Furniture and other wood products	09100, 09200
22. Paper and social articles	Paper and paper products, Printing, Articles for cultural activities, education	10100, 10200, 10300
23. Electricity	Electricity, steam and hot water	11000
24. Petroleum refineries	Petroleum refineries	12000
25. Coking and coal	Coking, Gas and coal products	13001, 13002
26. Chemicals	Basic chemicals, Chemical fertilizers, Chemical pesticides, Organic chemical products, Chemical products for daily use, Synthetic chemicals, Other chemicals, Medicines, Chemical fibers, Rubber for production, Rubber for daily use, Plastics for production, Plastics for daily use	14101, 14102, 14103, 14104, 14105, 14106, 14109, 14200, 14300, 14401, 14402, 14501, 14502
27. Building materials	Cement, Cement and asbestos products, Bricks, tiles, lime and lightweight building materials, Glass and glass products, Pottery, china and earthenware, Fireproof materials, Nonmetallic mineral products not elsewhere classified	15001, 15002, 15003, 15004, 15005, 15006, 15009
28. Basic metals	Primary iron and steel, Primary nonferrous metals manufacturing	16100, 16200
29. Metal products	Metal products for production use, Metal products for daily use	17001, 17002
30. Machinery	Boilers, engines and turbines, Metal-working machinery, Special industrial machinery and equipment, Agricultural, forestry, animal husbandry and fishing machinery, Machinery for daily use, Special equipment, Machinery not elsewhere classified	18001, 18002, 18003, 18004, 18005, 18006, 18009
31. Road vehicles	Motor vehicles	19002

32. Other transport equipment	Railroad, Ship building, Aircraft, Transport equipment not elsewhere classified	19001, 19003, 19004, 19009
33. Electrical machinery	Generators Household electrical appliances, Electric machinery not elsewhere classified	20001, 20002, 20009
34. Electronics	Computers, Electronic appliances, Electronic and telecommunication equipment not elsewhere classified, Instruments, meters	21001, 21002, 21009
35. Instruments	Instruments, meters	22000
36. Machinery repairing	Maintenance and repair of machinery and equipment	23000
37. Other industries	Products for production use not elsewhere classified, Products for daily use not elsewhere classified, Scrap and waste	24101, 24102, 24200
38. Construction	Construction	25000
39. Freight transport and communication	Railway freight transport, Highway freight transport, Water freight transport, Air freight transport, Pipe transport, Communications	26101, 26102, 26103, 26104, 26105, 26200
40. Commerce	Supply and marketing of materials and storage, Domestic and foreign trade, Trade of grain and cooking oils	27100, 27201, 27202
41. Restaurants	Restaurants	28000
42. Passenger transport	Railway passenger transport, Highway passenger transport, Water passenger transport, Air passenger transport	29001, 29002, 29003, 29004
43. Public utilities	Real estate Public utilities, Services to household	30100, 30200, 30300
44. Social cultural	Health service, Sports, Social welfare institutions, Education services, Cultural services, arts, radio and television broadcasting, Research and scientific institutions, General technical services	31101, 31102, 31103, 31201, 31202, 31301, 31302
45. Finance and insurance	Financial institutions, Insurance	32001, 32002
46. Services	Public administration	33000

Appendix B Algebraic Specification of CGE Model for China

This appendix provides a detailed description of the algebraic specification of the CGE model for China. The sector definition is given first, followed by definition of variables and parameters, as well as a complete equation list.

1 Sector Definition

i   Production sectors. *j* is an alias for *i* (including *e, nf, tex* and *ag* as a subset).

      nf   Represents non-fuel commodities.

      e   Represents fuel commodities.

      tex   Represents textile and clothing commodities.

      ag   Represents food and agricultural commodities subject to import quotas.

      comm Represents commerce sectors.

l   Represents labor types.

      aglb   Represents agricultural labor forces

      uslb   Represents production workers.

      slb   Represents professionals.

h   Represents households.

f   Represents final demand expenditure categories (including *s, zp* as a subset).

      s   Represents the social consumption category.

      zp   Represents the fixed asset investment category.

c   Represents firm types (including *O, P* as a subset).

      O   Represents ordinary enterprises.

      P   Represents export processing enterprises.

m   Represents import types (including *n, P* as subsets).

      n   Represents the import of non-intermediate export processing.

P Represents the import of processing trade.

v Represents capital vintages.

t Time index.

I=46, NF+E=I, L=3, H=10, F=2, c=2, m=4, v=2

2 Definition of Variables

VARIABLE   DEFINITION   NO. OF VARIABLES

Production variables

Variable	Definition	No. of Variables
Xp_{ic}	Output	IxCxV
Xpv_{vic}	Output by vintage	IxCxV
ND_{vic}	Demand for ND bundle	IxCxV
KEL_{vic}	Demand for KEL bundle	IxCxV
PXA_{ijc}	Price for intermediate demand	IxIxC
PX_{ic}	Producer price exclusive of taxes	IxC
PXv_{vic}	Producer price exclusive of taxes	IxCxV
PP_i	Producer price inclusive of taxes	I
$PKEL_{vic}$	Price of KEL bundle	IxCxV
PN_{ic}	Price of ND bundle	IxC
XAp_{ijc}	Intermediate consumption	IxIxC
AL_{jc}	Aggregate demand for labor	IxC
KE_{vjc}	Demand for KE bundle	IxCxV
AW_i	Average sectoral wage rate	I
PKE_{vjc}	Price of KE bundle	IxCxV
Ev_{vic}	Demand for energy bundle	IxCxV
KT_{vjc}	Demand for capital-land bundle by vintage	IxCxV
PE_{vic}	Aggregate price of energy bundle	IxCxV
PKT_{vjc}	Price of capital-land bundle	IxCxV
Kv_{vjc}	Capital demand by vintage	IxCxV
K_j^d	Aggregate capital demand	I
Tv_{vjc}	Land demand by vintage	IxCxV
T_j^d	Aggregate land demand	I

| $L_{ljc}^{\ d}$ | Demand for labor by sector and skill | LxIxC |
| W_l | Wage by skill | L |

Capital income distribution variables

CY	Retained capital income	1
$sTax^c$	Business direct tax	1
Sav_c^p	Business retained earnings	1
Fee^c	Value of enterprise fee	1

Household income variables

YL_l	Net labor income by type of labor	L
$YMIG$	Income of migratory agricultural labor	1
YH_h	Household income by type of household	H
RMQ	NTBs rent	1
REQ	MFA quota rent	1
$Tax_h^{\ h}$	Household direct taxes	H
$Fee_h^{\ h}$	Household fee by household type	H
YD_h	Household disposable income	H

Consumer variables

PC_{ih}	Consumer prices inclusive of taxes and subsidies	IxH
Y_h^*	Supernumerary income	H
XAC_{ih}	Household consumption	IxH
$HSav_h$	Household saving	H
S_h	Total household saving	1
cpi_h	Consumer price index	H

Final demand variables

$XAFD_{if}$	Armington final demand	IxF
$TFDV_f$	Value of final demand expenditures	F
TFD_{zp}	Volume of fixed assets investment	1
PFD_{if}	Final demand price inclusive of taxes	IxF

Government revenue and expenditure variables

$GExp$	Government expenditure	1
VA_{ic}	Sectoral value-added	IxC
$VATx$	Value of value-added tax	1
$IMDITx$	Value of intermediate demand indirect taxes	1
$PITx$	Value of production indirect taxes	1
$HITx$	Value of household indirect taxes	1
$FDITx_f$	Value of final demand indirect taxes	F
$TIndTax$	Total value of indirect taxes	1
$ExVAT$	Value of VAT rebate for export	1
$YTrade$	Revenue from tariffs	1
$Grev$	Total government revenues	1
S^g	Nominal government saving	1
$ExBRev$	Extra-budget revenues	1
$ExBC$	Extra-budget consumption	1
S^{ExB}	Extra-budget saving	1

Armington prices and volumes

PA_i	Economy-wide Armington price 1	
PMO_i	Domestic price of aggregated ordinary Imports	I
	PM_{im} Domestic price of imports	IxM
XD_i	Aggregate domestic sales of domestic Production	I
XMo_i	Aggregate ordinary imports	I
XM_{im}	Imports	IxM
XA_i	Economy-wide Armington demand	I
$XAPpd_{ij}$	Intermediate Armington demand for export processing	IxJ
$XAPpm_{ij}$	Intermediate demand for processing imports for export processing	IxJ

CET variables

PD_i	Producer price for domestic sales	I
WPE_i	Export price at the border	I

PE_{ic}	Export price before the border	IxC
ESW_i	Aggregate export supply	I
ES_{ic}	Export supply	IxC
ED_i	Export demand	I
FTC	FTC export margin	1

Factor market variables

$MigAg$	Migration of agricultural labor to production worker	1
$Pland$	Aggregate price of land	1
PT_i	Sector specific land price	I
TR	Rental rate on mobile capital	1
R_j^v	Sectoral rental rate by vintage	IxV
X_{ic}^{Old}	Old capital-output ratio	IxC
$RR_{i,t}$	Relative rental rate of old capital	I
$K_{ic,0}^s$	Initial installed capital by sector	IxC
K_t	Aggregate capital stock	1
K_t^s	Aggregate capital supply	1
γ^i	Annual growth rate of investment	1

Aggregate variables

$GDPVA$	GDP value at market price	1
$RGDP$	Real GDP at market price	1
ER	Exchange rate	1

Exogenous variables

P	GDP price deflator	1
L_l^s	Labor supply by type of labor	L
TK^s	Aggregate capital supply	1
$Tland$	Aggregate quantity of land	1
Pop_h	Population	H
S_f	Foreign saving	1
$TR^h_{g,h}$	Government transfers to households	H
$Subs^h_{g,h}$	Government subsidies to households	H

$TR^h_{f,h}$	ROW transfers to households	H
StB	Aggregate volume of stock building	1
RGc	Government real spending	1
WPM_{im}	World import price	IxM
$WPINDEX_i$	Price index of world exports	I
λ^t_j	Land efficiency factor	I
λ^k_j	Capital efficiency factor	I
λ_{ij}	Labor efficiency factor	LxI
λ^e_{vj}	Energy efficiency factor	IxV
λ_j	Hicks productivity factor	I
δ^H	Household direct tax shifter	1
δ^{Tar}	Tariff adjustment shifter	1
δ^{ntb}_i	Tariff equivalent of NTBs adjustment factor	I
δ^c	Corporate tax adjustment shifter	1
δ^x	Intermediate demand indirect tax adjustment shifter	1
δ^v	VAT adjustment shifter	1
δ^{vm}	VAT for import adjustment shifter	1
δ^{ve}	VAT rebate for export adjustment shifter	1
δ^p	Production tax adjustment shifter	1
δ^{HTr}	Government to households transfer adjustment factor	1
δ^E	Export tax adjustment shifter	1
$AgQuota_{ag}$	Import quota of food and agricultural products	AG
$TexQuota_{tex}$	Export quota of textiles and clothing	TEX

3. Definition of Parameters

σ^p_{vj}	Top level CES elasticity between non-energy intermediate input and capital-energy-labor bundle
σ^v_{vj}	CES substitution elasticities between labor and apital-land-energy bundle
σ^k_{vj}	CES substitution elasticities between capital-land bundle and energy bundle
σ^t_{vj}	CES substitution elasticities between capital and land
σ^e_{vj}	CES substitution elasticities between different types of energy
σ^l_j	CES substitution elasticities between different types of labor

σ^x_j	CES substitution elasticities of intermediate input for export processing
α^{nd}_{vjc}	CES share parameter for ND bundle
α^{kel}_{vjc}	CES share parameter for KEL bundle
α^l_{vjc}	CES labor share parameter
α^k_{vjc}	CES capital share parameter
α^e_{vjc}	CES energy share parameter
α^{kt}_{vjc}	CES capital land share parameter
α^t_{vjc}	CES land share parameter
α^k_{vjc}	CES capital share parameter
$\alpha^t_{e,vjc}$	CES share parameters in energy bundle
α^l_{ljc}	CES share parameters for different types of labor
α^m_{ij}	CES share parameters for intermediate input of processing imports
α^d_{ij}	CES share parameters for intermediate input of Armington goods
Φ_{ljc}	Relative wages across sectors for same skill labor
$\alpha_{i,j,c}$	Leontief coefficients
χ^k	Retained capital earnings
Ξ_{hl}	Wage income distribution matrix
ϕ^k_h	Distribution shares for land income
ϕ^k_h	Distribution shares for capital income
ϕ^c_h	Distribution shares for corporate earnings
ϕ^t_h	Distribution shares for quota rent
μ_{ih}	Marginal propensity to consume
θ_{ih}	Subsistence minima
afd^f_i	Final demand share parameters
α^{st}_i	Change in stock share parameters
κ^c	Corporate tax rate
κ^h_h	Household direct tax rate
η_c	Enterprise fee rate
η^h_h	Households fee rate
τ^p_{ic}	Indirect taxation of production
τ^h_{ih}	Consumer indirect tax rate
τ^f_i	Final demand indirect tax rates
τ^x_i	Intermediate demand indirect tax rates
τ^E_{ic}	Export tax rate (export tax equivalent of VER)
τ^v_{ic}	VAT rate
τ^{ve}_{ic}	VAT rebate rate for export
τ^{ftc}_{ic}	FTC export margin rate
$\tau^{vm}_{i,m}$	VAT rate for import
$\tau^m_{i,m}$	Import tariffs
$\tau^{ntb}_{i,m}$	Tariff equivalent of NTBs
φ^p_{ic}	Production subsidies
σ^m_i	Armington elasticity

σ_i	Second level Armington elasticity
σ_i	CET elasticity
σ^2_i	CES elasticity between processing export and ordinary export
σ^f_i	Export demand elasticity
α^f_i	Initial export demand shifter
$\alpha_{d,i}$	CET domestic share parameter
$\alpha_{e,i}$	CET export share parameter
$\beta^e_{i,c}$	CES export share parameter
β^d_i	Economy-wide Armington domestic share parameter
β^m_i	Economy-wide Armington import share parameter
$\beta_{i,n}$	Second level Armington import share parameter
σ^{agl}	Transformation elasticity of agricultural labor
w^0_l	Initial wage shifter
η^k_i	Disinvestment elasticity of old capital
δ	Depreciation rate of capital

4 Equation List

Production

Top-level Production Equations

$$(1.1) \quad ND_{vjc} = \alpha^{nd}_{vjc} \left[\frac{PXv_{vjc}}{PN_{jc}} \right]^{\sigma^P_{vj}} XPv_{vjc}$$

$$(1.2) \quad KEL_{vjc} = \alpha^{kel}_{vjc} \left[\frac{PXv_{vjc}}{PKEL_{vjc}} \right]^{\sigma^P_{vj}} XPv_{vjc}$$

$$(1.3) \quad PXv_{vjc} = \left[\alpha^{nd}_{vjc} (PN_{jc})^{1-\sigma^P_{vj}} + \alpha^{kel}_{vjc} (PKEL_{vjc})^{1-\sigma^P_{vj}} \right]^{1/(1-\sigma^P_{vj})}$$

$$(1.4) \quad PX_{jc} XP_{jc} = \sum_v PXv_{vjc} XPv_{vjc}$$

$$(1.5) \quad PP_{jc} = PX_{jc} (1 + \delta^P \tau^P_{jc} - \varphi^P_{jc})$$

Second-level CES Production Equations

(1.6) $\quad XAp_{nf,jc} = \sum_v a_{nf,jc} ND_{vjc}$

(1.7) $\quad PN_{jc} = \sum_{nf} a_{nf,jc} PXA_{nf,jc}$

(1.8) $\quad PXA_{ij,O} = (1 + \delta^x \tau_i^x) PA_i$

(1.9) $\quad PXA_{ij,P} = \left[\alpha_{ij}^m (PM_{i,P})^{1-\sigma_j^x} + \alpha_{ij}^d (PXA_{ij,O})^{1-\sigma_j^x} \right]^{1/(1-\sigma_j^x)}$

(1.10) $\quad AL_{jc} = \sum_v \alpha_{vjc}^l \left[\frac{PKEL_{vjc}}{AW_{jc}} \right]^{\sigma_{vj}^v} KEL_{vjc}$

(1.11) $\quad KE_{vjc} = \alpha_{vjc}^k \left[\frac{PKEL_{vjc}}{PKE_{vjc}} \right]^{\sigma_{vj}^v} KEL_{vjc}$

(1.12) $\quad PKEL_{vjc} = \left[\alpha_{vjc}^l (AW_{jc})^{1-\sigma_{vj}^v} + \alpha_{vjc}^k (PKE_{vjc})^{1-\sigma_{vj}^v} \right]^{1/(1-\sigma_{vj}^v)}$

Labour Demand

(1.13) $\quad L_{ljc}^d = \frac{\alpha_{ljc}^l}{\lambda_j \lambda_{lj}} \left[\frac{\lambda_j \lambda_{lj} AW_{jt}}{(1 + \tau_{jc}^v) \Phi_{ljc} W_l} \right]^{\sigma_j^l} AL_{jc}$

(1.14) $\quad AW_{jc} = \left[\sum_l \alpha_{ljc}^l \left(\frac{(1 + \tau_c^v) \Phi_{ljc} W_l}{\lambda_{lj}} \right)^{1-\sigma_j^l} \right]^{1/(1-\sigma_j^l)}$

Capital-Land Bundle and Energy Bundle Demand

$$(1.15) \quad Ev_{vjc} = \alpha^e_{vjc} \left[\frac{PKE_{vjc}}{PEv_{vjc}} \right]^{\sigma^k_{vj}} KE_{vjc}$$

$$(1.16) \quad KT_{vjc} = \alpha^{kt}_{vjc} \left[\frac{PKE_{vjc}}{PKT_{vjc}} \right]^{\sigma^k_{vj}} KE_{vjc}$$

$$(1.17) \quad PKE_{vjc} = \left[\alpha^e_{vjc} (PEv_{vjc})^{1-\sigma^k_{vj}} + \alpha^{kt}_{vjc} (PKT_{vjc})^{1-\sigma^k_{vj}} \right]^{1/(1-\sigma^k_{vj})}$$

Capital and Land Demand

$$(1.18) \quad Tv_{vjc} = \frac{\alpha^t_{vjc}}{(\lambda_j \lambda^t_j)^{1-\sigma^s_{vj}}} \left[\frac{PKT_{vjc}}{(1+\tau^v_{jc})PT_j} \right]^{\sigma^s_{vj}} KT_{vjc}$$

$$(1.19) \quad Kv_{vjc} = \frac{\alpha^k_{vjc}}{(\lambda_j \lambda^k_j)^{1-\sigma^s_{vj}}} \left[\frac{PKT_{vjt}}{(1+\tau^v_t)R^v_j} \right]^{\sigma^s_{vj}} KT_{vjc}$$

$$(1.20) \quad PKT_{vjc} = \left[\alpha^t_{vjc} \left(\frac{PT_j}{\lambda_j \lambda^t_j} \right)^{1-\sigma^s_{vj}} + \alpha^k_{vjt} \left(\frac{R^v_j}{\lambda_j \lambda^k_j} \right)^{1-\sigma^s_{vj}} \right]^{1/(1-\sigma^s_{vj})}$$

$$(1.21) \quad T^d_j = \sum_v \sum_c Tv_{vjc}$$

$$(1.22) \quad K^d_j = \sum_v \sum_c Kv_{vjc}$$

Decomposition of the Energy Bundle

$$(1.23) \quad XAP_{e,jc} = \sum_v \frac{\alpha^f_{e,vjc}}{\lambda^e_{vj}} \left[\frac{\lambda^e_{vj} PEv_{vjc}}{PXA_{e,jc}} \right]^{\sigma^f_{vj}} Ev_{vjc}$$

$$(1.24) \quad PEv_{vjc} = \left[\sum_e \alpha_{e,vjc}^f \left(\frac{PXA_{ejc}}{\lambda_{vj}^e} \right) \right]^{1/(1-\sigma_{vj}^f)}$$

Income Distribution

Corporate Earnings Equations

$$(2.1) \quad CY = \chi^k \sum_i \sum_v \sum_c R_i^v Kv_{vic}$$

$$(2.2) \quad Tax^c = \delta^c \kappa^c CY$$

$$(2.3) \quad Fee^c = \eta^c CY$$

$$(2.4) \quad Sav_c^p = (1 - \sum_h \phi_h^c)(1 - \delta^c \kappa^c)CY - Fee^c$$

Household Income Equations

$$(2.5) \quad YL_l = \sum_i \sum_c \Phi_{lic} W_l L_{lic}^d$$

$$(2.6) \quad YMIG = W_{aglb} \min(MigAg,0) + W_{uslb} \max(MigAg,0)$$

$$(2.7) \quad \begin{aligned} YH_h &= \sum_l \Xi_{hl} YL_l + (\Xi_{h,aglb} - \Xi_{h,uslb})YMIG \\ &+ \phi_h^t \sum_i \sum_v \sum_c PT_i Tv_{vic} + \phi_h^k (1 - \chi^k)KY + \phi_h^c (1 - \chi^c)CY \\ &+ \phi_h^r (RMQ + REQ) + P\delta^{HTr} TR_h^{gh} + P Subs_h^{gh} + ERTR_h^{fh} \end{aligned}$$

$$(2.8) \quad RMQ = ER \sum_i \sum_m \delta_i^{ntb} \tau_{i,m}^{ntb} WPM_{i,m} XM_{i,m}$$

$$(2.9) \quad REQ = \sum_c \sum_{tex} PE_{tex,c} \tau_{tex,c}^E (1 + \tau_{tex,c}^{ftc}) ES_{tex,c}$$

(2.10) $\quad Tax_h^h = \delta^h \kappa_h^h YH_h$

(2.11) $\quad Fee_h^h = \eta_h^h YH_h$

(2.12) $\quad YD_h = YH_h - Tax_h^h - Fee_h^h$

Household Consumption and Savings

Household Consumption and Savings Equations

(3.1) $\quad PC_{ih} = PA_i(1 + \tau_{ih}^h)$

(3.2) $\quad Y_h^* = YD_h - Pop_h \sum_i PC_{ih}\theta_{ih}$

(3.3) $\quad XAc_{ih} = Pop_h\,\theta_{ih} + \mu_{ih}Y_h^* / PC_{ih}$

(3.4) $\quad HSav_h = YD_h - \sum_i PC_{ih}XAc_{ih}$

(3.5) $\quad cpi_h = \dfrac{\displaystyle\sum_i PC_{ih}XAc_{ih}}{\displaystyle\sum_i PC_{ih,0}XAc_{ih}}$

Other Final Demands

Final Demand Expenditure Equations

(4.1) $\quad PA_iXAFD_{if} = afd_i^f TFDV_f$

(4.2) $\quad TFD_f = \sum_i XAFD_i^f$

(4.3) $\quad PFD_{if} = PA_i\left(1 + \tau_i^f\right)$

$$(4.4) \quad GExp = P\,RGc + P\sum_h \left(\delta^{HTr}TR_h^{gh} + HSubs_h^{gh} \right)$$

$$(4.5) \quad TFDV_s = P\,RGc + ExBC$$

Government Revenues and Saving

Indirect Tax Equations

$$(5.1) \quad VA_{ic} = \sum_l \Phi_{lic}W_l L_{lic}^d + PT_i \sum_v Tv_{vic}^d + R_i \sum_v K_{vic}^d$$

$$(5.2) \quad VATx = \sum_i \sum_c \tau_{ic}^v VA_{ic} + \sum_i \tau_{i,O}^{vm} PM_{i,O} XM_{i,O}$$

$$(5.3) \quad PITx = \sum_i \sum_c (\delta^P \tau_{ic}^p - \varphi_{ic}^p) PX_{ic} XP_{ic}$$

$$(5.4) \quad IMDITx = \sum_i PA_i \delta_i^x \tau_i^x XAp_{i,O}$$

$$(5.5) \quad HITx = \sum_h \sum_i PA_i \tau_{ih}^h XAc_{ih}$$

$$(5.6) \quad FDITx_f = \sum_i PA_i \tau_i^f XAFD_i^f$$

$$(5.7) \quad TIndTax = PITx + IMDITx + HITx + \sum_f FDITx_f + {+}VATx$$

$$(5.8) \quad ExVAT = \sum_i \sum_c \tau_{ic}^{ve} PE_{ic} ES_{ic}$$

Government Revenues and Closure Equations

$$(5.9) \quad YTrade = ER\delta^{Tar} \sum_m \sum_i \tau_{i,m}^m WPM_{i,m} XM_{i,m}$$

$$(5.10) \quad GRev = Tax^c + TIndTax + YTrade + \sum_h Tax_h^h - ExVAT$$

(5.11) $S^g = GRev - GExp$

(5.12) $ExBRev = Fee^c + \sum_h Fee_h^h$

(5.13) $S^{ExB} = ExBRev - ExBC$

(5.14) $S^{ExB} = \xi^{ExB} ExBRev$

Trade, Domestic Supply and Demand

Armington Equations

(6.1) $XA_i = \sum_j XAp_{i,j,o} + \sum_j XAPpd_{ij} + \sum_h XAc_{ih} + \sum_f XAFD_{if}$

(6.2) $XD_i = \beta_i^d \left(\dfrac{PA_i}{PD_i} \right)^{\sigma_i^m} XA_i$

(6.3) $XMo_i = \hat{A}_i^m \left(\dfrac{PA_i}{PMo_i} \right)^{\sigma_i^m} XA_i$

(6.4) $PA_j = \left[\beta_i^d PD_i^{1-\sigma_i^m} + \beta_i^m (PMo_i)^{1-\sigma_i^m} \right]^{/(1-\sigma_i^m)}$

(6.5) $XM_{i,n} = \hat{A}_{i,n}^s \left(\dfrac{PMo_i}{PM_{i,n}} \right)^{\sigma_i^r} XMo_i$

(6.6) $PMo_i = \left[\sum_n \beta_{i,n}^s ((1+\delta^{vm}\tau_i^{vm})PM_{i,n})^{1-\sigma_i^r} \right]^{1/(1-\sigma_i^r)}$

(6.7) $PM_{i,m} = ER\,WPM_{i,m}(1+\delta^{Tar}\tau_{i,m}^m + \delta_i^{ntb}\tau_{i,m}^{ntb})$

$$(6.8) \qquad XAPpd_{ij} = \alpha_{ij}^d \left[\frac{PXA_{ij,P}}{PM_{i,P}} \right]^{\sigma_j^x} XAP_{ij,P}$$

$$(6.9) \qquad XAPpm_{ij} = \alpha_{ij}^m \left[\frac{PXA_{ij,P}}{PXA_{ij,O}} \right]^{\sigma_j^x} XAP_{ij,P}$$

$$(6.10) \quad XM_{i,P} = \sum_j XAPpm_{ij}$$

$$(6.11) \quad \sum_m XM_{ag,m} \le AgQouta_{ag}$$

CET Equations

$$(6.12) \quad XD_i = \alpha_{d,i}^t \left(\frac{PD_i}{PP_{i,O}} \right)^{\sigma_i^t} (XP_{i,O} - \alpha_i^{st} StB - bool_i \frac{FTC}{PP_{comm,O}})$$
$$\text{if } i = comm \quad bool_i = 1 \quad else \quad bool_i = 0$$

$$(6.13) \quad ES_{i,O} = \alpha_{e,i}^t \left(\frac{(1 + \delta^{ve}\tau_{i,O}^{ve})PE_{i,O}}{PP_{i,O}} \right)^{\sigma_i^t} (XP_{i,O} - \alpha_i^{st} StB - bool_i \frac{FTC}{PP_{comm,O}})$$
$$\text{if } i = comm \quad bool_i = 1 \quad else \quad bool_i = 0$$

$$(6.14) \quad PP_{i,O} = \left[\alpha_{d,i}^t PD_i^{1+\sigma_i^t} + \alpha_{d,i}^t ((1 + \delta^{ve}\tau_{i,O}^{ve})PE_{i,O})^{1+\sigma_i^t} \right]^{/(1+\sigma_i^t)}$$

$$(6.15) \quad ES_{i,P} = XP_{i,P}$$

$$(6.16) \quad PP_{i,P} = (1 + \delta^{ve}\tau_{i,P}^{ve})PE_{i,P}$$

$$(6.17) \quad WPE_i = \left[\sum_c \beta_{ic}^e ((1 + \delta^E\tau_{ic}^E)(1 + \tau_{ic}^{ftc})PE_{ic})^{1-\sigma_i^{e2}} \right]^{1/(1-\sigma_i^{e2})}$$

$$(6.18) \quad ES_{ic} = \hat{a}_{ic}^e \left(\frac{WPE_i}{(1 + \delta^E \tau_{ic}^E)(1 + \tau_{ic}^{ftc}) PE_{ic}} \right)^{\sigma_i^{e2}} ESW_i$$

FTC Export Margin

$$(6.19) \quad FTC = \sum_c \sum_i \tau_{i,c}^{ftc} PE_{i,c} ES_{i,c}$$

Export Demand and Market Equilibrium

$$(6.20) \quad ED_i = \alpha_i^e \left(\frac{ER\overline{WPINDEX}_i}{WPE_i} \right)^{\sigma_i^e}$$

$$(6.21) \quad ED_{tex} \leq TexQouta_{tex}$$

$$(6.22) \quad ESW_i = ED_i$$

Equilibrium Conditions

Labor, Land Supply and Market Equilibrium

$$(7.1) \quad \sum_i \sum_c L_{ic,slb}^d = L_{slb}^s$$

$$(7.2) \quad \frac{\sum_i \sum_c L_{ic,aglb}^d}{\sum_i \sum_c L_{ic,uslb}^d} = \frac{L_{aglb}^s}{L_{uslb}^s} \left(\frac{W_{aglb}}{W_{uslb}} \frac{w_{aglb}^0}{w_{uslb}^0} \right)^{\sigma^{agl}}$$

$$(7.3) \quad \sum_i \sum_c L_{ic,aglb}^d + \sum_i \sum_c L_{ic,uslb}^d = L_{aglb}^s + L_{uslb}^s$$

$$(7.4) \quad MigAg = L_{aglb}^s - \sum_i \sum_c L_{ic,aglb}^d$$

(7.5) $\quad TLand = \sum_i T_i^d$

(7.6) $\quad PT_i = PLand$

Output by vintage

(7.7) $\quad \chi_{ic}^{Old} = \dfrac{Kv_{ic,Old}}{XPv_{ic}^{Old}}$

(7.8) $\quad XPv_{ic}^{Old} = \min\left(K_{ic,0}^s / \chi_{ic}^{Old}, XP_{ic}\right)$

(7.9) $\quad XPv_{ic}^{New} = XP_{ic} - XPv_{ic}^{Old}$

Capital Market Equilibrium

(7.10) $\quad RR_{i,t} = \min\left(1, RR_{i,t-1}\left(\dfrac{\sum_c Kv_{ic,Old}}{\sum_c K_{ic,0}^s}\right)^{1/\eta_i^k}\right)$

(7.11) $\quad \sum_i K_i^d = K^s$

(7.12) $\quad R_i^{New} = TR$

(7.13) $\quad R_i^{Old} = TR\, RR_i$

(7.14) $\quad K_{ic,0,t}^s = (1-\delta)^n K_{ic,t-n}^d$

Aggregated Capital Stock

(7.15) $\quad K_t = (1-\delta)^n K_{t-n} + \dfrac{(1+\gamma^i)^n - (1-\delta)^n}{\gamma^i + \delta} TFD_{zp,t-n}$

(7.16) $\quad \gamma^i = \left(\dfrac{TFD_{zp}}{TFD_{zp,t-n}} \right)^{1/n} - 1$

(7.17) $\quad K_t^s = \dfrac{K_{t-n}^s}{K_{t-n}} K_t$

Macro Closure

(8.1) $\quad TFDV_{zp} = Sav_c^p + \sum_h HSav_h + ERS_f + S^g + S^{ExB} - \sum_i \alpha_i^{st} PP_{i,O} StB$

(8.2) $\quad \begin{aligned} GDPVA &= \sum_l W_l \sum_i \Phi_{li} L_{li}^d + \sum_i PT_i T_i^d + \sum_i R_i K_i^d \\ &\quad + PITx + VATx + YTrade + REQ + RMQ - ExVAT \end{aligned}$

(8.3) $\quad \begin{aligned} RGDP &= \sum_i \sum_h XAC_{ih} + \sum_i \sum_f XAFD_{if} + StB \\ &\quad + \sum_i ED_i WPE_{i,0} - \sum_i XM_i WPM_{i,0} ER_0 \end{aligned}$

(8.4) $\quad P = \dfrac{GDPVA}{RGDP}$

6 NATURAL DECOMPOSITION OF TOTAL FACTOR PRODUCTIVITY GROWTH

Zhou Fang

Institute of Quantitative and Technical Economics, CASS

1. Abstract

Natural decomposition of total factor productivity (TFP) growth is carried out in this chapter. Total factor productivity growth consists of two components: (1) Solow's technical progress and (2) economies of scale. The former is independent of the change in production scale and referred to as "disembodied technological change", while the latter is associated with a change of production scale and depends upon the output elasticities of input factors. It is referred to as "embodied technological change". Product output growth can be divided into two components: extensive growth and intensive growth. The former is numerically equal to the total factor (TF) growth, and the latter equals the total factor productivity (TFP) growth. The purpose of this paper is to reveal the natural decomposition of total factor productivity growth and product output growth. The method of decomposition, developed in this paper, can be used for measuring the TFP growth components and the output growth components at either a micro-level (for firm, industry) or a macro-level (for regional or national economy). In illustration of the methodology, an example is presented.

2. Growth in Total Factor Productivity

Using Divisia indexes, we define total factor productivity (TFP) as follows [1]:

$$(TFP) = \frac{\overline{Q}}{Q_c} \tag{1}$$

where $\overline{Q}$ is an output index, and Q_c is an input (total factor input) index.

From eq.(1) we get the growth in total factor productivity as follows:

$$\frac{d \ln(TFP)}{dt} = \frac{d \ln \overline{Q}}{dt} - \frac{d \ln Q_c}{dt} \tag{2}$$

For simplicity, without loss of generality, we suppose that the production system uses only two inputs: capital input K, with the cost of capital P_k, and labor input L, with wage rate W. Then, the production cost (total factor input cost) is given by

$$C = Q_c P_c = P_k K + WL \tag{3}$$

where P_c is price index of Q_c and assumed to be constant.

From eq.(3) we get the growth of Q_c due to the growth in factor inputs K and L:

$$\frac{d \ln Q_c}{dt} = \frac{P_k K}{C} \frac{d \ln K}{dt} + \frac{WL}{C} \frac{d \ln L}{dt} \tag{4}$$

Substitute eq.(4) into eq.(2), and we obtain the growth in total factor productivity:

$$\frac{d \ln(TFP)}{dt} = \frac{d \ln \overline{Q}}{dt} - \left(\frac{P_k K}{C} \frac{d \ln K}{dt} + \frac{WL}{C} \frac{d \ln L}{dt} \right) \tag{5}$$

3. Output Elasticities in Terms of Costs [2]

The technical relationship between output and factor inputs under fixed technology can be expressed in the form of a function as

$$Q = Q(K,L)$$

from which we get the growth of Q due to the growth in K and L:

$$\frac{d \ln Q}{dt} = \alpha \frac{d \ln K}{dt} + \beta \frac{d \ln L}{dt},$$

(6)

where α - output elasticity with respect to capital input;

β - output elasticity with respect to labor input.

The cost elasticity with respect to output is:

$$E_c = \frac{d \ln C}{dt} \Big/ \frac{d \ln Q}{dt} = \frac{d \ln C}{d \ln Q} = \frac{dC}{C} \Big/ \frac{dQ}{Q}$$

$$= \frac{dC/dQ}{C/Q} = \frac{C_M}{C_A}$$

(7)

where $C_M = dC/dQ$ – marginal cost;

$C_A = C/Q$ – average cost.

From eq.(6) and eq.(7) we obtain the growth of cost C due to the growth in output Q (or due to the growth in factor inputs K and L):

$$\frac{d \ln C}{dt} = \frac{C_M}{C_A} \bullet \frac{d \ln Q}{dt}$$

$$= \left(\frac{C_M}{C_A} \alpha\right) \frac{d \ln K}{dt} + \left(\frac{C_M}{C_A} \beta\right) \frac{d \ln L}{dt}$$

(8)

On the other hand, from eq.(3) we obtain the growth of cost C due to the growth in factor inputs K and L (with P_c assumed to be constant):

$$\frac{d \ln C}{dt} = \frac{P_k K}{C} \frac{d \ln K}{dt} + \frac{WL}{C} \frac{d \ln L}{dt}$$

(9)

Since eq.(8) and eq.(9) are the same, we have:

(1) $\quad \dfrac{C_M}{C_A} \alpha = \dfrac{P_k K}{C}$, which leads to:

$$\alpha = \frac{C_A}{C_M}\frac{P_k K}{C} = \frac{P_k K/Q}{C_M} = \frac{C_{AK}}{C_M} \tag{10}$$

where $C_{AK} = P_k K/Q$ – average capital cost (unit capital cost).

(2) $\quad \dfrac{C_M}{C_A}\beta = \dfrac{WL}{C}\quad$ which yields

$$\beta = \frac{C_A}{C_M}\frac{WL}{C} = \frac{WL/Q}{C_M} = \frac{C_{AL}}{C_M} \tag{11}$$

where $C_{AL} = WL/Q$ – average labor cost (unit labor cost).

From eq.(10) and eq.(11) we obtain

$$\alpha + \beta = \frac{C_{AK} + C_{AL}}{C_M} = \frac{C_A}{C_M}$$

and

$$\left.\begin{aligned}
\frac{\alpha}{\alpha + \beta} &= \frac{C_{AK}/C_M}{C_A/C_M} = \frac{C_{AK}}{C_A} \\[2mm]
\frac{\beta}{\alpha + \beta} &= \frac{C_{AL}/C_M}{C_A/C_M} = \frac{C_{AL}}{C_A}
\end{aligned}\right\} \tag{12}$$

4. Decomposition of Total Factor Productivity Growth

Considering eq.(12), from eq.(5) we have

$$\frac{d\ln(TFP)}{dt} = \frac{d\ln\overline{Q}}{dt} - \left(\frac{P_k K/\overline{Q}}{C/\overline{Q}}\frac{d\ln K}{dt} + \frac{WL/\overline{Q}}{C/\overline{Q}}\frac{d\ln L}{dt}\right)$$

$$= \frac{d\ln\overline{Q}}{dt} - \left(\frac{C_{AK}}{C_A}\frac{d\ln K}{dt} + \frac{C_{AL}}{C_A}\frac{d\ln L}{dt}\right) \tag{13}$$

$$= \frac{d\ln\overline{Q}}{dt} - \left(\frac{\alpha}{\alpha+\beta}\frac{d\ln K}{dt} + \frac{\beta}{\alpha+\beta}\frac{d\ln L}{dt}\right)$$

From the input-output relationship of production $\overline{Q} = F(K,L,t)$ we get

$$\frac{d\ln\overline{Q}}{dt} = \frac{\partial\ln F}{\partial t} + \frac{\partial\ln F}{\partial\ln K}\frac{d\ln K}{dt} + \frac{\partial\ln F}{\partial\ln L}\frac{d\ln L}{dt}$$

$$= \frac{\partial\ln F}{\partial t} + \alpha\frac{d\ln K}{dt} + \beta\frac{d\ln L}{dt} \tag{14}$$

Substitute eq.(14) into eq.(13) and re-arrange the expression. We obtain the natural decomposition for total factor productivity growth:

$$\frac{d\ln(TFP)}{dt} = \frac{\partial\ln F}{\partial t} + \left(1 - \frac{1}{\alpha+\beta}\right)\left(\alpha\frac{d\ln K}{dt} + \beta\frac{d\ln L}{dt}\right) \tag{15}$$

It can be seen that total factor productivity growth *dln(TFP)/dt*, representing and measuring overall technological change, can be resolved into two components:

(1) $\dfrac{\partial\ln F}{\partial t}$

-- advances in knowledge, which stem from such factors as, improvements in technical efficiency, education, invention and innovation, etc. and all other advances in knowledge, which can be achieved independently of the changes in production scale. It is known as "Solow's technical progress", which is disembodied technological change.

$$(2) \quad \left(1 - \frac{1}{\alpha + \beta}\right)\left(\alpha \, \frac{d \ln K}{dt} + \beta \, \frac{d \ln L}{dt}\right)$$

--economies of scale, which accompany changes in production scale and depend upon the output elasticities of input factors. The output elasticities reflect the quality and capability of input factors. The economies of scale are determined by both internalities and externalities of production. Division of labor, organization and coordination of work, contribution to output by earlier inputs, *e.g.* earlier investment and experience of production (learning-by-doing) *etc.* are internalities. Environmental pollution, market mechanisms, *etc.* are typical examples of externalities of production. In summary, all matters affecting the change in returns to production scale are to be included. Economies of scale represent technological change, embodied in input factors.

In eq.(15), it can be seen that Solow's technical progress $(\partial \ln F / \partial t)$ is only a part of total factor productivity growth $[d \ln (TFP)/dt]$, and only in the case of constant returns to scale $(\alpha + \beta = 1)$ are Solow's technical progress $(\partial \ln F / \partial t)$ and the total factor productivity growth $[d \ln(TFP)/dt]$ identical:

$$\frac{d \ln(TFP)}{dt} = \frac{\partial \ln F}{\partial t}$$

Thus, overall technological change, quantified by TFP growth rate, consists of two ingredients: disembodied technological change (Solow's technical progress) and embodied technological change (economies or diseconomies of scale).

5. Decomposition of Product Output Growth

If we substitute eq.(15) into eq.(13), we obtain a decomposition of product output growth as follows:

$$\frac{d\ln\overline{Q}}{dt} = \frac{\partial\ln F}{\partial t} + \left(1 - \frac{1}{\alpha+\beta}\right)\left(\alpha\frac{d\ln K}{dt} + \beta\frac{d\ln L}{dt}\right) + \frac{1}{\alpha+\beta}\left(\alpha\frac{d\ln K}{dt} + \beta\frac{d\ln L}{dt}\right)$$

On the right hand side of the equation, the first two terms taken together stand for TFP growth, which is referred to as "intensive growth in product output"; the last term is referred to as "extensive growth in product output". It is in quantity equal to the growth in total factor input.

Let us consider the relationships in eq.(12). From eq.(4) we obtain growth in total factor input:

$$\frac{d\ln Q_c}{dt} = \frac{P_k K/\overline{Q}}{C/\overline{Q}}\frac{d\ln K}{dt} + \frac{WL/\overline{Q}}{C/\overline{Q}}\frac{d\ln L}{dt}$$

$$= \frac{C_{AK}}{C_A}\frac{d\ln K}{dt} + \frac{C_{AL}}{C_A}\frac{d\ln L}{dt}$$

$$= \frac{\alpha}{\alpha+\beta}\frac{d\ln K}{dt} + \frac{\beta}{\alpha+\beta}\frac{d\ln L}{dt}$$

$$= \frac{1}{\alpha+\beta}\left(\alpha\frac{d\ln K}{dt} + \beta\frac{d\ln L}{dt}\right)$$

The decomposition of product output growth is summarized in the following table:

Growth in product output :
$$\frac{d\ln \overline{Q}}{dt} = \frac{\partial \ln F}{\partial t} + \alpha\frac{d\ln K}{dt} + \beta\frac{d\ln L}{dt}$$

Growth in total factor input ⇔ Extensive growth in product output : $$\frac{1}{\alpha+\beta}\left(\alpha\frac{d\ln K}{dt} + \beta\frac{d\ln L}{dt}\right)$$	Total factor productivity growth ⇔ Intensive growth in product output: $$\frac{\partial \ln F}{\partial t} + \left(1 - \frac{1}{\alpha+\beta}\right)\left(\alpha\frac{d\ln K}{dt} + \beta\frac{d\ln L}{dt}\right)$$	
	Economies of scale: $$\left(1 - \frac{1}{\alpha+\beta}\right)\times$$ $$\left(\alpha\frac{d\ln K}{dt} + \beta\frac{d\ln L}{dt}\right)$$	**Advances in knowledge ⇔ Solow's technical progress:** $$\frac{\partial \ln F}{\partial t}$$
Part of the product output growth that is attributed to factor input growth: $$\left(\alpha\frac{d\ln K}{dt} + \beta\frac{d\ln L}{dt}\right)$$		**Part of the product output growth that is not attributed to factor input growth:** $$\frac{\partial \ln F}{\partial t}$$

It is important to note that we omitted the subscript "t", which is the time variable that dates the quantities in the equations. All quantities in the equations are related to an instantaneous time point, but for practical calculation the time point values of the quantities in equations must be replaced with their time interval values, e.g. their annual values.

For obtaining the average annual values of the components of output growth over a period of years, one can make use of two methods: (1) First we use the equations to compute the annual values, and then form an average of these computed annual values; (2) We might utilize the equations directly to compute the average annual values over the period being considered, provided that all quantities in equations should be annual averages over the period. But such a method for computing seems to be only approximate , and even rough.

The output elasticities of input factors (α, β) can either be directly computed if cost data are available, or estimated by econometric methods if statistical data are available. Production functions of translog, CES or Cobb-Douglas type can be specified for estimation of output elasticities.

For obtaining the aggregate output elasticities of input factors for the whole economy, it is recommended that we could, by making use of input-output tables [3] or in some other way, at first compute or estimate the output elasticities for industries, and then in some way [4] aggregate them.

To illustrate the methodology of decomposition presented in this paper, we carried out a calculation of the components of product output growth for the American economy over the period 1909—1949, for China's state-owned industry over the period 1953—1977 with 1960, 1961 and 1962 (3 years of natural calamities) excluded, and for China's economy over the period 1978—1996, respectively. For simplicity, the input-output relationship of the Cobb-Douglas type was chosen for estimating the output elasticities of capital and labor (average annual value over the period), and the method (2), mentioned above, was chosen for computing the average annual values of economies of scale and extensive growth in output. Results of calculation are listed in Table 1.

It can be seen in Table 1 that the results for the US economy over the period 1909—1949 are quite close to the results obtained by R. Solow [5]. The contributions of technical progress and of economies of scale to output growth account for 57.8% of the total. However, as shown in Table 1, there are some small economies of scale (3.1% of output growth), which had been omitted by R. Solow, assuming the returns to scale to be constant.

Table 1 Comparison of China's and the US Economies

Average annual values	USA 1909—1949	China's industrial economy 1953—1977	China's total economy 1978—1996
Output elasticity of capital α	0.2037	0.5514	0.7676
Output elasticity of labor β	0.8733	0.5180	0.8706
$\alpha + \beta$	1.077	1.069	1.638
Growth in product output (%)	2.87 (100 %)	9.87 (100%)	9.34 (100%)
Solow's technical progress (%)	1.57 (54.7%)	0 (0%)	0 (0%)
Economies of scale (%)	0.09 (3.1%)	0.64 (6.5%)	3.64 (39.0%)
Extensive growth in output (%)	1.21 (42.2%)	9.23(93.5%)	5.70 (61.0%)
	Appendix I	Appendix II	Appendix III

As shown in Table 1, for China's state-owned industry over the period 1953—1977 (1960, 1961, 1962 excluded), no technical progress and small economies of scale were present. That is to say, the average annual technological change over the period of those years was very small. Therefore, output growth was basically "extensive". The extensive growth in output is equal to the growth in total factor inputs.

It can be seen in Table 1 that for China's economy over the period 1978—1996 there are considerable economies of scale, the contribution of which accounts for 39% of output growth. The large economies of scale stem from the introduction of advanced foreign equipment and technology, with improvement in management and organization of work since 1978, when the policy of "Reform and Opening to the Outside World" began. It is generally the case for developing countries that economies of scale (embodied technological change) are much larger than technical progress (disembodied technological change).

A decomposition of TFP growth and product output growth can also be made for a multi-factor production process with labor as a necessary input factor. The input-output relationship of production is:

$$\overline{Q} = F(K_1, K_2, ..., K_n, L, t)$$

where $\overline{Q}$ – product output; L – labor input; K_i – the i–th factor input, $(i=1,2,...,n)$; and t – time.

Omitting the derivations here, we write down only the final equations:

$$(1) \quad \frac{d \ln(TFP)}{dt} = \frac{\partial \ln F}{\partial t} + \left(1 - \frac{1}{\sum_{1}^{n} \alpha_i + \beta}\right) \left(\sum_{1}^{n} \alpha_i \frac{d \ln K_i}{dt} + \beta \frac{d \ln L}{dt}\right)$$

$$(2) \quad \frac{d\ln\overline{Q}}{dt} = \frac{\partial\ln F}{\partial t} + \left(1 - \frac{1}{\sum\limits_{1}^{n}\alpha_i + \beta}\right)\left(\sum\limits_{1}^{n}\alpha_i\frac{d\ln K_i}{dt} + \beta\frac{d\ln L}{dt}\right)$$

$$+ \frac{1}{\sum\limits_{1}^{n}\alpha_i + \beta}\left(\sum\limits_{1}^{n}\alpha_i\frac{d\ln K_i}{dt} + \beta\frac{d\ln L}{dt}\right)$$

References

Yoshioka Kanji, Takanobu Nakajima, Masao Nakamura: "Sources of Total Factor Productivity", *Keio Economic Observatory*, Keio University, Monograph No. 5, 1994.

Zhou Fang: "On the Measurement of Output Elasticities of Input Factor", *Quantitative & Technical Economics*, No. 6, 1995 (in Chinese).

Zhou Fang: "Directly Computing the Output Elasticities Using Input-Output Tables", *Quantitative & Technical Economics*, No. 2, 1997 (in Chinese).

Wang-Li: "On the Measurement of Technical Progress for Industry and the Issue of Production Scale", *Quantitative & Technical Economics*, No. 9, 1995 (in Chinese).

R.M. Solow: "Technical Change and the Aggregate Production Function", *The Review of Economics and Statistics*, Vol. 39, August, 1957.

APPENDIX I

T	Output Q(t)/1909=1.0	Capital Input K(t)/1909=1.0	Labor Input L(t)/1909=1.0
1909	1.000000	1.000000	1.000000
10	1.014371	1.045818	1.025898
11	1.048860	1.063882	1.009953
12	1.090100	1.117460	1.041614
13	1.143697	1.134300	1.047828
14	1.103958	1.076990	1.008454
15	1.089476	1.113066	1.014564
16	1.241608	1.255230	1.105031

17	1.307345	1.286867	1.199523
18	1.438764	1.325061	1.229561
19	1.364071	1.328494	1.107974
20	1.254710	1.357840	1.084167
21	1.162039	1.163834	0.940195
22	1.312067	1.253863	1.037332
23	1.488675	1.452488	1.146408
24	1.481155	1.468134	1.103779
25	1.627747	1.586345	1.162943
26	1.701548	1.699523	1.219867
27	1.721941	1.751816	1.231652
28	1.753661	1.832576	1.250035
29	1.879354	1.943246	1.308198
30	1.687975	1.914335	1.195009
31	1.524054	1.697841	1.050316
32	1.277746	1.441950	0.905615
33	1.166665	1.352011	0.898433
34	1.418355	1.397228	0.959430
35	1.535814	1.413610	1.014647
36	1.766589	1.479836	1.120758
37	1.853038	1.564067	1.188921
38	1.733735	1.457633	1.080117
39	1.917810	1.492064	1.155509
40	2.125175	1.562226	1.223645
41	2.465112	1.714290	1.368774
42	2.701484	1.898667	1.481535
43	2.939039	1.973538	1.551713
44	3.120708	1.962181	1.536918
45	3.053247	1.895219	1.467726
46	2.952817	1.837473	1.514078
47	3.041584	1.926000	1.587024
48	3.146535	1.987366	1.605480
49	3.156132	2.021294	1.542173

RESULTS OF OLS ESTIMATION

$$dLnQ(t) = 0.0157 + 0.2037 \; dLnK(t) + 0.8733 \; dLnL(t)$$
$$(2.352) \quad (1.082) \qquad\quad (4.907)$$
R-squared = 0.7706, DW = 2.455, F-statistic = 62.144

where *dLnQ(t)* – annual growth in product output;
    dLnK(t) – annual growth in capital input;
    dLnL(t) – annual growth in labor input.

Output elasticity of capital: $\alpha = 0.2037$,
Output elasticity of labor: $\beta = 0.8733$

(I) Technical progress (disembodied technological change) = *1.57%*

(II) Economies of scale (embodied technological change): *ES*:

$$ES = \left(1 - \frac{1}{\alpha + \beta}\right)\left[\alpha \times MdLnK(t) + \beta \times MdLnL(t)\right]$$

$$= \left(1 - \frac{1}{0.2037 + 0.8733}\right)\left[0.2037 \times 0.017593 + 0.8733 \times 0.010830\right]$$

$$= 0.09\%$$

where *MdLnK(t)* – average annual growth in capital input;
    MdLnL(t) – average annual growth in labor input

(III) Extensive growth in product output-growth in total factor input:

$$EXTGR = \frac{1}{\alpha + \beta}\left[\alpha \times MdLnK(t) + \beta \times MdLnL(t)\right]$$

$$= \frac{1}{0.2037 + 0.8733}\left[0.2037 \times 0.017593 + 0.8733 \times 0.010830\right]$$

$$= 1.21\%$$

Source of data: R.M. Solow, "Technical Change and the Aggregate Production Function", *The Review of Economics and Statistics*, Vol. 39, August, 1957.

APPENDIX II

T	Output Q(t)	Capital Input K(t)	Labor Input L(t)
1953	15.30	17.68	58.60
54	17.70	21.17	59.20
55	18.80	23.83	55.90
56	24.50	27.28	68.60
57	30.00	33.32	71.10
58	50.20	47.55	218.00
59	65.30	67.99	186.40
63	39.50	87.09	104.00
64	50.20	90.55	107.80
65	63.90	98.32	115.30
66	79.60	106.23	123.40
67	65.30	115.50	128.90
68	60.60	122.58	139.20
69	81.90	130.23	152.20
70	110.10	152.29	183.10
71	127.60	170.17	209.00
72	134.10	194.65	220.30
73	140.40	218.41	225.10
74	138.50	234.91	234.40
75	159.80	255.49	253.20
76	144.20	274.44	269.80
77	157.90	294.80	283.80

Source: Chen Kuan *et al.*, "Productivity Change in Chinese Industry: 1953—1985", *Journal of Comparative Economics* 12, 1988; pp. 570—591.

RESULTS OF OLS ESTIMATION

$$LnQ(t) = -0.8992 + 0.5514\, LnK(t) + 0.5180\, LnL(t)$$
$$(-2.754)\quad (7.777)\qquad\quad (4.422)$$

R – squared = 0.9734   *DW = 1.277*   *F – statistic = 347.292*
where Output elasticity of capital: $\alpha = 0.5514$
Output elasticity of labor: $\beta = 0.5180$

(I) Technical progress (disembodied technological change) = 0

(II) Economies of scale (embodied technological change) : *ES*:

$$ES = \left(1 - \frac{1}{\alpha + \beta}\right)\left[\alpha \times MdLnK(t) + \beta \times MdLnL(t)\right]$$

$$= \left(1 - \frac{1}{0.5514 + 0.5180}\right)\left[0.5514 \times 0.117244 + 0.5180 \times 0.065731\right]$$

$$= 0.64\%$$

(III) Extensive growth in product output *EXTGR*:

$$EXTGR = \frac{1}{\alpha + \beta}\left[\alpha \times MdLnK(t) + \beta \times MdLnL(t)\right]$$

$$= \frac{1}{0.5514 + 0.5180}\left[0.5514 \times 0.117244 + 0.5180 \times 0.065731\right]$$

$$= 9.23\%$$

APPENDIX III

T	Output Y(t)	Labor Input L(t)	Capital-Output Ratio
	1978 = 1.00	1978 = 1.00	
1978	1.00	1.00	2.35
79	1.07	1.02	2.36
80	1.16	1.05	2.31
81	1.22	1.08	2.32
82	1.33	1.12	2.29
83	1.47	1.15	2.22
84	1.70	1.20	2.11
85	1.92	1.24	2.08
86	2.10	1.27	2.15
87	2.34	1.31	2.17
88	2.60	1.35	2.19
89	2.71	1.37	2.28
90	2.81	1.41	2.35
91	3.07	1.45	2.32
92	3.51	1.48	2.23
93	3.98	1.49	2.20
94	4.49	1.53	2.20
95	4.96	1.55	2.24
96	5.44	1.58	2.30

Source: *CSYB* 1996: Macro-economic Data Bank, IQTE, CASS

RESULTS OF OLS ESTIMATION

$$LnY(t) = -0.6496 + 0.7676\,LnK(t) + 0.8706\,LnL(t)$$
$$(-9.888)\quad (8.950)\qquad\qquad (2.869)$$

R – squared = 0.9969,   *DW* = 0.5690,   *F-statistic* = 2547.111

Output elasticity of capital α = 0.7676
Output elasticity of labor β = 0.8706

(I) Technical progress (disembodied technological change) = 0

(II) Economies of scale (embodied technological change)   *ES*:

$$ES = \left(1 - \frac{1}{\alpha + \beta}\right)\left[\alpha \times MdLnK(t) + \beta \times MdLnL(t)\right]$$

$$= \left(1 - \frac{1}{0.7676 + 0.8706}\right)\left[0.7676 \times 0.092904 + 0.8706 \times 0.025412\right]$$

$$= 3.64\%$$

(III) Extensive growth in product output *EXTGR*:

$$EXTGR = \frac{1}{\alpha + \beta}\left[\alpha \times MdLnK(t) + \beta \times MdLnL(t)\right]$$

$$= \frac{1}{0.7676 + 0.8706}\left[0.7676 \times 0.092904 + 0.8706 \times 0.025412\right]$$

$$= 5.70\%$$

7   CHINA'S MACRO ECONOMETRIC ANNUAL MODEL

Shen Lisheng

The Institute of Quantitative and Technical Economics, CASS

1. Summary of the model

In 1987, the Institute of Quantitative & Technical Economics, CASS began a project entitled, "Macro Economic Linkage Model of China, Japan and United States" in collaboration with Professor Lawrence R. Klein of the University of Pennsylvania and Professor Lawrence J. Lau of Stanford Uni-versity. In this project, we took up the task of building a Chinese macroeconometric annual model under the supervision of Professor Lau. Our purposes were two. One purpose was to link models of China, Japan and US and then deal with the feed-back relationship between China's economy and the world economy. Another purpose was to analyze and forecast China's economic situation with relevant policy simulations. After several years' efforts, this model was gradually improved and applied to the linkage analysis of the three countries. In the meantime, we began to use this model for the analysis and forecast of China's economic situation since 1990.

The Chinese Academy of Social Sciences set up a research group in 1990 headed by the then Vice-president of CASS, Prof. Liu Guoguang, a well-known economist in China. The Institute of Quantitative and Technical Economics was in charge of the underlying research work while collaborating with the Comprehensive Department of the State Statistical Bureau.[1] We used this China model to forecast and analyze the Chinese economy. Our forecast reports have been regularly announced. The first forecast meeting

---

[1] China's Macro Econometric Annual Model has been prepared, on a collaborative basis by the Institute of Quantitative & Technical Economics, Chinese Academy of Social Sciences (CASS) and Comprehensive Department of the State Statistical Bureau (See Wang Huijong, Li Boxi and Li Shantong ed. *China's Practical Macroeconomic Model*, Chinese Finance and Economy Publishing House, 1993.8, pp-41). The following persons have participated: Zhang Shouyi, Wang Tongsan, Shen Lisheng, Zhou Mingwu, Zhu Yunfa, Zhang Xinzhu, Zhang Yanqun, Zhang Siqi, Wang Li, Liu Geping. This explanatory chapter is written by Shen Lisheng.

was held in the fall of 1990. Participants, who came from various research institutions and universities, also presented their reports about forecasts and economic analyses for the current and next year. These meetings came to the attention of government departments concerned, and some news reports proved to be well received. Thus, we could lay a firm foundation for the holding of a regular forecast meeting in the spring and the fall every year. At the same time, the project of "Analysis and Forecast of China's Economic Situation" was given a grant by the Premier Fund of the State Council, which assured the continuation of this project. Since the fall of 1991, we began to publish an Economic Blue Book which collected various forecast reports presented at the fall meeting. The Blue Book is now published before the end of each year.

"Analysis and Forecast for the Economic Situation" has become an important contribution of the Institute of Quantitative & Technical Economics. Accordingly the maintenance and updating of the model has become a routine task. All data used in the model are taken from *China Statistical Yearbook*. Since the *Yearbook* is usually published after September each year, we cannot make use of this *Yearbook* in the fall forecast. However, we can rely on some revised figures in *A Statistical Survey of China*, and some figures are published in newspapers. At the end of each year or the beginning of next year, we update all data used in the model, re-estimate every equation, then make forecasts. After 1994, some data in the *Statistical Year-book* were changed from MPS to SNA. For example Social Gross Value and Net Output Value were changed to such concepts as Gross Domestic Project and Value-added; variables in our model were correspondingly changed.

2. Model Structure

China's macroeconometric annual model is a large model. It describes circulation and turnover in the whole national economy including production, distribution, exchange and consumption, as well as finance, banking, price formation and foreign trade. In other words, it reflects many aspects of the national economy. First we consider the steps of data collection, then we divide the whole model into 8 blocks. Roughly, they are: production, investment and capital stock, population and labor force, income, consumption, finance and banking, price formation, foreign capital movement and foreign trade. The relations among these blocks are shown in figure 1. The model includes

153 equations, of which 89 are stochastic equations and 64 are identities. There are 37 exogenous variables (of which there are 12 dummy variables). The model documentation and variable list are appended. Following is a brief description of some main equations.

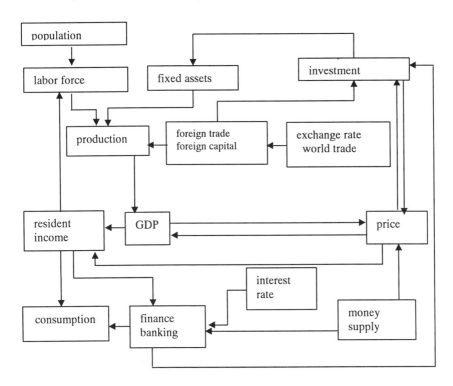

Figure 1 Diagram of China's Macro Econometric Annual Model

2.1. Production block

The production block includes production functions for 7 sectors — agriculture; light industry; heavy industry; construction; post, transportation and telecommunication; commerce; and non-material production. Production functions are of the Cobb-Douglas type, i.e. the output of a sector is determined by its capital stock and labor force in log-linear form. Output of a sector is its value-added, except that agricultural output is stated as gross output value. For the example of heavy industry, its production function is:

VHIC=EXP(−.943 + .720 * LOG(KHIC) + .530 * LOG(LHI)
      (−2.50) (9.62)   (5.40)

           + .286 * D70 + .309 * D92(−1)) ;
            (3.76)   (4.70)

    R^2=0.994   D.W.=2.02   (1965—1996)

where, VHIC: value-added of heavy industry (in constant price), KHIC: capital stock of heavy industry (in constant price), LHI: labor force (employment) in heavy industry, D70, D92: dummy variables for 1970 and 1992. In parentheses below the estimated coefficients, we list t-statistics.

Having value-added of each sector, we can get value-added of three (primary, secondary and tertiary) industries V1C, V2C, V3C, and gross domestic product GDPC (in constant price). We then convert constant price values into current price values by multiplying by corresponding deflators.

2.2. Population and labor force block

The total population equation is an auto-regressive equation in log-linear form:

TPOP=EXP(0.0428 + 2.419 * LOG(TPOP(−1)) − 2.012 * LOG(TPOP(−2))
       (2.20)   (15.71)   (−6.81)

           + .587*LOG(TPOP)(−3))
            (3.94)
    R^2=0.999   D.W.=1.62   (1968—1996)

where, TPOP is total population (mid-year). There is no other variable in this equation, so that we can obtain a forecast directly. The forecast up to 2010 is shown in Table 1. These figures indicate an optimistic pattern of decreasing natural growth year-by-year.

In this block, the equations of labor force LFR and of urban population TPN are both determined by total population TPOP. Total population *minus* urban population is rural population TPA.

The labor force of each sector is determined by its value in the previous period (one period time-lag) and the sector's value-added, divided by average wages of staff and workers. If average wages of staff and workers is constant, the demand for labor force will increase along with the increase of the sector's value-added; or the demand for labor force will decrease when the increase of average wages of staff and workers is faster than the sector's value-added. Taking the example of labor force demand in light industry:

Table 1 Total Population and Forecast (mid-year)

Year	Population	Annual Increase	Growth Rate (%)
1980	981.24	12.23	1.262
1981	993.88	12.65	1.289
1982	1008.63	14.75	1.484
1983	1023.31	14.68	1.455
1984	1036.82	13.52	1.321
1985	1051.04	14.21	1.371
1986	1066.79	15.75	1.499
1987	1084.03	17.24	1.617
1988	1101.63	17.60	1.623
1989	1118.65	17.02	1.545
1990	1135.19	16.54	1.478
1991	1150.78	15.59	1.374
1992	1164.97	14.19	1.233
1993	1178.44	13.47	1.156
1994	1191.84	13.40	1.137
1995	1204.85	13.02	1.092
1996	1217.55	12.70	1.054
1997	1229.67	12.12	0.995
1998	1241.09	11.42	0.929
1999	1251.81	10.72	0.863
2000	1261.87	10.06	0.804
2001	1271.37	9.50	0.753
2002	1280.40	9.03	0.710
2003	1289.05	8.66	0.676
2004	1297.41	8.35	0.648
2005	1305.50	8.10	0.624
2006	1313.38	7.88	0.603
2007	1321.05	7.67	0.584
2008	1328.51	7.46	0.565
2009	1335.77	7.26	0.546
2010	1342.82	7.05	0.528

Notes: observed values before 1996. unit: million

$$LLI=EXP(.627 + .819 * LOG(LLI(-1)) + .218 * LOG(VLIC/WGAVC)$$
$$(4.18) \quad (16.62) \qquad (3.66)$$
$$+0.0734 * D76 - 0.0737 * D88 - 0.0837 * D94),$$
$$(2.69) \qquad (-2.72) \qquad (-3.11)$$

$$R^2=0.998 \quad D.W.=2.13 \qquad (1966—1996)$$

where, LLI: employment in light industry (annual average), VLIC: value-added of light industry (in constant prices), WGAVC: average wages of workers and staff.

2.3. Residents' income block

Residents' income includes two parts: the annual income available for living costs of urban residents and annual net income of rural residents. Residents' income is usually stable, so we use its value in the previous period as one of independent variables; at the same time, we consider that the growth of income is determined by production. Therefore, net income of rural residents is determined by the income of the previous year and value-added of primary industry; while income available for living costs of urban residents is determined by the income of last year and value-added of secondary and tertiary industry. Taking income available for living cost of urban residents as an example, we have:

$$YUC=EXP(.391 + .306 * LOG(YUC(-1)) + .274 * LOG(V2C) +$$
$$(2.08) (2.44) \qquad\qquad (3.46)$$
$$.310 * LOG(V3C) + .177 * D79 - .117 * D84(-3) + 0.0585 * D90) ;$$
$$(3.69) \qquad\qquad (5.90) \qquad (-4.54) \qquad\qquad (2.47)$$

$$R^2=0.998 \quad D.W.=2.63 \qquad (1978—1996)$$

where, YUC: income available for living cost of urban residents (in constant price), V2C, V3C: value-added of secondary and tertiary industry (in constant price), D79, D84, D90: dummy variable.

The income available for living costs of urban residents YUC and net income of rural residents YAC divided by urban populations and rural populations separately, gives annual per capita income available for living costs of urban residents YUAVC and annual per capita net income of rural residents YAAVC.

In the residents' income block, there are equations of total wages of staff and workers WGC and equations of numbers of staff and workers (year average) SW. They are behavior equations. Total wages divided by the number of staff and workers is average wages of staff and workers used in the labor force block.

2.4. Consumption block

This block includes four behavior equations: peasants' consumption, non-peasants' consumption, social consumption and total retail sales of consumer goods.

The behavior of consumers is influenced by the habits of consumers; so previous period consumption is one of the explanatory variables of consumption. In addition, the size of consumption is also determined by income; therefore, we put different income variables into different consumption equations. Peasants' consumption is determined by value in the previous period and net income of rural residents. Non-peasants' consumption is determined by its previous value and income available for living costs of urban residents. Social consumption is determined by its previous value and government expenditure (divided by the GDP deflator to convert into constant prices). The sum of peasants' consumption, non-peasants' consumption and social consumption is total consumption. Total retail sales of consumer goods is determined by its previous period value and total consumption. The following is the equation of non-peasants' consumption:

$$CRNC = EXP(-.218 + .682 * LOG(CRNC(-1)) + .361 * LOG(YUC));$$
$$\quad\quad\quad (-0.98)\ (4.29)\quad\quad\quad\quad\quad (1.98)$$

$$R^2 = 0.996 \quad\quad D.W. = 1.64 \quad\quad\quad\quad (1979 - 1996)$$

where, CRNC: non-peasants consumption (in constant prices), YUC: income available for living costs of urban residents (in constant prices).

2.5. Investment and capital stock block

Investment here means total investment in fixed assets. It plays a very important role in this model. The equation is:

$$IIC = EXP(.930 + .335 * LOG(IIC(-1)) + .439 * LOG(GEXE/PI)$$
$$\quad\quad\quad (0.82)\quad (2.43)\quad\quad\quad (2.43)$$
$$+ .191 * LOG(LOANFA/PI) + 0.0941 * LOG(FCU * EXRA/PI)$$
$$\quad\quad (4.22)\quad\quad\quad\quad\quad\quad\quad (1.33)$$
$$- .469 * D80 + .194 * D92);$$

$$(-3.10) \qquad (2.99)$$
$$R^2 = 0.990 \qquad D.W. = 2.04 \qquad (1979—1996)$$

where, IIC: total investment in fixed assets (in constant prices), IIC(-1): one period time-lag (it reflects *continuity* of economic operation, as well as the demand for projects in process of construction), GEXE: construction expenditure in government outlays, PI: the price deflator of investment goods, LOANFA: mid- and long-term loans (mainly used in capital construction), FCU: total amount of foreign capital actually used, EXRA: the exchange rate, D80, D92: dummy variables.

In the investment equation, in addition to last period's value, we considered main resources of various investments, but did not consider any index of the stock market, which appeared only after 1990.

A sector's investment in fixed assets is obtained from the behavior equation of each sector which generally has the same form, *i.e.* one determined by last period's value and total investment. Taking the example of heavy industry we find:

$$IHIC = -17.065 + .312 * IHIC(-1) + .219 * IIC + 133.801 * D82$$
$$(-1.16) \quad (4.61) \qquad (11.01) \qquad (4.02)$$
$$-262.302 * D94 ;$$
$$(-4.35)$$
$$R^2 = 0.998 \qquad D.W. = 2.50 \qquad (1966—1996)$$

where IHIC: investment in fixed assets of heavy industry (in constant prices), IIC: total investment in fixed assets (in constant prices), D82, D94: dummy variables.

A sector's capital stock is: its last previous value minus depreciation, then plus its investment in fixed assets of the current year. The example of light industry gives:

$$KLIC = KLIC(-1) * (1-DLI) + ILIC$$

where, KLIC: capital stock of light industry (in constant prices), DLI: depreciation rate of light industry, ILIC: investment in fixed assets of light industry (in constant prices).

2.6. Finance and banking block

This block includes government revenue and government expenditure. Government revenue is the sum of sectors' revenue, which is obtained in a behavior equation, which is determined by its last period value and value-added. Taking the example of commerce we have:

GORVCOM= –44.667 + .715 *GORVCOM(–1) + .186 * VCOM ;
$\quad\quad$ (–1.85) $\quad$ (4.99) $\quad\quad\quad\quad\quad\quad$ (3.66)
$\quad\quad$ R^2=0.991 $\quad\quad\quad\quad$ D.W.=2.34 $\quad\quad\quad\quad\quad$ (1978—1995)

where, GORVCOM: government revenue of commerce (in current prices), VCOM: value-added of commerce (in current prices).

Government expenditure includes: expenditure for economic construction, expenditure for culture and education, expenditure for national defense, expenditure for administration, and other expenditure. Among these expenditures, culture and education, and national defense are influenced by government policy, thus they are exogenous. Others are obtained from behavior equations. Taking the example of expenditures for economic construction we have:

GEXE=EXP(–.498 + .111*LOG(GEXE(–1)) +.891 * LOG(GORV) –.177 * D84(–2)) ;
$\quad\quad$ (–2.17) $\quad$ (1.25) $\quad\quad\quad\quad\quad$ (10.68) $\quad\quad\quad\quad$ (–3.19)
$\quad\quad$ R^2=0.988 $\quad\quad\quad\quad$ D.W=1.44 $\quad\quad\quad\quad$ (1966—1996)

where, GEXE: expenditure for economic construction, GORV: government revenue, D84: dummy variable.

The balance from equations for government revenue and expenditure is given by government revenue *minus* government expenditure. It is a deficit value when it is negative, to be accommodated by issuing state bonds.

Banking includes two parts: banks as sources and as lenders. Bank sources include: currency in circulation (exogenous), deposits, and other funds. Deposits are further divided into: savings deposit of enterprises, savings deposit of government, savings deposits of urban households, savings deposits of rural households. The different savings deposits are determined by different independent variables. Each equation has an interest rate to reflect its adjustment function in financial market clearing. Taking the example of de-posits of enterprises, we have:

M1DD=EXP(–1.806 + .602 * LOG(M1DD(–1)) + .513 * LOG(GDP) +
$\quad\quad$ (–3.94) $\quad$ (6.11) $\quad\quad\quad\quad\quad$ (4.14)
$\quad\quad\quad$ 0.0251 * RSAV + .194 * D84 –.404 *D88 +.230 *D90) ;
$\quad\quad\quad\quad$ (1.99) $\quad\quad\quad\quad$ (3.19) $\quad\quad$ (–5.87) $\quad\quad$ (3.62)
$\quad\quad$ R^2=0.998 $\quad\quad\quad\quad\quad\quad$ D.W.=1.91 $\quad\quad\quad\quad$ (1965—1996)

where, M1DD: deposit of enterprises, GDP: gross domestic product (in current prices), RSAV: interest rate of deposit for one year, D84, D88, D90 are dummy variables.

Loans are the main uses of funds of banking institutions; thus total loans are determined by funds of all banks' sources:

$$
\begin{aligned}
\text{LOANTT}=\text{EXP}(.134 &+ .978 * \text{LOG(MASSET)} - 0.0470 * \text{D78} \\
(1.60) &\quad (82.16) \qquad\qquad\qquad (-2.32) \\
&+ .163 * \text{D88}(-1) - .249 * \text{D94}) \\
&\quad (6.88) \quad (-10.30) \\
\text{R}^2 = 0.990 &\qquad\qquad \text{D.W.}=1.74 \qquad\qquad (1965\text{--}1996)
\end{aligned}
$$

where, LOANTT: total loans, MASSET: funds of all banks' sources, D78, D88, D94 are dummy variables.

Loans include: loans to industry, loans to commerce, loans to agriculture, mid- and long-term loans, and other loans, with each having a behavior equation.

2.7. Price block

In the price block, there are three main price indexes: the price index of investment goods, a general consumer price index, a general retail price index, and various deflators. The function of the price block is to provide various indexes to convert some indicators between current prices and constant prices. The price index of investment and the general consumer price index are two basic indexes. Other indexes are mainly determined by these two indexes. These two indexes are determined by their last period values and other (same period) independent variables, *i.e.* ratio of currency in circulation to GDP, ratio of investment to GDP. Taking the example of a general consumer price index:

$$
\begin{aligned}
\text{PCR}=\text{EXP}(.292 &+ .847 * \text{LOG(PCR}(-1)) + .106 * \text{LOG(M1CUR/GDP)} + \\
(5.11) &\ (14.00) \qquad\qquad\qquad (3.53) \\
&\ 0.0716 * \text{LOG(IIC/GDPC)} + .130 * \text{D88} - 8.960 * \text{D90} \\
&\ (2.35) \qquad\qquad\qquad\quad (5.33) \qquad\ (-3.07) \\
&+ 0.0524 * \text{D92} + .118 * \text{D94}) ; \\
&\ (2.21) \qquad\quad (3.60) \\
\text{R}^2 = 0.997 &\qquad\qquad \text{D.W.}=1.82 \qquad\qquad (1965\text{---}1996)
\end{aligned}
$$

where, PCR: the general consumer price index, M1CUR: currency in circulation, GDP: gross domestic product (in current prices), IIC: total investment (in constant prices), GDPC: gross domestic product (in constant prices), D88, D90, D92, D94: dummy variables.

In the above equation, the ratio of currency in circulation to GDP reflects State monetary policy, whereby currency in circulation depends on money issued each year, which will directly affect price determination; while the ratio of investment to GDP is the investment rate, which is also an important factor in price changes.

The GDP deflator is a basic deflator among all deflators, the equation is:

$$PGDP = EXP(0.00967 + .505 * LOG(PGDP(-1)) + .310 * LOG(PI) +$$
$$\quad\quad (0.68) \quad\quad (5.35) \quad\quad\quad\quad\quad\quad (4.18)$$
$$\quad\quad .165 * LOG(PCR) + 0.0233 * D78 - 0.0372 * D80(-1)$$
$$\quad\quad (1.82) \quad\quad\quad\quad (1.72) \quad\quad\quad\quad (-2.47)$$
$$\quad\quad + 0.0495 * D84) ;$$
$$\quad\quad\quad (3.48)$$

$$R^2 = 0.998 \quad\quad\quad D.W.=1.74 \quad\quad\quad\quad (1966—1996)$$

where, PGDP: the deflator of gross domestic product, PI: the price index of investment, PCR: the general consumer price index, D78, D80, D84: dummy variables. Most other deflators are determined by PGDP.

2.8. Foreign capital and foreign trade block

Foreign trade includes imports and exports. In the model, we divide import and export goods into five categories according to SITC (Standard International Trade Category): 0+1 (food, beverages, tobacco, etc); 2+4 (non-edible raw materials, animal and vegetable oils, etc.); 3 (mineral fuels, related materials, etc.); 7 (machinery and transportation equipment); and 5–9 (manufactured goods except 7). Each category has its own import equation and export equation. We consider competitiveness of domestic production in the import equation by using value-added of a corresponding sector as an independent variable. Taking the example of import goods of SITC 7:

$$M7C = EXP(-1.674 + .451 * LOG(M7C(-1)) + .553 * LOG(VHIC)$$
$$\quad\quad (-2.81) \quad (3.55) \quad\quad\quad\quad\quad\quad (4.09)$$
$$\quad\quad - .367 * D82 + .862 * D84 - .438 * D84(-2)) ;$$
$$\quad\quad (-2.36) \quad\quad (4.47) \quad\quad (-2.60)$$
$$\quad\quad R^2 = 0.967 \quad\quad\quad D.W.=1.88 \quad\quad\quad\quad (1966—1996)$$

where, M7C: import goods of SITC 7, *i.e.* machinery and transportation equipment (constant price), VHIC: value-added of heavy industry, D82, D84: dummy variables.

Exports are mainly dependent on the total amount of world trade (exogenous variable) and the exchange rate. For example, the equation of manufactured goods exports (except machinery and transportation equipment) is:

$$XNC = EXP(-1.709 + .692 * LOG(XNC(-1)) + .329 * LOG(WTNC) +$$
$$\quad\quad (-1.94) \quad (7.96) \quad\quad\quad\quad (2.55)$$
$$\quad\quad 0.0460 * EXRA + .233 * D78) ;$$
$$\quad\quad (1.99) \quad\quad\quad (2.48)$$
$$R^2 = 0.989 \quad\quad\quad D.W. = 1.53 \quad\quad\quad\quad\quad (1966\text{--}1996)$$

where, XNC: export goods of SITC 5, 6, 8 and 9 (constant price), WTNC: the total amount of world trade of SITC 5, 6, 8, 9, EXRA: exchange rate (RMB/US$), D78: dummy variables.

Moreover, we have two bridge equations in the model. They are error equations: the error between GDP (constant price) and value added of secondary industry. This is because the value-added sum (constant price) of primary, secondary and tertiary industry is not equal to GDP (constant price) after converting them from values in current prices. There exists an error which is remedied by a bridge equation. For the same reason we have a bridge equation for value added of secondary industry (constant price). There is an error between the value-added of secondary industry (constant price) and the sum of value-added (constant price) of light industry, heavy industry and construction.

3. Model Application and Problems

We have held 15 meetings and presented 15 forecast reports since the first fall meeting in October 1990 to October 1997. In the meantime, we have updated the model 7 times. We present forecasts for the current year and the next year in the fall meeting, and make a forecast for the current year in the spring meeting. The fall forecast is published in *the Economic Blue Book*. Through practical applications for 8 years, we feel, in general, that the results are good, and that this model has passed the forecast test. However, we also have had some problems, which should be dealt with carefully. These problems are as follows:

(1) This model still keeps the same specification from its beginning, and basically is a supply-oriented model, which reflects features of the central planning economic system. For example, all goods can be sold out after production in a shortage economy. It is thought that labor force and capi-

tal stock are fully utilized. But now we can say "good-bye" to the shortage economy. Some goods have been produced in surplus, which means that some excess production capacities exist. Some enterprises, even a whole industry, are producing in terms of assumed sales. The most obvious example is the textile industry. Market forces have begun to adjust production. Although we have considered the demand side in some equations of the model, we still need to improve the model further.

(2) China is now in transition from a planned economic system to a socialist market economic system. Some phenomena are not consistent with economic theory. In agriculture, as we all know, the labor force has begun to shift toward secondary and tertiary industry on a large scale. This is reflected in the data. Employment in primary industry has been declining, year by year, since 1992, and had fallen one-tenth by 1996, compared with 1992. The employment share of primary industry in total employment has decreased from 59.7% in 1991 to 50.5% in 1996 (see *China Statistical Yearbook 1997*, pp. 94), about two percentage points reduction per year. But output (value-added) of primary industry is still increasing year-by-year. It is predicted that such a situation will continue for many years, until the employment share of primary industry in total employment is reduced to a relatively low level (say, 15% or lower). Then, how should one reflect such a fact in a production function, with output of primary industry increasing while the input of labor force is declining?

(3) Investment in fixed assets is changing with deepening economic reform. We can already see profound changes in investment patterns. State planning of investment held a dominant position in the past, but is replaced now in various main sectors. The share of state appropriations in total investment has declined from 28.1% in 1981 to 2.7% in 1996. Domestic loans in the same period have increased from 12.7% to 19.5%. Foreign investment has increased from 3.8% to 11.7%. Fundraising and other forms of financing have increased from 55.4% to 66.1% (see *China Statistical Yearbook 1997*, pp. 151). Our investment equation should reflect such changes.

(4) In the field of banking, China has opened two stock exchanges, one in Shanghai and another in Shenzhen, in the early 90s. Some enterprises' share certificates have gone on the market to raise financial capital. The history of stock markets in modern China is very short; the scale of Chinese stock markets is not very big, but it is developing quickly. The de-

velopment of stock markets gives residents new opportunities for invest-ment, and affects their savings deposits. It is obviously inadequate that our model does not include stock market activity as yet. It is necessary to add some corresponding equations to the model, if we want to use the model to analyze banking and finance.

(5) There is an unemployment problem. We did not consider unemployment explicitly in our model, because there are no proper data at this time. That means, implicitly, that we assume that there is not unemployment. The assumption of full employment is not consistent with current reality. In fact, there exists serious hidden unemployment in some enterprises, especially in some state-owned enterprises. Furthermore, with the conti-nuous adjustment of economic structure, waiting for jobs will be a social phenomenon for a relatively long time. The labor force provides a kind of merchandise in a market economy, Government will no longer main-tain a policy of giving every person (even merely every urban resident) a job. Together with the formation of a *labor market*, there will be some people who are willingly off duty (temporarily unemployed and under-taking skill training to pursue a better job). In a word, it is normal that there is some unemployment in the operation of the macro economy. We hope to find data support so that there can be an unemployment equation in our macro economic model. Now we are waiting for the State Statis-tical Bureau to provide underlying data.

(6) In our model, we have used many dummy variables and had to do this for two reasons. On the one hand, we wanted to have this model simulate better. As we all know, China's economic development in the past gene-rated fluctuations, and using dummy variables will help to isolate "out-liers" better. Of course we incur the risk of distorting trends. On the other hand, if there is no dummy variable in some behavior equations, regression coefficients will be biased. For example, some coefficients should be less than 1 instead of greater than 1; some coefficients should be positive and not negative, and vice versa. The violent data changes made some coefficients inconsistent with economic analysis. The use of dummy variables can help to handle such problems, if used sensibly, with economic guidance.

8 A RETROSPECTIVE VIEW OF THE ASIAN FINANCIAL CRISIS: SPECIAL REFERENCE TO EXCHANGE RATE POLICY

Yoshihisa Inada, Lawrence Klein and Junichi Makino[1]

Konan University, the University of Pennsylvania, and Daiwa Institute of Research

1. Introduction

The financial crisis in Asia has been most evident in four ASEAN countries (Indonesia, Malaysia, the Philippines, and Thailand) and in the Republic of Korea. At this point it can be considered as an East Asian crisis, but the contagious dynamics of 1997 provide a warning that it can be confined only with great effort, and its ultimate path like those of tropical storms is difficult to predict in the earliest stages.

There has been a multitude of analyses, which we *hope* are post-mortems. The consensus view is that many factors contributed to the fast build-up of disturbances, but in this paper we are going to concentrate on what appears to be one of the significant factors; namely, the exchange rate policies of developing and newly industrializing economies of East Asia. The spot rate of the ASEAN-4 and ROK were closely pegged to the US dollar until mid-1997. Of these, the won per dollar rate tilted gently upward for two years before the crisis, but that was not enough to withstand crisis pressures.

There has been no corresponding crisis in Hong Kong or Taiwan, where reserve positions are so large that predatory speculation can be withstood without severe damage to the economy. At worst, there will be a moderation of growth and an uptick of inflation. Singapore should experience a similar outcome, but there was some depreciation of the exchange rate in 1997. As for China, there is presently a policy to hold the exchange rate in place, keep the currency market under control, and allow the growth rate of the economy to dip slightly while introducing fundamental reforms in the interest of overall efficiency.

---

[1] We are indebted to Lawrence J. Lau for critical commentary and assistance with data preparation.

By and large, possibly unanimously, the large scale crisis was not foreseen, and the consensus prognosis is that East Asian expansion will resume in 1998 or 1999 but at rates that average one or two percentage points below those of 1996 and *early* 1997. While the magnitude of the crisis was not foreseen, many international economic forecasts of 1995 and 1996 projected a moderate slowing of East Asian growth, something like a maturing of the economies. It should be remarked that the Philippines and Vietnam were, for many institutional reasons, latecomers in joining the expansion and, correspondingly, may incur lighter set-backs.

The East Asian financial crisis of 1997 was not the first of such financial breakdowns. Others have been:

1. Polish Debt Crisis of 1979,
2. The World Debt Crisis of the 1980s (mainly among developing countries)
3. The Savings and Loan Crisis of the mid 1980s (the USA),
4. The Mexican Crisis of 1994.

In each case there were some area-specific factors at work but also some lessons for the future. Unfortunately, the lessons were not always taken to heart; so crises have continued to occur. Yet none has got so far out of control that it brought down the whole international system; *i.e.* none has been of the order of magnitude of the Great Depression of the 1930s.

In the present East Asian crisis, it is possible to identify several important issues:

1. Ill-considered banking or general financial practices,
2. Vulnerable mixture of international capital flows giving rise to "flight capital,"
3. Speculative activity of a predatory nature,
4. Political instability,
5. High concentration of income and wealth,
6. Inadequate early-warning-systems,
7. Inadequate financial institutions in developing economies,
8. Inflexible exchange rate policies.

All these issues deserve careful consideration but in this paper, we are going to pay special attention to exchange rate policy.

2. Dollar Pegs

On different occasions in the past, developing countries have tied their currency values (exchange rates) to that of advanced countries with which they have close ties. In many cases since World War II, this tie has been to the US dollar and some of the East Asian economies maintained such ties in the past few years.

A rigid tie sacrifices flexibility in exchange rate or monetary policy, and when the key currency, in this case the US dollar, becomes very strong as in 1996-97, the competitive position of the tying country can become extremely awkward. This proved to be the case for Thailand and some other East Asian economies during the period leading up to the crisis. Although the crisis erupted in full public view in July 1997 in Thailand, it was building up in 1996 and early 1997 in South Korea and in Thailand, too.

It is instructive to consult Table 1, where we have displayed the recent annual values of current accounts for some important East Asian economies. It is evident that China was forging ahead in world markets and Japan was maintaining a large surplus position after a brief dip in 1996. The ASEAN-4 and Korea, on the other hand, were slipping and building up large deficit positions by 1996 or earlier. The small deficit values, on average, for 1989-94, were much more sustainable than the large negative jumps that occurred in 1996. The values for 1997 look much better, but they involve a half-year of severe import restraint in a crisis situation. The projections for 1998 assume a gradual emergence from rock bottom.

Table 1 Current Account of East Asian Economies (US$, billions)

Country	1989-94 (average)	1996	1997	1998*
China	3.8	12.45	39.56	31.49
Indonesia	-2.7	-6.27	-0.98	3.71
South Korea	-1.9	-23.07	-8.96	14.29
Malaysia	-2.4	-4.46	-4.18	-3.23
The Philippines	-2.0	-3.47	-2.81	-1.78
Thailand	-6.5	-14.69	-2.83	5.23
Japan	91.7	65.86	87.39	101.01

* Taken from Project LINK, United Nations, 1998

Trends in the current balance serve as one among many candidates for inclusion in an early-warning-system. If that were all that mattered, the USA would have cracked up, too, but it is only one component and needs to be studied in the context of the world and national environment. The current account trends are only suggestive and not definitive in our search for some explanations of the East Asian Crisis. It is, however, evident that the competitive position of some of these countries (ASEAN-4 and ROK) deterio-rated. A deeper econometric investigation involves the estimation of elasti-cities of substitution between the world exports of each of the ASEAN-4 and ROK, on the one hand, and China on the other. The specification that we have chosen, for ease of interpretation, is log linear and eventually involves two competing price relations–that between each of the ASEAN-4 and ROK prices in comparison with Chinese and Japanese prices.

We specify two export functions of Thailand's and China's to the world:

TH_EXMN
$$= A \cdot (\text{TH\_PEX/ WO\_PEX})_t^{\alpha} \cdot (\text{WO\_EXMN/WO\_PEX})_t^{\beta} \cdot u_t$$
CH_EXMN
$$= B \cdot (\text{CH\_PEX/ WO\_PEX})_t^{\alpha} \cdot (\text{WO\_EXMN/WO\_PEX})_t^{\gamma} \cdot v_t,$$

where

TH_EXMN = current dollar value of Thai merchandise exports,
CH_EXMN = current dollar value of Chinese merchandise exports,
WO_EXMN= current dollar value of world exports
TH_PEX = Thai export price index (dollar denominated),
CH_PEX = Chinese export price index (dollar denominated),
WO_PEX = World export price index (dollar denominated).

We then form an export share equation:

$$\ln \frac{TH\_EXMN}{CH\_EXMN} = const + \alpha \ln \frac{TH\_PEX}{CH\_PEX} + (\beta - \gamma) \ln \frac{WO\_EXMN}{WO\_PEX} + \varepsilon$$

where

$$\varepsilon_t = \ln u_t - \ln v_t$$

In order to simplify the equation to be estimated, we have assumed that is similar for both countries. Our problem is to regress the logarithm of relative export values on the logarithm of relative prices and the volume of world trade. It is not, however, a straightforward regression. In the first place it is well known in the econometric study of international trade that there is significant time delay in reaction to price changes. For that reason we must use previous values of ln(TH_PEX/CH_PEX) in the estimation process. There should also be lags in the use of world trade volume, which is an activity variable that stands in the place of world income or some similar macroeconomic magnitude.

But it is not only an issue that lagged values of price relatives must be used, but also that the time lag is exceptionally long in international trade adjustment. Full effects have been found to be as long as 5 years–20 quarters or 60 months of lags. In the present context we have used 24 month lags, employing the technique of estimating Almon polynomial lag distributions. Most of the effect seems to be present in the first two years in the present case.

On examining the monthly data assembled for this investigation, we noticed very strong seasonal movements, especially in the trade values associated with individual countries. Chinese data, for example, show very large exports in the month of December for every year – possibly toys or other nondurables. In order to deal with this statistical problem, we examined the monthly series for each country and then decided upon appropriate monthly indicators for seasonal phenomena. In our log linear equation, this suggests the use of particular "dummy variables". These contribute a great deal to the overall degrees of correlation.

In addition to the problem of estimating long lag distributions for relative price adjustments and treating the problems of seasonal variation, country-by-country, we also had to place every country's variables in comparable units of measurement. We measured country exports, world exports, and associated prices in US dollar units. That required the stating of monthly price data in dollars by converting own-price measurements at prevailing exchange rates to dollar price measurements. In that respect, China's price data, measured in yuan, were converted to US dollars at the SWAP rate for the period prior to 1994, at which time the Chinese official and SWAP rates were unified. This means effectively that the Chinese currency underwent much smaller depreciation between 1992-93 and 1994 than many people had thought, looking at official rates. The period 1992-93 is very important in our analysis because of the long lag distribution that we employ–having a 24 months "tail" prior to January 1994.

The data used in our calculations are not ideal. We would have liked to be using international trade indexes of import/export prices, but these are not available at the time-frequency of our investigation. Our monthly frequency is of great importance because there is no other good basis for building a respectable sample that includes pre-crisis and crisis period data together.

For the volume of world trade, our activity variable, we used a four-month lag, while for the relative price we used the longer adjustment period of 24 months. The equations with 24-months' lag (Almon quadratic, constrained to be zero at 25 months) have estimated coefficients that are usually, not always, significant and sum to a negative value for relative price effects. They are negative, and usually significant for the activity effect at all lags and very significant for seasonal effects. The Durbin-Watson statistics indicate no 12-months serial correlation but some tendency for 1-month serial correlation. The correlations are quite high, thanks to the strong seasonal effects, that are captured by (0,1) dummy variables.

A summary tabulation given in **Appendix B** Table 2 shows the total cumulative effect of all 24 lag-coefficients of relative price. The sum of activity effects is also given in Table 2.

We have taken the analysis one step further; we introduced a distributed lag in the logarithm of relative price between each of the crisis countries and Japan; *e.g.,* other variables left unchanged. In this case, we found that the one-month serial correlation was not very strong, with the 12-month also showing very little serial correlation, if the lag distributions of the two relative price variables – that involving China and that involving Japan – were each distributed along a quadratic curve at lag points 12-months to 24-months. These specifications had higher degrees of correlation and very significant seasonal effects. The long run elasticity estimates are in Table 3.

From the viewpoint of parameter estimation, these estimates for crisis or non-crisis countries show that exchange rate policy, working through elasticities of substitution effects did have something to do with the precipitation of the financial crisis in East Asia. The general hunch that we get from Table 1 has deeper foundations, as we can see from the estimated equations.

3. How Large is the Effect of Exchange Rate Policy?

Our estimates of derived trade equations may be looked upon as "semi-reduced forms" to show the effect of clinging to US dollar-pegs.

The data of the SWAP rate in the accompanying **Appendix C** shows that China did not devalue abruptly between late 1993 and early 1994; the average SWAP rate in 1992 was 6.56 yuan per US dollar. In 1994 the rate was fixed at approximately 8.7. We can say roughly that the number of yuan per dollar was raised by 30 *percent.* We have accordingly simulated the estimated with the exchange rate increased for each country by 30 *percent*.[2] If nothing else were to be changed, the countries involved would have had exports that reached approximately 10~20 *percent* more after 1994. The estimates are above 20 percent for Malaysia and the Philippines, but under 5 percent for the other three countries. The figures in Table 1 indicate that the current account trends in the Philippines were not showing any particular adverse direction before the crisis and may not have needed depreciation of their currency in order to stay competitive.

4. Conclusions

We cannot decide from the kind of econometric analysis that we have conducted so far about a recommended or optimal exchange rate policy for Asian developing countries, but we do find that there is evidence of a significant role for a policy. Certainly an inflexible tie to a rate of a single major partner is not to be recommended, especially when that currency is known to move from very high to quite low absolute valuations. It can very well be at an awkward position in the course of policy formation in developing countries that are aiming at making steady progress toward high levels of living.

A tie to a basket is to be preferred to a tie to any one country, as a means of holding down risk of misjudgment. Some, as yet to be discovered, international system still stands as an alternative, in fact a multiplicity of alternatives, is yet to be introduced. All the reasons cited earlier for the onset of the East Asian currency crisis remain to be dealt with effectively, but our findings do show that exchange rate policy is one of those reasons.

---

[2] This simulation was made for the first set of equations involving the elasticity of substitution only *vis-à-vis* China. Those for the second set that included Japanese prices, too, are shown in Table 4 in Appendix B.

Appendix A: Estimated Equations and the Coefficents

A complete set of the estimated equations used in these analyses is attached as Appendix A, with diagnostic statistics significance of coefficients, goodness of fit, serial correlation of residual error.

Thailand
Restricted Ordinary Least Squares
MONTHLY data for 60 periods from JAN 1994 to DEC 1998

LOG (TH_EXMN/CH_EXMN)
=   0.05351 * LOG((TH_CPI/TH_RATE)/(CH_CPI/CH_RATE))
           0.04380 * LOG((TH_CPI/TH_RATE)/(CH_CPI/CH_RATE))[-1]
           0.03472 * LOG((TH_CPI/TH_RATE)/(CH_CPI/CH_RATE))[-2]
           0.02627 * LOG((TH_CPI/TH_RATE)/(CH_CPI/CH_RATE))[-3]
           0.01845 * LOG((TH_CPI/TH_RATE)/(CH_CPI/CH_RATE))[-4]
           0.01127 * LOG((TH_CPI/TH_RATE)/(CH_CPI/CH_RATE))[-5]
           0.00471 * LOG((TH_CPI/TH_RATE)/(CH_CPI/CH_RATE))[-6]
          -0.00122 * LOG((TH_CPI/TH_RATE)/(CH_CPI/CH_RATE))[-7]
          -0.00651 * LOG((TH_CPI/TH_RATE)/(CH_CPI/CH_RATE))[-8]
          -0.01117 * LOG((TH_CPI/TH_RATE)/(CH_CPI/CH_RATE))[-9]
          -0.01521 * LOG((TH_CPI/TH_RATE)/(CH_CPI/CH_RATE))[-10]
          -0.01861 * LOG((TH_CPI/TH_RATE)/(CH_CPI/CH_RATE))[-11]
          -0.02138 * LOG((TH_CPI/TH_RATE)/(CH_CPI/CH_RATE))[-12]
          -0.02352 * LOG((TH_CPI/TH_RATE)/(CH_CPI/CH_RATE))[-13]
          -0.02503 * LOG((TH_CPI/TH_RATE)/(CH_CPI/CH_RATE))[-14]
          -0.02591 * LOG((TH_CPI/TH_RATE)/(CH_CPI/CH_RATE))[-15]
          -0.02616 * LOG((TH_CPI/TH_RATE)/(CH_CPI/CH_RATE))[-16]
          -0.02578 * LOG((TH_CPI/TH_RATE)/(CH_CPI/CH_RATE))[-17]
          -0.02476 * LOG((TH_CPI/TH_RATE)/(CH_CPI/CH_RATE))[-18]
          -0.02312 * LOG((TH_CPI/TH_RATE)/(CH_CPI/CH_RATE))[-19]
          -0.02084 * LOG((TH_CPI/TH_RATE)/(CH_CPI/CH_RATE))[-20]
          -0.01793 * LOG((TH_CPI/TH_RATE)/(CH_CPI/CH_RATE))[-21]
          -0.01440 * LOG((TH_CPI/TH_RATE)/(CH_CPI/CH_RATE))[-22]
          -0.01023 * LOG((TH_CPI/TH_RATE)/(CH_CPI/CH_RATE))[-23]
          -0.00543 * LOG((TH_CPI/TH_RATE)/(CH_CPI/CH_RATE))[-24]
              SUM -0.124

(cont'd)

-0.42854 * LOG(WO_EXMN/WO_PEX)
-0.32141 * LOG(WO_EXMN/WO_PEX)[-1]
-0.21427 * LOG(WO_EXMN/WO_PEX)[-2]
-0.10714 * LOG(WO_EXMN/WO_PEX)[-3]
    SUM -1.071
+0.22885 *D1&2M   +0.15333 *D3M   -0.2618 *D12M +7.69298
(7.20541)   (3.77552)   (6.31870)   (3.60049)

POLYNOMIAL LAGS:
LOG((TH_CPI/TH_RATE)/(CH_CPI/CH_TATE))
FROM 0 TO 24 DEGREE 2 FAR
LOG(WO_EXMN/WO_PEX)
FROM 0 TO 3 DEGREE 1 FAR
SUM SQ   0.3828 STD ERR   0.085 LHS MEAN -1.0459
RSQ   0.8467 R BAR SQ 0.8294 F 6, 53   48.7918
D.W.(1)   1.1689 D.W.(12) 1.8188

Malaysia
Restricted Ordinary Least Squares
MONTHLY data for 60 periods from JAN 1994 to DEC 1998
LOG (MAL_EXMN/CH_EXMN)
=   0.10602 * LOG((MAL_CPI/MAL_RATE)/(CH_CPI/CH_RATE))
    0.08191 * LOG((MAL_CPI/MAL_RATE)/(CH_CPI/CH_RATE))[-1]
    0.05945 * LOG((MAL_CPI/MAL_RATE)/(CH_CPI/CH_RATE))[-2]
    0.03865 * LOG((MAL_CPI/MAL_RATE)/(CH_CPI/CH_RATE))[-3]
    0.01951 * LOG((MAL_CPI/MAL_RATE)/(CH_CPI/CH_RATE))[-4]
    0.00203 * LOG((MAL_CPI/MAL_RATE)/(CH_CPI/CH_RATE))[-5]
  -0.01380 * LOG((MAL_CPI/MAL_RATE)/(CH_CPI/CH_RATE))[-6]
  -0.02798 * LOG((MAL_CPI/MAL_RATE)/(CH_CPI/CH_RATE))[-7]
  -0.04050 * LOG((MAL_CPI/MAL_RATE)/(CH_CPI/CH_RATE))[-8]
  -0.05136 * LOG((MAL_CPI/MAL_RATE)/(CH_CPI/CH_RATE))[-9]
  -0.06057 * LOG((MAL_CPI/MAL_RATE)/(CH_CPI/CH_RATE))[-10]
  -0.06812 * LOG((MAL_CPI/MAL_RATE)/(CH_CPI/CH_RATE))[-11]
  -0.07402 * LOG((MAL_CPI/MAL_RATE)/(CH_CPI/CH_RATE))[-12]
  -0.07826 * LOG((MAL_CPI/MAL_RATE)/(CH_CPI/CH_RATE))[-13]
  -0.08084 * LOG((MAL_CPI/MAL_RATE)/(CH_CPI/CH_RATE))[-14]
  -0.08177 * LOG((MAL_CPI/MAL_RATE)/(CH_CPI/CH_RATE))[-15]
  -0.08105 * LOG((MAL_CPI/MAL_RATE)/(CH_CPI/CH_RATE))[-16]
  -0.07866 * LOG((MAL_CPI/MAL_RATE)/(CH_CPI/CH_RATE))[-17]
  -0.07463 * LOG((MAL_CPI/MAL_RATE)/(CH_CPI/CH_RATE))[-18]
  -0.06893 * LOG((MAL_CPI/MAL_RATE)/(CH_CPI/CH_RATE))[-19]
  -0.06158 * LOG((MAL_CPI/MAL_RATE)/(CH_CPI/CH_RATE))[-20]
  -0.05258 * LOG((MAL_CPI/MAL_RATE)/(CH_CPI/CH_RATE))[-21]
  -0.04192 * LOG((MAL_CPI/MAL_RATE)/(CH_CPI/CH_RATE))[-22]
  -0.02960 * LOG((MAL_CPI/MAL_RATE)/(CH_CPI/CH_RATE))[-23]
  -0.01563 * LOG((MAL_CPI/MAL_RATE)/(CH_CPI/CH_RATE))[-24]
    SUM -0.774
  -0.71969 * LOG(WO_EXMN/WO_PEX)
  -0.53977 * LOG(WO_EXMN/WO_PEX)[-1]
  -0.35985 * LOG(WO_EXMN/WO_PEX)[-2]
  -0.17992 * LOG(WO_EXMN/WO_PEX)[-3]
    SUM -1.799
  +0.18143 *D1M   +0.08830 *D2M   -0.23801 *D12M   +14.5680
   (4.15804)   (1.95028)   (5.39908)   (5.39883)

POLYNOMIAL LAGS:
LOG((MAL_CPI/MAL_RATE)/(CH_CPI/CH_TATE))
FROM 0 TO 24 DEGREE 2 FAR
LOG(WO_EXMN/WO_PEX)
FROM 0 TO 3 DEGREE 1 FAR

SUM SQ	0.4430 STD ERR	0.0914 LHS MEAN	-0.7505	
RSQ	0.7962 R BAR SQ	0.7731 F 6, 53	34.5047	
D.W.(1)	1.2319 D.W.(12)	1.6061		

Indonesia
Restricted Ordinary Least Squares
MONTHLY data for 60 periods from JAN 1994 to DEC 1998

LOG (IND_EXMN/CH_EXMN)
=   0.03806 * LOG((IND_CPI/IND_RATE)/(CH_CPI/CH_RATE))
         0.03044 * LOG((IND_CPI/IND_RATE)/(CH_CPI/CH_RATE))[-1]
         0.02332 * LOG((IND_CPI/IND_RATE)/(CH_CPI/CH_RATE))[-2]
         0.01671 * LOG((IND_CPI/IND_RATE)/(CH_CPI/CH_RATE))[-3]
         0.01061 * LOG((IND_CPI/IND_RATE)/(CH_CPI/CH_RATE))[-4]
         0.00502 * LOG((IND_CPI/IND_RATE)/(CH_CPI/CH_RATE))[-5]
        -0.00007 * LOG((IND_CPI/IND_RATE)/(CH_CPI/CH_RATE))[-6]
        -0.00464 * LOG((IND_CPI/IND_RATE)/(CH_CPI/CH_RATE))[-7]
        -0.00871 * LOG((IND_CPI/IND_RATE)/(CH_CPI/CH_RATE))[-8]
        -0.01226 * LOG((IND_CPI/IND_RATE)/(CH_CPI/CH_RATE))[-9]
        -0.01531 * LOG((IND_CPI/IND_RATE)/(CH_CPI/CH_RATE))[-10]
        -0.01785 * LOG((IND_CPI/IND_RATE)/(CH_CPI/CH_RATE))[-11]
        -0.01988 * LOG((IND_CPI/IND_RATE)/(CH_CPI/CH_RATE))[-12]
        -0.02141 * LOG((IND_CPI/IND_RATE)/(CH_CPI/CH_RATE))[-13]
        -0.02242 * LOG((IND_CPI/IND_RATE)/(CH_CPI/CH_RATE))[-14]
        -0.02292 * LOG((IND_CPI/IND_RATE)/(CH_CPI/CH_RATE))[-15]
        -0.02292 * LOG((IND_CPI/IND_RATE)/(CH_CPI/CH_RATE))[-16]
        -0.02241 * LOG((IND_CPI/IND_RATE)/(CH_CPI/CH_RATE))[-17]
        -0.02139 * LOG((IND_CPI/IND_RATE)/(CH_CPI/CH_RATE))[-18]
        -0.01986 * LOG((IND_CPI/IND_RATE)/(CH_CPI/CH_RATE))[-19]
        -0.01782 * LOG((IND_CPI/IND_RATE)/(CH_CPI/CH_RATE))[-20]
        -0.01527 * LOG((IND_CPI/IND_RATE)/(CH_CPI/CH_RATE))[-21]
        -0.01222 * LOG((IND_CPI/IND_RATE)/(CH_CPI/CH_RATE))[-22]
        -0.00865 * LOG((IND_CPI/IND_RATE)/(CH_CPI/CH_RATE))[-23]
        -0.00458 * LOG((IND_CPI/IND_RATE)/(CH_CPI/CH_RATE))[-24]
             SUM -0.166
        -0.34394 * LOG(WO_EXMN/WO_PEX)
        -0.25795 * LOG(WO_EXMN/WO_PEX)[-1]
        -0.17197 * LOG(WO_EXMN/WO_PEX)[-2]
        -0.08598 * LOG(WO_EXMN/WO_PEX)[-3]
             SUM -0.860
        +0.21569 *D1&2M   -0.24351 *D12M   +4.96858
         (7.27215)   (6.10452)   (4.00751)

POLYNOMIAL LAGS:
LOG((IND_CPI/IND_RATE)/(CH_CPI/CH_TATE))
FROM 0 TO 24 DEGREE 2 FAR
LOG(WO_EXMN/WO_PEX)
FROM 0 TO 3 DEGREE 1 FAR

SUM SQ	0.3677 STD ERR	0.0825 LHS MEAN	-1.1729
RSQ	0.8111 R BAR SQ	0.7936 F 5, 54	46.3761
D.W.(1)	1.2031 D.W.(12)	2.0071	

The Philippines
Restricted Ordinary Least Squares
MONTHLY data for 60 periods from JAN 1994 to DEC 1998
LOG   (PHI_EXMN/CH_EXMN)
=   0.00044 * LOG((PHI_CPI/PHI_RATE)/(CH_CPI/CH_RATE))
        -0.00856 * LOG((PHI_CPI/PHI_RATE)/(CH_CPI/CH_RATE))[-1]
        -0.01682 * LOG((PHI_CPI/PHI_RATE)/(CH_CPI/CH_RATE))[-2]
        -0.02433 * LOG((PHI_CPI/PHI_RATE)/(CH_CPI/CH_RATE))[-3]
        -0.03109 * LOG((PHI_CPI/PHI_RATE)/(CH_CPI/CH_RATE))[-4]
        -0.03710 * LOG((PHI_CPI/PHI_RATE)/(CH_CPI/CH_RATE))[-5]
        -0.04236 * LOG((PHI_CPI/PHI_RATE)/(CH_CPI/CH_RATE))[-6]
        -0.04687 * LOG((PHI_CPI/PHI_RATE)/(CH_CPI/CH_RATE))[-7]
        -0.05063 * LOG((PHI_CPI/PHI_RATE)/(CH_CPI/CH_RATE))[-8]
        -0.05365 * LOG((PHI_CPI/PHI_RATE)/(CH_CPI/CH_RATE))[-9]
        -0.05591 * LOG((PHI_CPI/PHI_RATE)/(CH_CPI/CH_RATE))[-10]
        -0.05743 * LOG((PHI_CPI/PHI_RATE)/(CH_CPI/CH_RATE))[-11]
        -0.05819 * LOG((PHI_CPI/PHI_RATE)/(CH_CPI/CH_RATE))[-12]
        -0.05821 * LOG((PHI_CPI/PHI_RATE)/(CH_CPI/CH_RATE))[-13]
        -0.05748 * LOG((PHI_CPI/PHI_RATE)/(CH_CPI/CH_RATE))[-14]
        -0.05600 * LOG((PHI_CPI/PHI_RATE)/(CH_CPI/CH_RATE))[-15]
        -0.05377 * LOG((PHI_CPI/PHI_RATE)/(CH_CPI/CH_RATE))[-16]
        -0.05079 * LOG((PHI_CPI/PHI_RATE)/(CH_CPI/CH_RATE))[-17]
        -0.04707 * LOG((PHI_CPI/PHI_RATE)/(CH_CPI/CH_RATE))[-18]
        -0.04259 * LOG((PHI_CPI/PHI_RATE)/(CH_CPI/CH_RATE))[-19]
        -0.03736 * LOG((PHI_CPI/PHI_RATE)/(CH_CPI/CH_RATE))[-20]
        -0.03139 * LOG((PHI_CPI/PHI_RATE)/(CH_CPI/CH_RATE))[-21]
        -0.02467 * LOG((PHI_CPI/PHI_RATE)/(CH_CPI/CH_RATE))[-22]
        -0.01719 * LOG((PHI_CPI/PHI_RATE)/(CH_CPI/CH_RATE))[-23]
        -0.00897 * LOG((PHI_CPI/PHI_RATE)/(CH_CPI/CH_RATE))[-24]
        SUM -0.968
        -0.09805 * LOG(WO_EXMN/WO_PEX)
        -0.07354 * LOG(WO_EXMN/WO_PEX)[-1]
        -0.04903 * LOG(WO_EXMN/WO_PEX)[-2]
        -0.02451 * LOG(WO_EXMN/WO_PEX)[-3]
        SUM -0.245
        +0.20166 *D1M   +0.30548 *D2M   -0.33097 *D12M   -2.07165
        (2.08037)   (3.06524)   (3.39226)   (0.50760)

POLYNOMIAL LAGS:
LOG((PHI_CPI/PHI_RATE)/(CH_CPI/CH_TATE))
FROM 0 TO 24 DEGREE 2 FAR
LOG(WO_EXMN/WO_PEX)
FROM 0 TO 3 DEGREE 1 FAR
SUM SQ   2.1808 STD ERR   0.2028 LHS MEAN   -2.0393
RSQ   0.3920 R BAR SQ   0.3232 F 6, 53   5.6948
D.W.(1)   1.5502 D.W.(12)   1.1042

Korea
Restricted Ordinary Least Squares
MONTHLY data for 60 periods from JAN 1994 to DEC 1998
LOG   (KOR_EXMN/CH_EXMN)
=   0.08921 * LOG((KOR_CPI/KOR_RATE)/(CH_CPI/CH_RATE))
         0.07390 * LOG((KOR_CPI/KOR_RATE)/(CH_CPI/CH_RATE))[-1]
         0.05958 * LOG((KOR_CPI/KOR_RATE)/(CH_CPI/CH_RATE))[-2]
         0.04623 * LOG((KOR_CPI/KOR_RATE)/(CH_CPI/CH_RATE))[-3]
         0.03385 * LOG((KOR_CPI/KOR_RATE)/(CH_CPI/CH_RATE))[-4]
         0.02246 * LOG((KOR_CPI/KOR_RATE)/(CH_CPI/CH_RATE))[-5]
         0.01205 * LOG((KOR_CPI/KOR_RATE)/(CH_CPI/CH_RATE))[-6]
         0.00261 * LOG((KOR_CPI/KOR_RATE)/(CH_CPI/CH_RATE))[-7]
        -0.00585 * LOG((KOR_CPI/KOR_RATE)/(CH_CPI/CH_RATE))[-8]
        -0.01333 * LOG((KOR_CPI/KOR_RATE)/(CH_CPI/CH_RATE))[-9]
        -0.01983 * LOG((KOR_CPI/KOR_RATE)/(CH_CPI/CH_RATE))[-10]
        -0.02536 * LOG((KOR_CPI/KOR_RATE)/(CH_CPI/CH_RATE))[-11]
        -0.02990 * LOG((KOR_CPI/KOR_RATE)/(CH_CPI/CH_RATE))[-12]
        -0.03347 * LOG((KOR_CPI/KOR_RATE)/(CH_CPI/CH_RATE))[-13]
        -0.03606 * LOG((KOR_CPI/KOR_RATE)/(CH_CPI/CH_RATE))[-14]
        -0.03768 * LOG((KOR_CPI/KOR_RATE)/(CH_CPI/CH_RATE))[-15]
        -0.03831 * LOG((KOR_CPI/KOR_RATE)/(CH_CPI/CH_RATE))[-16]
        -0.03797 * LOG((KOR_CPI/KOR_RATE)/(CH_CPI/CH_RATE))[-17]
        -0.03664 * LOG((KOR_CPI/KOR_RATE)/(CH_CPI/CH_RATE))[-18]
        -0.03434 * LOG((KOR_CPI/KOR_RATE)/(CH_CPI/CH_RATE))[-19]
        -0.03106 * LOG((KOR_CPI/KOR_RATE)/(CH_CPI/CH_RATE))[-20]
        -0.02681 * LOG((KOR_CPI/KOR_RATE)/(CH_CPI/CH_RATE))[-21]
        -0.02157 * LOG((KOR_CPI/KOR_RATE)/(CH_CPI/CH_RATE))[-22]
        -0.01536 * LOG((KOR_CPI/KOR_RATE)/(CH_CPI/CH_RATE))[-23]
        -0.00817 * LOG((KOR_CPI/KOR_RATE)/(CH_CPI/CH_RATE))[-24]
          SUM -0.112
        -0.18738 * LOG(WO_EXMN/WO_PEX)
        -0.14054 * LOG(WO_EXMN/WO_PEX)[-1]
        -0.09369 * LOG(WO_EXMN/WO_PEX)[-2]
        -0.04685 * LOG(WO_EXMN/WO_PEX)[-3]
          SUM -0.468
        +0.15641 *D1&2M   -0.20002 *D12M   +3.14123
        (4.03120)   (3.86832)   (1.52673)

POLYNOMIAL LAGS:
LOG((KOR_CPI/KOR_RATE)/(CH_CPI/CH_TATE))
FROM 0 TO 24 DEGREE 2 FAR
LOG(WO_EXMN/WO_PEX)
FROM 0 TO 3 DEGREE 1 FAR
SUM SQ   0.6093 STD ERR   0.1062 LHS MEAN   -0.2207
RSQ   0.5821 R BAR SQ   0.5434 F 5, 54   15.0412
D.W.(1)   0.9051 D.W.(12)   1.5725

Thailand
Restricted Ordinary Least Squares
MONTHLY data for 60 periods from JAN 1994 to DEC 1998
LOG (TH_EXMN/CH_EXMN)
=　　　-0.11289 * LOG((TH_CPI/TH_RATE)/(CH_CPI/CH_RATE))[-12]
　　　-0.08668 * LOG((TH_CPI/TH_RATE)/(CH_CPI/CH_RATE))[-13]
　　　-0.06339 * LOG((TH_CPI/TH_RATE)/(CH_CPI/CH_RATE))[-14]
　　　-0.04302 * LOG((TH_CPI/TH_RATE)/(CH_CPI/CH_RATE))[-15]
　　　-0.02557 * LOG((TH_CPI/TH_RATE)/(CH_CPI/CH_RATE))[-16]
　　　-0.01104 * LOG((TH_CPI/TH_RATE)/(CH_CPI/CH_RATE))[-17]
　　　 0.00056 * LOG((TH_CPI/TH_RATE)/(CH_CPI/CH_RATE))[-18]
　　　 0.00925 * LOG((TH_CPI/TH_RATE)/(CH_CPI/CH_RATE))[-19]
　　　 0.01501 * LOG((TH_CPI/TH_RATE)/(CH_CPI/CH_RATE))[-20]
　　　 0.01785 * LOG((TH_CPI/TH_RATE)/(CH_CPI/CH_RATE))[-21]
　　　 0.01777 * LOG((TH_CPI/TH_RATE)/(CH_CPI/CH_RATE))[-22]
　　　 0.01477 * LOG((TH_CPI/TH_RATE)/(CH_CPI/CH_RATE))[-23]
　　　 0.00884 * LOG((TH_CPI/TH_RATE)/(CH_CPI/CH_RATE))[-24]
　　　-0.03257 * LOG((TH_CPI/TH_RATE)/(JP_CPI/JP_RATE))[-12]
　　　-0.03266 * LOG((TH_CPI/TH_RATE)/(JP_CPI/JP_RATE))[-13]
　　　-0.03232 * LOG((TH_CPI/TH_RATE)/(JP_CPI/JP_RATE))[-14]
　　　-0.03154 * LOG((TH_CPI/TH_RATE)/(JP_CPI/JP_RATE))[-15]
　　　-0.03033 * LOG((TH_CPI/TH_RATE)/(JP_CPI/JP_RATE))[-16]
　　　-0.02869 * LOG((TH_CPI/TH_RATE)/(JP_CPI/JP_RATE))[-17]
　　　-0.02662 * LOG((TH_CPI/TH_RATE)/(JP_CPI/JP_RATE))[-18]
　　　-0.02411 * LOG((TH_CPI/TH_RATE)/(JP_CPI/JP_RATE))[-19]
　　　-0.02118 * LOG((TH_CPI/TH_RATE)/(JP_CPI/JP_RATE))[-20]
　　　-0.01781 * LOG((TH_CPI/TH_RATE)/(JP_CPI/JP_RATE))[-21]
　　　-0.01400 * LOG((TH_CPI/TH_RATE)/(JP_CPI/JP_RATE))[-22]
　　　-0.00977 * LOG((TH_CPI/TH_RATE)/(JP_CPI/JP_RATE))[-23]
　　　-0.00510 * LOG((TH_CPI/TH_RATE)/(JP_CPI/JP_RATE))[-24]
　　　SUM(CHINA) -0.259　　　SUM(JAPAN)　　　-0.307
　　　-0.52804 * LOG(WO_EXMN/WO_PEX)
　　　-0.39603 * LOG(WO_EXMN/WO_PEX)[-1]
　　　-0.26402 * LOG(WO_EXMN/WO_PEX)[-2]
　　　-0.13201 * LOG(WO_EXMN/WO_PEX)[-3]
　　　　SUM -1.320
　　　+0.22436 *D1&2M　 +0.15248 *D3M　　　-0.26687 *D12M　　+9.90188
　　　 (6.24776)　　　　　 (3.68223)　　　　　(6.69460)　　　　　(4.17721)

POLYNOMIAL LAGS:
LOG((TH_CPI/TH_RATE)/(CH_CPI/CH_TATE))
FROM 12 TO 24 DEGREE 2 FAR
LOG((TH_CPI/TH_RATE)/(JP_CPI/JP_TATE))
FROM 12 TO 24 DEGREE 2 FAR
LOG(WO_EXMN/WO_PEX)
FROM 0 TO 3 DEGREE 1 FAR
SUM SQ　　　0.3319 STD ERR　　　0.0807 LHS MEAN　 -1.0459
RSQ　　　　　0.8671 R BAR SQ　　　0.8463 F 8, 51　　　41.6014
D.W.(1)　　　1.3960 D.W.(12)　　　1.8153

Malaysia
Restricted Ordinary Least Squares
MONTHLY data for 60 periods from JAN 1994 to DEC 1998
LOG   (MAL_EXMN/CH_EXMN)
=   -0.21913 * LOG((MAL_CPI/MAL_RATE)/(CH_CPI/CH_RATE))[-12]
          -0.18348 * LOG((MAL_CPI/MAL_RATE)/(CH_CPI/CH_RATE))[-13]
          -0.15097 * LOG((MAL_CPI/MAL_RATE)/(CH_CPI/CH_RATE))[-14]
          -0.12159 * LOG((MAL_CPI/MAL_RATE)/(CH_CPI/CH_RATE))[-15]
          -0.09534 * LOG((MAL_CPI/MAL_RATE)/(CH_CPI/CH_RATE))[-16]
          -0.07222 * LOG((MAL_CPI/MAL_RATE)/(CH_CPI/CH_RATE))[-17]
          -0.05223 * LOG((MAL_CPI/MAL_RATE)/(CH_CPI/CH_RATE))[-18]
          -0.03538 * LOG((MAL_CPI/MAL_RATE)/(CH_CPI/CH_RATE))[-19]
          -0.02165 * LOG((MAL_CPI/MAL_RATE)/(CH_CPI/CH_RATE))[-20]
          -0.01106 * LOG((MAL_CPI/MAL_RATE)/(CH_CPI/CH_RATE))[-21]
          -0.0036 * LOG((MAL_CPI/MAL_RATE)/(CH_CPI/CH_RATE))[-22]
           0.00073 * LOG((MAL_CPI/MAL_RATE)/(CH_CPI/CH_RATE))[-23]
           0.00193 * LOG((MAL_CPI/MAL_RATE)/(CH_CPI/CH_RATE))[-24]
          -0.05104 * LOG((MAL_CPI/MAL_RATE)/(JP_CPI/JP_RATE))[-12]
          -0.0516 * LOG((MAL_CPI/MAL_RATE)/(JP_CPI/JP_RATE))[-13]
          -0.05141 * LOG((MAL_CPI/MAL_RATE)/(JP_CPI/JP_RATE))[-14]
          -0.05047 * LOG((MAL_CPI/MAL_RATE)/(JP_CPI/JP_RATE))[-15]
          -0.04879 * LOG((MAL_CPI/MAL_RATE)/(JP_CPI/JP_RATE))[-16]
          -0.04636 * LOG((MAL_CPI/MAL_RATE)/(JP_CPI/JP_RATE))[-17]
          -0.04318 * LOG((MAL_CPI/MAL_RATE)/(JP_CPI/JP_RATE))[-18]
          -0.03925 * LOG((MAL_CPI/MAL_RATE)/(JP_CPI/JP_RATE))[-19]
          -0.03458 * LOG((MAL_CPI/MAL_RATE)/(JP_CPI/JP_RATE))[-20]
          -0.02916 * LOG((MAL_CPI/MAL_RATE)/(JP_CPI/JP_RATE))[-21]
          -0.02299 * LOG((MAL_CPI/MAL_RATE)/(JP_CPI/JP_RATE))[-22]
          -0.01607 * LOG((MAL_CPI/MAL_RATE)/(JP_CPI/JP_RATE))[-23]
          -0.00841 * LOG((MAL_CPI/MAL_RATE)/(JP_CPI/JP_RATE))[-24]
          SUM(CHINA) -0.964   SUM(JAPAN)   -0.493
          -0.79726 * LOG(WO_EXMN/WO_PEX)
          -0.59795 * LOG(WO_EXMN/WO_PEX)[-1]
          -0.39863 * LOG(WO_EXMN/WO_PEX)[-2]
          -0.19932 * LOG(WO_EXMN/WO_PEX)[-3]
             SUM -1.993
          +0.18563 *D1M   +0.07728 *D2M   -0.24056 *D12M   +18.0269
          (4.61579)   (1.73195)   (6.10782)   (7.62105)
POLYNOMIAL LAGS:
LOG((MAL_CPI/MAL_RATE)/(CH_CPI/CH_TATE))
FROM 12 TO 24 DEGREE 2 FAR
LOG((MAL_CPI/MAL_RATE)/(JP_CPI/JP_TATE))
FROM 12 TO 24 DEGREE 2 FAR
LOG(WO_EXMN/WO_PEX)
FROM 0 TO 3 DEGREE 1 FAR
SUM SQ   0.3248 STD ERR   0.0798 LHS MEAN   -0.7505
RSQ   0.8505 R BAR SQ   0.8271 F 8, 51   36.2794
D.W.(1)   1.6861 D.W.(12)   1.5897

Indonesia

Restricted Ordinary Least Squares

MONTHLY data for 60 periods from JAN 1994 to DEC 1998

LOG (IND_EXMN/CH_EXMN)

= 0.0905 * LOG((IND_CPI/IND_RATE)/(CH_CPI/CH_RATE))[-12]
0.04542 * LOG((IND_CPI/IND_RATE)/(CH_CPI/CH_RATE))[-13]
0.00668 * LOG((IND_CPI/IND_RATE)/(CH_CPI/CH_RATE))[-14]
-0.02569 * LOG((IND_CPI/IND_RATE)/(CH_CPI/CH_RATE))[-15]
-0.05172 * LOG((IND_CPI/IND_RATE)/(CH_CPI/CH_RATE))[-16]
-0.07139 * LOG((IND_CPI/IND_RATE)/(CH_CPI/CH_RATE))[-17]
-0.08470 * LOG((IND_CPI/IND_RATE)/(CH_CPI/CH_RATE))[-18]
-0.09167 * LOG((IND_CPI/IND_RATE)/(CH_CPI/CH_RATE))[-19]
-0.09227 * LOG((IND_CPI/IND_RATE)/(CH_CPI/CH_RATE))[-20]
-0.08653 * LOG((IND_CPI/IND_RATE)/(CH_CPI/CH_RATE))[-21]
-0.07443 * LOG((IND_CPI/IND_RATE)/(CH_CPI/CH_RATE))[-22]
-0.05597 * LOG((IND_CPI/IND_RATE)/(CH_CPI/CH_RATE))[-23]
-0.03116 * LOG((IND_CPI/IND_RATE)/(CH_CPI/CH_RATE))[-24]
-0.05799 * LOG((IND_CPI/IND_RATE)/(JP_CPI/JP_RATE))[-12]
-0.05670 * LOG((IND_CPI/IND_RATE)/(JP_CPI/JP_RATE))[-13]
-0.05488 * LOG((IND_CPI/IND_RATE)/(JP_CPI/JP_RATE))[-14]
-0.05253 * LOG((IND_CPI/IND_RATE)/(JP_CPI/JP_RATE))[-15]
-0.04965 * LOG((IND_CPI/IND_RATE)/(JP_CPI/JP_RATE))[-16]
-0.04625 * LOG((IND_CPI/IND_RATE)/(JP_CPI/JP_RATE))[-17]
-0.04232 * LOG((IND_CPI/IND_RATE)/(JP_CPI/JP_RATE))[-18]
-0.03785 * LOG((IND_CPI/IND_RATE)/(JP_CPI/JP_RATE))[-19]
-0.03287 * LOG((IND_CPI/IND_RATE)/(JP_CPI/JP_RATE))[-20]
-0.02735 * LOG((IND_CPI/IND_RATE)/(JP_CPI/JP_RATE))[-21]
-0.02130 * LOG((IND_CPI/IND_RATE)/(JP_CPI/JP_RATE))[-22]
-0.01473 * LOG((IND_CPI/IND_RATE)/(JP_CPI/JP_RATE))[-23]
-0.00763 * LOG((IND_CPI/IND_RATE)/(JP_CPI/JP_RATE))[-24]
SUM(CHINA) -0.523 SUM(JAPAN) -0.502
-0.45356 * LOG(WO_EXMN/WO_PEX)
-0.34017 * LOG(WO_EXMN/WO_PEX)[-1]
-0.22678 * LOG(WO_EXMN/WO_PEX)[-2]
-0.11339 * LOG(WO_EXMN/WO_PEX)[-3]
SUM -1.134
+0.20136 *D1&2M -0.21899 *D12M +3.36942
(6.52281) (5.99016) (1.48474)

POLYNOMIAL LAGS:
LOG((IND_IND/TH_RATE)/(CH_CPI/CH_TATE))
FROM 12 TO 24 DEGREE 2 FAR
LOG((IND_IND/TH_RATE)/(JP_CPI/JP_TATE))
FROM 12 TO 24 DEGREE 2 FAR
LOG(WO_EXMN/WO_PEX)
FROM 0 TO 3 DEGREE 1 FAR

SUM SQ	0.2823 STD ERR	0.0737 LHS MEAN	-1.1729
RSQ	0.8550 R BAR SQ	0.8355 F 7, 52	43.8038
D.W.(1)	1.4872 D.W.(12)	1.9113	

The Philippines
Restricted Ordinary Least Squares
MONTHLY data for 60 periods from JAN 1994 to DEC 1998
LOG (PHI_EXMN/CH_EXMN)
=   -0.24087 * LOG((PHI_CPI/PHI_RATE)/(CH_CPI/CH_RATE))[-12]
       -0.20562 * LOG((PHI_CPI/PHI_RATE)/(CH_CPI/CH_RATE))[-13]
       -0.17316 * LOG((PHI_CPI/PHI_RATE)/(CH_CPI/CH_RATE))[-14]
       -0.14349 * LOG((PHI_CPI/PHI_RATE)/(CH_CPI/CH_RATE))[-15]
       -0.11660 * LOG((PHI_CPI/PHI_RATE)/(CH_CPI/CH_RATE))[-16]
       -0.09250 * LOG((PHI_CPI/PHI_RATE)/(CH_CPI/CH_RATE))[-17]
       -0.07119 * LOG((PHI_CPI/PHI_RATE)/(CH_CPI/CH_RATE))[-18]
       -0.05266 * LOG((PHI_CPI/PHI_RATE)/(CH_CPI/CH_RATE))[-19]
       -0.03692 * LOG((PHI_CPI/PHI_RATE)/(CH_CPI/CH_RATE))[-20]
       -0.02396 * LOG((PHI_CPI/PHI_RATE)/(CH_CPI/CH_RATE))[-21]
       -0.01379 * LOG((PHI_CPI/PHI_RATE)/(CH_CPI/CH_RATE))[-22]
       -0.00641 * LOG((PHI_CPI/PHI_RATE)/(CH_CPI/CH_RATE))[-23]
       -0.00181 * LOG((PHI_CPI/PHI_RATE)/(CH_CPI/CH_RATE))[-24]
       0.35056 * LOG((PHI_CPI/PHI_RATE)/(JP_CPI/JP_RATE))[-12]
       0.26543 * LOG((PHI_CPI/PHI_RATE)/(JP_CPI/JP_RATE))[-13]
       0.18999 * LOG((PHI_CPI/PHI_RATE)/(JP_CPI/JP_RATE))[-14]
       0.12424 * LOG((PHI_CPI/PHI_RATE)/(JP_CPI/JP_RATE))[-15]
       0.06819 * LOG((PHI_CPI/PHI_RATE)/(JP_CPI/JP_RATE))[-16]
       0.02183 * LOG((PHI_CPI/PHI_RATE)/(JP_CPI/JP_RATE))[-17]
       -0.01483 * LOG((PHI_CPI/PHI_RATE)/(JP_CPI/JP_RATE))[-18]
       -0.04179 * LOG((PHI_CPI/PHI_RATE)/(JP_CPI/JP_RATE))[-19]
       -0.05906 * LOG((PHI_CPI/PHI_RATE)/(JP_CPI/JP_RATE))[-20]
       -0.06664 * LOG((PHI_CPI/PHI_RATE)/(JP_CPI/JP_RATE))[-21]
       -0.06452 * LOG((PHI_CPI/PHI_RATE)/(JP_CPI/JP_RATE))[-22]
       -0.05271 * LOG((PHI_CPI/PHI_RATE)/(JP_CPI/JP_RATE))[-23]
       -0.03120 * LOG((PHI_CPI/PHI_RATE)/(JP_CPI/JP_RATE))[-24]
       SUM(CHINA) -1.179   SUM(JAPAN)   0.689
       -0.50261 * LOG(WO_EXMN/WO_PEX)
       -0.37696 * LOG(WO_EXMN/WO_PEX)[-1]
       -0.25130 * LOG(WO_EXMN/WO_PEX)[-2]
       -0.12565 * LOG(WO_EXMN/WO_PEX)[-3]
          SUM -1.257
      +0.11431 *D1M   +0.18174 *D2M   -0.27665 *D12M   +5.05674
      (1.19511)   (1.69496)   (2.91330)   (0.79833)

POLYNOMIAL LAGS:
LOG((PHI_CPI/TH_RATE)/(CH_CPI/CH_TATE))
FROM 12 TO 24 DEGREE 2 FAR
LOG((PHI_CPI/TH_RATE)/(JP_CPI/JP_TATE))
FROM 12 TO 24 DEGREE 2 FAR
LOG(WO_EXMN/WO_PEX)
FROM 0 TO 3 DEGREE 1 FAR
SUM SQ   1.8452 STD ERR   0.1902 LHS MEAN   -2.0393
RSQ   0.4856 R BAR SQ   0.4049 F 8, 51   6.01698
D.W.(1)   1.6091 D.W.(12)   1.2002

Korea
Restricted Ordinary Least Squares
MONTHLY data for 60 periods from JAN 1994 to DEC 1998
LOG   (KOR_EXMN/CH_EXMN)
=   -0.37147 * LOG((KOR_CPI/KOR_RATE)/(CH_CPI/CH_RATE))[-12]
           -0.27978 * LOG((KOR_CPI/KOR_RATE)/(CH_CPI/CH_RATE))[-13]
           -0.19860 * LOG((KOR_CPI/KOR_RATE)/(CH_CPI/CH_RATE))[-14]
           -0.12794 * LOG((KOR_CPI/KOR_RATE)/(CH_CPI/CH_RATE))[-15]
           -0.06780 * LOG((KOR_CPI/KOR_RATE)/(CH_CPI/CH_RATE))[-16]
           -0.01819 * LOG((KOR_CPI/KOR_RATE)/(CH_CPI/CH_RATE))[-17]
            0.02091 * LOG((KOR_CPI/KOR_RATE)/(CH_CPI/CH_RATE))[-18]
            0.04949 * LOG((KOR_CPI/KOR_RATE)/(CH_CPI/CH_RATE))[-19]
            0.06754 * LOG((KOR_CPI/KOR_RATE)/(CH_CPI/CH_RATE))[-20]
            0.07507 * LOG((KOR_CPI/KOR_RATE)/(CH_CPI/CH_RATE))[-21]
            0.07209 * LOG((KOR_CPI/KOR_RATE)/(CH_CPI/CH_RATE))[-22]
            0.05858 * LOG((KOR_CPI/KOR_RATE)/(CH_CPI/CH_RATE))[-23]
            0.03455 * LOG((KOR_CPI/KOR_RATE)/(CH_CPI/CH_RATE))[-24]
            0.06375 * LOG((KOR_CPI/KOR_RATE)/(JP_CPI/JP_RATE))[-12]
            0.03834 * LOG((KOR_CPI/KOR_RATE)/(JP_CPI/JP_RATE))[-13]
            0.01635 * LOG((KOR_CPI/KOR_RATE)/(JP_CPI/JP_RATE))[-14]
           -0.00222 * LOG((KOR_CPI/KOR_RATE)/(JP_CPI/JP_RATE))[-15]
           -0.01738 * LOG((KOR_CPI/KOR_RATE)/(JP_CPI/JP_RATE))[-16]
           -0.02912 * LOG((KOR_CPI/KOR_RATE)/(JP_CPI/JP_RATE))[-17]
           -0.03744 * LOG((KOR_CPI/KOR_RATE)/(JP_CPI/JP_RATE))[-18]
           -0.04235 * LOG((KOR_CPI/KOR_RATE)/(JP_CPI/JP_RATE))[-19]
           -0.04383 * LOG((KOR_CPI/KOR_RATE)/(JP_CPI/JP_RATE))[-20]
           -0.04190 * LOG((KOR_CPI/KOR_RATE)/(JP_CPI/JP_RATE))[-21]
           -0.03655 * LOG((KOR_CPI/KOR_RATE)/(JP_CPI/JP_RATE))[-22]
           -0.02779 * LOG((KOR_CPI/KOR_RATE)/(JP_CPI/JP_RATE))[-23]
           -0.01560 * LOG((KOR_CPI/KOR_RATE)/(JP_CPI/JP_RATE))[-24]
            SUM(CHINA) -0.686   SUM(JAPAN)   -0.176
           -0.70412 * LOG(WO_EXMN/WO_PEX)
           -0.52809 * LOG(WO_EXMN/WO_PEX)[-1]
           -0.35206 * LOG(WO_EXMN/WO_PEX)[-2]
           -0.17603 * LOG(WO_EXMN/WO_PEX)[-3]
              SUM -1.760
           +0.10408 *D1&2M   -0.17150 *D12M   +10.3853
           (2.50383)   (3.51011)   (3.48492)

POLYNOMIAL LAGS:
LOG((KOR_CPI/TH_RATE)/(CH_CPI/CH_TATE))
FROM 12 TO 24 DEGREE 2 FAR
LOG((KOR_CPI/TH_RATE)/(JP_CPI/JP_TATE))
FROM 12 TO 24 DEGREE 2 FAR
LOG(WO_EXMN/WO_PEX)
FROM 0 TO 3 DEGREE 1 FAR
SUM SQ   0.5106 STD ERR   0.0991 LHS MEAN   -0.2207
RSQ   0.6498 R BAR SQ   0.6026 F 7, 52   13.7825
D.W.(1)   1.1456 D.W.(12)   1.4371

Appendix B: Summary of Simulation Results

Appendix B gives some summary tables of our findings. Table 2 and 3 show the estimates of the long run elasticities of substitution with respect to relative price changes and world trade changes (proxy for income effects) for the case only *vis-à-vis* China and the case *vis-à-vis* China and Japan. Table 3 gives some findings of policy simulations. These tables show marginal *ceteris paribus* effects for changes made, one at a time.

A more interesting simulation can, however, be generated along the following lines:

1. Suppose that the five East Asian economies, being studied here in relation to China, did not peg their currencies to the US dollar. That was, in any case, a highly inappropriate policy. Many economies just emerging into the global competitive markets were often warned not to be so rigid in exchange rate policy.
2. Suppose instead that the five nations had devalued (or depreciated) their currencies by the same amount as China implicitly did by unifying its rates. On average, for all five as a group, they would have improved their exports by as much as 10% if we use the set of equations without introduction of substitution *vis-à-vis* Japan. If the Japanese prices are introduced, the elasticity of substitution becomes larger on average. In this case, the same rule of behavior indicates that exports value would have been 20% larger, assuming no change in the yen-dollar exchange rate.[3]

Table 2 Long run elasticity of relative prices and real income

Sum of coefficients	Relative price against China	Real income
Thailand	-0.124	-1.071
Malaysia	-0.774	-1.799
Indonesia	-0.166	-0.860
The Philippines	-0.968	-0.245
Republic of Korea	-0.112	-0.468

---

[3] The results presented here are a revision and updating of those cited in the UN's *World Economic and Social Survey,* United Nations, NY 1998. See Box III 1, "Trade and the Devaluation Question in China", *op cit.*, pp. 61-64.

Table 3 Long run elasticity of relative prices and real income

Sum of coefficients	Relative price against China	Relative price against Japan	Real income
Thailand	-0.259	-0.307	-1.320
Malaysia	-0.964	-0.493	-1.993
Indonesia	-0.523	-0.502	-1.134
The Philippines	-1.179	0.689	-1.257
Republic of Korea	-0.686	-0.176	-1.760

Table 4 Summary of Simulation Result   ($ Million)

Thailand	Baseline	Difference	% Difference
1994	45261.2	-1915.5	-4.2
1995	56439.7	180.3	0.3
1996	55725.0	1785.8	3.2
1997	57533.2	1962.7	3.4
1998	54456.3	1844.7	3.4

Malaysia	Baseline	Difference	%,Difference
1994	58735.1	-3340.1	-5.7
1995	74047.3	8960.4	12.1
1996	78356.1	16901.2	21.6
1997	78738.6	18203.8	23.1
1998	73291.5	16860.5	23.0

Indonesia	Baseline	Difference	%,Difference
1994	40053.4	-1018.5	-2.5
1995	45417.0	891.6	2.0
1996	49814.0	2129.6	4.3
1997	53444.0	2403.3	4.5
1998	48846.5	2186.6	4.5

The Philippines	Baseline	Difference	%,Difference
1994	13304.3	717.1	5.4
1995	17501.5	4050.8	23.1
1996	20415.7	5684.9	27.8
1997	25088.5	6947.6	27.7
1998	27783.4	7678.9	27.6

Republic of Korea	Baseline	Difference	%,Difference
1994	96013.0	-7238.1	-7.5
1995	124985.0	-1445.5	-1.2
1996	129713.0	3678.8	2.8
1997	136171.0	4249.2	3.1
1998	132315.0	3933.0	3.0

Appendix C: Swap rate

The Data used in our esimation are listed in Appendix C: Swap Rate and D: New Data for estimation of the Equations for Appendix A. Note that these are monthly data and not available in *statistical year books.*

88M01	5.73	89M07	6.71	91M01	5.69	92M07	6.69
88M02	5.73	89M08	6.52	91M02	5.72	92M08	7.10
88M03	5.90	89M09	6.23	91M03	5.74	92M09	6.95
88M04	6.70	89M10	6.06	91M04	5.78	92M10	6.96
88M05	6.75	89M11	5.80	91M05	5.83	92M11	7.08
88M06	6.75	89M12	5.81	91M06	5.87	92M12	7.37
88M07	6.75	90M01	5.95	91M07	5.86	93M01	7.76
88M08	6.80	90M02	5.95	91M08	5.81	93M02	8.38
88M09	6.75	90M03	5.91	91M09	5.84	93M03	8.09
88M10	6.44	90M04	5.91	91M10	5.79	93M04	8.11
88M11	6.56	90M05	5.89	91M11	5.85	93M05	8.14
88M12	6.59	90M06	5.87	91M12	5.87	93M06	10.61
89M01	6.58	90M07	5.72	92M01	5.97	93M07	8.89
89M02	6.65	90M08	5.77	92M02	5.95	93M08	8.82
89M03	6.67	90M09	5.72	92M03	5.96	93M09	8.74
89M04	6.70	90M10	5.64	92M04	6.07	93M10	8.70
89M05	6.70	90M11	5.59	92M05	6.21	93M11	8.69
89M06	6.75	90M12	5.68	92M06	6.38	93M12	8.69

Appendix D: New Data

1-1

	CH_RATE	CH_CPI	CH_EXMN	CH_RATE	IND_RATE
1987M1	3.722	105.096	1757.073	3.722	1631.190
1987M2	3.722	105.399	2517.396	3.722	1639.420
1987M3	3.722	105.801	3003.681	3.722	1647.130
1987M4	3.722	106.698	2888.155	3.722	1641.680
1987M5	3.722	107.603	3043.981	3.722	1641.770
1987M6	3.722	107.798	3420.112	3.722	1645.150
1987M7	3.722	107.796	3258.913	3.722	1645.150
1987M8	3.722	108.200	3237.420	3.722	1640.960
1987M9	3.722	107.699	3387.872	3.722	1645.540
1987M10	3.722	107.502	3549.072	3.722	1649.300
1987M11	3.722	108.297	3809.677	3.722	1648.250
1987M12	3.722	108.902	5668.843	3.722	1650.640
1988M1	3.722	114.876	2683.969	3.722	1657.880
1988M2	3.722	116.364	2726.955	3.722	1661.240
1988M3	3.722	117.756	3530.265	3.722	1660.350
1988M4	3.722	119.715	3995.057	3.722	1665.680
1988M5	3.722	122.876	4392.682	3.722	1670.550
1988M6	3.722	125.375	3729.078	3.722	1678.190
1988M7	3.722	128.499	3852.664	3.722	1690.350
1988M8	3.722	133.734	4016.550	3.722	1696.480
1988M9	3.722	136.136	3981.623	3.722	1702.320
1988M10	3.722	136.628	4255.662	3.722	1709.760
1988M11	3.722	137.328	3997.743	3.722	1709.620
1988M12	3.722	139.287	6378.120	3.722	1726.030
1989M1	3.722	146.345	2810.242	3.722	1735.920
1989M2	3.722	149.406	2915.021	3.722	1741.960
1989M3	3.722	149.665	3930.577	3.722	1751.290
1989M4	3.722	151.565	3935.950	3.722	1755.920
1989M5	3.722	153.480	4427.608	3.722	1765.410
1989M6	3.722	153.952	4220.736	3.722	1771.540
1989M7	3.722	153.426	4403.428	3.722	1773.600
1989M8	3.722	154.196	4811.800	3.722	1780.300
1989M9	3.722	151.783	4744.633	3.722	1787.380
1989M10	3.722	148.386	4612.987	3.722	1787.680
1989M11	3.722	147.488	4822.546	3.722	1794.230
1989M12	4.238	148.480	5990.751	4.238	1795.480
1990M1	4.722	152.645	2839.838	4.722	1804.850
1990M2	4.722	155.983	3250.672	4.722	1809.870

1-2

1990M3	4.722	154.758	4690.710	4.722	1820.350
1990M4	4.722	156.414	4798.712	4.722	1826.050
1990M5	4.722	157.622	4934.245	4.722	1831.400
1990M6	4.722	155.654	5118.485	4.722	1841.000
1990M7	4.722	155.111	5118.485	4.722	1846.960
1990M8	4.722	158.056	5506.025	4.722	1854.920
1990M9	4.722	156.194	5095.191	4.722	1860.350
1990M10	4.722	152.988	5849.093	4.722	1865.850
1990M11	4.955	152.944	5519.232	4.955	1860.480
1990M12	5.222	154.859	8199.766	5.222	1891.680
1991M1	5.222	156.006	3977.327	5.222	1907.540
1991M2	5.222	158.794	4059.670	5.222	1914.000
1991M3	5.222	157.235	5342.678	5.222	1927.120
1991M4	5.266	158.444	5165.309	5.266	1934.610
1991M5	5.314	163.298	5766.010	5.314	1942.920
1991M6	5.354	162.500	5727.094	5.354	1950.960
1991M7	5.356	162.406	6217.907	5.356	1956.650
1991M8	5.359	165.794	6306.794	5.359	1961.350
1991M9	5.374	163.221	6048.200	5.374	1966.050
1991M10	5.379	160.327	6060.606	5.379	1973.590
1991M11	5.401	159.671	6406.577	5.401	1980.620
1991M12	5.413	161.829	9212.836	5.413	1988.400
1992M1	5.448	164.582	3991.000	5.970	1998.230
1992M2	5.464	167.208	4970.000	5.950	2006.630
1992M3	5.473	165.568	6000.000	5.960	2014.830
1992M4	5.497	169.696	6349.000	6.070	2019.610
1992M5	5.504	170.968	6601.000	6.210	2024.520
1992M6	5.475	170.298	7658.000	6.380	2030.080
1992M7	5.443	170.847	7159.000	6.690	2033.380
1992M8	5.429	175.409	7650.000	7.100	2033.920
1992M9	5.495	175.455	7064.000	6.950	2037.720
1992M10	5.537	172.988	7686.000	6.960	2045.330
1992M11	5.613	172.766	8527.000	7.080	2054.800
1992M12	5.798	176.069	11323.000	7.370	2060.000
1993M1	5.764	181.534	3357.000	7.760	2064.780
1993M2	5.770	185.260	5823.000	8.380	2066.630
1993M3	5.731	185.764	6906.000	8.090	2069.130
1993M4	5.706	191.072	6895.000	8.110	2070.730
1993M5	5.722	194.909	7213.000	8.140	2076.630
1993M6	5.737	196.010	6948.000	10.610	2083.410
1993M7	5.761	198.527	7627.000	8.890	2093.000

1-3

1993M8	5.776	204.177	7638.000	8.820	2097.380
1993M9	5.787	203.011	8842.000	8.740	2105.420
1993M10	5.787	200.500	8052.000	8.700	2107.900
1993M11	5.795	201.618	8946.000	8.690	2102.190
1993M12	5.807	209.174	13486.430	8.690	2108.040
1994M1	8.700	219.835	4881.000	8.700	2116.900
1994M2	8.703	228.247	5733.000	8.703	2129.000
1994M3	8.703	227.374	8488.000	8.703	2140.220
1994M4	8.696	232.543	8935.000	8.696	2147.950
1994M5	8.665	236.424	9491.000	8.665	2151.950
1994M6	8.657	240.308	10900.000	8.657	2158.000
1994M7	8.640	246.169	10346.000	8.640	2164.270
1994M8	8.590	256.862	10110.000	8.590	2171.520
1994M9	8.540	258.428	10436.000	8.540	2178.770
1994M10	8.529	256.033	10430.000	8.529	2184.050
1994M11	8.517	257.065	12569.000	8.517	2189.270
1994M12	8.485	262.514	18508.000	8.485	2197.140
1995M1	8.441	272.819	9179.000	8.441	2203.680
1995M2	8.435	279.369	8885.000	8.435	2209.750
1995M3	8.428	275.810	12880.000	8.428	2215.000
1995M4	8.423	280.674	11991.000	8.423	2222.320
1995M5	8.318	284.410	12817.000	8.318	2231.890
1995M6	8.301	285.731	14037.000	8.301	2241.360
1995M7	8.301	287.286	12268.000	8.301	2251.570
1995M8	8.308	294.100	12520.000	8.308	2262.000
1995M9	8.319	292.541	12431.000	8.319	2271.810
1995M10	8.316	287.012	12344.000	8.316	2280.860
1995M11	8.314	285.851	12179.000	8.314	2290.640
1995M12	8.316	289.024	17244.000	8.316	2302.420
1996M1	8.319	297.374	9175.000	8.319	2306.250
1996M2	8.313	305.353	8654.000	8.313	2317.500
1996M3	8.329	302.840	10407.000	8.329	2330.760
1996M4	8.332	307.903	11382.000	8.332	2339.250
1996M5	8.329	309.722	12155.000	8.329	2349.000
1996M6	8.323	310.308	12266.000	8.323	2344.000
1996M7	8.316	311.126	12426.000	8.316	2348.500
1996M8	8.308	317.921	14134.000	8.308	2358.500
1996M9	8.304	314.190	13419.000	8.304	2344.000
1996M10	8.300	307.109	15219.000	8.300	2344.040
1996M11	8.299	305.579	13621.000	8.299	2348.000
1996M12	8.299	309.259	18326.000	8.299	2377.750

1-4

1997M1	8.296	314.913	11692.000	8.296	2393.000
1997M2	8.293	322.458	9847.000	8.293	2403.000
1997M3	8.296	314.944	14046.000	8.296	2413.800
1997M4	8.296	317.751	14795.000	8.296	2426.800
1997M5	8.292	318.399	15192.000	8.292	2438.300
1997M6	8.291	318.997	15373.000	8.291	2446.590
1997M7	8.289	319.526	15583.000	8.289	2518.300
1997M8	8.287	323.961	16027.000	8.287	2800.370
1997M9	8.290	319.845	16563.000	8.290	3055.300
1997M10	8.280	311.716	17817.000	8.280	3616.300
1997M11	8.280	308.940	16752.000	8.280	3492.000
1997M12	8.280	310.496	19190.000	8.280	4908.797
1998M1	8.280	315.858	12676.000	8.280	9662.500
1998M2	8.280	319.233	12158.000	8.280	8950.000
1998M3	8.280	317.149	15238.000	8.280	9687.570
1998M4	8.280	316.798	15952.000	8.280	7950.000
1998M5	8.280	315.215	14927.000	8.280	9897.300
1998M6	8.280	314.850	15609.000	8.280	13535.000
1998M7	8.280	315.053	16157.000	8.280	13962.500
1998M8	8.280	319.426	15557.000	8.280	11950.000
1998M9	8.280	315.048	15476.000	8.280	10843.800
1998M10	8.280	308.287	14730.000	8.280	8287.500
1998M11	8.280	305.233	15100.000	8.280	7685.300
1998M12	8.280	307.391	20009.000	8.280	7752.000
1999M1	8.280	312.067	11390.000	8.280	8714.300
1999M2	8.280	315.083	11000.000	8.280	8726.000
1999M3	8.280	311.440	14900.000	8.280	8886.800
1999M4	8.280	312.679	14800.000	8.280	8547.800
1999M5	8.280	308.280	15500.000	8.280	7990.300
1999M6	N.A	N.A	N.A	N.A	7225.500

2-1

	IND_CPI	IND_EXMN	JP_RATE	JP_CPI	KOR_RATE
1987M1	50.620	1180.000	154.480	87.190	858.750
1987M2	51.360	1123.000	153.480	87.190	856.300
1987M3	51.220	1225.000	151.540	87.470	852.010
1987M4	51.260	1103.000	142.980	88.310	840.900
1987M5	52.210	1467.000	140.540	88.500	828.220
1987M6	52.370	1412.000	144.480	88.310	814.270
1987M7	52.570	1535.000	150.210	87.840	808.110
1987M8	52.860	1662.000	147.560	87.940	808.140
1987M9	53.230	1552.000	143.000	88.680	806.380
1987M10	53.960	1666.000	143.540	88.680	804.480
1987M11	54.910	1510.000	135.250	88.310	798.510
1987M12	55.110	1698.000	128.590	88.220	794.740
1988M1	55.300	1540.000	127.560	87.940	787.460
1988M2	55.590	1537.000	129.160	87.750	773.440
1988M3	55.620	1638.000	127.280	88.120	753.490
1988M4	56.020	1547.000	124.930	88.590	741.800
1988M5	56.540	1514.000	124.770	88.680	735.670
1988M6	56.760	1669.000	127.140	88.500	729.460
1988M7	57.390	1759.000	133.070	88.310	725.810
1988M8	57.620	1718.000	133.630	88.590	722.810
1988M9	57.590	1647.000	134.440	89.240	720.300
1988M10	57.820	1481.000	129.020	89.710	709.350
1988M11	58.070	1665.000	123.190	89.340	693.000
1988M12	58.190	1750.000	123.630	89.060	685.030
1989M1	58.490	1683.400	127.230	88.870	682.420
1989M2	59.230	1540.000	127.770	88.680	676.990
1989M3	59.360	1840.100	130.360	89.060	672.970
1989M4	60.300	1785.000	132.080	90.650	667.360
1989M5	60.680	1703.000	138.350	91.210	666.560
1989M6	60.550	1852.000	143.790	91.110	666.710
1989M7	60.820	1927.000	140.720	90.930	667.280
1989M8	60.880	1892.000	141.110	90.830	668.380
1989M9	61.010	1918.000	145.050	91.580	670.030
1989M10	61.470	1988.000	141.930	92.330	671.270
1989M11	61.770	1876.000	143.520	91.390	672.330
1989M12	61.750	2155.000	143.660	91.390	675.170
1990M1	62.310	1909.000	145.090	91.860	683.430

2-2

1990M2	62.930	1845.200	145.530	91.950	689.870
1990M3	62.680	2055.000	153.080	92.330	697.800
1990M4	63.390	1803.000	158.470	93.080	706.030
1990M5	63.940	1802.000	153.520	93.540	709.200
1990M6	64.760	1750.000	153.770	93.170	715.330
1990M7	66.190	1812.000	149.280	92.980	715.940
1990M8	66.590	2124.000	147.420	93.360	715.470
1990M9	66.920	2603.000	138.990	94.100	714.990
1990M10	67.620	2639.000	129.730	95.130	715.040
1990M11	67.840	2681.200	129.080	94.940	714.320
1990M12	67.880	2650.500	133.550	94.850	715.750
1991M1	68.390	2554.000	133.880	95.500	718.140
1991M2	68.610	2361.000	130.480	95.220	721.600
1991M3	68.630	2115.000	137.200	95.690	725.080
1991M4	69.930	2667.000	137.100	96.250	725.480
1991M5	70.060	2378.000	138.040	96.720	725.130
1991M6	70.370	2433.000	139.790	96.350	725.370
1991M7	71.710	2538.000	138.010	96.250	728.960
1991M8	73.060	2414.000	138.890	96.440	731.120
1991M9	73.150	2441.000	134.580	96.630	739.730
1991M10	73.720	2544.000	130.720	97.650	749.250
1991M11	74.510	2409.000	129.680	97.840	753.100
1991M12	74.650	2689.000	128.110	97.370	757.280
1992M1	74.980	2358.000	125.090	97.190	762.660
1992M2	75.170	2487.000	127.500	97.090	765.740
1992M3	75.660	2627.000	132.700	97.560	771.100
1992M4	76.360	2390.000	133.530	98.590	778.280
1992M5	76.440	2703.000	130.570	98.680	782.780
1992M6	76.930	2694.000	126.810	98.590	789.070
1992M7	77.110	2844.000	125.650	97.840	787.150
1992M8	77.230	2017.000	126.310	98.120	789.230
1992M9	77.380	2851.000	122.720	98.590	785.550
1992M10	77.700	3453.000	121.040	98.680	783.590
1992M11	77.900	3313.000	123.870	98.500	784.040
1992M12	78.410	3351.000	124.030	98.500	788.620
1993M1	80.700	3002.000	125.010	98.400	791.990
1993M2	82.340	2893.000	120.960	98.500	796.590
1993M3	83.570	3009.000	117.070	98.780	793.250
1993M4	83.690	2958.000	112.450	99.430	795.840
1993M5	83.800	3118.000	110.400	99.520	799.990
1993M6	84.010	2981.200	107.340	99.430	802.680

2-3

1993M7	84.570	3025.700	107.730	99.710	806.200
1993M8	84.840	3128.400	103.710	99.990	810.210
1993M9	85.080	3084.100	105.290	100.080	808.570
1993M10	85.580	3218.400	106.920	99.990	810.210
1993M11	85.930	3212.100	107.800	99.430	807.120
1993M12	86.390	3194.700	109.700	99.520	809.400
1994M1	87.470	2666.500	111.510	99.590	810.480
1994M2	89.010	2799.600	106.210	99.590	805.120
1994M3	89.630	3032.300	105.140	100.090	807.730
1994M4	89.850	3133.900	103.530	100.290	808.540
1994M5	90.320	3209.800	103.730	100.390	806.550
1994M6	90.430	3567.800	102.720	99.990	806.640
1994M7	91.660	3514.900	98.500	99.490	805.120
1994M8	92.480	3592.200	99.850	99.990	803.460
1994M9	92.980	3481.200	98.810	100.290	800.730
1994M10	93.810	3646.300	98.420	100.690	798.790
1994M11	94.230	3640.900	97.960	100.490	796.330
1994M12	94.720	3768.000	100.120	100.190	791.860
1995M1	95.810	3259.000	99.750	100.190	790.480
1995M2	97.070	3431.000	98.240	99.890	790.920
1995M3	97.630	3485.000	90.790	99.790	778.690
1995M4	99.270	3414.000	83.670	100.090	767.500
1995M5	99.760	3822.000	85.100	100.290	761.440
1995M6	99.920	3834.000	84.530	100.190	761.040
1995M7	100.630	3775.000	87.220	99.690	757.010
1995M8	100.950	3953.000	94.550	99.790	767.960
1995M9	101.340	3940.000	100.490	100.390	772.350
1995M10	101.990	3900.000	100.660	100.090	767.400
1995M11	102.420	4080.000	101.920	99.790	769.410
1995M12	103.230	4524.000	101.820	99.790	771.080
1996M1	106.410	3601.000	105.840	99.690	787.270
1996M2	107.820	3685.000	105.730	99.490	780.280
1996M3	107.110	3955.000	105.820	99.690	781.250
1996M4	107.420	4030.000	107.460	100.290	780.430
1996M5	108.110	4075.000	106.450	100.490	780.160
1996M6	107.310	4136.000	108.860	100.190	797.960
1996M7	108.060	4069.000	109.320	100.090	812.760
1996M8	108.010	4322.000	107.750	99.990	816.810
1996M9	108.210	4331.000	109.750	100.390	821.760
1996M10	108.650	4472.000	112.360	100.590	827.610
1996M11	109.090	4456.000	112.260	100.290	828.130

2-4

1996M12	109.460	4682.000	113.770	100.390	839.020
1997M1	111.320	4243.000	118.020	100.290	849.880
1997M2	112.160	4078.000	123.010	100.090	866.850
1997M3	112.190	4084.000	122.640	100.190	896.200
1997M4	112.640	4231.000	125.510	102.190	893.560
1997M5	112.990	4508.000	118.990	102.390	892.050
1997M6	112.950	4417.000	114.210	102.390	889.490
1997M7	113.850	4535.000	115.160	101.990	890.500
1997M8	114.900	4700.000	117.900	102.090	895.900
1997M9	116.150	4707.000	120.750	102.790	909.530
1997M10	117.770	4558.000	121.060	103.090	921.850
1997M11	118.700	4679.000	125.270	102.390	1025.580
1997M12	120.740	4704.000	129.380	102.190	1484.080
1998M1	129.040	4149.000	129.450	102.090	1701.530
1998M2	145.510	3812.000	126.000	101.990	1626.750
1998M3	153.500	4555.000	128.690	102.390	1488.870
1998M4	160.470	3652.000	131.670	102.590	1388.320
1998M5	169.110	3920.000	135.000	102.890	1400.130
1998M6	176.950	4481.000	140.570	102.490	1395.260
1998M7	192.100	4579.000	140.730	101.890	1293.730
1998M8	204.200	4091.770	144.660	101.790	1312.120
1998M9	211.870	4009.420	134.590	102.590	1372.580
1998M10	211.290	3825.580	121.300	103.290	1336.240
1998M11	211.470	3865.440	120.580	103.190	1290.210
1998M12	214.470	3906.320	117.620	102.790	1211.500
1999M1	220.840	N.A	113.180	102.290	1174.000
1999M2	223.620	N.A	116.660	101.890	1189.050
1999M3	223.220	N.A	119.780	101.990	1228.790
1999M4	221.700	N.A	119.810	102.490	1205.760
1999M5	221.080	N.A	122.110	102.490	1196.750
1999M6	N.A	N.A	120.900	N.A	1168.450

3-1

	KOR_CPI	KOR_EXMN	MAL_RATE	MAL_CPI	MAL_EXMN
1987M1	58.470	2831.000	2.580	75.100	1183.333
1987M2	58.580	2900.000	2.540	75.100	1226.772
1987M3	59.040	3653.000	2.520	74.750	1391.667
1987M4	59.380	3673.000	2.490	75.040	1422.490
1987M5	60.290	4029.000	2.470	75.220	1344.534
1987M6	60.230	4241.000	2.510	75.400	1450.199
1987M7	60.060	4224.000	2.540	75.280	1511.811
1987M8	60.920	3479.000	2.540	75.340	1548.425
1987M9	61.320	4441.000	2.520	75.450	1600.794
1987M10	61.370	4042.000	2.530	74.920	1767.194
1987M11	61.260	4424.000	2.500	75.100	1748.400
1987M12	61.770	5245.000	2.490	75.510	1746.988
1988M1	62.110	3959.000	2.540	75.630	1603.150
1988M2	63.140	4121.000	2.580	75.750	1459.690
1988M3	64.050	4792.000	2.570	75.810	1809.728
1988M4	63.930	4627.000	2.570	75.810	1712.062
1988M5	64.270	4773.000	2.580	75.870	1626.744
1988M6	64.670	5052.000	2.590	76.580	1869.884
1988M7	64.780	5203.000	2.630	77.050	1744.106
1988M8	65.130	5310.000	2.650	77.110	1889.434
1988M9	65.300	5393.000	2.660	77.340	1862.030
1988M10	65.130	5256.000	2.680	77.220	1814.925
1988M11	65.640	5811.000	2.680	77.580	1790.672
1988M12	66.210	6401.000	2.700	78.170	1924.444
1989M1	66.320	4401.000	2.720	78.230	1851.103
1989M2	66.550	4337.000	2.730	78.280	1583.150
1989M3	67.000	5330.000	2.750	78.280	2075.636
1989M4	67.290	4784.000	2.730	78.340	2036.996
1989M5	68.140	4950.000	2.700	78.580	1971.111
1989M6	68.250	5427.000	2.710	78.580	2096.679
1989M7	68.200	5233.000	2.680	78.870	2282.836
1989M8	68.710	5268.000	2.680	78.930	2236.455
1989M9	69.330	5475.000	2.700	79.110	2210.333
1989M10	69.510	5304.000	2.700	79.170	2138.000
1989M11	69.620	5655.000	2.700	79.580	2313.926
1989M12	69.560	6214.000	2.700	79.820	2261.630
1990M1	70.240	3958.000	2.700	79.830	2238.889
1990M2	70.870	4669.000	2.700	80.310	2013.704

3-2

1990M3	71.780	5273.000	2.720	80.310	2370.956
1990M4	72.860	4950.000	2.730	80.720	2129.304
1990M5	74.230	5215.000	2.700	80.880	2268.519
1990M6	74.680	5689.000	2.710	80.800	2382.657
1990M7	75.020	5490.000	2.710	80.550	2316.605
1990M8	75.250	5321.000	2.700	80.550	2565.926
1990M9	75.820	6112.000	2.700	80.880	2544.922
1990M10	75.990	5278.000	2.700	81.280	2921.719
1990M11	75.880	6051.000	2.690	81.930	2844.227
1990M12	76.100	7023.000	2.700	82.500	2817.052
1991M1	77.700	4643.000	2.720	82.820	2779.029
1991M2	78.780	4857.000	2.700	83.220	2366.781
1991M3	79.800	5760.000	2.740	83.390	2798.485
1991M4	80.200	5854.000	2.750	83.950	2381.502
1991M5	80.650	6385.000	2.760	84.360	2854.906
1991M6	80.800	6497.000	2.780	84.920	2714.755
1991M7	81.310	5446.000	2.790	84.600	3040.502
1991M8	81.980	5763.000	2.780	84.840	3106.363
1991M9	82.430	5680.000	2.760	84.600	2994.203
1991M10	82.570	6637.000	2.750	84.840	3126.545
1991M11	82.940	6677.000	2.740	85.330	3078.102
1991M12	83.090	7697.000	2.740	85.970	3098.175
1992M1	83.680	5392.000	2.690	86.460	2805.985
1992M2	84.200	5144.000	2.600	86.780	2364.577
1992M3	85.090	6429.000	2.580	86.940	3418.605
1992M4	85.610	6361.000	2.550	87.670	2987.608
1992M5	86.130	6337.000	2.530	88.480	3380.553
1992M6	86.280	7053.000	2.520	88.560	3457.183
1992M7	86.650	6352.000	2.500	88.800	3824.160
1992M8	86.800	6177.000	2.500	89.210	3501.240
1992M9	87.090	6626.000	2.500	89.210	3717.640
1992M10	87.020	7126.000	2.500	88.970	3893.240
1992M11	86.570	6629.000	2.520	89.860	3606.706
1992M12	86.800	7007.000	2.570	90.180	3766.265
1993M1	87.460	5325.000	2.600	90.340	3215.538
1993M2	88.050	5937.000	2.630	90.580	3290.494
1993M3	89.170	6915.000	2.610	90.750	3728.736
1993M4	89.680	6751.000	2.580	90.990	4112.016
1993M5	89.980	6743.000	2.570	91.310	3878.599
1993M6	90.420	7248.000	2.570	91.550	3838.132
1993M7	90.350	6662.000	2.570	91.960	4330.350

3-3

1993M8	90.650	6544.000	2.550	91.720	3961.961
1993M9	91.090	7186.000	2.550	91.800	4367.843
1993M10	91.460	7481.000	2.550	92.060	4174.118
1993M11	91.310	7345.000	2.550	92.610	3936.078
1993M12	91.830	8098.000	2.570	93.250	4270.817
1994M1	93.020	6068.000	2.710	93.980	4006.642
1994M2	94.050	6202.000	2.760	95.110	3617.029
1994M3	94.870	7613.000	2.720	94.710	4454.412
1994M4	95.020	7668.000	2.690	94.550	4684.387
1994M5	95.090	7858.000	2.620	94.710	4624.809
1994M6	95.760	8304.000	2.590	96.000	4930.502
1994M7	96.570	7611.000	2.600	96.580	5100.000
1994M8	97.310	7601.000	2.570	96.780	5272.763
1994M9	97.020	8301.000	2.560	97.160	5358.594
1994M10	96.720	8867.000	2.560	97.450	5591.797
1994M11	96.870	9225.000	2.560	97.940	5410.156
1994M12	96.940	10695.000	2.560	98.230	5683.984
1995M1	97.790	7730.000	2.560	98.610	5333.594
1995M2	98.190	8391.000	2.550	99.290	5112.549
1995M3	99.190	9998.000	2.550	99.190	5471.765
1995M4	99.790	10158.000	2.480	99.190	6023.387
1995M5	99.990	10646.000	2.470	99.770	5946.559
1995M6	99.690	11246.000	2.440	99.770	6402.869
1995M7	99.990	10485.000	2.450	99.970	6333.061
1995M8	100.590	10613.000	2.430	100.260	6755.144
1995M9	101.490	10974.000	2.510	100.550	6756.972
1995M10	100.990	11524.000	2.530	100.740	6304.743
1995M11	100.790	11463.000	2.540	101.230	6711.417
1995M12	101.490	11757.000	2.540	101.420	6895.276
1996M1	102.490	9923.000	2.560	102.000	6304.688
1996M2	102.890	9883.000	2.540	102.680	5137.795
1996M3	103.590	11689.000	2.540	102.390	7170.472
1996M4	104.290	10637.000	2.510	102.770	6360.558
1996M5	104.890	11236.000	2.490	103.350	6813.253
1996M6	104.890	11302.000	2.500	103.550	6490.000
1996M7	105.390	9897.000	2.490	103.740	6381.526
1996M8	105.890	9687.000	2.490	103.740	6924.498
1996M9	106.090	9992.000	2.500	104.130	6628.800
1996M10	106.090	11848.000	2.510	104.130	6753.785
1996M11	106.090	11399.000	2.520	104.610	6556.349
1996M12	106.490	12220.000	2.530	104.800	6834.387

3-4

1997M1	107.290	9034.000	2.490	105.290	6728.514
1997M2	107.890	9362.000	2.490	105.870	5430.120
1997M3	108.290	11327.000	2.480	105.670	7531.452
1997M4	108.790	11402.000	2.500	105.480	6253.600
1997M5	108.890	11745.000	2.510	105.960	6873.705
1997M6	109.090	12392.000	2.520	105.870	6564.683
1997M7	109.290	11807.000	2.570	105.960	6674.319
1997M8	110.090	11041.000	2.740	106.250	7012.409
1997M9	110.590	11334.000	3.010	106.540	6673.422
1997M10	110.590	12465.000	3.290	106.930	6549.240
1997M11	110.690	11834.000	3.390	107.320	6362.537
1997M12	113.490	12428.000	3.770	107.800	6084.615
1998M1	116.190	9001.000	4.410	108.860	5125.170
1998M2	118.190	11222.000	3.830	110.510	5849.347
1998M3	117.990	12009.000	3.750	111.090	6467.733
1998M4	118.390	12061.000	3.730	111.380	5982.306
1998M5	117.790	11309.000	3.820	111.670	5854.974
1998M6	117.290	11509.000	3.990	112.440	5890.727
1998M7	117.290	10024.000	4.160	112.150	5753.846
1998M8	117.690	9709.000	4.200	112.250	5790.238
1998M9	118.190	10748.000	3.810	112.440	6576.115
1998M10	118.590	10634.000	3.800	112.540	6707.632
1998M11	118.190	11670.000	3.800	113.310	6486.579
1998M12	117.990	12419.000	3.800	113.500	6806.842
1999M1	117.890	9266.000	3.800	114.470	5752.632
1999M2	118.390	9344.000	3.800	114.860	5770.526
1999M3	118.590	11721.000	3.800	N.A	N.A
1999M4	118.890	11588.000	3.800	N.A	N.A
1999M5	118.690	11556.000	3.800	N.A	N.A
1999M6	117.990	N.A	3.800	N.A	N.A

4-1

	PHI_RATE	PHI_CPI	PHI_EXMN	TH_RATE	TH_CPI
1987M1	20.460	46.960	365.543	25.960	67.190
1987M2	20.530	47.220	390.940	25.920	67.120
1987M3	20.560	47.260	447.422	25.720	67.190
1987M4	20.500	47.210	408.341	25.670	67.460
1987M5	20.470	47.630	471.764	25.620	67.790
1987M6	20.460	48.230	474.096	25.760	68.190
1987M7	20.450	48.770	497.213	25.940	68.260
1987M8	20.440	48.940	498.043	25.900	68.660
1987M9	20.600	49.350	492.087	25.730	69.060
1987M10	20.710	49.370	518.204	25.770	68.920
1987M11	20.820	49.620	518.252	25.470	69.520
1987M12	20.810	50.150	566.939	25.230	69.520
1988M1	20.850	50.940	481.871	25.230	69.320
1988M2	20.900	51.380	540.431	25.310	69.920
1988M3	21.030	51.710	526.724	25.220	70.250
1988M4	21.030	51.790	530.480	25.150	70.450
1988M5	20.950	52.040	555.943	25.150	70.590
1988M6	20.950	52.580	613.938	25.260	70.720
1988M7	21.020	52.920	613.701	25.500	70.720
1988M8	21.060	53.140	635.185	25.540	71.120
1988M9	21.250	53.100	623.435	25.530	71.790
1988M10	21.360	53.210	588.202	25.360	72.050
1988M11	21.380	54.110	604.958	25.120	71.850
1988M12	21.360	54.690	716.573	25.150	71.720
1989M1	21.340	52.370	570.056	25.300	72.190
1989M2	21.360	52.720	558.661	25.360	73.050
1989M3	21.340	52.720	628.538	25.480	73.050
1989M4	21.410	53.210	644.932	25.520	73.250
1989M5	21.580	53.750	671.826	25.750	73.780
1989M6	21.680	54.740	654.336	25.920	74.120
1989M7	21.890	55.380	701.827	25.800	75.180
1989M8	21.880	56.610	660.375	25.850	75.920
1989M9	21.970	57.100	671.643	25.990	76.250
1989M10	21.960	57.540	671.129	25.850	76.650
1989M11	22.100	58.090	644.615	25.860	76.510
1989M12	22.340	59.170	676.947	25.750	76.110
1990M1	22.460	59.330	581.434	25.730	76.580
1990M2	22.620	59.520	610.345	25.710	77.380
1990M3	22.760	59.800	691.257	25.910	77.650

4-2

1990M4	22.760	60.260	619.200	26.000	78.110
1990M5	22.900	60.630	691.921	25.870	78.650
1990M6	23.100	61.280	637.403	25.860	78.850
1990M7	23.560	62.200	724.533	25.680	79.040
1990M8	24.450	62.390	674.969	25.560	79.310
1990M9	25.350	63.040	739.408	25.370	79.640
1990M10	25.750	64.150	688.117	25.110	81.240
1990M11	28.000	65.260	681.179	25.050	81.580
1990M12	28.000	67.480	728.607	25.190	81.180
1991M1	28.000	69.610	621.321	25.220	81.310
1991M2	28.000	71.000	656.107	25.120	81.840
1991M3	28.000	71.640	734.536	25.450	81.840
1991M4	27.930	72.110	690.763	25.570	82.970
1991M5	27.820	72.480	676.600	25.630	83.570
1991M6	27.800	73.310	761.799	25.750	83.710
1991M7	27.620	74.050	787.581	25.740	83.370
1991M8	27.200	74.980	762.868	25.710	84.040
1991M9	26.980	75.720	758.821	25.610	84.910
1991M10	26.990	75.720	751.315	25.540	85.500
1991M11	26.740	76.090	745.363	25.490	85.240
1991M12	26.670	76.460	819.873	25.380	84.970
1992M1	26.540	77.010	654.559	25.320	85.370
1992M2	26.160	77.380	705.772	25.440	85.700
1992M3	25.810	77.850	898.954	25.610	85.440
1992M4	25.670	78.310	639.657	25.630	85.770
1992M5	26.150	79.050	792.964	25.530	87.040
1992M6	26.120	79.880	823.775	25.390	87.440
1992M7	25.260	80.530	828.029	25.280	87.640
1992M8	24.670	81.090	890.596	25.250	88.370
1992M9	24.730	81.730	861.059	25.190	88.430
1992M10	24.780	81.920	843.543	25.240	88.300
1992M11	24.940	82.100	805.573	25.450	87.840
1992M12	25.320	82.200	1007.070	25.470	87.500
1993M1	25.280	82.840	777.097	25.530	87.810
1993M2	25.310	83.120	810.549	25.490	88.530
1993M3	25.370	83.310	830.508	25.420	88.530
1993M4	26.080	83.590	854.179	25.230	89.240
1993M5	27.010	83.770	925.139	25.220	89.480
1993M6	27.210	84.600	923.117	25.210	89.790
1993M7	27.570	85.710	990.751	25.310	90.350
1993M8	27.950	86.270	986.905	25.180	90.580

4-3

1993M9	28.230	87.290	1010.769	25.190	91.370
1993M10	29.160	87.940	1004.115	25.260	91.290
1993M11	28.480	88.120	978.862	25.360	91.060
1993M12	27.790	88.490	996.653	25.450	91.530
1994M1	27.720	90.250	940.837	25.530	91.770
1994M2	27.650	91.270	910.958	25.380	92.560
1994M3	27.590	91.270	1042.334	25.290	93.350
1994M4	27.530	91.450	950.309	25.250	93.350
1994M5	27.050	91.920	1074.455	25.200	94.140
1994M6	26.980	92.380	1109.155	25.140	94.930
1994M7	26.460	93.030	1130.385	24.970	94.930
1994M8	26.310	93.670	1240.669	25.020	95.730
1994M9	25.910	93.860	1230.181	24.980	96.520
1994M10	25.390	93.860	1289.799	24.960	96.520
1994M11	24.260	93.860	1115.293	24.980	95.730
1994M12	24.150	93.950	1269.938	25.100	95.730
1995M1	24.620	96.170	1149.878	25.070	96.520
1995M2	25.030	96.640	1380.743	25.020	96.910
1995M3	25.860	97.010	1285.499	24.760	97.310
1995M4	26.010	97.380	1361.323	24.560	98.100
1995M5	25.850	98.300	1388.627	24.660	99.210
1995M6	25.670	99.140	1489.014	24.670	99.840
1995M7	25.510	99.880	1636.299	24.740	100.230
1995M8	25.710	101.360	1572.190	24.950	101.110
1995M9	25.970	103.490	1566.808	25.120	102.130
1995M10	25.970	103.580	1579.900	25.110	102.920
1995M11	26.170	103.390	1394.498	25.160	102.920
1995M12	26.210	103.670	1696.681	25.160	102.920
1996M1	26.220	106.630	1409.344	25.290	103.590
1996M2	26.160	107.370	1580.810	25.240	104.060
1996M3	26.200	107.750	1651.794	25.230	104.440
1996M4	26.190	108.120	1488.163	25.270	104.920
1996M5	26.180	108.300	1599.656	25.280	105.290
1996M6	26.190	109.040	1778.351	25.350	105.390
1996M7	26.200	109.230	1680.763	25.340	105.580
1996M8	26.200	110.150	1760.344	25.270	106.620
1996M9	26.240	110.060	1889.901	25.360	106.810
1996M10	26.270	110.150	1871.526	25.460	107.370
1996M11	26.270	110.240	1835.782	25.450	107.850
1996M12	26.290	111.080	1869.304	25.550	107.850
1997M1	26.320	112.470	1653.419	25.710	108.130

4-4

1997M2	26.340	112.930	1827.183	25.930	108.600
1997M3	26.330	113.480	1996.658	25.950	109.170
1997M4	26.360	113.670	2053.490	26.050	109.360
1997M5	26.370	113.850	2002.882	25.870	109.830
1997M6	26.380	115.240	2257.013	25.780	110.020
1997M7	27.670	115.520	2088.110	30.320	110.780
1997M8	29.330	116.170	2246.983	32.480	113.710
1997M9	32.390	117.190	2290.954	36.300	114.180
1997M10	34.460	117.740	2319.443	37.400	115.120
1997M11	34.520	118.480	2177.433	39.300	116.070
1997M12	37.170	119.130	2174.980	45.290	116.070
1998M1	42.660	120.330	2099.391	53.810	117.390
1998M2	40.410	122.090	2211.854	46.140	118.240
1998M3	39.000	123.110	2455.872	41.330	119.570
1998M4	38.440	123.850	2267.560	39.480	120.420
1998M5	39.300	125.330	2345.471	39.150	121.080
1998M6	40.400	127.550	2368.713	42.360	121.740
1998M7	41.780	127.830	2157.946	41.190	121.830
1998M8	43.040	128.480	2846.213	41.580	122.310
1998M9	43.780	128.940	4266.012	40.410	122.120
1998M10	42.890	129.680	2074.353	38.140	121.930
1998M11	39.940	131.720	782.098	36.460	121.550
1998M12	39.070	131.440	1907.909	36.260	121.080
1999M1	38.400	134.220	2845.755	36.620	121.550
1999M2	38.780	134.220	2509.335	37.060	121.650
1999M3	38.910	133.850	2503.058	37.510	121.460
1999M4	38.240	133.660	N.A	37.600	120.890
1999M5	37.840	133.760	N.A	37.020	120.420
1999M6	37.900	134.960	N.A	36.910	120.320

5-1

	TH_EXMN	WO_EXMN	WO_PEX	D1M	D2M	D3M	D1&2M	D12M
1987M1	781.972	162660.000	79.700	1	0	0	1	0
1987M2	771.219	179180.000	80.670	0	1	0	1	0
1987M3	986.781	201500.000	81.010	0	0	1	0	0
1987M4	910.401	196490.000	82.410	0	0	0	0	0
1987M5	919.984	195450.000	82.800	0	0	0	0	0
1987M6	982.919	200640.000	82.140	0	0	0	0	0
1987M7	1034.695	202210.000	81.880	0	0	0	0	0
1987M8	913.900	176980.000	81.730	0	0	0	0	0
1987M9	1032.647	208790.000	83.430	0	0	0	0	0
1987M10	1040.357	216990.000	84.510	0	0	0	0	0
1987M11	1130.349	221390.000	87.750	0	0	0	0	0
1987M12	1147.840	243410.000	89.350	0	0	0	0	1
1988M1	978.993	191380.000	87.990	1	0	0	1	0
1988M2	1084.947	209230.000	87.410	0	1	0	1	0
1988M3	1443.299	242390.000	88.180	0	0	1	0	0
1988M4	1191.650	226950.000	90.540	0	0	0	0	0
1988M5	1242.147	234130.000	90.900	0	0	0	0	0
1988M6	1373.713	237630.000	90.470	0	0	0	0	0
1988M7	1287.059	219380.000	86.480	0	0	0	0	0
1988M8	1459.280	208960.000	86.130	0	0	0	0	0
1988M9	1499.412	230670.000	86.070	0	0	0	0	0
1988M10	1432.571	241120.000	87.250	0	0	0	0	0
1988M11	1390.525	247520.000	89.440	0	0	0	0	0
1988M12	1570.577	261170.000	89.930	0	0	0	0	1
1989M1	1423.320	225800.000	89.250	1	0	0	1	0
1989M2	1381.703	229460.000	89.280	0	1	0	1	0
1989M3	1806.515	261460.000	88.670	0	0	1	0	0
1989M4	1607.759	248080.000	91.400	0	0	0	0	0
1989M5	1691.650	245710.000	89.740	0	0	0	0	0
1989M6	1906.636	258350.000	90.090	0	0	0	0	0
1989M7	1554.264	242830.000	88.810	0	0	0	0	0
1989M8	1860.735	229740.000	87.750	0	0	0	0	0
1989M9	1725.664	249400.000	87.060	0	0	0	0	0
1989M10	1605.416	266380.000	88.980	0	0	0	0	0
1989M11	1677.108	263540.000	89.520	0	0	0	0	0
1989M12	1837.670	270430.000	91.970	0	0	0	0	1
1990M1	1549.553	252440.000	92.560	1	0	0	1	0
1990M2	1677.557	253630.000	94.960	0	1	0	1	0
1990M3	2022.771	289600.000	93.360	0	0	1	0	0

5-2

1990M4	1647.692	262820.000	92.910	0	0	0	0	0
1990M5	1908.002	279680.000	93.920	0	0	0	0	0
1990M6	2002.320	279980.000	93.670	0	0	0	0	0
1990M7	1907.710	277790.000	95.980	0	0	0	0	0
1990M8	2166.275	266380.000	96.710	0	0	0	0	0
1990M9	1921.561	288520.000	98.310	0	0	0	0	0
1990M10	2034.648	327810.000	101.190	0	0	0	0	0
1990M11	2192.415	318700.000	102.000	0	0	0	0	0
1990M12	2037.316	307660.000	101.050	0	0	0	0	1
1991M1	2081.285	288000.000	99.980	1	0	0	1	0
1991M2	2004.777	282280.000	100.740	0	1	0	1	0
1991M3	2493.910	298450.000	95.970	0	0	1	0	0
1991M4	2145.874	287570.000	93.040	0	0	0	0	0
1991M5	2246.196	288580.000	92.330	0	0	0	0	0
1991M6	2177.476	282200.000	90.840	0	0	0	0	0
1991M7	2710.956	288460.000	90.810	0	0	0	0	0
1991M8	2510.696	259430.000	91.530	0	0	0	0	0
1991M9	2465.053	287960.000	93.150	0	0	0	0	0
1991M10	2496.085	317050.000	93.630	0	0	0	0	0
1991M11	2539.820	307420.000	95.330	0	0	0	0	0
1991M12	2555.556	313970.000	97.400	0	0	0	0	1
1992M1	2615.719	284050.000	96.640	1	0	0	1	0
1992M2	2279.481	290410.000	95.860	0	1	0	1	0
1992M3	2700.117	319100.000	93.920	0	0	1	0	0
1992M4	2571.986	305030.000	94.840	0	0	0	0	0
1992M5	2390.913	300040.000	96.090	0	0	0	0	0
1992M6	2894.840	320510.000	97.380	0	0	0	0	0
1992M7	2870.253	329170.000	100.370	0	0	0	0	0
1992M8	2725.941	285670.000	100.680	0	0	0	0	0
1992M9	2909.488	330470.000	100.720	0	0	0	0	0
1992M10	2876.387	343190.000	97.760	0	0	0	0	0
1992M11	2664.833	311600.000	93.820	0	0	0	0	0
1992M12	2973.302	324010.000	94.320	0	0	0	0	1
1993M1	2410.889	270006.974	89.010	1	0	0	1	0
1993M2	2763.437	290960.136	88.750	0	1	0	1	0
1993M3	2966.955	329888.168	88.930	0	0	1	0	0
1993M4	2736.821	315955.980	90.030	0	0	0	0	0
1993M5	2819.191	308716.559	90.400	0	0	0	0	0
1993M6	3074.177	319310.974	89.560	0	0	0	0	0
1993M7	3252.469	307094.631	88.170	0	0	0	0	0
1993M8	3020.651	281757.826	87.870	0	0	0	0	0

5-3

1993M9	3625.645	326238.815	89.050	0	0	0	0	0
1993M10	3395.883	329015.172	88.440	0	0	0	0	0
1993M11	3375.789	321441.650	87.310	0	0	0	0	0
1993M12	3331.238	336505.359	87.390	0	0	0	0	1
1994M1	3018.410	291079.868	87.120	1	0	0	1	0
1994M2	2966.509	300109.175	87.720	0	1	0	1	0
1994M3	4108.343	358885.858	88.930	0	0	1	0	0
1994M4	3370.297	334301.541	89.330	0	0	0	0	0
1994M5	3595.238	343466.324	90.100	0	0	0	0	0
1994M6	3843.675	369804.802	91.100	0	0	0	0	0
1994M7	3739.688	347702.815	93.210	0	0	0	0	0
1994M8	3804.556	341432.315	92.740	0	0	0	0	0
1994M9	4295.837	379776.227	93.650	0	0	0	0	0
1994M10	4031.250	388684.988	94.870	0	0	0	0	0
1994M11	4278.223	394212.467	94.490	0	0	0	0	0
1994M12	4209.163	402648.491	94.170	0	0	0	0	1
1995M1	3987.635	366583.675	96.600	1	0	0	1	0
1995M2	3985.612	383024.545	97.840	0	1	0	1	0
1995M3	5205.574	455529.132	99.910	0	0	1	0	0
1995M4	4072.476	416523.778	101.410	0	0	0	0	0
1995M5	4836.983	436432.408	100.780	0	0	0	0	0
1995M6	4984.597	449534.113	101.420	0	0	0	0	0
1995M7	4624.495	412735.697	101.790	0	0	0	0	0
1995M8	4876.954	399980.018	99.530	0	0	0	0	0
1995M9	5025.080	436865.242	99.130	0	0	0	0	0
1995M10	4837.515	449586.956	100.230	0	0	0	0	0
1995M11	5179.650	448821.194	100.760	0	0	0	0	0
1995M12	4823.132	438883.115	100.610	0	0	0	0	1
1996M1	4486.358	406305.976	100.060	1	0	0	1	0
1996M2	4679.477	413571.074	100.240	0	1	0	1	0
1996M3	4888.625	456539.886	100.360	0	0	1	0	0
1996M4	4246.537	434059.444	99.270	0	0	0	0	0
1996M5	5006.725	441130.375	99.210	0	0	0	0	0
1996M6	4396.844	433044.883	98.810	0	0	0	0	0
1996M7	4492.107	438131.536	98.990	0	0	0	0	0
1996M8	4779.185	409995.187	99.410	0	0	0	0	0
1996M9	4537.461	442092.974	98.980	0	0	0	0	0
1996M10	4665.357	482098.418	99.160	0	0	0	0	0
1996M11	4878.585	461681.083	99.740	0	0	0	0	0
1996M12	4667.710	455910.542	98.990	0	0	0	0	1
1997M1	4624.660	432210.000	97.990	1	0	0	1	0

5-4

1997M2	4324.720	418150.000	96.440	0	1	0	1	0
1997M3	5178.420	463400.000	95.550	0	0	1	0	0
1997M4	4340.499	468010.000	94.570	0	0	0	0	0
1997M5	4934.287	460630.000	95.450	0	0	0	0	0
1997M6	4752.909	470710.000	94.810	0	0	0	0	0
1997M7	4752.968	469690.000	94.130	0	0	0	0	0
1997M8	4811.576	417100.000	93.520	0	0	0	0	0
1997M9	4984.848	476480.000	93.720	0	0	0	0	0
1997M10	5163.102	508610.000	93.820	0	0	0	0	0
1997M11	4855.725	474030.000	93.860	0	0	0	0	0
1997M12	4809.450	475860.000	92.240	0	0	0	0	1
1998M1	4072.477	420130.000	90.500	1	0	0	1	0
1998M2	4786.736	431100.000	90.370	0	1	0	1	0
1998M3	5011.372	484650.000	89.740	0	0	1	0	0
1998M4	4292.300	458020.000	89.320	0	0	0	0	0
1998M5	4251.852	446900.000	89.740	0	0	0	0	0
1998M6	4521.483	465180.000	88.540	0	0	0	0	0
1998M7	4671.522	453310.000	87.930	0	0	0	0	0
1998M8	4287.398	403030.000	87.130	0	0	0	0	0
1998M9	4689.928	468710.000	98.800	0	0	0	0	0
1998M10	4684.845	487090.000	89.250	0	0	0	0	0
1998M11	4565.551	464630.000	87.700	0	0	0	0	0
1998M12	4620.794	467270.000	87.960	0	0	0	0	1
1999M1	4043.965	410900.000	N.A	1	0	0	1	0
1999M2	4184.296	411130.000	N.A	0	1	0	1	0
1999M3	4743.002	479870.000	N.A	0	0	1	0	0
1999M4	4515.957	N.A	N.A	0	0	0	0	0
1999M5	N.A	N.A	N.A	0	0	0	0	0
1999M6	N.A	N.A	N.A	0	0	0	0	0

9   OUTPUT AND PRICE DETERMINATION IN CHINESE MACROECONOMETRIC MODELS

Soshichi Kinoshita

Sugiyama Jogakuen University

1. Introduction

The purpose of this note is to make a brief review of output and price determination in two Chinese econometric models.   One is the model constructed by Youcai Liang and the other is the model by Lisheng Shen. The price and output determination mechanisms in these models show quite contrasting features in assessing the role of demand- and supply-side factors.

2. The case of Liang's Model

Price determination in the Liang Model is summarized in the following flow-chart Figure 1:

It is clear from this chart that, given the exogenous variables, output prices and expenditure deflators are determined recursively by supply-side and are not affected by demand-side factors.

On the other hand, aggregate real output or GDP is determined by demand-side factors.   GDP is determined as the sum of individual expenditure components, as in the case of a Keynesian income determination model.   Given the various policy and other exogenous variables, gross domestic investment, private consumption and GDP are determined interdependently.   Income variables in the consumption function are explained by agricultural and non-agricultural value added.

Exports and imports are both demand-determined, without resort to supply factors.

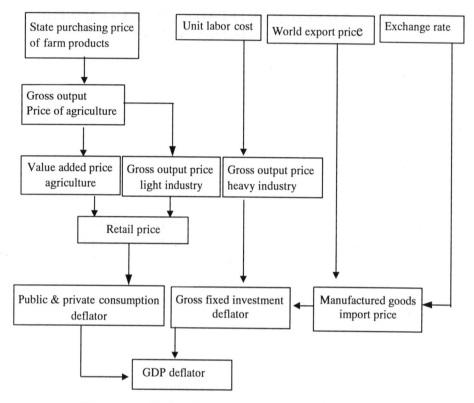

Figure 1: Price Determination in Liang Model

3. The case of Shen's Model

Price determination in the Shen Model is summarized in the following way: First, the GDP deflator is expressed as a weighted average of two expenditure deflators, both of which are determined by monetary and excess demand factors as in Figure 2.

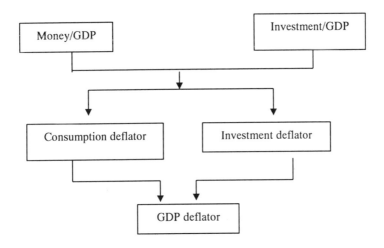

Figure 2: Price Determination in Shen Model

Output price by sector is basically determined as a linear function of the GDP deflator.

Real GDP is defined as the sum of real value added by sector. Sectoral value added is explained by capital stock and employment using a Cobb-Douglas-type production function. The demand situation in commodity markets does not affect output level but does affect price level.

Sectoral employment is determined by partial adjustment of a cost minimization process, for a Cobb-Douglas technology, output level and real wage.

$$Ln(L^*) = ln(V) - ln(w/p)$$

$$Ln(L) = aln(L^*) + (1-a)ln(L-1) = (1-a)ln(L-1) + a[ln(V) - ln(w/p)]$$

4. Concluding Remarks

As we have observed, alternative specifications are quite possible to describe the price and output determination mechanism in the Chinese economy. If we accept the view expressed in the Liang model, inflation in the Chinese economy is a cost-push process. On the contrary, if we specify the price and output determination mechanism based on the Shen model, monetary and fiscal policy will be highly responsible for stability of the general price level. Thus it can be said that the policy implications derived from simulations with the Chinese models are heavily dependent on the specification of the price and output determination mechanism in the Chinese economy.

References

Kinoshita, Soshichi, "On Macro Econometric Model Building in ASEAN Countries – The Case of Thailand," in *Review of National Economies and Econometric Models*, ed. By Statistics Department, IDE, Institute of Developing Economies, Tokyo, 1984.
Liang, Youcai, "China's Econometric Model for Project PAIR," in Chapter 4.
Shen, Lisheng, "China's Macro Econometric Annual Model," in Chapter 7.

10   A NOTE ON THE STATISTICAL DATA OF CHINA: POPULATION AND LABOR

Shoichi Ito

Kwansei Gakuin University

1. Introduction

In the case of analyzing the economy of China, we face the problem of un-reliability of the statistical data. The purpose of this short note is to pursue the possible problems that may exist in the data of such variables as population and labor of China. For this purpose, we shall use only Chinese Statistical Yearbooks from 1983 through 1998, although some other data sources of population and labor of China are available.

2. Data of Population and Labor

The Population Censuses of China taken in 1982 and 1990 are said to be very reliable, because of the well-organized ways of conducting the censuses. These censuses have affected the data of Chinese population and labor. The total population from 1952 to 1981 is the same in all the *Chinese Statistical Yearbooks* (CSY) from 1983 to 1998. The figures (unit: 10,000 persons) for total population from 1982 to 1986 differ, however, from one year of *Chinese Statistical Yearbooks* to another year of CSY. For example, the total population in 1982 is 101,541 in CSY for 1987 and earlier years; 101,590 in CSY for 1988, 1989, and 1990; and 101,654 in CSY for 1991 and later years. In the same manner, the total population in 1986 is 105,721 for CSY for 1987; 106,529 in CSY for 1988, 1989, and 1990; and 107,507 in CSY for 1991 and later years. The figures for total population from 1987 to 1989 differ in *Chinese Statistical Yearbooks* in various years. For example, the total population in 1987 is 108,073 for CSY for 1988, 1989, and 1990; but 109,300 in CSY for 1991 and later years. In the same manner, the total population in 1989 is 111,191 for CSY for 1990; but 112,704 in CSY for 1991 and later years. From these figures, we may be able to argue that following the population census in 1990, the total population from 1982 to 1989 was adjusted in CSY for 1991. Thus, the time series of total population in 1981 and earlier years may be a different time series after 1982. However, the difference seems to be very small (64) in 1982 and then become large (1,513) in 1989.

Urban population and rural population have exactly the same problem as total population. Thus, it may be said that the time series data of total population before 1981 are different from those after 1982.

3. Economically Active Population and Employed Persons

Economically Active Population was included for the first time in CSY for 1996. The particular figures for this variable are given for 1978, 1980, and 1985 and later years. The figures for 1978, 1980 and from 1985 to 1989 are the same in CSY for various years, but those figures from 1990 to 1995 are different in the CSY's for 1996, 1997 and 1998. The Economically Active Population in 1990 is 57,123 in CSY for 1996 but 64,483 in CSY's for 1997 and 1998. In the same manner, the Economically Active Population in 1995 is 69,660 in CSY for 1996 but 68,737 in CSY's for 1997 and 1998. We may argue that the data of Economically Active Population before 1989 is a different time series data from that of after 1990.

The Numbers of Employed Persons from 1952 to 1978 are the same in all the Chinese Statistical Yearbooks (CSY) for 1983 through 1998. The figures for Number of Employed Persons from 1978 to 1984 are different, however, in Chinese Statistical Yearbooks for various years. For example, the number of employed persons in 1978 is 39,856 in CSY for 1987 and earlier years, but 40,152 in CSY after 1988. In the same manner, the number of employed persons in 1984 is 47,597 in CSY for 1987 and earlier years, but 48,197 in CSY's after 1988. The figures for the number of employed persons from 1990 to 1995 differ in Chinese Statistical Yearbooks in various years. For example, the number of employed persons in 1990 is 56,740 in CSY for 1996 and earlier years but 63,909 in CSY's for 1997 and 1998. In the same manner, the number of employed persons in 1995 is 62,388 in CSY for 1996 but 67,947 in CSY's for 1997 and 1998. Thus, the three sets of time series data for the number of employed persons exist for the periods before 1977, from 1978 to 1989, and after 1990. They seem to differ from each other.

4. The Number of Staff and Workers

Although we showed the different time series data for the same variable in the above, the number of *staff and workers* from 1952 to 1997 are the same in CSY's for various years. This is the figure concerning the workers in the urban areas and has been well covered by the government. This seems to provide the consistent data for the number of staff and workers over the years.

In the case of the number of persons employed in the primary industry, the problem is different from the above ones. The CSY's for 1983 and 84 provide the full data of the number of employed persons in the primary industry. The CSY for 1985 partially provides its time series data, and CSY for 1986 provides only 1985 data, and CSY for 87 does so only 1986 data. CSY for 88 again provides the full time series of number of employed persons in the primary industry from 1952 to 1987, but their figures are different from those in CSY for 84. The figures for the data from 1953 to 1984 in CSY for 1988, 1989, and 1990 are different from those in CSY for1983 to 1985. The figures for that variable form 1952 to 1989 in CSY for 1991 are different from those in CSY for 1990 and earlier years. However, those differences seem to be minimal. In the same manner, the data from 1978 to 1989 in CSY in 1998 are slightly different from those in CSY from 1991 to 1997. The data from 1990 to 1995 in CSY for 1997 and 1998 are different from those in CSY for 1996 and earlier years. For example, the number of employed persons of primary industry in 1997 is 34,049 in CSY for 1996 and earlier years but 38,428 in CSY for 1997 and 1998. In the same manner, the number of employed persons of primary industry in 1995 is 33,018 in CSY for 1996 and 35,468 in CSY's for 1997 and 1998. Thus, the number of employed persons in the primary industry consists of three different sets of time series data; that is to say, the data from 1952 to 1977, another from 1978 to 1989, and the third after 1990.

Next, as for the number of employed persons of construction, the CSY's for 1986 and 87 provided only the data in 1985 and 1986 respectively. The CSY for 88 provided the full set of data for the number of employed persons in construction industry from 1978 to 87 for the first time. The figures for the same data from 1978 to 1992 in CSY for 94 are, however, different from those in CSY for 1993 and earlier years. But the differences are small. For example, the figure of that variable for 1978 in CSY for 94 is 854, whereas that in CSY for 93 is 879. Similarly, the figure that variable for 92 in CSY in 94 is 2,660, whereas that in CSY for 93 is 2,702.

We may conclude finally that when we use the data concerning population and labor in Chinese Statistical Yearbooks, we should be very careful of the possibility that different sets of time series data exist for the same particular variables.

INDEX

A

Accumulation, 32, 156, 157, 223, 260, 261
Activity variable, 325, 326
Agricultural gross output, 210, 211, 221
Almon lag, 325, 326
Armington composite commodity, 256
Armington, Paul S., 256, 257, 258, 269, 275, 276, 279, 280, 286

B

Balance of Payments, 9, 10, 11, 12, 31, 47
Balance of Payments Manual, 11
Beghin, John, 250, 252, 269
Burmeister, Edwin, 248

C

Capital items, 10
Capital-output ratio, 277
CES, 253, 255, 256, 258, 278, 279, 280, 281, 299
CES aggregation function, 255, 256
Cheon, Munkun, 248
Chinese Statistical Yearbook (CSY), 76, 81
Chiu, Yi-chung, 248
Chou, Win-Lin, 248
Chow, G.C., 78, 95
Cobb-Douglas type of production function, 73, 74, 207, 299, 309, 365
Commerce, 70, 202, 212, 222, 244, 247, 263, 273, 309, 315, 316
Comparable prices, 76, 156
Computable General Equilibrium (CGE), 5, 249
Construction, 70, 72, 78, 87, 94, 202, 212, 259, 266, 309, 314, 315, 318, 369

CSCPRC–US National Academy of Sciences, Social Science Research Council, 2
Cultural Revolution, 1, 2
Currency in circulation, 35, 38, 211, 213, 221, 224, 225, 243, 247, 315, 317
Current items, 9

D

Deng, Xiaoping, 1
Depreciation, 21, 22, 74, 78, 166, 167, 169, 170, 171, 258, 314, 321, 325, 327
Dessus, Sèbastien, 249, 269
Disembodied technological change, 291, 295, 296, 300, 303, 304, 306
Distributed profits, 258
Durbin-Watson statistic, 326
Dynamic simulation test, 223

E

Eckstein, Alexander, 1
Economically active population, 368
El-Said, Mooatax, 264, 269
Embodied technological change, 291, 296, 303, 305, 306
Employed persons, 368
Employed persons of construction, 369
Environmental planning and assessment, 265
Errors and omissions, 10
Extensive growth in output, 299, 300
Extra-budget public sectors, 259
Ezaki, M., 2, 3, 248

F

Fang, Zhou, 5, 151, 291, 301
Final test, 42, 165
Financial crisis in Asia, 321
Flight capital, 322
Foreign Direct Investment (FDI), 19, 24, 51, 52, 55, 57, 73, 103, 115, 117, 214

Foreign exchange reserves, 19, 22, 24, 27, 31, 32, 42
Foreign-funded enterprises, 18, 20, 22, 23, 25, 29, 31
Formation of labor market, 320
Fujikawa, K., 67, 95
Funds, 27, 30, 78, 79, 164, 202, 207, 267, 268, 315, 316

G

Galenson, Walter, 1
GDP deflator, 39, 86, 92, 120, 121, 124, 125, 128, 129, 132, 133, 136, 137, 204, 224, 225, 226, 243, 247, 313, 317, 364, 365
Goldberger, Arthur S., 248
Government corporate income taxes, 258
Government revenue, 87, 212, 314, 315

H

Heavy industry, 208, 210, 221, 222, 225, 309, 310, 314, 317, 318
Hicks neutral efficiency factor, 261
Hiratsuka, D., 151
Households Survey, 262
Howe, H., 257, 269

I

Ichimura, Shinichi, 1, 2, 3, 6, 47, 68, 95, 96, 151, 248
Ichino, Y., 67, 95
ICSEAD World LINK model, 67
Inada, Yoshihisa, 6, 7, 67, 68, 95, 151, 152, 321
Industrial policy, 265
Infrastructure, 202
Input-Output Table of 1995, 262
Institute for Developing Economies, 6
Investment function, 78
Investment price index, 211
Ishikawa, Shigeru, 1
Ito, Shoichi, 6, 367

J

Joint Economic Committee of the US Congress, 1
Jorgenson, D.W., 261, 269

K

Kim, Yangwoo, 248
Kinoshita, Soshichi, 6, 363, 366
Klein, Lawrence, 1, 68, 248, 307, 321
Kravis, Irving B., 2, 3
Krugman, P., 95

L

Labor, 23, 68, 69, 70, 73, 74, 75, 82, 84, 85, 86, 94, 202, 242, 247, 253, 254, 255, 258, 260, 273, 274, 275, 277, 278, 279, 280, 292, 293, 294, 296, 299, 300, 303, 304, 306, 308, 309, 310, 311, 313, 318, 319, 320, 367, 369
Labor force, 82, 202, 242, 247, 260, 308, 309, 310, 311, 313, 318, 319, 320
Land, 17, 73, 253, 254, 258, 274, 277, 278, 279
Lau, Lawrence J., 2, 5, 68, 95, 307, 321
Lee, Yuang-San, 248
Li, Boxi, 4, 307
Li, Shantong, 4, 5, 151, 249, 269, 307
Liang, Y., 95, 162
Liang, Youcai, 5, 6, 151, 201, 248, 363
Light industrial gross output, 208
Light industry, 210, 221, 225, 309, 311, 312, 314, 318
Lin, Tzong-Biau, 248
Liu Xuesheng, 47
Liu, Geping, 307
Liu, Ta-chung, 1

M

Makino, Junichi, 7, 321
Mansur, A., 261, 269
Material Production System (MPS), 68, 70, 202, 203, 308
Matsumoto, Y., 3, 6, 47, 95, 96

Mensbrugghe, Dominique van der, 249, 250, 269
Minimizing entropy difference method, 264
Monetary multiplier, 35, 36, 37
Monetary policy, 31, 37, 38, 88, 89, 317, 323
Money plus quasi-money, 35
Moriguchi, Chikashi, 3
Motamen, Homa, 248

N

Natural resources, 202
Naughton, Barry, 252, 269
Neoclassical macroeconomic closure, 260
Niwa, Haruki, 2, 68
Nogami, K., 67, 96
Nominal *GDP*, 38, 39, 42, 78, 86, 93, 94, 95
Non state-owned enterprises (NSOE), 70
Non-material production, 309
Non-tradable goods, 264
Number of staff and workers, 81, 313, 368

O

OECD Development Center, 250
Open-door policy, 11
Opportunity cost, 257

P

PAIR project, 5, 6, 151, 152, 156, 161, 202, 225, 366
Persons employed in the primary industry, 368
Pindyck, R.S., 166
Pomfret, Richard, 255, 269
Population, 6, 26, 40, 82, 83, 84, 202, 205, 222, 247, 260, 308, 310, 367, 368, 369
Post, 309, 321
Price determination, 6, 317, 363
Primary factors of production, 253

Private consumption, 203, 204, 213, 214, 221, 222, 225
Production function, 2, 5, 71, 73, 74, 75, 207, 208, 299, 309, 319, 365
Project LINK, 2, 5, 68, 226, 239, 323
Purchased goods, 204, 205, 206, 208, 220

R

Recursive dynamics, 260
Re-export, 157, 168, 169, 180, 181
Re-export Margin (RRXM), 158
Reform and Open Door Policy, 68
Representative equilibrium, 261
Reserve money, 33, 34, 35, 89
Reserves and related items, 10
Retained earnings, 258
Robinson, Sherman, 264, 269
Rubinfeld, D.L., 166
Rural household consumption, 204, 205, 224

S

Saving/investment relation, 260
Scarf, H.E., 269
Self-produced goods, 204, 205
Semi-reduced forms, 326
Shen, Lisheng, 5, 6, 151, 307, 363, 364, 365, 366
Shoven, J., 269
Sideline product purchasing price index, 84
Social accounting matrix (SAM), 250, 251, 252, 262, 263, 264, 266
Standard International Trade Classification (SITC), 15, 16, 156, 317, 318
State Information Center, 6, 68, 113, 152, 201
State-owned enterprises (SOE), 70, 207, 320
Stock exchange, 319
Structure of production, 254
System of National Accounts (SNA), 68, 69, 70, 75, 152, 153, 203, 308

T

Tang, Guoxing, 3, 4, 9, 47, 68, 96
Tao, L., 162
Tax revenue, 93, 94, 212
Technological progress, 75
The price index of private consumption (CPI), 211
Third national industrial census of 1995, 262
Toida, M., 70, 96, 151, 161, 162, 248
Total factor productivity (TFP), 261, 291, 295, 296, 297, 300
Total factor productivity growth, 291, 298
Town and Village Enterprise, 82
Transportation and telecommunication, 202, 309

U

Umezaki, So, 6, 151
Urban household consumption of goods, 204, 206
Utilization of foreign capital, 24

W

Walrasian type, 252
Wang, Huijiong, 4, 249, 269

Wang, Li, 307
Wang, Tongsan, 307
Wang, Zhi, 269
Watanabe, Mariko, 151, 161
Wescott, R.F., 67, 95
Whalley, John, 252, 261, 262, 269
Wilcoxen, Peter J., 251, 269

X

Xu, Bin, 47

Y

Young, Richard M., 248
Yu, Tzong-Shian, 248

Z

Zhai, Fan, 5, 249, 250, 252, 262, 265, 269, 270
Zhang, Shou Yi, 96
Zhang, Shouyi, 307
Zhang, Siqi, 307
Zhang, Xinzhu, 307
Zhang, Yanqun, 307
Zhou, Mingwu, 307
Zhu, Baoliang, 96
Zhu, Yunfa, 307